# Religious Texts and Material Contexts

Edited by

Jacob Neusner
BARD COLLEGE

James F. Strange
UNIVERSITY OF SOUTH FLORIDA

Studies in Ancient Judaism

University Press of America,® Inc.
Lanham · New York · Oxford

4720 Boston Way
Lanham, Maryland 20706

12 Hid's Copse Rd.
Cumnor Hill, Oxford OX2 9JJ


Printed in the United States of America
British Library Cataloging in Publication Information Available

**Library of Congress Cataloging-in-Publication Data**

Religious texts and material contexts /
edited by Jacob Neusner, James F. Strange.
p. cm. – (Studies in ancient Judaism)
Papers delivered at a conference held Feb. 24-25, 2001 at the
University of South Florida, St. Petersburg Campus.
Includes bibliographical references.
1. Archaeology and religion—Congresses. I. Neusner, Jacob, 1932-
II. Strange, James F. III. Studies in ancient Judaism (University
Press of America)
BL65.A72 R45 2001 200'.9 dc21 2001027756 CIP

ISBN 0-7618-2062-0 (cloth : alk. paper)

™ The paper used in this publication meets the minimum
requirements of American National Standard for Information
Sciences—Permanence of Paper for Printed Library Materials,
ANSI Z39.48—1984

# Studies in Ancient Judaism

# Table of Contents

## Islam



## Asian Religions/Hinduism



## North American Religions

# Preface

If the medium is the message, then how shall learning proceed when data come from distinct media: writing and rubbish, for instance? No problem so vexes learning as how to balance the claims of the written record of humanity against the actualities of man's material detritus. Speaking of particular locations and times, the books tell of worlds that, when dug up, do not correspond at all. And without books in hand, archaeologists find themselves dumb, unable ultimately to account for the meaning and use of what they find except by appealing to surmise and committing anachronism. The result is an impasse: the books tell one story, the dirt yields a different story or none at all. In well-known cases, the absence of literary records leaves the stones silent. In others, the written record completely contradicts the corresponding material evidence. And rare are the archaeologists who read critically and imaginatively and thoroughly—rarer still, the historians who dig. More common are the archaeologists who ask the written record the wrong questions, the historians who afford recognition only to the material evidence that tells them what they already think they know.

The contemporary debate about the status of the tales of the Hebrew Scriptures of ancient Israel (a.k.a., "the Old Testament") illustrates where we now stand. A long generation ago, archaeology promised to "validate" the biblical narrative. Those promises were kept, then badly broken. Archaeology today, in the biblical context, produces an anti-history, a record of what did not happen, of what cannot be documented in the shards and remnants yielded by the spade. And for their part, archaeologists propose an account of what did happen so sharply at variance with the expectations of the generality of biblical culture as to defy comprehension. But the archaeology of the Land of Israel in conflict with the narrative of the Scriptures of ancient Israel forms only a single example of what happens when those that master the written record do not leave the library for the field, and those that work in the fields find no harvest to bring home other than broken pots and mute stones. Jacob, who dwelled in tents studying the Torah, and Esau, a man of the field and the hunt, continue their struggle.

In the first editor's decade at the University of South Florida, there was no struggle between archaeology and text-scholarship, only constant interchange. The daily discussions of what people were finding and the meanings of those finds, not to mention of the character of the documents and the implications thereof—these led the two editors to suppose that discussions like theirs would prove stimulating for others. We determined to bring together scholars of the written record and those of the material realm beyond, especially those working in the academic study of religion. No field in the humanities—not literature, not history, not philosophy, not languages—derives more, or more important, insight from archaeology than the study of religion. For mankind has expressed yearnings for heaven not only or mainly in writing, but in constructions that leave a material mark, statues, buildings, even whole cities. Indeed, religion, more than any other single factor, accounts for the character of man's civilization, men's cultures. It follows, in our view, that the academic study of religion bears a special responsibility to inform itself of the workings of dirt-archaeologists and to keep a close eye on the outcome: the data and their problems.

At stake is not only the conventional areas of inquiry, ancient Israelite history and archaeology for example, but the entire range of religions and cultures that contribute to the academic study of religion. To provide for a conversation between archaeology and the study of religion in the context of comparative religions, the Department of Religious Studies at the University of South Florida, sponsored a conference, "Religious Texts and Material Contexts," on February 24-25, 2001, at the St. Petersburg Campus of the University of South Florida. Our criterion for success is, depth at some few places, Christianity for example, breadth at many others, the range represented by Hindu India and Aztec Mexico, with much in-between.

The organizers, the editors of this volume, determined to engage a wide variety of religions and their attendant archaeologies, not only the familiar ones of the ancient Near East. We spread our net to encompass both the old world and the new, the Etruscans for the old, and Mayan and Aztec archaeology and textual artifacts, for the new. We considered texts and material culture as these derive from the worlds of Judaism, Christianity, and Islam. We took cases of archaeology not supported by written evidence, e.g., the Etruscans, and of archaeology overwhelmed by written evidence, American Christianity. We dealt with written evidence correlated with archaeological findings, and written evidence that, if taken at face value, would mislead archaeology. Most of the papers stressed particular problems, but at least some of them spilled over into theoretical problems, e.g., what should we expect to find, how do we think about what we do find, what are the regularities that transcend the cases at hand? And all of them bear evidence of a theoretical framework that guides the respective authors. Hence at no point do we limit ourselves to the case at hand, and throughout we aim at raising the question, why this, not that? Both the archaeologists and the scholars of religious texts took risks, stretched to the outer limits of their learning and beyond. That is what a productive conference means to make possible.

The publication of the papers renders the conference accessible to a wider public than could participate in person. The conference was organized by the two editors of this volume. The actual management passed into the hands of Professor Strange when in May, 2000, after ten years of service, 1990-2000, Professor Neusner left the University of South Florida for his full-time appointment at Bard College, where he had taught on a part-time basis from 1994. From that time, Professor Strange single-handedly managed the entire project. He also taught a seminar for USF students at which the conference papers were read and discussed in advance of the event itself. The students actively participated in the discussions and some of them made important contributions to the discussion.

Dean William Heller, University of South Florida St. Petersburg Campus, now Vice President for USF-SP of the University, hosted the conference, as he hosted the prior ones. This he did not only through material support via facilities and grants but through his own presence on both days of the conference. He embodies all that is exemplary in academic administration and leadership. In addition to grants from USF-SP, the conference was supported by funds provided by former University of South Florida President Betty Castor, former University of South Florida Provost Thomas Tighe, Dean of the Honors Program of the University of South Florida Stuart Silverman, and the Acting Dean of the College of letters and Science at University of South Florida, Tampa, Acting Dean Renu Khator. These same offices of the University supported the prior three conferences in the same ongoing project. We take note, especially, of support for the research seminar-conference projects of past years accorded to the Department of Religious Studies at USF by Dean Rollin Richmond, who originally encouraged the project of student-centered research conferences and helped make the first three of them possible.

Funds for the preparation of camera ready copy for this book derived from the 1999-2000 Research Grant provided by the University of South Florida to Professor Neusner, supplemented by the Research Grant of 2000-2001 accorded to him by Bard College.

JACOB NEUSNER
Research Professor of Religion and Theology
Program in Religion and Institute of Advanced Theology
Bard College
Annandale-on-Hudson, New York 12504

JAMES F. STRANGE
Professor of Religious Studies
University of South Florida
Tampa, Florida 33620

ANCIENT ISRAEL AND CLASSICAL ROME

# 1

# A Near Eastern Ethnic Element Among the Etruscan Elite[1]

Jodi Magness
*Tufts University*

"Virtually all archaeologists now agree that the evidence is overwhelmingly in favour of the 'indigenous' theory of Etruscan origins: the development of Etruscan culture has to be understood within an evolutionary sequence of social elaboration in Etruria" (Barker and Rasmussen 1998:44).

The archaeological evidence now available shows no sign of any invasion, migration, or colonisation in the eighth century... the formation of Etruscan civilisation occurred in Italy by a gradual process, the final stages of which can be documented in the archaeological record from the ninth to the seventh centuries BC... For this reason the problem of Etruscan origins is nowadays (rightly) relegated to a footnote in scholarly accounts (Cornell 1995:47).

## Introduction: The Problem of Etruscan Origins

The origins of the Etruscans are shrouded in mystery and have been the subject of debate since classical antiquity. Traditionally, there have been three schools of thought (also referred to as "models" or "theories") regarding Etruscan origins, based on a combination of literary, archaeological, and linguistic evidence.[2] According to the first school of thought, the Etruscans (or Tyrrhenians' *Tyrsenoi*, *Tyrrhenoi*) originated in

[1]I am grateful to Tony Tuck, Louise Hitchcock, and Hanan Eshel for their valuable advice and assistance with this paper. I assume sole responsibility for its contents and views.
[2]For a review of the literary evidence, see Hencken 1968:603-18.

the eastern Mediterranean. This is based partly on Herodotus's testimony (*Histories* 1.94) that the Lydians of Asia Minor, forced by famine to leave their homeland, sailed westwards under their leader Tyrrhenus and established themselves in Etruria (Barker and Rasmussen 1998:43).[3] Other sources identify the Tyrrhenians with the Pelasgians, who had already colonized the Aegean islands of Lemnos and Imbros (Hellanicus, quoted by Dionysius, I.28; Anticleides, in Strabo 5:2, 4; see Pallottino 1975:64). A second school of thought, which has never gained wide acceptance, posits a "northern" origin—somewhere across the Alps, in the region of the Danube river (see Pallottino 1975:65; Barker and Rasmussen 1998:43).[4] According to the third school of thought, based partly on the testimony of Dionysius of Halicarnassus (1.30.2), the Etruscans were autochthonous. The theory of an eastern origin was popular among scholars until the middle of the twentieth century, since which time the autochthonous theory has gained steadily in popularity, and is (as indicated by the passages quoted above) almost universally accepted today.

In this paper, I wish to reconsider the origin of the Etruscans, in light of the archaeological evidence and changing interpretive models. I believe the evidence indicates that during the seventh century, Near Eastern immigrants (perhaps from different parts of the Near East) settled in southern Etruria.[5] These should not be confused with the Near

---

[3]For the possible connection of the term "Tyrsenoi" or "Tyrrhenians"with the *Trš.w* mentioned in Egyptian hieroglyphs as one of the Sea Peoples, see Pallottino 1975:67; Torelli 1986:47; Tykot 1994. Scholars have noted that there is a chronological discrepancy in Herodotus's account, since the Lydian migration occurred shortly after the Trojan war—that is, centuries earlier than the beginning of the Etruscan orientalizing period. This has led some scholars to dismiss Herodotus's testimony as unreliable, while others have posited two waves of immigration from the Near East—one shortly after the Trojan War, and a second one centuries later (Pallottino 1975:74; Hencken 1968:618, 640-41). However, the chronologies provided by ancient classical sources are notoriously unreliable. I agree with Reich that the fact that these sources preserve a tradition that the Etruscans originated in the East cannot be easily dismissed (Reich 1979:77-78). In this paper, I focus on the period beginning ca. 700. Unless otherwise indicated, all dates refer to B.C.E.

[4]The theory of a northern origin is based partly on the notion that the rite of cremation was introduced to Etruria by new people from the north at the transition from the Bronze Age to the Villanovan Iron Age (ca. 900) (see Barker and Rasmussen 1998:60). Other evidence that has been cited in support of this theory is the equation of the term "Rasenna" (the word the Etruscans used to describe themselves) with Raetia, as well as a passage in Livy (see Pallottino 1975:75-78; Torelli 48; Harrel-Courtes 1964:7-8).

[5]I focus on southern Etruria because it is there that the rock-cut tombs with benches are found; also see Strøm 1971:201, who noted that, "the origin and early development of the Etruscan Orientalizing style can be restricted largely to the

Eastern craftsmen who some scholars believe immigrated to Etruria at this time (see below). Instead, these immigrants became part of the elite in Etruria, as attested by their tombs and burial customs. Their arrival and influence served as one catalyst for the transformation of the Iron Age Villanovan culture to Etruscan civilization ca. 700.

## The Transformation of Iron Age Etruria

The Iron Age of Etruria (ca. 900-700) is usually referred to as "Villanovan" (named after a cemetery near Bologna; see Barker and Rasmussen 1998:60). Although there are signs of nucleation in the settlement pattern during this period, the characteristic feature of Villanovan culture is the use of cremation tombs, in which the ashes are contained within large biconical urns of dark impasto with incised linear decoration. The largest Villanovan cemeteries in Etruria are associated with sites that became the main cities in historical times, especially near the coast (Veii, Cerveteri, Tarquinia, Vulci, Vetulonia, Populonia) (see Pallottino 1975:48; Barker and Rasmussen 1998:61). During the course of the eighth century, inhumation appeared alongside cremation, and graves became richer (Pallottino 1975:48; Reich 1979:60). However, around 700, the local and still quite provincial Iron Age Villanovan culture was transformed by Near Eastern influence into what we know as Etruscan civilization (see Barker and Rasmussen 1998:118; "Whereas the earlier archaeology of Etruria can in large part be explained without recourse to moving beyond the confines of central Italy, Etruscan culture emerges now, after 700 BC, as one of the leading lights on the Mediterranean stage..."). The Orientalizing phase of the seventh century is characterized by monumental tombs containing inhumation burials with a wealth of rich grave goods (Pallottino 1975:49; Strong 1968:21).

The size and wealth of these tombs indicate they contained elite burials (Ridgeway 1988:663-64; Rathje 1979:177; Strong 1968:23; Brendel 1978:43). In fact, the largest and richest—such as the Regolini-Galassi tomb at Caere (Cerverteri), the Barberini and Bernardini tombs at Praeneste (Palestrina), and the Bocchoris tomb at Tarquinia—have been described as princely tombs (*tombe principesche*) (Barker and Rasmussen 1998:118; also see Reich 1979:82).[6] The closest parallels to these tombs,

---

artistic position of Southern Etruria from the late 8th century B.C. to about the middle of the 7th century..."

[6]For the Regolini-Galassi tomb see Paretti 1947; for the Bernardini tomb see Curtis 1919; for the Barberini tomb see Curtis 1925; for a summary of the finds from the Bocchoris tomb and references, see Strøm 1971:149-50. The burials in these tombs were made at different times; for summaries and references see Richardson 1966:45-58; Brendel 1978:439-40, nn. 47.6, 48.8. The burials in the Regolini-Galassi tomb included a woman in the cella (apparently named Larthia,

which have rock-cut burial chambers modeled after houses and were sometimes covered by earthen tumuli, are found in Asia Minor, Cyprus, and the Near East. These tombs contained a wealth of Near Eastern imports and local imitations of imports (Grant 1980:38). However, the appearance of rich burials in monumental tombs is just one aspect of the emergence of Etruscan civilization at this time. By ca. 700, the Etruscans had adopted a modified version of the Phoenician alphabet that was used by the Greek (Euboean) settlers on Pithecoussa and Cumae (Penney 1988: 721). Unlike Greek and Latin, however, Etruscan is not an Indo-European language; in fact, it was the only non-Indo-European language written (and perhaps spoken) in Italy in historic times.[7] Although Etruscan can be read, it is poorly understood, and there is no consensus on the language group to which it belongs or is related (which might shed light on the ethnic origin of the Etruscans) (see Penney 1988; Richardson 1986:215-16; Reich 1979:79-80). The only evidence found to date that might indicate the origin of the Etruscan language is a sixth century funerary stele from the Aegean island of Lemnos, which is inscribed in a language closely related to Etruscan. Interestingly, Thucydides (4.109.4) noted that there were Tyrsenoi living on Lemnos before the island was annexed by Miltiades for Athens. Although the Lemnos inscription represents an isolated find, even Pallottino, one of the most vocal advocates of the theory of autochthonous origins, admitted that, "the similarities between Etruscan and Lemnian are certainly remarkable when considered in light of the legends that give Lemnos as the original home of the Etruscans" (Pallottino 1975:75; but see his reservations on p. 73).[8] Recent scholarship has suggested that the Etruscan language spread from a single center in Italy, where it was introduced not long before it was first written down ca. 700 (Richardson 1986:215). It is interesting (and perhaps significant?) that in contrast to the Greeks and Latins, the Etruscans always wrote retrograde; that is, from right to left, like the Semites. Thus, although the language family to

according to inscriptions on several silver vases), a warrior in the antechamber, and an urn burial in a niche. The woman's burial is the earliest and richest of the three, dating to the mid-seventh century at the latest. The warrior's burial, which is the last of the three, was made ca. 625 (see Strøm 1971:162-68).

[7]For the suggestion that the Etruscan language represents a relic of a pre-Indo-European substratum, see Pallottino 1991:29.

[8]Also see Penney 1988:725-26; Barker and Rasmussen 198694-95; Richardson 1986:218; VII-5; Torelli 1986:49; Cornell 1995:410, n. 35; Cristofani 1979:391; Reich 1979:79, who notes that this inscription has been cited in support of Herodotus's theory of eastern origins. For a recent suggestion that the Lemnian alphabet represent a development independent of the Etruscans, see Malzahn 1999.

which Etruscan belongs is still unknown, the archaeological and linguistic evidence supports the idea of an eastern origin.[9]

Evidence for Near Eastern ethnic presence in Etruria is most strongly suggested by certain cultural features (Turfa 1986:68; Harrel-Courtes 1964:11-12). For example, the Etruscan system of divination has clear affinities with ancient Mesopotamian religious practices. The Etruscans, like some Near Eastern peoples such as the Babylonians, interpreted the omens of thunder and lightening and the livers of sacrificed animals. Parallels to Etruscan terracotta liver models come from Mari, Bogazkoy, Hazor, and Megiddo (these are much earlier in date than the Etruscan models; see Cryer 1994:173-80, who notes that in the Near East, the positions right and left with respect to the diviner played an important part in the reading of the entrails; also see Henckel 1968:599; Barker and Rasmussen 1998:228-30; Harrel-Courtes 1964:12-13; also see Richardson 1986:222-24).[10] The idea of constructing monumental tombs modeled after and furnished in imitation of the houses of the living is clearly Near Eastern in inspiration (see below). Etruscan clothing and shoes of the seventh century have Oriental prototypes, including the laced, pointed shoes (*calcei repandi*), pointed caps, and knee-length chitons (Bonfante 1986:259; Harrel-Courtes 1964:11). Locally manufactured bronze statuettes in an orientalizing style depict women wearing a long pigtail down their back, in the Syro-Phoenician manner (Brendel 1978:91; for a woman depicted in this manner in one of the Boccanera plaques, see Macnamara 1991:68).[11] The parasols and fans carried by members of the

---

[9]A fragmentary bronze vase of the mid-seventh century from a tomb in Falerii bears a Babylonian inscription in cuneiform script that reads, "Belonging to Nabû-iddin, son of Baniya, the *qīpu*" (Cristofani and Fronzaroli 1971).

[10]In the first half of the sixth century, two temples dedicated to Astarte-Uni and Apollo-Suri were erected in a sanctuary at Pyrgi, the main port of Caere. Excavations in the sanctuary brought to light three sheets of gold, two inscribed in Etruscan and one in Phoenician. These plaques document the establishment of the cult of Astarte at this site by the king of Caere. See Reich 1979:80-81; Acquaro 1988:533-34.

[11]Richardson has also discussed the "Syrian braid" worn by these female figures, one of the which she described as follows: "One of the first of these Etruscan figures is a small votive bronze from Arezzo... The hair is very elaborately dressed; the back part is drawn into a heavy braid that forms a hump on the shoulders and hangs to the hem of the skirt; the front is brushed forward in a bang from a transverse parting that runs from ear to ear over the crown, while a corkscrew curl on either side of the face in front of the ear hangs to the shoulder. This arrangement of the hair is, again, Syrian... Such an arrangement is never found in Greece; its appearance on this little bronze and others from Etruria looks like more than a simple copy of an Oriental object. It is took carefully reproduced with too much understanding to be anything but a contemporary Etruscan fashion. And if Etruscan ladies of the mid-seventh century were

Etruscan elite are paralleled in ancient Near Eastern reliefs (Turfa 1986:68). At banquets, which are represented in Etruscan art from earliest times, men and women dined while reclining on couches (at least in southern Etruria), in contrast to Greek and Roman custom, where respectable women were seated on chairs or were excluded altogether. (Richter 1966:93, noted that "The greater freedom of the Etruscan women in this respect [banqueting] is paralleled by Egyptian practice"). Although the custom of reclining on a banqueting couch was adopted by the Greeks ca. 600, it originated in the Near East (Barker and Rasmussen 1998:248).[12] Just as the *kline* (dining couch) originated in the Near East, so did the idea of the permanent funerary couches found in the tombs of southern Etruria (Barker and Rasmussen 1998:249; see below). In paintings, the Etruscans are depicted banqueting at tables laden with food and wine, surrounded by musicians, dancers, and servants (Bonfante 1986:233-34). The musicians are shown playing the Oriental flute, instead of the lyre or trumpet (Harrel-Courtes 1964:12). The Etruscans' love of luxury, which was ridiculed by ancient Greek authors, is also considered to be typically Near Eastern (Harrel-Courtes 1964:12; Bonfante 1986:235). The use of the chariot in warfare may be linked to the East, where chariots were retained by the Phoenicians even after they were superseded elsewhere (Turfa 1986:68). Chariots with horse-trappings have been found in the seventh century princely Etruscan tombs (see for example Pareti 1947:Pl. 25), in the tumuli at Gordion (for a miniature bronze quadriga from Tumulus P, see Young 1981:21-26; for horse trappings and a horse burial from other tumuli, see Kohler 1995:75-76, 80-81), and in the so-called royal tombs at Salamis on Cyprus (together with the skeletal remains of horses; see Muhly 1997:94; Karageorghis 1967:10, 22, 31, 50, 78, 86, 117-19). Other military innovations were also adopted from the Near East (Turfa 1968:68; Markoe 1985:80). It has even been suggested that the concept of the city-state (*polis*) was introduced to Etruria by the Phoenicians (Turfa 1986:68).[13]

---

wearing their hair as Syrian ladies did somewhat earlier—the Syrian ivories from Nimrod are dated between the end of the ninth and the end of the eighth centuries—it looks as though they must have learned the fashion in the East and brought it with them as part of their heritage" (1966:60-61; my emphasis).

[12]According to Collon 1992:28, "The reclining banquet probably spread eastwards from Syria to Assyria and westwards into Anatolia and the Greek world, where it is first attested about 600 BC, and it came to be associated with the funerary meal."

[13]Turfa (1986250-51) also noted that the closest parallels to Etruscan dentistry skills are found in Phoenicia.

The Etruscans were renowned for their sophisticated hydraulic technology. The draining of the marshy forum area in Rome is traditionally attributed to the Etruscan kings of the sixth century, and some of the oldest stretches of the Cloaca Maxima have the corbeled vaulting characteristic of early Etruscan tombs (Strong 1968:14). *Cuniculi* (sgl., *cuniculus*)—sometimes described as "chains of wells"—are perhaps the most distinctive feature of Etruscan hydraulic technology. *Cuniculi* were created by cutting an underground tunnel through a hillside, to tap a deep aquifer. The tunnel has just enough of a downward slope for the water to run down and into the open air by gravity. Vertical shafts were dug down to the tunnel at intervals of 20 meters or so (Hodge 1995:20; also see Cressey 1958:27). Over seventy *cuniculi* are known in Etruria, many of which are several hundred meters long (Barker and Rasmussen 1998:197). Although this type of hydraulic system was eventually adopted by the Romans (perhaps from the Etruscans), it originated in the Near East—specifically, in Iran. The Near Eastern and later Arab examples are known as "qanats," "karez," or "foggaras" (Cressey 1958:27). Since the construction of qanats is a specialized trade, they probably spread through diffusion, rather than representing an independent development in different regions (see Cressey 1958:29; Hodge 1995:21-22, is cautious: "As for the Etruscans, it must remain unclear whether their *cuniculi* were derived from the qanat or an independent development"). Though qanats originated in Iran, by ca. 800 they were apparently being used in Iraq (Cressey 1958:41). They are also found elsewhere around the Mediterranean, including in Palestine, Cyprus, and Egypt (at least some of these examples date to the Roman and Islamic periods; see Cressey 1958; Hodge 1995:21; Avner and Magness 1998:46-47). Hodge suggested that the Etruscans learned about this technology Avia the Phoenicians of Carthage, *though it is not entirely sure that even they themselves knew about qanats in pre-Roman days* "(1995:22; my emphasis). In light of the other evidence presented here, it is reasonable to assume that this technology was introduced to Etruria in the seventh century by Near Eastern immigrants. The *cuniculi* are concentrated in southern Etruria, the same area where the other Near Eastern features described here are located (see Strong 1968:14; Barker and Rasmussen 1998:197). It interesting to note that qanats are a by-product of mining (Hodge 1995:22), since the wealth of metal ores formed the basis of Etruria's prosperity. In southern Etruria, the La Tolfa region behind Caere is rich in deposits of iron, copper, and argentiferous lead (Strong 1968:13).

The monumental Etruscan tombs of the seventh century were filled with Near Eastern imports and their imitations (Rathje 1979:177).[14] The imports include a group of Phoenician bowls, most which come from the Bernardini and Barberini tombs at Praeneste and the Regolini-Galassi tomb at Caere (Markoe 1985:11, 27, 141). One bowl from Praeneste and another from Pontecagnano bear Phoenician inscriptions, apparently referring to their manufacturers (Markoe 1985:72). Other Near Eastern imports include silver jugs, carved ivories, jewelry, and glass and faience vessels (Markoe 1985:91-98; Strøm 1971:113-37; Rathje 1979). Some of the Near Eastern objects found in these rich tombs were apparently the products of orientalizing workshops in Etruria.[15] Most come from the same tombs that yielded Near Eastern imports (Markoe 1985:129).[16] These objects not only show Near Eastern influence in their forms and motifs, but were produced using Near Eastern techniques or technologies not previously attested in Etruria. This suggests that some of the craftsmen who produced them were Near Eastern immigrants (Markoe 1985:138, 144, 146-48; Strøm 1971:216). At least one of these ateliers has been described as "Cypro-Phoenician" (Markoe 1985:148). For example, a group of core-formed glass vessels of seventh century date is thought to have been produced by eastern artisans working in Etruria (see Markoe 1985:97). Another example is gold jewelry decorated with filigree, a technique widely employed and perfected by the Phoenicians (Markoe 1985:129). Other examples include silver and bronze objects (such as kotylai, cistae, paterae, and belt ornaments), and ivory plaques (Markoe 1985:132-48). Depending on the type of object, its material and technology, and the specific motif(s) and style used, various parts of the Near East have been cited as sources of inspiration, especially Syria-Palestine (Phoenicia and north Syria), Assyria, and Egypt (see Strøm 1971:202-5). The Etruscans' fondness for blood and gore also seems to have its source in the Near East (for example, Barker and Rasmussen 1998:256, suggest Assyrian prototypes for a depiction of dead soldiers being decapitated by their victors while vultures peck at other parts of their anatomy; also see Brendel 1978:59, 66).

---

[14]There is an enormous amount of literature on these imports and their imitations. Here I cite only a few. For native bucchero pottery with Near Eastern and Greek influence, see Ridgway 1988:663; Brendel 1978:47, 49-51, 82.

[15]There were also Near Easterners at Pithecoussa, on the island of Ischia; for example, Barker and Rasmussen 1998:119, refer to "a mixed community of Greek and Phoenician traders"; also see Markoe 1985:145, n. 278; and see below.

[16]These rich tombs and their contents (and by way of extension, the workshops that produced some of the objects) are dated to the seventh century, especially the first half of that century (Strøm 1971:171; Markoe 1985:146, 154-55; Reich 1979:82).

The introduction of wine making to Etruria has been attributed to Phoenician influence (Turfa 1986:67). Interestingly, a group of local amphorae in seventh century Italian fabric imitate Canaanite jars in form and surface treatment (Turfa 1986:67; recent analysis of examples from Carthage suggest an origin on the island of Ischia and in northern Etruria; see Doctor et al. 1997). These amphorae were produced by local potters borrowing Phoenician models, or by Phoenician immigrants living on the island of Ischia and perhaps in Etruria (see Doctor et al. 1997:28, n. 35; 57).[17]

The objects found in the tombs point to the presence of Near Eastern craftsmen in Etruria in the seventh century. However, the form of the tombs themselves, combined with the other features of seventh century Etruscan culture mentioned above point to the presence of Near Easterners among the elite. Here I wish to focus on certain elements of Etruscan tomb design that point to the presence of Near Eastern immigrants.

## Monumental Etruscan Tombs of the Seventh Century, and Near Eastern Parallels

Ca. 700, chamber tombs first appeared in Etruria (in southern Etruria in particular). Some of the rock-cut chambers have a gabled or barrel-vaulted ceiling. In chambers where the upper part of the walls and ceiling were built, the roof could be constructed of flat stone slabs. Some consist only of a single corridor-like chamber, while others have a more spacious chamber reached by a dromos (passage). The Regolini-Galassi tomb represents a monumental variant of the latter, with its lower walls and floor cut out of rock and the walls and ceiling constructed of corbelled masonry. Some of the chamber tombs are covered with a tumulus (Hencken 1968:594; for another basic study of Etruscan tombs see Akerstrom 1934). The tumuli rest on a circular drum that was rock-cut and/or constructed of masonry. Some tumuli contain tombs of various dates, and sometimes the tumulus was constructed over existing tombs (Barker and Rasmussen 1998:120-21). The most impressive and best preserved necropolis with tumuli is located at Caere. Prayon has distinguished a development from partly rock-cut and partly constructed passages and tomb chambers (as in the Regolini-Galassi tomb) to tombs in which the long dromos and burial chambers were

---

[17]At Carthage these amphorae are found in levels dating from ca. 760 to the second quarter of the seventh century (Doctor et al. 1997:55). Their initial production thus antedates most of the other cultural features and Near Eastern influence discussed here. For a locally produced imitation of a Phoenician mushroom-lipped jug from Cerveteri, see Sodo 1999.

completely cut out of the tufa (Prayon 1986:180). In the earliest tombs (such as Regolini-Galassi), all kinds of furniture, implements, weapons, and food were left for the dead. By the second half of the seventh century, the interiors of the tomb chambers were being carved in imitation of houses, with imitation roof beams in the ceilings (sometimes "supported" by columns with capitals), imitation doors and windows cut into the walls, and beds, chairs, and other furnishings carved out of the tufa (Prayon 1986:182). And whereas large tumuli predominate at Caere in the seventh century, during the sixth century smaller tomb structures become more frequent. From the mid-sixth century on, square "cube" tombs (*tomba a dado*) become common at Caere and elsewhere (Prayon 1986:185; Barker and Rasmussen 1998:281-82; for the parallels between these tombs and a group of monolithic tombs in the Silwan village in Jerusalem, see Avigad 1954:29-30).

Most of the monumental tombs of southern Etruria had rock-cut benches for the dead—a feature to which we shall return (Barker and Rasmussen 1998:121; Hencken 1968:594; for the distribution of benches in seventh century Etruscan tombs, see Steingräber 1979:8).[18] This reflects the fact that in southern Etruria, inhumation replaced cremation, which was the prevailing rite during the Villanovan period (although inhumation had appeared during the later Villanovan phases, and cremation continued to prevail in northern Etruria; Pallottino 1975:72 Barker and Rasmussen 1975:122). Some scholars have argued that these tombs represent the evolution of Villanovan fossa graves, enlarged and provided with an entrance (Hencken 1968:595; Pallottino 1975:71-72; Barker and Rasmussen 1998:123). Similarly, it has been suggested that the desire to model the tomb chamber after the house of the living should be sought among the Villanovans, who made cinerary urns in the shape of their own houses (Prayon 1986:180). However, the size, layout, and specific elements of the design and decoration of these monumental tombs have no precedents in Etruria, and instead reflect Near Eastern influence (Prayon 1986:174). General (and contemporary) parallels to the Etruscan tombs are found in Asia Minor, Cyprus, and in the vicinity of Van in Urartu (see Hencken 1968:596; Barker and Rasmussen 1998:249). Prayon has noted the "remarkable similarity" between tombs in Ugarit and the Regolini-Galassi tomb, with its elongated ground plan and corbelled masonry ceiling (Prayon 1986:176).

The Tomb of the Statues at Ceri near Caere contains some of the earliest examples of monumental Etruscan sculpture, and shows clear

---

[18]It has been suggested that benches in Etruscan tombs were used for male burials, whereas females were laid in carved burial troughs; see Steingraber 1979:140, with references in n. 7.

Near Eastern influence. The tomb, dated ca. 690-670, consists of two successive rock-cut chambers, which were originally entered through a dromos. It was not covered by a tumulus (Colonna and von Hase 1984:18-24, 29; Prayon 1975:108 cites a date around the mid-seventh century). The inner (second) chamber had two rock-cut benches with a slightly raised parapet around the edges, one on each side of the room. The outer (first) chamber had two seated figures carved in high relief on the side walls, facing each other across the interior of the tomb (Colonna and von Hase 1984:23). Both figures represent bearded, enthroned men, in a hieratically frontal pose. One figure holds a scepter topped with a Phoenician palmette, while the other holds a staff with a rounded top that might represent a scepter or *lituus* (Colonna and von Hase 1984:30-34). The feet of both figures rest on carved footstools, one of which sits on a carved plinth (perhaps indicating a distinction in status between the two figures; Colonna and von Hase 1984:34). These enthroned figures were apparently not intended to represent the deceased laid on the two burial couches in the inner chamber, since these tombs were made for the nuclear family of husband and wife. Perhaps they represent ancestors (recalling the *imagines maiorum*) or gods (Colonna and von Hase 1984:37-38; Barker and Rasmussen 1998:128).[19] Other rock-cut tombs in southern Etruria were furnished with carved stone seats in the outer chamber, as in the Tomb of the Five Chairs at Caere, where terracotta seated statuettes had originally been placed on a row of chairs (Colonna and von Hase 1984:38, 55-57; Barker and Rasmussen 1998:127).[20] The outer chambers with chairs and statues recall the atrium of a Roman house, where the *pater familias* received his clients (Colonna and von Hase 1984:38; Prayon 1975:109-12). However, the statues themselves are clearly Near Eastern in style and inspiration. Their frontal, hieratic pose, straight-hemmed gowns, carved footstools, and the scepter topped with a palmette have late Hittite, north Syrian, or Phoenician parallels. Colonna and von Hase have therefore suggested that the sculptors were immigrant Syrian stonemasons who were active in the area of Caere and

---

[19]According to Tony Tuck (personal communication), the fact that one of the figures is smaller than the other (the one seated on a raised platform) suggests it is a woman. In this case, the statues would represent the husband and wife who were presumably buried inside the tomb. I am grateful to Tuck for sharing with me this observation.

[20]These rock-cut seats are stone imitations of the kind of wooden chair or throne found, for example, in the Regolini-Galassi tomb (see Steingraber 1979:22-34; Richter 1966:98-101; Prayon 1975:109; Pl. 58:1).

Bologna (1984:47-48, 52, 54; also see Ridgway and Ridgway 1994:8; 14 n. 26).[21]

Scholars have noted that many features of the monumental Etruscan tombs are paralleled in Asia Minor (Phrygia, Caria, Lydia), on Cyprus (in particular at Amathus, Tamassos, and Salamis), and in the vicinity of Van in Urartu.[22] These features include burial chambers approached by a dromos, flat or gabled ceilings carved with imitation wood beams, imitation doors and windows cut into the walls, stone benches for the dead, and earthen tumuli above (for a discussion and references, see Ussishkin 1993:303-16).[23] These similarities have been attributed to Near Eastern influence on Etruscan culture, or at the most, to the work of immigrant craftsmen (as in the case of the Tomb of the Statues). However, I believe that several minor but highly specific elements must have been introduced directly by Near Eastern immigrants who were buried inside these tombs, and therefore were members of the Etrurian elite. The proto-Ionic capitals carved on top of the columns in some Etruscan tombs represent one such element (see for example the Tomb of the Capitals at Caere, illustrated in Pallottino 1950:25). Similar capitals are represented in ancient Near Eastern reliefs and on carved ivories (see Dinsmoor 1975:61), and actual examples have been found in association with monumental ashlar architecture in Iron Age Palestine (at Dan, Hazor, Megiddo, Samaria, Jerusalem [the City of David], Ramat Rahel, Medebiyeh [in Moab], and perhaps at Gezer) (Barkay 1992:317-19). Others come from seventh century contexts in Cyprus and in areas of Phoenician colonization in the western Mediterranean (Barkay 1992:319). These include examples from the tombs at Tamassos (see Westholm 1941:37) and Salamis (Karageorghis 1970:Pl. 92:A-B) in Cyprus. Variants of these capitals were also used in buildings in western Asia Minor

---

[21]The carved figures in the Tomb of the Statues recall a ninth-eighth century tomb at Tell `Aitun in Palestine (west of Hebron). This two-chambered rock-cut tomb has five arcosolia cut into the side and rear walls. Crude lions (and perhaps bulls) were carved in relief on the walls flanking the entrances to the tomb chambers and the arcosolia. This is apparently related to the contemporary Syro-Hittite custom of depicting lions and bulls guarding the entrances to gates, palaces, and temples (see Edelstein et al. 1971:88-89; Barkay 1994:134-35).

[22]Although a number of Israelis have noted the similarities between Etruscan and Judean tombs (except for the carved headrests) (see for example Avigad 1954:26, 29-31; Ussishkin 1993:316; Barkay 1994:158-60), they have been overlooked by other scholars.

[23]Karageorghis (1967:121-24), noted that whereas tumuli are common in Anatolia (for example, at Gordion), they are very rare on Cyprus. He suggested that the built tombs at Tamassos might represent "stone versions of Phrygian tombs" (p. 123), reflecting Anatolian influence on Cypriot tomb architecture.

(including the offshore islands) dating to the first half of the sixth century (see Dinsmoor 1975:61-63; Pl. 18).

One feature of the Etruscan tombs that has been overlooked in discussions of Near Eastern parallels are the carved stone headrests on the burial benches. The only close parallels I have found for this element come from Judean tombs, especially in the region of Jerusalem and Hebron. More than 100 tomb caves of the latter part of the Iron Age (eighth to sixth centuries) have been discovered in Jerusalem and its environs. They are concentrated in three areas representing three distinct cemeteries. The eastern necropolis lies in the present-day Silwan (Siloam) village, across from the City of David; the northern necropolis is located to the north of the Damascus Gate in the Old City; and the western necropolis extends over the western slopes of the Ben Hinnom Valley, to the west of the western hill (Barkay 1992:370-71). Caves that have benches with carved headrests are found in all three necropoli (for other parallels between the tombs in the eastern necropolis [Silwan village] and Etruscan tombs, see Avigad 1954:29-31; Ussishkin 1993:316). The best preserved examples are found in two elaborate eighth-seventh century burial caves on the grounds of the Dominican monastery of St. Etienne (the Ecole Biblique et Archeologique Francaise de Jerusalem), in the northern necropolis (Barkay 1992:371). Both caves have a central entrance chamber surrounded by burial chambers. The chambers in these two caves have flat ceilings. Recessed panels, ceiling cornices, and door frames which imitate architectural elements are carved into the stone walls of the large entrance chambers and in some of the burial chambers (the double ceiling cornices found in some of the chambers are paralleled in Urartu and Phyrgia; Barkay 2000:257). Most of the burial chambers have benches lining three of the walls (a few contained carved burial troughs), with a hollowed out area under each right-hand bench that served as a repository for gathered bones and burial goods (Barkay and Kloner 1986:30; Barkay, Mazar, and Kloner 1975). The benches have a low parapet about two inches high around the outer edge, and carved headrests at the ends. The headrests are shaped like horseshoes with rounded ends. In one of the caves, the headrests are heavier and higher, with a thickened curve at the two ends that gives them the appearance of the wig typically worn by the Egyptian goddess Hathor (Barkay and Kloner 1986:29-36). Carved headrests are also found on burial benches in the tombs in Jerusalem's eastern necropolis. They occur both on benches and inside carved burial troughs; some of the tombs in which they are found have gabled ceilings (Ussishkin 1993:99-103; Ill. 77; 269; 277-79; Barkay 2000:250, and 1994:156 notes that carved burial troughs and gabled ceilings represent Egyptianizing features that are also found in tombs in Cyprus, Asia Minor, and Etruria). Some of the benches have a low parapet around the outer edge (Ussishkin 1993:279). Carved headrests are also attested in the burial caves at Ketef Hinnom, in Jerusalem's western necropolis. Instead of the raised horseshoe shape characteristic of the other Jerusalem examples, these were created by hollowing out oval depressions in the raised borders at the ends of the bench (see Barkay 1988:49-50; Barkay 1994:117). One intact repository discovered in this cemetery contained the remains of about 95 individuals and 1000 objects (including pottery vessels and jewelry; see Barkay 1992:371). Rock-cut tombs containing benches with carved headrests have been found elsewhere around Jerusalem and Judea (Barkay 1994:150-51; for references see Barkay 1988:50, n. 1; Ussishkin 1993:301, including n. 24; Bloch-Smith 1992:42, with references to carved parapets, headrests, and other features; also see pp. 46-47).[24]

Carved headrests and raised parapets are found on benches in Phrygian tombs, whose rock-cut interiors have pitched ceilings with imitation beams (see Haspels 1971:Pls. 56; 542:5-6 [the "Triclinium" Tomb]; Barker and Rasmussen 1998:249; Ussishkin 1993:309-12). These elements are also found in many of the tombs at Salamis (see Karagheorghis 1970:11, 25, 27, 33, 36, 38, 39, 43, 55, 61, 92, 111, 121, 133, 139, 143, 146; all with references to figure and plate numbers). However, the rectangular, pillow-shaped Phrygian and Cypriot headrests differ significantly from the semicircular Judean and Etruscan examples (for pillow-shaped headrests in Judea see Bloch-Smith 1992:42). The Etruscan headrests are carved in low relief and tend to be C-shaped, with a more open form than the horseshoe-shaped Judean examples (for examples see Barker and Rasmussen 1998:235, Fig. 89; Prayon 1975:67, Fig. 12; 70, Fig. 13; Pallottino 1950:25). They can terminate in thickened, rounded ends, or in upturned ends that give them the shape of the Greek letter omega (see Steingräber 1979:8; Brocato 1996:69; Fig. 2; Pls. 17-19; these are found on benches used for male burials). Some of the benches with headrests have low parapets and/or carved bed legs (see Steingräber 1979:8; Richter 1966: 91-92; Brocato 1996:Pls. 17-19; for stone couches with carved legs at Salamis see Karageorghis 1970:30). Headrests are even attested inside carved stone troughs, recalling those in the Silwan village in Jerusalem (see Pallottino 1950:29).

A complete bed made of bronze from the Regolini-Galassi tomb shows how closely the features found on the stone burial benches in these rock-cut tombs imitate real furniture (see Pareti 1947:285-86; Pl. 30,

---

[24]For Iron Age tumuli in Judea, see Barkay 1994:159. For a suggested typology of rock-cut tombs in Iron Age Palestine, see Loffreda 1968.

no. 236).[25] The low parapets on the stone benches mimic the wood frame of a real bed (and perhaps prevented the body and burial gifts from rolling off the bench, as suggested by Barkay 1986:29; Bloch-Smith 1992:149). The Regolini-Galassi bed has a raised bronze strip that served as a headrest at one end. The strip is decorated in relief with a semicircle that marks the place for the head, with rosettes on either side. The ends of the strip are thickened and turned upwards (see Pareti 1947:Pl. 30). In contrast, the wooden child's bed in Tumulus P at Gordion (TumP 155) had headboards and footboards, and railings along the sides, but no headrests (Young 1981:70-71, 187-90; see below).[26]

According to Barkay, just as the benches in the burial caves are copies of the beds in houses, the carved headrests are imitations of portable headrests. These headrests were probably influenced by Egyptian prototypes (as seen especially in those shaped like a Hathor wig), and should perhaps be identified with the *rosh-mitta* ("head of the bed") referred to in Genesis 47:31 (Barkay 1988:50; Barkay 1994:156; for the suggestion that the headrests are of Mesopotamian inspiration and symbolize the womb of mother earth, see Keel 1987). The Regolini-Galassi bed is a bronze example of the kind of wood frame bed that was common in Egypt, in which the mattress was made of a webbing of leather thongs or fiber cords woven through slots in the rails (see Brovarski 1997:184; also see Edwards 1976 [no page numbers], for a portable wooden bed from the tomb of Tutankhamum). The child's bed from Tumulus P at Gordion represents this kind of bed, with interwoven narrow strips of heavy cloth stretched between the frame.[27] In contrast, the king's bed from Tumulus MM had a platform made of wooden planks laid lengthwise. Thick layers of blanket-like cloth were laid over the platform to create a mattress. The excavators noted that the cloth was thicker and ended in rolls against the headboard and near the footboard, creating pillows (Young 1981:70, 189-90, 260). The bed from Tumulus MM had apparently been used by the king while he was alive, before being buried with him in the tomb. Because the bed from Tumulus P is much too large for a child, the excavators suggested that it

---

[25]A poorly preserved iron bed comes form the Tomba Marsiliana at Albegna; see Richter 1966:92; Steingräber 1979:8, n. 11. The Regolini-Galassi bed provides a prototype for Steingräber's Kline Type 1a, dated from the mid-seventh century to the beginning of the sixth century (Steingräber 1979:8; 139-40).

[26]Some scholars have suggested that the male buried inside Tumulus MM is an earlier ruler than Midas—perhaps his father; see Voigt 1997:430.

[27]The wooden planks from Tumulus MM that Young identified as the remains of the king's bed (1981:189-90, 260) have now been identified as a coffin (see Simpson and Spirydowicz 1999:51; Fig. 57). I am grateful to Elizabeth Simpson for bringing the latter reference to my attention.

represents a full-sized version from the palace that was placed in the tomb, instead of the smaller bed or crib used by the child while alive. It is probably representative of the kind of bed used by upper class Phrygians (Young 1981:260). The most popular type of headrest used in Egypt consisted of a curved neck piece supported by a pillar with an oblong base, usually made of wood (Brovarski 1997:184; 222, no. 71; also see Strouhal 1992:71, Fig. 73; for an example of an elaborately carved and decorated ivory headrest from the tomb of Tutankhamun, see Edwards 1976 [no page numbers]). The headrests were used with a pad, with the body turned on its side instead of lying on its back (Brovarski 1997:184). This was the position assumed by Middle Kingdom mummies as they lay on a headrest, facing one side of their coffins (Brovarski 1997:184). In contrast, in the case of the bed from the Regolini-Galassi tomb, the bed from Tumulus P at Gordion, and the burial benches in Etruscan, Judean, Cypriot, and Phrygian tombs, the body was laid out supine on its back (for examples of skeletons found lying on the benches inside the tombs at Salamis, see Karageorghis 1970:112; Pl. 171:3; for the Judean tombs see Bloch-Smith 1992:48, 149).

The Judean tombs reflect Egyptian influence not only in their design and interior layout, but also in the riches that were buried with those interred (which include Egyptian and Egyptianizing objects). In other words, members of the Judean elite were buried with their wealth (and with provisions of food and drink), in the manner of Egyptian rulers (Barkay 1994:157). Similar Egyptian influence on tombs and burial customs is evident in Asia Minor, Cyprus, and in Etruria (Barkay 1994:155). That at least some of this Egyptian influence was spread by Phoenicians is indicated by the Phoenician style of some features of these tombs and the objects placed in them (such as the proto-Ionic capitals and window treatments; see Ussishkin 1993:314). As Ussishkin has noted, however, although distinctive Phoenician elements are found in these tombs, "it seems unlikely that Phoenicia was the principal source of these funerary architectural styles, especially as they were not widespread in Phoenicia itself" (Ussishkin 1993:319). Instead, these features were spread by the Phoenicians, who were strongly influenced by Egypt and whose culture absorbed many Egyptian elements (Ussishkin 1993:319). Barkay has attributed the similarities between the tombs in Judea, Asia Minor, Cyprus, and Etruria to a *koine* of goods, knowledge, and ideas that existed during the eighth to sixth centuries (Barkay 1994:160). There is no reason to associate the appearance of these features in Judean tombs with a foreign population, given Judea's physical proximity to and direct connections with Egypt and Phoenicia (Barkay 1994:160; Ussishkin 1993:319). On the other hand, the population buried in the Cypriot tombs apparently included a

Phoenician element that was directly or indirectly influenced by Egyptian funerary customs (Barkay 1994:158; but see Ussishkin 1993:317, who states that these funerary architectural styles "appear to have reached Etruria from Asia Minor, together with other cultural influences brought from there. Karageorghis assumes that Cyprus, too, was subjected to influences from Asia Minor. The main source of inspiration—though not the only one—was undoubtedly Egypt").

**A Near Eastern Ethnic Element in Etruria?**

According to Barkay, the similarities between tombs located in different parts of the Mediterranean can be explained by the movement of peoples between distant cultural centers (Barkay 1994:160). Several factors suggest that in Etruria, these features should be associated with Near Eastern immigrants who were buried in the tombs and were therefore members of the local elite. The heavy dose of orientalizing influence in seventh century Etruria has been attributed by many scholars to trading contacts with Greece and the Near East, through Phoenician intermediaries or, in some cases, to immigrant craftsmen from the Near East. Near Eastern imports or orientalizing influence on Etruscan objects can easily be explained by trading contacts, with imported objects furnishing prototypes for local imitations. In cases where orientalizing objects appear to have been manufactured in Etruria using a previously unattested technology, they have been attributed to immigrant craftsmen. Similarly, the reliefs in the Tomb of the Statues are thought to have been carved by Near Eastern artisans. Greece also experienced an orientalizing period during the seventh century; indeed, some of the Near Eastern influence on Etruscan culture has been attributed to Greek intermediaries (such as Euboean traders) or imported Greek orientalizing objects (including the Etruscans' adoption of the Phoenician alphabet from the Greeks). However, the situation in Greece differs significantly from that in Etruria. First, the objects found in Greece and Etruria differ in type and origin (see Strøm 1971:203-5). As Strøm noted, "although Greece and Etruria to a great extent imported Near Eastern objects of the same origin... Etruria also received Near Eastern goods immediately from their place of origin and, consequently, had Near Eastern cultural relations which are not registered in Greece. The trade routes in question appear, therefore, to have by-passed Greece. These commercial relations are to the Phoenician area and are datable later than the main wave of Phoenician imports into Greece of the latter half of the 8th Century B.C.; they are from the years shortly before or after 700 B.C. They point more distinctly towards Cyprus than to any other Phoenician region, but not unquestionably to this specific island;

an exact localization within the Phoenician cultural area does not seem possible to-day" (Strøm 1971:205). Strøm attributed the earliest Near Eastern imports found in Etruria to direct and independent contacts with the Near East, first with Syria in particular, and shortly afterwards also with Phoenicia (Strøm 1971:212; also see Rathje 1979:179).[28] Not until the first half of the seventh century is there evidence for Greek involvement in this trade, and for Greek orientalizing influence on Etruscan objects (Strøm 1971:206, 213). Second, whereas in Greece most of the Near Eastern imports and orientalizing objects come from sanctuaries, in Etruria they are found in tombs (Strøm 1971:203-4; Hoffman 1997:257-58; Rathje 1979:179).

In her analysis of evidence for the presence of Near Eastern immigrants in Iron Age Crete, Hoffman posed the following question: "What evidence is required to establish the residence of foreigners as distinguished from the transient visits of traders?" (Hoffman 1997:5). In attempting to answer this question, she noted that, "contrary to previous assumptions, typologies of tools, dwellings, and even burial forms do not unerringly identify ethnicity" (Hoffman 1997:11; also see Hall 1997:111-13). Although Hoffman is convinced that people from the Near East must have been living on Iron Age Crete, she believes it is currently impossible to identify with certainty their presence in the archaeological record (Hoffman 1997:17, 255). Hoffman demonstrates that even the Tekke Tholos tomb (to which she devotes an entire chapter), does not provide unequivocal evidence for Near Eastern ethnic presence (Hoffman 1997:191-245). The burial in the Tekke Tholos tomb was identified as a Near Eastern jeweler because of the nature of the grave goods, and because the manner in which those goods were buried was thought to resemble a "foundation deposit." However, the tomb itself is a reused Minoan building (Hoffman 1997:191).[29]

Rathje has noted that, "Oriental influence is much more extensive in Etruria than in Greece" (Rathje 1979:147). In fact, despite the orientalizing style of art and architecture in the seventh century, there is no evidence in Greece for the other types of Near Eastern cultural influence found in Etruria. The oriental imports and their local imitations which flooded Etrucan markets in the seventh century were placed inside Near Eastern style tombs that have no analogs in Greece, or even in Italy outside of Etruria (Richardson 1966:51). The Etruscan

---

[28]On the other hand, Buchner (1979:138) finds Strøm's arguments that some of the Oriental and Orientalizing objects in Etruria were imported directly from the Near East or made by immigrant craftsmen "too thin to be convincing." He believes that these objects were imported through the mediation of the Greek colonies of Pithecoussa and Cumae.

[29]For possible Near Eastern burials at Arkades see Hoffman 1997:165-72.

tombs not only resemble contemporary rock-cut (and tumulus) tombs in Cyprus, Asia Minor, Urartu, and Judea, but they have highly specific elements that could hardly have been introduced through trade contacts. These include the proto-Ionic capitals and the burial benches with parapets and carved headrests (as well as some of the burial goods, such as horse-trappings and chariots). This contradicts Pallottino's description of these similarities as being of "a rather vague and generic nature" (Pallottino 1975:73, referring to Atumuli, chamber tombs, rock facades, etc."). As we have seen, Etruscan culture in the seventh century provides evidence for other kinds of Near Eastern influence not attested in contemporary Greece, including religious beliefs and practices (divination), clothing, banqueting, and hydraulic technology (*cuniculi*). This evidence, combined with the testimony of Herodotus and other ancient sources (however imprecise), and the Lemnian inscription and Etruscan language (whatever its language family) strongly suggest that Near Eastern immigrants settled in southern Etruria beginning ca. 700. These immigrants must have introduced the new monumental tomb types and burial customs, as well as some of the other cultural features. This corresponds well with indications that the Etruscan language spread from a single center in Italy, and was not introduced there much before it was first written down (see Richardson 1986:215). The elements of continuity between the Iron Age Villanovan culture and the Etruscan culture of the seventh century suggest that the immigrants assimilated with the native population and became members of the elite.

Who were these immigrants to Etruria, and what was their place of origin? I have deliberately used the ambiguous term "Near Eastern," since it is difficult to pinpoint their place(s) of origin. As we have seen, the Near Eastern features found in Etruria reflect influence from various parts of the eastern Mediterranean. The possible sources of influence include Mesopotamia/Babylonia (divination; *cuniculi*), north Syria (the carved reliefs in the Tomb of the Statues), and Urartu (rock-cut tombs) (according to Brown 1960:1; 27, n. 1, an almost complete absence of Egyptian influence distinguishes Phoenician art styles from north Syrian styles, which instead show strong Hittite survivals). However, most of the influence seems to come from Cyprus, Asia Minor, and Syria-Palestine (primarily ancient Phoenicia, but extending to the area of Judea). (Ridgway 1988:659, noted that "it is not a coincidence that the two strands of the Orientalizing movement in early Etruscan art have ben defined as the Syrian and Phoenician, and still less that they are interwined to a particularly inextricable degree"). The cultural features found in Etruria that probably were introduced from these regions include wine making; the use of chariots in warfare; banqueting while reclining; locally-produced amphorae in the shape of Canaanite jars;

some of the technologies used for manufacturing locally-produced orientalizing objects (including core-formed glass vessels and gold jewelry decorated with filigree); rock-cut tombs with gabled ceilings carved with imitation beams, sometimes covered with tumuli; proto-Ionic capitals; and burial benches with low parapets and carved headrests. Egyptian or Egyptianizing features probably reached Etruria indirectly, through these intermediaries.

It is reasonable to assume that at least some of the Near Eastern immigrants were Phoenicians. After all, many of the Near Eastern elements found on Cyprus are attributed to Phoenicians, and by this time Phoenicians were living on Sardinia and Ischia, in close proximity to Etruria.[30] On the other hand, the tomb types and burial customs that have been described here are not attested in Phoenicia. This could be due to two factors: 1) few Iron Age cemeteries have been excavated in Phoenicia proper; and 2) different types of tombs, and different rites (cremation and inhumation) seem to have been used in Iron Age Phoenicia (see Bienkowski 1982:85). Phoenician art is characterized by its tendency to adapt or use foreign, and especially Egyptian, motifs (Hoffman 1997:14). This same eclecticism is evident in Phoenician tomb types and burial customs. The Phoenician cemetery at Akhziv includes deep shaft tombs dating to the eighth to sixth centuries which have burial chambers with benches lining three walls. Other tombs at Akhziv that were used from the tenth to seventh centuries consisted of rock-cut and built burial chambers entered through a shaft (Prausnitz 1993:34).[31]

As Hoffman has noted, "our use of the term 'Phoenician' has confused matters by implying the existence of a coherent ethnic group when... the term was and frequently still is (at least in Greek archaeology) an overarching term rather loosely used to describe eastern material and the people or peoples who transported it into the Aegean" (Hoffman 1997:9). In fact, the term "Phoenician" as used by modern scholars does not define a self-consciously perceived ethnic group.

---

[30]For Phoenician presence on Cyprus and Ischia, see Ridgway 1988:657; Moscati 1968:103-10; Aubet 1993:42-45; Holloway 1981:141; Muhly 1985:182-83, 185; also see Culican 1970:34; for Sardinia see Bernardini 1993; Moscati 1968:206-29; Aubet 1993:138-39, 203-7, 313-16. I do not include the Nora stele, because no matter which chronology is followed, it is earlier than the period under consideration here. Aubet 1993:139, describes Kition as a "bridgehead" for Phoenician expansion to the west.

[31]Some of the eighth century tombs at Akhziv are cists with gabled ceilings, lined with ashlar masonry (see Bloch-Smith 1992:29, 41; Mazar 1993:35). Other types of graves at Phoenician sites along the coast include simple graves and jar burials (Bloch-Smith 1992:57). According to Bloch-Smith (1992:55), "Phoenicians cremated and inhumed their dead at sites along the coast from Khalde in the north to Tell er-Ruqueish in the south and at Tell el-Farah (S)."

Instead, it is frequently used to describe any objects or cultural features thought to be of Levantine origin (Hoffman 1997:15). Based on the available evidence, it is impossible to pinpoint the origin of the Near Eastern immigrants in Etruria, though I believe it is likely there were groups from different places around the eastern Mediterranean (including Phoenicia and/or Cyprus and/or Asia Minor, and perhaps from north Syria or Assyria) (see Hoffman 1997:254, on the problem of distinguishing the origins of Near Eastern craftsmen in the Aegean; for the problems of distinguishing Phoenician imports from objects made by resident oriental craftsmen, see Muhly 1985:183; Ridgway 1988:663, noted that "These master craftsmen cannot possibly be distinguished satisfactorily into Etruscan 'natives' and oriental 'guest-workers').

Contemporary political events in the Near East provide plenty of opportunities for the migrations of groups to the west, although it is impossible to identify specific occasions with certainty. During the second half of the eighth century, Syria, Phoenicia, and Cyprus were conquered by Assyria (Brown 1960:1-2; for Phoenicia see Moscati 1968:18-23; Aubet 1993:46-49). A number of scholars have suggested that the Assyrian invasions of these territories caused the migration of craftsmen to the west (Brown 1960:2; Strøm 1971:216; Richardson 1966:44-45, suggested that "an actual shift of population" took place). According to Strøm (1971:216), "the historic events in the Near East resulted for Etruria in an absorption of various craftsmen working from essentially different local traditions." Markoe noted that the main production of Cypriote paterae (late eighth century through the third quarter of the seventh century) coincides precisely with the period of presumed Assyrian domination (Markoe 1985:8; Cypriot stone sculpture also exhibits Assyrian influence). He suggested that, "it is within the second half of this period (ca. 690-675 B.C.) that Cyprus exports her wares, or more probably her craftsmen, overseas to Etruria" (Markoe 1985:155). Holloway has noted that although there were Phoenicians in western waters by about 800, "their activity increased in the 7th century following the Assyrian conquest" (Holloway 1981:137).

## Ex Oriente Lux

Although the question of Near Eastern immigrants in Iron Age and Orientalizing Greece has been the subject of intense debate in recent years (see Hoffman 1997), Etruria has been overlooked. Instead, as noted at the beginning of this paper, the current consensus is that Etruscan civilization should be understood as an indigenous, autochthonous development. Although scholars readily acknowledge Near Eastern influence on the Etruscans, it has been attributed either to trading contacts or to immigrant craftsmen (individuals or small groups) working in Etruria.[32] Why is it legitimate to attribute this influence to trading contacts or the occasional immigrant craftsman, but not to immigrants who became members of the local elite? Or, to repeat Hoffman's question, "What evidence is required to establish the residence of foreigners as distinguished from the transient visits of traders?" (Hoffman 1997:5). It is easy to dismiss the evidence for Near Eastern presence in Etruria when considering the elements individually, but taken together this body of material points to a Near Eastern ethnic element among the Etrurian elite. On the other hand, the differences between the cultures of seventh century Etruria and the Phoenician colonies in the west indicate that there was no massive or formal "colonization" of Etruria by Near Eastern immigrants (for an overview of the Phoenician colonies in the west, see Aubet 1993). I am also not suggesting that all of the Near Eastern elements found in seventh century Etruria were introduced by these immigrants, since some elements could have been transmitted through other mechanisms, including Near Eastern traders and immigrant craftsmen, as well as Greek traders and Greek orientalizing objects.

The case of the Philistine settlement in Canaan provides a useful analogy with seventh century Etruria.[33] Biblical accounts and Egyptian reliefs provide some information on the settlement of the 'Sea Peoples' along the coast of Palestine. Their route can be traced through "beachheads" that they established along the shores of the eastern Mediterranean and on the coasts of Cyprus (Stager 1995:336-37). The Philistine settlement on the southern coastal plain of Canaan is well documented in the archaeological record. The Philistines brought with

---

[32]See for example Holloway 1981:141, "The impact of Ischian trade and the Phoenician trade, which may at times have been carried on the same ships from the same ports or competed from its own bases, was to create the Italic and Etruscan orientalizing period"; Rathje 1979:179, "Why did the Greek and Phoenician colonists stop short of Etruria, the former to the south and the latter to the west? Probably the answer is simply that by the eighth century B.C. the Etruscans were sufficiently well organized to resist direct colonization"; Strong 1968:23, "Prosperity was due mainly to the successful exploitation of the mineral resources of the country which drew the Greeks, through their Italian colonies, and other oriental traders into contact with Etruria and provided vital stimuli for the development of Etruscan civilization"; Cornell 1995:45, "As far as the archaeological evidence goes, this social, economic and political transformation was internally generated, though undoubtedly stimulated by contacts and exchange with the outside world." In contrast, Richardson has argued in favor of Near Eastern presence in Etruria; see for example Richardson 1966:45, 51, 60-61.

[33]The literature on the Philistine settlement in Palestine is vast. Here I cite only a few sources. For overviews see T. Dothan 1982; Mazar 1992; T. Dothan and M. Dothan 1992; Stager 1995; for a cautionary note see Bunimovitz 1990.

them an urban tradition that was foreign to Canaan (Stager 1995:345). The cultural elements they introduced (and which can be distinguished in the archaeological record) include new types of pottery, tombs and burial customs, cultic buildings and objects, food (such as pork) and drinking habits (including the Aegean custom of mixing wine with water), and (still undeciphered) epigraphic remains (Mazar 1992:262-81; Stager 1995:345; Dever 1989:103; anthropoid clay coffins are associated with Egyptians rather than Sea Peoples; see Stager 1995:341-42). Naturally, no single site exhibits all of the elements of Philistine material culture (Dever 1989:103).

Unlike the case of Etruria, the Philistine settlement in Canaan consisted of a mass migration accompanied by violent destructions (see Dever 1989:103; Stager 1995:342-43). However, it provides a useful parallel for examining archaeological, literary, and linguistic evidence for the arrival and settlement of a foreign ethnic element. In the context of Biblical archaeology, Philistine culture has been described as "the most conspicuous case of the identification of a material culture with a specific 'ethnic' group" (Bunimovitz 1990:210). Although the exact origin of the Philistines cannot be pinpointed with certainty, there is no doubt they came from somewhere (perhaps from more than one place) in the Aegean world (for a recent overview see T. Dothan and M. Dothan 1992). Based on the nearly universal agreement among our ancient sources, and the appearance of new types of tombs and burial customs, clothing, dining habits, religious practices and beliefs, language, and technologies (as well as a wealth of imports and local imitations), is it not logical to conclude that some Near Eastern immigrants settled in southern Etruria ca. 700-650? In fact, Strong has noted that, "if the idea of a mass migration has few adherents nowadays there is still a variant suggesting that an elite element, preferably from the east, arrived to give the vital spark—*a more insidious doctrine*, hard to prove or disprove, which might very well be true" (Strong 1968:16; my emphasis). His description of this idea as "insidious"—even while acknowledging it might be true—reveals a bias characteristic of modern Etruscan studies. This is so pervasive that the most recent studies of the Etruscans (such as those quoted at the beginning of this paper) allow for no other possibility than that of autochthonous origins.

The reluctance of Etruscan specialists to consider the possibility that Near Eastern immigrants settled in southern Etruria during the seventh century and became part of the elite has its roots in modern intellectual attitudes. As Stager has noted, "Social archaeologists have usually shunned migration (and even diffusion) as an explanation of cultural change. Partly this aversion is due to an earlier generation of archaeologists who suffered from the 'Tower of Babel' syndrome in which cultural creations were thought to emanate from a single source and spread to the rest of an uncreative world... Partly this negative attitude toward migration and diffusion springs from premises of the newer archaeology in which internal developments, more often than external ones, were assumed to explain cultural change. For this cadre of archaeologists, all archaeology (like politics) is local" (Stager 1995:332). The three schools of thought regarding Etruscan origins are paralleled in Greek archaeology, as summarized in Bernal's controversial work, *Black Athena*.[34] The theory of eastern origins corresponds with Bernal's "Ancient Model," according to which Greek culture arose as the result of colonization by and influence from the Egyptians and Phoenicians (Bernal 1987:1). The theory of northern origins resembles Bernal's "Aryan Model" (which has two subtypes—the "Broad" and "Extreme" forms), according to which northern invaders overran Greece (Bernal 1987:2). Bernal noted that these models "share one paradigm, that of the possibility of diffusion of language or culture through conquest. Interestingly, this goes against the dominant trend in archaeology today, which is to suggest indigenous development. The latter is reflected in Greek prehistory by the recently proposed Model of Autochthonous Origin" (Bernal 1987:7). The theory of Etruscan autochthonous origins parallels Bernal's "Model of Autochthonous Origin," which he also called the "Ultra-Europeanist Model" (Bernal 1987:407-8; Berlinerblau 1999:24-25). Bernal noted that, "This model belongs to the isolationist or anti-diffusionist paradigm which has been dominant in archaeology and anthropology since the 1940's; its dominance seems to be related to a reaction against colonialism, of which diffusionism is clearly an academic reflex" (Bernal 1987:407). The autochthonous model also developed in response to the racial (and racist) theories of Nazi archaeologists (such as Kossinna and others), which focused on the identification of ethnic groups or peoples through material culture traits (see Jones 1997:16). It is probably fair to say that the most prominent advocate of the autochthonous origin model for Greece is Renfrew (see Bernal 1987:407), and for the Etruscans, Pallottino. Renfrew developed his model in response to Childe's theory of diffusion, which was at the time he wrote was believed to account for the origins of Minoan and Mycenean civilization (Renfrew 1972:58-60; Childe's work was influenced by Kossinna and others, although he rejected their Indo-Germanic interpretation of European prehistory; see Jones 1997:16; Hall 1997:129). According to Renfrew, the "emergence of Aegean civilisation

---

[34]Bernal's thesis has been criticized by numerous scholars; see for example Lefkowitz 1997; Lefkowitz and Rogers 1996. For a review of the reactions to Bernal's work, see Berlinerblau 1999.

has to be explained in terms of the positive interactions between the various subsystems which can be detected during the third millennium" (Renfrew 1972:489). In other words, Renfrew's model uses systems theory to posit entirely internal (cultural) developments created by a "multiplier effect" (Renfrew 1972). Similarly, Pallottino argued that all ancient Italic cultures developed indigenously: "The notion of a 'beginning', a particular moment, is giving way to the notion of 'formation' or 'development' spread out over time. Scholars no longer pursue the will-o'-the-wisp of a 'point of departure', conceived in deterministic fashion as containing in embryo all future developments, located in the distant past, and identified either with immigrations or with the indigenous cultures... Nor is it now thought reasonable to trace the existence, for example, of a Latin or Etruscan nation or civilisation back beyond this 'point of arrival', seeking them (as they were once sought) in far-off times and places" (Pallottino 1991:31). According to Pallottino, Etruscan civilization developed out of the local Villanovan (and even pre-Villanovan) cultures (Pallottino 1991:53). This view, now almost universally accepted, was recently expressed by Cornell (1995:46) as follows: "it looks as if the Etruscan civilisation emerged directly from the Villanovan, and consequently that the people who professed the Villanovan culture in iron-age Etruria were in fact Etruscans."

The main thrust of Pallottino's model is that Etruscan civilization developed indigenously and gradually (Pallottino 1975:78). That the model of autochthonous origins reflects modern world views and represents an academic reaction to colonialism (as Bernal suggested for Greece) is apparent in Pallottino's wording: "It also becomes clear that in this process an essential factor is the geographical one: the actual territory of a nation is where its formative process has taken place" (Pallottino 1975:79). It is not a coincidence that the model of autochthonous origins proposed for Greece and for the Etruscans developed during a period of increasing specialization among archaeologists and other scholars working in the ancient Mediterranean world (as pointed out by Stager 1995:332, "They [archaeologists] take comfort in the assumption that explanations of cultural change reside within the confines of regional research, which, in turn, justifies their ignorance of the broader field of comparative archaeology"). Whereas earlier generations of scholars were broadly trained in Classical and Near Eastern languages, history, texts, and archaeology, archaeologists today tend to specialize in either the Classical or Near Eastern worlds. Ironically, this is partly a result of the explosion of information due to technological advances, which has made it difficult for scholars to keep abreast of developments and publications even in their own narrow field of specialization. It also reflects the manner in which the archaeology of the Mediterranean world is compartmentalized at North American universities, with Classical Archaeology (and archaeologists) in departments of Classics or Art History, Biblical Archaeology (and archaeologists) in departments of Bible or Religious Studies, and so on.

Almost twenty years ago, Cherry questioned the notion that the emergence of palatial society on Crete was the inevitable outcome of slow growth and cumulative development during the preceding Early Bronze Age (Early Minoan period) (Cherry 1983:33). He cited three main problems with this "gradualist" view: 1) it lacks explanatory power, since time is seen as the main causal mechanism of change; 2) the gradualist view carries with it unacceptable orthogenetic concepts inherited from nineteenth century theories of social evolution; 3) the belief that change (on Bronze Age Crete) was slow and incremental is derived not so much from observed facts as from a particular philosophy of change which must be tested (Cherry 1983:33). Archaeologists have spoken of "the evolution of Minoan society," using the word in a loose metaphorical sense to refer to gradual, incremental change from simple to complex conditions (Cherry 1983:35). In other words, the culture itself has been viewed as growing due to some inherent potential. Cherry described this as an "idealist position" expressed by the use of organic metaphors such as birth, growth, fluorescence, and maturity. Under this paradigm of culture change, a civilization, like an organism, is viewed as having a definite life-cycle (Cherry 1983:36). I believe that the same problems apply to the theory of Etruscan autochthonous origins. The kind of view described by Cherry is evident in Pallottino's descriptions of the development of Etruscan civilization: "Various ethnic, linguistic, political and cultural elements contributed to the formation of this historical reality, and this process must have occurred gradually, over a long period of time" (Pallottino 1975:78). Cherry noted that Renfrew's model "has had the effect of setting an *imprimatur* on the gradualist argument" (Cherry 1983:36). The gradualist view, which has its roots in the eighteenth and nineteenth century Darwinian notion of evolution, is taxonomic and descriptive (Cherry 1983:36-37). It does not provide an explanation for observed cultural changes. Systems models are also unable to account for threshold phenomena. Although these models can go some way towards accounting for growth or changes in a culture, they do not explain its structural reordering. Instead, Cherry suggested that generalized systems models can be combined with "self-organizing systems" or catastrophe theory. The latter have been used by paleobiologists and evolutionary biologists, who have noticed evidence for long periods of *stasis* punctuated by the sudden appearance of new species (punctuated equilibria) (Cherry 1983:37). Such a model would help explain the "quantum leap" or rapid set of linked changes that led to a social reordering and appearance of the palatial culture during the relatively short Early Minoan III/Middle Minoan I periods on Crete (Cherry 1983:38). A similar model might help account for the emergence of Etruscan civilization. In fact, Camporeale has recently suggested that there is some truth to all three schools of thought regarding Etruscan origins (Camporeale 1997:47).

The fact that Phoenician and Euboean colonies were established on Sardinia, Ischia, and Campania but not in Etruria suggests an active opposition—and by way of extension, the existence of a unified political entity or entities—among the local population (Ridgway 1988:654). The proximity of these foreign colonies to Etruria must have had a profound social effect on the native population (Ridgway 1988:66). According to Ridgway, by the second half of the eighth century, "the Etruscans had achieved a fully formed national identity" (Ridgway 1988:655). However, many of the distinctive features of Etruscan civilization appeared during the course of the seventh century. It is reasonable to assume that some of these were introduced through trading contacts (such as imported oriental objects, imported Greek orientalizing objects, and their local imitations), or by Near Eastern craftsmen who settled in Etruria. On the other hand, the absence of monumental rock-cut tombs with benches and other cultural features discussed here from areas outside of Etruria (including on nearby Pithecoussa) suggests that they were introduced directly by Near Eastern immigrants who became members of the local elite. The story of Demaratus of Corinth provides a historically documented (even if legendary) account of this kind of phenomenon, involving a Greek instead of a Near Easterner.[35] Demaratus, a Bacchiad, was forced to leave Corinth when the oligarchy there was overthrown by Cypselus (ca. 657-656 B.C.E.). As a nobleman and merchant who had visited Etruria many times before, Demaratus chose to settle in Tarquinia, bringing with him a number of craftsmen. There he married a local Etruscan noblewoman. Forty years later, one of their two sons took the name Lucius Tarquinius and became the fifth king of Rome (and the first Etruscan king of Rome) (see Ridgway and Ridgway 1994:6; Ridgway 1988:666; for evidence of a Greek named Hippocrates at Tarquinia see Camporeale 1997:47). The story of Demaratus is important because it attests to the absorption of a foreign immigrant into the Etrurian elite during the mid-seventh century. Small groups of immigrants from different places in the Near East were presumably assimilated in a similar manner at about the same time (Ridgway 1988:654, has described "the assimilation of aliens into local society"; and Camporeale 1997:49, refers to "the integration of individual

---

[35] I am grateful to Tony Tuck for bringing to my attention the Demaratus story.

elements or groups of a certain size"). Camporeale has described this as a "process of ethno-cultural osmosis" (Camporeale 1997:47).

The Etruscan elite in the seventh century thus included individuals of local, Villanovan descent, with groups of immigrants of Near Eastern, Greek (and perhaps other) origins. Because of their small numbers, these immigrants were absorbed or assimilated into the local elite (see Hall 1997:27, "the arrival of too small a number of settlers or families is not sufficient in itself either to provoke an instance of social closure, or to escape assimilation [particularly intermarriage]"). The customs introduced by the Near Eastern immigrants suggest that like Demaratus, they had been members of the elite in their native countries. Perhaps they included no more than a few families who settled mainly in the area of Caere. The debate over Etruscan origins in modern times has reflected nationalistic concerns with race and ethnicity. This is partly because of the location of Tuscany in the heart of Italy, and partly because the Etruscans provide an example of a bounded, continuous entity occupying an exclusive, spatio-temporal position (see Jones 1997:137). As Jones has stated, "within archaeology, the past will continue to be represented as a fixed and distant monolithic reality, either encouraging simplistic and exclusive associations with particular ethnic and national groups, or alienating present-day communities altogether. The acceptance that the past is never dead, and that archaeological remains are likely to be involved in the ongoing construction of potentially diverse and fluid identities, will facilitate the development of dynamic and engaged relationships between archaeology and living communities" (1997:141). The recognition of a Near Eastern ethnic element among the Etruscan elite means that they were a fluid and complex society, rather than an entirely autochthonous people who absorbed or borrowed outside influences through traded goods or occasional immigrant craftsmen.

## References

Acquaro, E.

1988 *Phoenicians* and Etruscans. Pp. 532-37 in *The Phoenicians*, S. Moscati. New York: Abbeville.

Åkerström, Å.

1934 *Studien uber die Etruskischen Graber, unter besonderer Berucksichtigung der Entwicklung des Kammergrabes.* Uppsala: Almquist and Wiksells Boktryckeri.

Aubet, M.E.

1993 *The Phoenicians and the West. Politics, Colonies and Trade.* New York: *Cambridge* University.

Avigad, N.

1954 *Ancient Monuments in the Kidron Valley.* Jerusalem: Bialik Institute (Hebrew).

Avner, U., and Magness, J.

1998 Early Islamic Settlement in the Southern Negev. *Bulletin of the American Schools of Oriental Research* 310:39-57.

Barkay, G.

1988 Burial Headrests as a Return to the Tomb—A Reevaluation. *Biblical Archaeology Review* 14.2:48-50.

1992 The Iron Age II-III. Pp. 302-73 in *The Archaeology of Ancient Israel*, ed. A. Ben-Tor. New Haven: Yale University.

1994 *Burial* Caves and Burial Practices in Judah in the Iron Age. Pp. 96-164 in *Graves and Burial Practices in Israel in the Ancient Period*, ed. I. Singer. Jerusalem: Yad Izhak Ben-Zvi (Hebrew).

2000 The Necropoli of Jerusalem in the First Temple Period. *Pp.* 233-70 in *The History of Jerusalem, The Biblical Period*, eds. S. Ahituv and A. Mazar. Jerusalem: Yad Izhak Ben-Zvi (Hebrew).

Barkay, G., and Kloner, A.

1986 *Jerusalem* Tombs from the Days of the First Temple. *Biblical Archaeology Review* 12.2:22-39.

Barkay, G.; Mazar, A.; and A. Kloner

1975 The *Northern* Cemetery of Jerusalem in First Temple Times. *Qadmoniot* 30-31:71-76 (Hebrew).

Barker, G., and Rasmussen, T.

1998 *The Etruscans. Malden,* MA: Blackwell.

Berlinerblau, J.

1999 *Heresy in the University. The Black Athena Controversy and the Responsibilities of American Intellectuals.* New Brunswick: Rutgers University.

Bernal, M.

1987 *Black Athena, The Afroasiatic Roots of Classical Civilization. Volume I: The Fabrication of Ancient Greece 1785-1985.* New Brunswick: Rutgers University.

1991 *Black Athena, The Afroasiatic Roots of Classical Civilization. Volume II: The Archaeological and Documentary Evidence.* New Brunswick: Rutgers University.

Bernardini, P.

1993 La Sardegna e i Fenici. Appunti sulla colonizzazione. *Rivista di Studi Fenici* 21:29-81.

Bienkowski, P.A.

1982 Some Remarks on the Practice of Cremation in the Levant. *Levant* 14:80-89.

Bloch-Smith, E.

1992 *Judahite Burial Practices and Beliefs about the Dead.* Sheffield: Sheffield Academic.

Bonfante, L.

1986 Daily Life and Afterlife. Pp. 232-78 in *Etruscan Life and Afterlife, A Handbook of Etruscan Studies,* ed. L. Bonfante. Detroit: Wayne State University.

Brendel, O.J.

1978 *Etruscan Art.* New York: Penguin.

Brocato, P.

1996 Sull'origine e lo sviluppo delle prime tombe a dado etrusche. *Studi Etruschi* 61:57-93.

Brovarski, E.

1997 *Searching for Ancient Egypt. Art, Architecture, and Artifacts from the University of Pennsylvania Museum of Archaeology and Anthropology,* ed. D.P. Silverman. Dallas: Dallas Museum of Art.

Brown, W.L.

1960 *The Etruscan Lion*. Oxford: Clarendon.

Buchner, G.

1979 Early Orientalizing: Aspects of the Euboean Connection. Pp. 139-44 in *Italy Before the Romans. The Iron Age, Orientalizing and Etruscan periods*, eds. D. and F.R. Ridgway. New York: Academic.

Bunimovitz, S.

1990 Problems in the "Ethnic" Identification of the Philistine Material Culture. *Tel Aviv* 17:210-22.

Camporeale, G.

1997 On Etruscan Origins, Again. *Etruscan Studies* 4:45-51.

Cherry, J.F.

1983 Evolution, Revolution, and the Origins of Complex Society in Minoan Crete. Pp. 33-45 in *Minoan Society, Proceedings of the Cambridge Colloquium 1981*, eds. O. Krzyszkowska and L. Nixon. Bristol: Bristol Classical.

Collon, D.

1992 Banquets in the Art of the Ancient Near East. *Res Orientales* 4 (Banquets d'Orient): 23-29.

Colonna, G., and von Hase, F.-W.

1984 Alle origini della statuaria etrusca: la tomba delle statua presso Ceri. *Studi Etruschi* 52:13-59.

Cornell, T.J.

1995 *The Beginnings of Rome. Italy and Rome from the Bronze Age to the Punic Wars (c. 1000-264 BC)*. New York: Routledge.

Cressey, G.B.

1958 Qanats, Karez, and Foggaras. *Geographical Review* 48:27-44.

Cristofani, M.

1979 Recent Advances in Etruscan Epigraphy and Language. Pp. 373-412 in *Italy Before the Romans. The Iron Age, Orientalizing and Etruscan Periods*, eds. D. and F.R. Ridgway. New York: Academic.

Cristofani, M., and Fronzaroli, P.

1971 Un'iscrizione cuneiforme su un vaso bronzeo da una tomba di Faleri. *Studi Etruschi* 39:313-31.

Cryer, F.H.

1994 *Divination in Ancient Israel and Its Near Eastern Environment, A Socio-Historical Investigation.* Sheffield: Sheffield Academic.

Culican, W.

1970 Almunecar, Assur and Phoenician Penetration of the Western Mediterranean. *Levant* 2: 28-36.

Curtis, C.D.

1919 The Bernardini Tomb. *Memoirs of the American Academy in Rome* 3: 9-90.

1925 the Barberini Tomb. *Memoirs of the American Academy in Rome* 5: 9-52.

Dever, W.G.

1989 The Late Bronze-Early Iron I Horizon in Syria-Palestine: Egyptians, Canaanites, 'Sea Peoples,' and Proto-Israelites. Pp. 99-110 in *The Crisis Years: The 12th Century B.C., From Beyond the Danube to the Tigris*, eds. W.A. Ward and M.S. Joukowsky. Dubuque: Kendall/Hunt Publishing Company.

Dinsmoor, W.B.

1975 *The Architecture of Ancient Greece.* New York: W.W. Norton and Company.

Doctor, R.F.; Annis, M.B.; Jacobs, L.; and G.H.M. Blessing

1997 Early Central Italian Transport Amphorae from Carthage: Preliminary Results. *Rivista di Studi Fenici* 25: 15-58.

Dothan, T.

1982 *The Philistines and Their Material Culture.* Jerusalem: Israel Exploration Society.

Dothan, T., and Dothan, M.

1992 *People of the Sea, The Search for the Philistines.* New York: Macmillan Publishing Company.

Edelstein, G.; Ussishkin, D.,; Dothan, T.; and V. Tzaferis

1971 The Necropolis at Tell `Aitun. *Qadmoniot* 15: 86-90 (Hebrew).

Edwards, I.E.S.

1976 *Tutankhamum: His Tomb and Its Treasures.* New York: Metropolitan Museum of Art.

Hall, J.M.

1997 *Ethnic identity in Greek antiquity*. New York: Cambridge University.

Harrel-Courtes, H.

1964 *Etruscan Italy*. New York: Orion.

Haspels, C.H.E.

1971 *The Highlands of Phyrgia, Sites and Monuments. Volumes 1-2 (Text and Plates)*. Princeton: Princeton University.

Hencken, H.

1968 *Tarquinia, Villanovans, and Early Etruscans*. Cambridge, MA: Peabody Museum.

Hodge, A.T.

1995 *Roman Aqueducts and Water Supply*. London: Duckworth.

Hoffman, G.L.

1997 *Imports and Immigrants, Near Eastern Contacts with Iron Age Crete*. Ann Arbor: University of Michigan.

Holloway, R.R.

1981 *Italy and the Aegean, 3000-700 B.C.* Louvain-la-Neuve: College Erasme.

Jones, S.

1997 *The Archaeology of Ethnicity, Constructing Identities in the past and present*. New York: Routledge.

Karageorghis, V.

1967 *Salamis Vol. 3: Excavations in the Necropolis of Salamis I.* Nicosia: Department of Antiquities.

1970 *Salamis Vol. 4: Excavations in the Necropolis of Salamis II.* Nicosia: Department of Antiquities.

Keel, O.

1987 The Peculiar Headrests for the Dead in First Temple Times. *Biblical Archaeology Review* 13.4: 50-53.

Kohler, E.L.

1995 *The Lesser Phrygian Tumuli, Part I: The Inhumations.* Philadelphia: The University Museum.

Lefkowitz, M.R.

1997 *Not Out of Africa: How Afrocentricism Became an Excuse to Teach Myth as History*. New York: New Republic Books.

Lefkowitz, M.R., and Rogers, G.M., eds.

1996 *Black Athena Revisited*. Chapel Hill: University of North Carolina.

Loffreda, S.

1968 Typological Sequence of Iron Age Rock-Cut Tombs in Palestine. *Liber Annuus* 18: 244-87.

Macnamara, E.

1991 *The Etruscans*. Cambridge, MA: Harvard University.

Malzahn, M.

1999 Das Lemnische Alphabet: eine eigenstandige Entwicklung. *Studi Etruschi* 63: 259-79.

Markoe, G.

1985 *Phoenician Bronze and Silver Bowls from Cyprus and the Mediterranean*. Berkeley: University of California.

Mazar, A.

1992 The Iron Age I. Pp. 258-301 in *The Archaeology of Ancient Israel*, ed. A. Ben-Tor. New Haven: Yale University.

Mazar, E.

1993 Achzib. Pp. 35-36 in *The New Encyclopedia of Archaeological Excavations in the Holy Land*, ed. E. Stern. New York: Simon and Schuster.

Moscati, S.

1968 *The World of the Phoenicians*. New York: Praeger.

Muhly, J.D.

1985 Phoenicia and the Phoenicians. Pp. 177-91 in *Biblical Archaeology Today, Proceedings of the International Congress on Biblical Archaeology, Jerusalem, April 1984*. Jerusalem: Israel Exploration Society.

1997 Cyprus. Pp. 89-96 in *The Oxford Encyclopedia of Archaeology in the Near East, Volume 2*, ed. E.M. Meyers. New York: Oxford University.

Pallottino, M.

1950 *The Necropolis of Cerveteri.* Rome: La libreria dello stato.

1975 *The Etruscans.* Bloomington: Indiana University.

Pareti, L.

1947 *La tomba Regolini-Galassi del Museo Gregoriano Etrusco e la civilta dell'Italia centrale nel sec. VII A.C.* Vatican City: Tipografia Poliglotta Vaticana.

Penney, J.H.W.

1988 *The Languages of Italy. Pp. 720-38 in The Cambridge Ancient History, Second Edition. Volume IV: Persia, Greece and the Western Mediterranean c. 525 to 479 B.C.,* eds. J. Boardman et al. New York: Cambridge University.

Prausnitz, M.W.

1993 Achzib. Pp. 32-35 in *The New Encyclopedia of Archaeological Excavations in the Holy Land,* ed. E. Stern. New York: Simon and Schuster.

Prayon, F.

1975 *Fruhetruskische Grab- und Hausarchitektur.* Heidelberg: G.H. Kerle Verlag.

1986 Architecture. Pp. 174-201 in *Etruscan Life and Afterlife, A Handbook of Etruscan Studies,* ed. L. Bonfante. Detroit: Wayne State University.

Rathje, A.

1979 Oriental Imports in Etruria in the Eighth and Seventh Centuries B.C.: Their Origins and Implications. Pp. 145-83 in *Italy Before the Romans. The Iron Age, Orientalizing and Etruscan Periods,* eds. D. and F.R. Ridgway. New York: Academic.

Reich, J.

1979 *Italy Before Rome.* Oxford: Elsevier-Phaidon.

Renfrew, C.

1972 *The Emergence of Civilisation, The Cyclades and the Aegean in the Third Millennium B.C.* London: Methuen and Company.

Richardson, E.

1966 *The Etruscans, Their Art and Civilization.* Chicago: University of Chicago.

1986 An Archaeological Introduction to the Etruscan Language. Pp. 215-31 in *Etruscan Life and Afterlife, A Handbook of Etruscan Studies,* ed. L. Bonfante. Detroit: Wayne State University.

Richter, G.M.A.

1966 *The Furniture of the Greeks, Etruscans, and Romans.* London: Phaidon.

Ridgway, D.

1988 *The Etruscans. Pp. 634-75 in The Cambridge Ancient History, Second Edition. Volume IV: Persia, Greece and the Western Mediterranean c. 525 to 479 B.C.,* eds. J. Boardman et al. New York: Cambridge University.

Ridgway, D., and Ridgway, F.R.

1994 Demaratus and the Archaeologists. Pp. 6-15 in *Murlo and the Etruscans, Art and Society in Ancient Etruria.* Madison: University of Wisconsin.

Simpson, E., and Spirydowicz, K.

1999 *Gordion, Wooden Furniture.* Ankara: Museum of Anatolian Civilizations.

Sodo, M.N.

1999 Un alabastron etrusco-fenicio da Cerveteri. *Rivista di Studi Fenici* 27:37-42.

Stager, L.E.

1995 The Impact of the Sea Peoples in Canaan (1185-1050 BCE). Pp. 332-48 in *The Archaeology of Society in the Holy Land,* ed. T.E. Levy. New York: Facts on File.

Steingräber, S.

1979 *Etruskische Mönbel.* Rome: Giorgio Bretschneider.

Strøm, I.

1971 *Problems Concerning the Origin and Early Development of the Etruscan Orientalizing Style.* Odense: Odense University.

Strong, D.

1986 *The Early Etruscans.* New York: G.P. Putnam's Sons.

Strouhal, E.

1992 *Life of the Ancient Egyptians.* Norman: University of Oklahoma.

Torelli, M.

1986 History: Land and People. Pp. 47-65 in *Etruscan Life and Afterlife, A Handbook of Etruscan Studies,* ed. L. Bonfante. Detroit: Wayne State University.

Turfa, J. MacIntosh

1986 International Contacts: Commerce, Trade, and Foreign Affairs. Pp. 66-91 in *Etruscan Life and Afterlife, A Handbook of Etruscan Studies,* ed. L. Bonfante. Detroit: Wayne State University.

Tykot, R.H.

1994 Sea Peoples in Etruria? Italian Contacts with the Eastern Mediterranean in the Late Bronze Age. *Etruscan Studies* 1:59-83.

Ussishkin, D.

1993 *The Village of Silwan, The Necropolis from the Period of the Judean Kingdom.* Jerusalem: Israel Exploration Society.

Voigt, M.M.

1997 Gordion. Pp. 426-31 in *The Oxford Encyclopedia of Archaeology in the Near East, Volume 2,* ed. E.M. Meyers. New York: Oxford University.

Young, R.S.

1981 *The Gordion Excavations Final Reports, Volume I: Three Great Early Tumuli.* Philadelphia: The University Museum.

# CHRISTIANITY

# 2

# The Archaeology of Religion at Capernaum, Synagogue and Church

James F. Strange
*University of South Florida*

The purpose of this paper is to make a contribution to the idea that one can infer propositions about religion from the materials of religion. Although one ordinarily interprets the realia of religious practice by using the texts of the religion in question, this paper is not about that. Rather, can we make inferences about religions from their artifacts and architecture that we might not otherwise make?

To accomplish this analysis, I place on the table the issue of interpretation. To accomplish this proximate goal I consider Christopher Tilley's idea of artifact as "solid metaphor". I will treat five theses about metaphors which appear to be applicable to material culture. Second, I will elaborate on six ideas about structures which did not originate with Tilley, but which he reports as a case study in the interpretation of houses. These ideas are examples of houses as "solid metaphors" and seem to have applicability in the analysis of synagogues and Churches. Third, I will repeat in brief the results of an earlier analysis of synagogues, which seemed to have some success. Finally I turn to synagogue and church at Capernaum in an attempt to extend and elaborate on the analysis. I will end with the conclusion that metaphorical analysis of structures can reveal to us something about the nature of the religions practiced with them.

What we come to see and know is itself slender when compared to the richness we derive from rigorous studies of texts. On the other hand we are venturing into difficult seas without a good compass or chart, so we are not surprised that this vast ocean at first appears almost featureless.

## Metaphor in Interpretation in Archaeology

An interesting development in interpretation of architecture and artifacts is the publication of Christopher Tilley, *Metaphor and Material Culture* (Blackwell, 1999). Tilley is Professor of Material Culture in the Department of Anthropology and the Institute of Archaeology at the University College London. He is best known for his sorties into theories of archaeology and of material culture, particularly in five books prior to the one under discussion.

He owes much of his position on interpretation to the structuralism of Claude Lévi-Strauss, about whose theory of interpretation he wrote a major article.[1] He has also been in constant dialogue with Daniel Miller, with whom he co-authored an important editorial in the *Journal of Material Culture* in 1996.[2]

In the 1999 volume Tilley boldly appropriates a major linguistic category for interpretation in archaeology, namely, the idea of artifact as "solid metaphor".

The question I wish to address is to what extent understanding architecture as a "solid metaphor" aids us in understanding the question of comparison of the religions of synagogue and church at fourth and fifth century CE Capernaum in ancient Galilee. Although I have treated the question of the earliest synagogues in Israel elsewhere, I will not simply assume those results.[3] This kind of interpretation is still too new to assume much. Rather, my objective is simply to see where it is possible that "synagogue as metaphor" and "church as metaphor" may move us towards deducing specific information about the religion practiced within the structures. If the inferred religious practices or beliefs are consistent with literary studies of synagogues and churches, then so much the better. If not, then perhaps we stand to enrich our understanding of both religions as they stood side by side in this small frontier town.

## "Metaphor and the Constitution of the World"

I have borrowed one of Tilley's section titles in order to summarize and re-present his findings on the nature of metaphor, especially on

---

[1]Christopher Tilley, "Claude Lévi-Strauss: structuralism and beyond." In *Reading Material Culture*, Edited by Christopher Tilley. Oxford: Blackwell Publishers, 1990.

[2]David Miller and Christopher Tilley, "Editorial," *The Journal of Material Culture*, vol. 1/1 (1996):5-14.

[3]James F. Strange, "The Synagogue as Metaphor," Ch. 5 in *Judaism in Late Antiquity (Part 3, vol. 4, Where We Stand)* edited by Jacob Neusner and Alan Avery-Peck. Leiden: E.J. Brill, 2000: 91-120, 7 figures.

metaphor as used in discussions and interpretations of material culture and archaeology. Tilley asserts five theses about linguistic metaphors that promise to change our understanding of artifacts:

1. "THE INEXPRESSIBILITY THESIS:" Linguistic metaphors give form to ideas and descriptions of the world which are impossible in a literal language. Metaphors elicit experiences and create meanings in a far richer manner than any literal expression. Specifically, metaphors allow emotions, insights, and intuitions to come to expression in a way that stretches our imagination. I understand this sense of metaphor, when applied to material culture, to mean that artifacts, buildings, and the humanly transformed landscape elicit meanings (including emotions, insights, and intuitions) directly from the people who normally and ordinarily enter them. These "solid metaphors" mediate meanings without discussion, as it were. In other words, we experience our emotions, insights, and intuitions directly when handling an artifact or entering architecture. Furthermore, meanings elicited by solid metaphors may come to expression as repeated non-linguistic behaviors, i.e., ritual. Of course solid metaphors surely elicit oral and written texts, that is, discussion, but we do not unearth those texts unless written down and preserved.
2. "THE COMPACTNESS THESIS:" Linguistic metaphors enable communication between members of the same culture in the simplest and most sparing way possible. It is more succinct to characterize someone as a fox than it is to enter into discursive descriptions of his or her character and behavior. By analogy, solid metaphors enable communication in the same simple and parsimonious way. It more efficient in terms of communication to wear a badge or a tie to communicate authority than it is to discuss your and my relative authoritative standing. It is more efficient to give a building a distinctive silhouette than to affix a sign to it, as the silhouette communicates the function and importance of the building non-verbally but sparingly.
3. "THE VIVIDNESS THESIS:" Linguistic metaphors link subjective and objective experience. They encode and recall information in a graphic or colorful manner that facilitates memory. For example, synagogue buildings and church buildings encode information in a manner that facilitates memory and therefore tradition. As users enter synagogue or church, they are reminded by their very presence within these distinctive structures of utterances, gestures, postures, clothing, material

symbols, and actions that are sometimes appropriate to the one space but not to the other, and sometimes appropriate to both.

4. METAPHOR AS MEDIATOR: Linguistic metaphors facilitate the production of novel understandings and interpretations of the world. Linguistic metaphors accomplish this by connecting concrete and abstract thought. By using the metaphor of the church as the body of Christ, Paul was able to remove the idea of unity from abstract thought and insert it into the realm of concrete thought and experience of the church at Corinth (I Corinthians 12:12-30). Similarly the rabbis could use a *minyan* at prayer as a metaphor for "all Israel" to mediate the abstraction "Israel" into concrete experience (y Megilla 4:4). By analogy, a solid metaphor such as a synagogue or church allows one to connect the realm of the divine with the here and now immediately and experientially in daily experience. This is not to suggest that other daily experiences could not or do not accomplish the same thing, it is simply that the solid metaphor embodies that purpose. The architectural design, spaces, decorations, sights, and smells of each building connect our abstract reasoning about God, world, time, history, and so forth with these concrete experiences in these spaces.

5. His fifth thesis is not so much about the nature of linguistic metaphor as it is about the nature of interpretation in archaeology. Tilley asserts that understanding metaphors, especially in the language of archeology, enables us to unmask "factual statements" about archaeology as interpretations. This unmasking has at least two implications. First, when archaeologists (and presumably others) learn about metaphors in their own discourse, then they learn about the culture of scholarship and the assumptions about language that inform it. Second, when they learn the metaphors in use by ancient peoples of their own world, they (the archaeologists) learn the culture and develop the ability to make authoritative statements about the culture of the ancient peoples.

"All social scientific texts," says Tilley, "are motivated by an act of persuasion in which authors employ the powers of metaphor in conjunction with a presentation of empirical materials, or evidence, to convince their readers of the veracity, significance, and importance of the statements they are making."[4] At the very least this statement alerts us to the significance of archaeological reports as rhetorical documents

---

[4]Op. cit., p. 10.

informed by the assumptions of archaeology as a discipline. We are also enabled to see that these reports are replete with the metaphors of interpretation of that discipline. This is also true of this paper and all the other papers read at this conference.

Tilley also points out that metaphor is not incidental to scholarly theories, Tilley says that certain theories of culture in anthropology rest upon particular root metaphors or images of the world. The functionalists think of society as an organism. The structuralists, on the other hand, see culture and society as languages. Cultural evolutionists mediate culture by means of a metaphor of species evolution. The ethnomethodologists conceive of culture as theater or as a game. These metaphors (sometimes called models) are essential to the transmission and preservation of the various forms of the discipline, just as linguistic metaphors and solid metaphors are essential to the transmission and preservation of a society.[5]

## Material Metaphors and Structures

Tilley devotes only a few pages to "Metaphor in Architecture".[6] Tilley appropriates Pierre Bourdieu's idea that the house provides a coherent language with which to organize reality.[7] This is similar to the idea that the house is a "structuring structure", that is, the house embodies a metaphorical relationship to the principles of social order.[8] For example, houses and other buildings are normally variations on a theme in terms of size, height, materials, location of doorways (entrance and egress), orientation, ground plan, and areas devoted to specific activities. By analogy, we might hypothesize that both synagogue and church were also a variation on themes derived from their social order in terms of size, materials, entrances and exits, orientation, ground plan, and areas devoted to specific activities, including rituals.

Tilley advances six key ideas about or characteristics of houses, several of which seem useful in our analysis of synagogue and church at Capernaum.

(1) Directional orientation, which has long been noticed of synagogues. About half of them are clearly oriented on Jerusalem. We are also accustomed to the idea that apses of churches pointed east.

---

[5]Op. cit., p. 17.

[6]Op. cit., pp. 40-49.

[7]Pierre Bourdieu, *Outline of a Theory of Practice*. Cambridge: Cambridge University Press, 1977, p. 89.

[8]See the relevant literature cited in Christopher Tilley, *Metaphor and Material Culture*, p. 41.

(2) "Silhouetting, in which an object is identified by its distinctive profile...".[9] It is arresting to think that the profile or silhouette of a synagogue is distinctive when compared to Middle Eastern houses. It so happens that most churches and synagogues in ancient Israel share the same silhouette, since the fundamental form of both buildings is related to the basilica.

(3) Nesting, or the positioning of one element inside another. Nesting is observable in the succession of perhaps five (sometimes four) architectural elements of a synagogue: from outside wall, to walk-around or corridor, to benches, to columns, to central floor. As we will see, nesting applies to the octagonal church of the fifth century CE at Capernaum, but less so to its fourth century predecessor.

(4) Skeuomorphs or the substitution for an original material in order to represent changes in place, time, or status. This is easy to illustrate with the synagogue. If the synagogue represents the temple courts, as is our contention, then we should be able to find skeuomorphs. For example, we find simple limestone rather than the marble of the temple forecourts. If the church represents an adaptation from royal structures (as the name "basilica" seems to suggest) we might expect to find a parallel phenomenon of the use of limestone rather than marble. On the other hand, if the architectural citation is literal rather than metaphoric, we might expect to find marble.

(5) "Key ritual actions, architectural elements, or the entire house may be used synecdochially to suggest essential features of the cosmos."[10] For example, the interior of both synagogue and church, when well lit by the sun, provides a metaphorical experience as well as a literal experience of light. The cosmos, as God's creation, declares the glory of God. The "glory of God' is to be found within both church and synagogue.

(6) Ideas of transition come to concrete visual expression in certain visual metaphors. This invites comparison to one noticeable feature of synagogues and churches; namely, that often one enters into a relatively darkened vestibule

---

[9]Op. cit., p. 43.
[10]Op. cit., p. 44.

or atrium from the street before entering worship space. The central area of the synagogue and of the church would have been bright from the clerestory above, but the vestibule would be relatively dark. This is clearest for the octagon and for the great white synagogue at Capernaum, but it is also visible in the fourth century church at Capernaum.

### Synagogue Space as Metaphor

In my previous analysis of the first century synagogue as metaphor, I took the position that the origins of synagogue architecture are to be found in the forecourts of the Second Temple.[11] If so, then the synagogue buildings at Gamala, Jericho, and now Kiriat Sefer "stand for" or are "solid metaphors" for the temple forecourt in Jerusalem. Furthermore, according to the "Inexpressibility Thesis", the feelings, insights, and intuitions appropriate to that temple forecourt environment will come to expression in the synagogue environment. These emotions, insights, and intuitions give subjective meaning to "sanctified space" for the user of both spaces.

"The Compactness Thesis" suggests that synagogues as metaphors provided the simplest or most parsimonious means of communication between the people of Israel about what it means to be Israel at work declaiming Torah. The synagogue building was the most appropriate structure Israel could imagine to give expression to certain core elements of Judaism. Our contention is that this is the synagogue as we know it from Gamala, Masada, Herodium, Herodian Jericho, and now Kiryat Sefer. All of these form a template derived from the forecourts of the Second Temple.

"The Vividness Thesis" tells us that solid metaphors link subjective and objective experience. In Tilley's terms, they encode and recall information in a graphic or colorful manner that facilitates memory. We can see that a synagogue building, if styled after the second Temple forecourts, encodes and re-presents the visual experience of the temple forecourts and evokes memories of experiences in that environment, as long as those memories are available. To put it another way, when one participates in reading Torah in the local synagogue, he or she links his or her subjective experience with the collective experience mediated by and in the architectural space of the synagogue. The synagogue evokes the experience of participation in Torah reading in the forecourts of the Second Temple. Therefore building the synagogue to mimic the Second

---

[11]See footnote 3.

Temple forecourts guarantees continuity between the experiences *there* with *here*.

If I understand Tilley correctly, synagogues as solid metaphors would actively facilitate the production of novel understandings and interpretations of Israel, God, worship, and so on. In more specific terms, a synagogue as solid metaphor mediates between concrete and abstract thoughts. I may have an abstract concept of worship or Torah reading as I discuss this idea with my neighbors, but when I enter the synagogue and participate, it is now a concrete, subjective experience. The same analysis pertains to the experiences of those who used church space at Capernaum.

## Fifth Century Synagogue Space at Capernaum

In addition to the general remarks about synagogue as metaphor, it is also necessary to discuss the Byzantine Synagogue at Capernaum specifically. That is, in addition to all the general remarks made in the previous section, we need to ask what we can learn about the Judaism or Judaisms practiced at Capernaum.

In previous work on the synagogue I concluded that the synagogue space is ideal for audition, but not for vision. In other words participants within the structure could hear, but the three rows of columns made vision difficult. This is because those not declaiming Torah evidently stand or sit on benches along two walls. They must arrange themselves between the columns to see what is going on. Simple viewshed analysis shows that vision is restricted by the columnization.

We notice that synagogue space is organized into two sections, namely, the space outside the columns and the space inside the columns.[12] The central, largest portal on the south face gives into the internal columniation. The other two entrances give directly into the side aisles. Therefore the design of the building presupposes that those entering shall divide themselves into two groups depending on which of three portals they choose. In other words, the porch itself embodies the idea of transition, much as a vestibule or atrium would in first century synagogues.

---

[12]Virgillio Corbo, *Cafarnao I: Gli edifici dell Città.* Jerusalem: Franciscan Printing Press, 1975, Fig. 10 on p. 116.

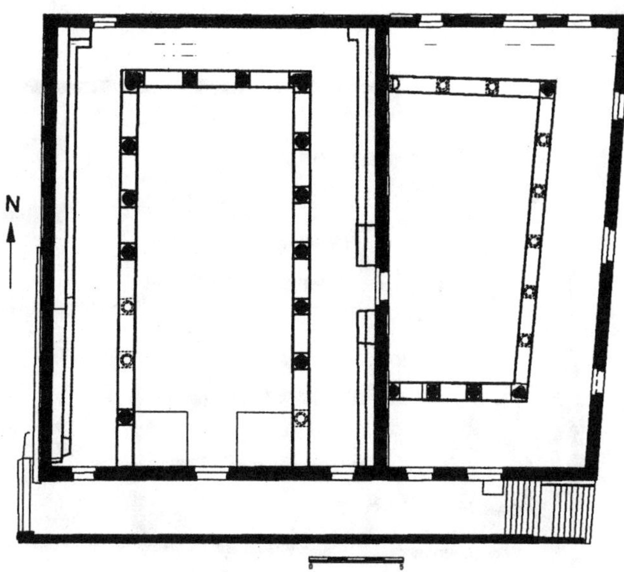


**The Capernaum Synagogue, Adapted from Corbo 1975.**

Another feature on either side of the central portal plays its role in defining the use of the space. Two similar square platforms evidently stood on either side of the central entrance inside the building. As excavated, no remains endure to tell us what these may have been. However, arguing from similar features found at Sardis, it is possible to propose a simple interpretation that these are platforms functioning as centers of attention. Those standing in the central space between the columns stand facing these two platforms. This helps us understand why there is a transverse row of columns across the end of the building. In the central space, we stand with our backs to the columns to focus on the central space. Specifically we stand facing the two raised platforms. Even more specifically, the two platforms may have contained on one side a menorah and on the other a synagogue ark.

If the whole edifice is primarily a metaphor for declamation of Torah, then it is reasonable to hypothesize that an ark was indeed the main feature on one of these raised platforms. We know Torah arks from gold glass images, from mosaics, and from the find of a pediment from an ark at Nabratein. We know of certain activities appropriate for synagogue space from M Megillah and all the later expositions of these texts. In sum, what we can infer of ritual behavior from the synagogue space, understanding it as a solid metaphor, coheres with what we read of synagogue use in the texts.

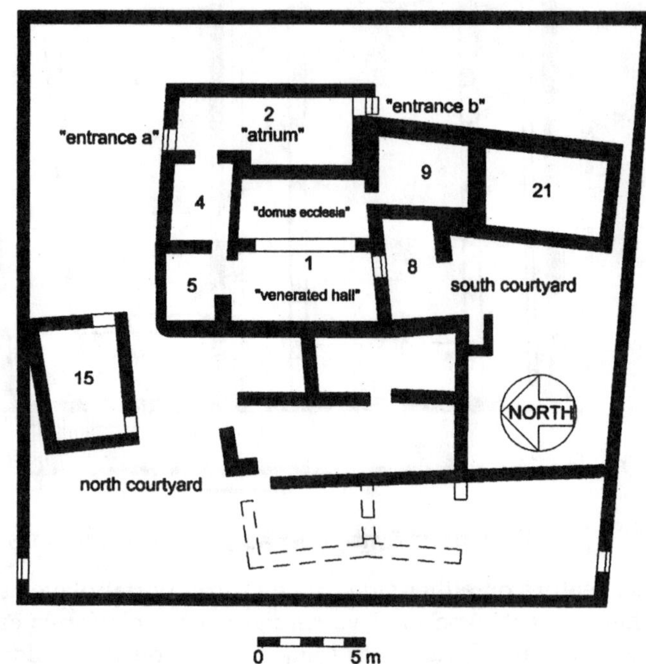

Capernaum: The Fourth Century Church, adapted from Corbo

## Fourth Century Church Space at Capernaum as Metaphor

We report here on an analysis of the floor plan in Insula I of the excavations at Capernaum.[13] In this case we are dealing with an enlargement and renovation of a house, evidently for public use. Two main features of the renovation suggest public space to the analyst. The first is the use of white plaster on all the walls, floors, and ceilings of almost all of the rooms. This feature would multiply the available light in a set of rooms otherwise not designed for strong light. Ancient houses of this period and place, as far as is known, were dimly lit by modern western standards, as they used only small windows hardly twenty centimeters square to allow sunlight inside and a few oil lamps. These windows normally were placed high under the eves, for they doubled as vents to allow smoke out from warming fires of for any smoke that

[13]Virgillio Corbo, *Cafarnao I: Gli edifici della Città.* Jerusalem: Franciscan Printing Press, 1975:59-105.

might have entered the rooms. The open-air courtyards that formed the central spaces of most of these houses provided prime space for cooking in ovens.

The second datum that suggests a change in the nature of the use of the space is that the pottery found in the renovated structure is storage jars and storage jars alone. In other words, the pottery assemblage of cooking pots, bowls, juglets, jars, lamps, and jugs has given way to an assemblage of solely storage jars. Evidently pottery vessels no longer served to store, prepare, and serve food in this structure. The sole function of pottery in the newly renovated and rebuilt structure is to store liquids such as wine, oil, water, and perhaps dry foods. No one is preparing food for consumption.

But let us return to the plastered walls. It is not simply that the users of this renovated space plastered the interior. According to the excavators they also decorated the plaster with painted elements which we expect to see from hundreds of excavations in contemporary buildings. These include rectangular panels of color, colored borders, checked patterns, flowers, and pomegranates. These are well-known painted plaster motifs seen everywhere in the Roman Empire. But there were other painted elements that we do not expect to see, such as geometric figures, "floral crosses," circles and circlets, something resembling architectural elements such as pediments, and possibly an uncial alpha and omega. If their reconstruction is correct, this room features a most unusual decoration.[14]

Of course painting rectangular panels of color is a well-known technique for aesthetic enhancement of a building. It is cheaper than cutting marble sheets to be fastened to the walls. In fact, it is possible to use Tilley's idea of the "skeuomorph" here and suggest that painting in this instance is a skeuomorph for marble elsewhere.

The building in question is surrounded by a wall about 35 x 35 m. in extent. The archaeologists excavated only two means of entrance and egress. These are labeled simply "northern entrance" and "southern entrance" on the published plans. The wall around the whole suggests isolation of his block of houses, but no different in isolation than all the other blocks of houses. By observation from the outside streets one would not know that the buildings had any significance unless the doorways were especially elaborate.

Entry from the south places one in a 20 x 7 meter unroofed courtyard. The low remains of two rooms stand in front of the person

---

[14]Emannuele Testa, *Cafarnao IV: I Graffiti della Casa di S. Pietro.* Jerusalem: Franciscan Printing Press, 1972, chapter 1 (pp. 13-48), esp. the reconstruction Plate X on p. 39.

entering. One must walk through the remains to the open space beyond where on can turn to the right and see the house-now-church. In other words, no one gets to see the structure, the center of attention, until one has turned right at the end of the wall which separates those who enter from the main space of the church grounds.

Entrance from the north, on the other hand, places one directly into the open space just mentioned, apparently an unroofed courtyard at the end of the 20 x 7 south entryway. This open space is about s 7 x 12 meters. Nevertheless, the walled space called room 15 in their plans effectively blocks the view of most of the "house church" of the fourth century.

This "house church" is nested within the four walls mentioned, but not centrally. The builders evidently intended to enlarge and use a specific room of the house in their church.

There is no convenient walkway to Entrance A of the edifice. One must walk east through the "north courtyard" and traverse a narrow area between the northwest corner of the edifice and a low wall remaining from room 15 to the left. From that corner one must still walk about 10 meters to Entrance A.

From Entrance A one enters immediately into part of the additions to the house of the earlier centuries. This part is a roofed "atrium" (according to the excavators), which is about three meters broad at Entrance A, widening to four meters broad about half way to Entrance B. The atrium is a bit longer than 10 meters overall. Whether one enters Entrance A or B, one is plunged into relative darkness, unless there is a series of small windows on the east side of the Atrium. The atrium represents or stands for the idea of transition from ordinary space to some other kind of space, presumably sacred space.

The rooms of this edifice are generally small. They do not bespeak large crowds. They also do not invite processions or pageants, as there is too little room. Furthermore nothing in the rooms as reconstructed suggests which direction one should face while standing. There is no provision for seating, so one would have to squat or stand, if not walk.

From the atrium one walks into room 4, another addition, which is a bit larger than 3 x 4 meters in extent. Nothing was found in this room to tell us its function. The southwest corner of room 4 features a doorway into room 5. Thus the only detected function of room 4 is to usher us into room 5. In like manner the main feature of room 5 is to open directly into the southwest end of Room 1, which the excavators call the "venerated hall." In other words, one must walk through three rooms to arrive at the Room 1.

This chain of rooms is quite unexpected, as most commonly one enters directly into a building's vestibule or atrium and thence directly into unroofed space. In the present instance, the entry to "venerated space" is a variant on what we expect. We first enter into unroofed space, make a turn, and turn again into an atrium. Then we pass through three rooms to get to our goal. The chain of three rooms appears to be a metaphor for the separation of room 1 from ordinary space, or even transitional space (the atrium). Intentional or not, all the walking from the outside street through a kind of maze is more like pilgrimage than it is like processional. The organization of the space continues the metaphor of pilgrimage even inside the building.

Note that one does not enter room 1 in the center of a side. Entrance is near a corner. We do not have a central portal to focus attention as in a synagogue or a church constructed as basilicas.

Room 1 is nearly 8 x 8 m., which is rather large by ancient standards. This room was dominated by an arch overhead with its piers on the north and south sides. The arch doubled the ceiling height for the walls, which were constructed of basalt about 75 cm. thick. The walls do not contain carefully cut, square stones, so they are not well suited for height. On the other hand construction of the arch with a span of nearly six meters allowed the builders to elevate the ceiling and transfer some of the load of the roof to the arch piers and thereby spare the walls.

The renovators plastered the whole interior of room 1 in white: all four walls, the floor, the ceiling, and the arch and its piers. The floor and ceiling featured this same, thick plaster. Light for this hall presumably came from windows in the added upper reaches of the walls. This new "upper story" therefore functioned as a clerestory.

The hall and its paintings, the special finish for the floor, walls, and ceiling, and the hall's placement at the end of three rooms suggests that this room stands for what takes place here. The excavators proposed that this activity was veneration and celebration of the memory of a special room in the first century house, the "House of St. Peter." Room 1 is itself a renovated room of this first century house. Therefore the special treatment of this room stands for its special religious status in its community.

One of the fascinating features of the venerated hall is the graffiti scratched into its plaster.[15] The graffiti are predominantly in Greek, but there are also words and phrases in Hebrew, Syriac, and Latin. Most are of the type "Lord Jesus Christ help your servant PN." The excavators therefore conclude that the graffiti found in this room suggest that this room was the goal of pilgrims coming from areas where these languages dominated. In any case the graffiti in effect form an imprint of their devotion. That is, the treatment of the room by the builders, then the

[15]Emannuele Testa, *Cafarnao IV: I Graffiti*, 1972, chs. 2-6.

scratching of pious graffiti into the plaster of the walls both suggest that the room is a metaphor for the goal of pilgrimage. The goal is to stand in the very spot where Jesus, Peter, and Andrew stood.

From the "venerated hall," also known as the "domus ecclesia" or "house church", one could exit into a dependency, room 9, which was not furnished with its own threshold. This would mean that there was no door swinging on a hinge, so the space could not be closed off with a door. This is a remnant of the former house. One could also exit into room 8, which probably only had a simple shed roof and let one into the south courtyard ("cortile sud").

The south courtyard is about 8 x 12 m. and could serve for gathering, but it is not roofed. This would not be a problem except during inclement weather.

Following the usual figures we use to calculate dense crowd size, or about one square meter per person, we find that a crowd of 64 could squat or stand in the "venerated hall." There is no sign of permanent furniture to tell us what they were doing.

The addition of the arch and the raised roof of room 1 changed the silhouette of the edifice. The new silhouette is not distinctive, as it resembles two-storied houses everywhere. On the other hand, the internal silhouette of room 1 is distinctive because of the height of the ceiling, the plastering of all walls, the ceiling, and the floor, and because of the painting and graffiti on the walls.

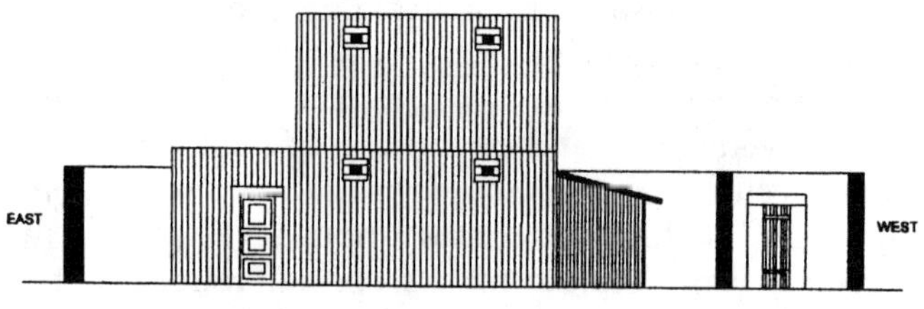


CAPERNAUM: VIEW TO SOUTH OF THE FOURTH CENTURY CHURCH

The lighting inside the venerated hall or room 1 must come from its clerestory, for otherwise there is no way to introduce sunlight into the interior. Room 1 would likely have been rather gloomy if it were not for the white plaster, which would have increased the reflectivity of the interior and served to multiply available light. Thus there are four features of room 1 which serve its metaphorical function as the goal of pilgrimage; (1) Its raised roof, therefore a clerestory, (2) Its internal raised silhouette, the result of moving the roof up, (3) Its white plaster with some colored paint, (4) Its lighting from two stories up beneath the beams of the roof. Visitors scratched a fifth feature of its metaphorical status, namely the graffiti in Greek, Syriac, Hebrew, and Latin.

Following Tilley, then, it seems that the House Church of the fourth century, and especially its Room 1, carries design features that do suggest that it is a metaphor for pilgrimage. If that is the case, then entrance into Room 1 would elicit emotions, insights, and intuitions and ritual action (prayer, confession, chanting or singing, kneeling, etc.) Room 1 would mediate meanings directly (the "inexpressibility thesis").

Furthermore the addition of the arch to room one and thereby the alteration of its internal silhouette, the plastering and painting, and the introduction of light through clerestory windows would all communicate the function and importance of this room to the community (the "compactness thesis").

Third, Room 1 by its construction and decoration facilitates memory and therefore tradition. One enters and remembers the gospel stories that connect Jesus, Peter, and Andrew, and other apostles (and Peter's mother-in-law) to this house at Capernaum. One may engage in relating these stories or reading them to those assembled (the "vividness thesis").

Fourth, Room 1 links the experiences of those early disciples and apostles with one's experience here and now. Written and oral stories about Jesus and the apostles gain a concrete context in Room 1. This space with its paintings, smells, and sounds now functions as one's concrete experience of those stories and memories which are otherwise abstractions.

Finally the Church of the Fourth Century exhibits several of the ideas which Tilley and Bourdieu have posited about houses having a coherent language to organize reality. In this case we have named the internal silhouette of Room 1, which is unique to Room 1. There is also a rudimentary nesting of Room 1 within the modified house, and the house is nested within its wall.

I have proposed that painted plaster is a skeuomorph for marble, or by analogy that painted plaster "stands for" high status marble.

I have also suggested that the lighting of Room 1 from high in the upper story is a metaphor for the spiritual illumination that one gains in this space. The light is a metaphorical experience of the "glory of God" for the experient.

Furthermore the excavators themselves understood that room 2, the addition to the east, was an atrium. Atriums embody the idea of transition from one space to another. In this case we have an extended transition in the form of rooms 2, 4, and 5 before one enters Room 1 or the "venerated hall."

## Fifth Century Church Space at Capernaum as Metaphor

In the course of the fifth century of three Common Era builders destroyed the rooms of the fourth century to their foundations. In their place they built an octagonal church of cut, black basalt. The central octagonal room of the octagonal church lay directly upon Room 1 of the church of the preceding century.[16]

The wall which surrounded the fourth century church also surrounded the new church. Since the builders placed the central octagon directly on top of the foundation of Room 1, the church is not centered in its block or insula. On the other hand it does exhibit nesting, and nesting to an extreme degree. In fact, one might term this building mainly an example of nesting. The architect built two other octagons concentrically around the central octagon.

The outermost octagon, with a diameter of about 28 meters north to south, is a surrounding porch. It is formed of five sides, since the other three sides of the external octagon are interrupted on the east by a series of rooms. The porch, also called an ambulatory by some, was paved with mosaics in repeated geometric patterns. There is no wall on the outside edge of the porch. Rather there are a series of arches that loop from corner to corner of the sides.

If one were to enter the porch at any point, one would soon realize that the porch conveys one around the outside of a centrally organized building. That is, the porch in its own way invites entry toward the center of the building, it does not merely invite one to walk around.

The second octagon has all eight of its sides. Doorways pierce the three sides (walls) of the octagon on the west. The doorway on the west-facing wall is the largest, which suggest that it stands on the axis of the building. This axis would be an east-west line drawn from the center of this portal to the center of the apse on the east. It does not escape us that the apse points east and the entrance west, like other churches of the fourth and fifth centuries.

The floor on the inside was also paved with mosaic. The small amount which has been preserved is floral in design, a very common motif in mosaic art at this period.

---

[16]Virgillio Corbo, *Cafarnao I: Gli edifici della Città.* Jerusalem: Franciscan Printing Press, 1975: 26-58.

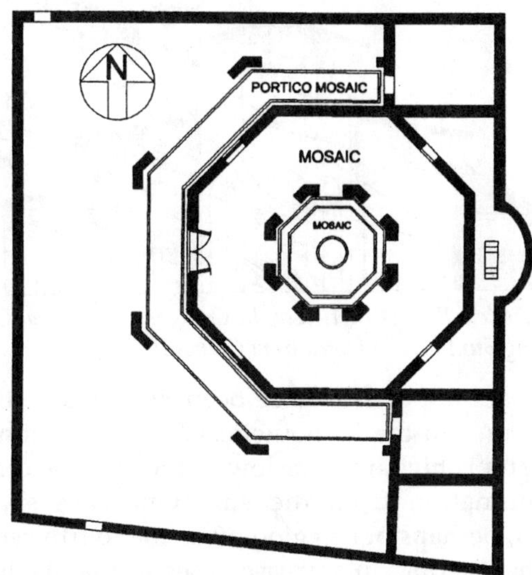


*Capernaum: Plan of the Octagonal Church of the 5th Century*

If one were to walk around in this area between the porch and central room, one would see no furniture. There is no altar, no altar rail, no pulpit, none of the accoutrements which one expects of churches of the fifth century. Rather, one sees a central, octagonal area which is not built of solid walls and a door, but of eight piers and eight openings. From any position within the second octagon one is thereby invited to enter the central octagon.

The central, octagonal space was paved with a mosaic of repeated circlets. In the very center was a circular medallion displaying a peacock in full presentation. There was no trace in the floor of attached furniture.

The nesting of this octagonal structure is a powerful feature in terms of its standing metaphor. Much as a bull's eye invites one to strike the center, so this nesting invites one to walk to the central octagonal space. When there, there is no provision for seating, nor was painted plaster found as though the piers were plastered and then painted, as for the fourth century church. Instead, one stands inside the octagon space, well able to see out the eight doorways, and quite visible to those outside this central octagon.

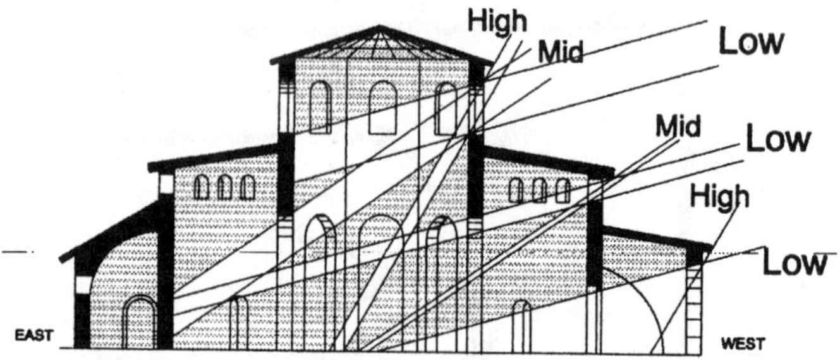


*Hypothetical Reconstruction of the Octagonal Church at Capernaum showing Sunlines. Adapted from Corbo, 1975.*

In fact, this space appears to have been designed so that it is very well lit from the sun. In the Hypothetical Reconstruction one can see that whether the sun is high, mid, or low in the sky, the central octagon shows high illumination from the sun. One sees shafts of light penetrating gloom, perhaps not as gloomy as the fourth century church, but darker than the exterior. In any case, it seems that the lighting of the interior from the sun may express the same metaphor for God's glory as in the fourth century church and in synagogues of the first to the fifth century.

Following Tilley, then, it seems that the Fifth Century Octagonal Church carries many of the design features of the fourth century church that preceded it. These features suggest that that the octagon is also a metaphor for pilgrimage. In that case those who walked to the center would experience emotions, insights, and intuitions and engage in the appropriate ritual action (prayer, meditation, chanting or singing, kneeling, etc.) Room 1 would mediate meanings directly (the "inexpressibility thesis").

Furthermore the nesting of the whole, the distinctive silhouette, and the introduction of light through clerestory windows would all communicate the function and importance of this room to the community (the "compactness thesis").

Third, the central octagon would also facilitate memory and therefore tradition. One enters and remembers the gospel stories that connect Jesus, Peter, and Andrew (and Peter's mother-in-law) to Capernaum. One may engage in relating these stories or reading them to those assembled (the "vividness thesis"). By this time the literal connection to this spot is invisible, but not inaudible. Above all it is metaphorical.

Fourth, the central octagon would function to link the experiences of those early disciples and apostles with one's experience here and now. Written and oral stories about Jesus and the apostles gain a concrete context in this building. This space with its interior finish, smells, and sounds now functions as one's concrete experience of those stories and memories which are otherwise abstractions. As an aside, a pilgrim may return home with a firm memory of a mosaic peacock in his or her mind. In that case the peacock would advance in importance among pilgrims as an operative symbol for their pilgrimage.[17]

I have proposed that painted plaster is a skeuomorph for marble. By analogy, I would suggest that cut stone in the fifth century church "stands for" high status just as surely as the marble does.

I have also suggested that the lighting of the central octagon from high in the upper story is a metaphor for the illumination that one gains in this space. By analogy light is a metaphorical experience of the "glory of God" for the experient in the central octagon.

The very nesting of porch, inner octagon, and central octagon embodies an idea of transition, similar to that of the movement from atrium to rooms 4 and 5 in the fourth century church. In this case we have a transition continuously from outside to porch to octagon to central octagon. We also have the continuous viewing of the goal (the central octagon) as one walks toward the center. In the fourth century church the goal was invisible, yet, both seem to embody the metaphor of the pilgrim's journey.

Finally, the Church of the Fifth Century exhibits several of the ideas of a structure having a coherent language to organize reality. In this case we have named the central octagon above Room 1 as the goal of pilgrimage. The nesting of the central octagon, its silhouette, the idea of transition embodied in its successive octagons, its finely cut stones, and its lighting all conspire to provide a powerful metaphor for the church as pilgrimage body. To be a pilgrim means to walk into and be present in this edifice with these specific features. Being a pilgrim also means many other things, some of them ritual behaviors, and these rituals would be appropriate for this space. We cannot infer much about the specific rituals, but we can infer the central idea of the church.

## Conclusions

The purpose of this analysis in the first place was to determine to what extent one might infer propositions about religion from certain elements of material culture, in this case a synagogue and two churches. Although the aim was not comparative religion, it is instructive to see how differently Christians and Jews solved the problem of erecting architecture appropriate to their local expressions. It is also instructive

---

[17]If so, it is reasonable to hypothesize that peacocks would appear in other pilgrimage churches of this century.

to see that one cannot easily infer detailed propositions about religion from architecture. We can tell that they gather, that they wish to set aside specific properties for their gatherings, and that they are willing to spend large amounts of money for their finish and fixtures. But these attitudes and values are not necessarily distinctive when considered from the point of view of other religions. In fact, we are making generalizations from Capernaum that seem to apply to almost any religion anywhere.

That which yields propositions specific to Judaism and Christianity are more concrete than abstract. Those who meet in the synagogue apparently wish to hear declamation of Torah. Some sit in one space to hear, others assemble in the central space between the columns and perform the ritual. In the case of the fourth century church, participants must thread their way through open spaces, between low, ruined walls, and then enter the building. Then they are obliged to walk though two more rooms before they realize their goal. In a sense, they are participating in the end of their pilgrimage journey, not a processional.

Even the Byzantine octagonal church seems to invite walking to the center. The walk may be understood as the final steps in pilgrimage so that the pilgrim arrives at a small, octagonal space without furniture, the goal of his or her journey. Pilgrimage is the idea.

## Works Cited

Pierre Bourdieu, *Outline of a Theory of Practice.* Cambridge: Cambridge University Press, 1977.

Virgillio Corbo, *Cafarnao I: Gli edifici dell Città.* Jerusalem: Franciscan Printing Press, 1975.

David Miller and Christopher Tilley, "Editorial," *The Journal of Material Culture*, vol. 1/1 (1996):5-14.

James F. Strange, "The Synagogue as Metaphor," Ch. 5 in *Judaism in Late Antiquity. Part 3, vol. 4, Where We Stand,* edited by Jacob Neusner and Alan Avery-Peck. Leiden: E.J. Brill, 2000: 91-120, 7 figures.

Emannuele Testa, *Cafarnao IV: I Graffiti.* Jerusalem: Franciscan Printing Press, 1972.

Christopher Tilley, "Claude Lévi-Strauss: structuralism and beyond." In *Reading Material Culture,* Edited by Christopher Tilley. Oxford: Blackwell Publishers, 1990.

Christopher Tilley, *Metaphor and Material Culture.* Oxford: Blackwell Publishers, 1999.

# 3

# From Economic Culture to Theological Interpretation: Nazareth, Capernaum, and Jerusalem as Environments of Jesus' Teaching

Bruce Chilton
*Bard College*

Three economies that influenced Jesus' teaching are chosen here, because recent archaeological and socially historical work has laid them bare in a way they have not been before. Nazareth, Capernaum, and Jerusalem each has a distinctive economic ethos, to which Jesus responds distinctively on the evidence of the Gospels.

But the approach taken here is not only a matter of taking account of the social anthropology of Jesus' environments, important thought that is. Even more fundamentally, the Gospels themselves need to be approached as the products, not of single, homogeneous communities, but of the different cultures and climes which fed the interpretation of Jesus over time, depending on their application of the tradition concerning him. For that reason, the translation of texts here is neither a rendering in smooth English, nor a representation of the Semitic forms presumably rendered by the Greek, but an approximation of the distinctive, mostly non-literary styles of the Synoptic Gospels.

Following an accepted (but by no means universal) chronology, Mark is placed in Rome c. 73 C.E., Matthew in Damascus c. 80 C.E., and Luke in Antioch c. 90 C.E. The stark reality of a considerable gap in culture, geography, and time – a distance exacerbated by the very different sociology produced by the emergence of Christianity itself – precludes simply embedding the texts of the Gospels in the material context of Galilee and Judea as suggested by archaeological and historical research. Instead, Jesus' movement in its initial phase, an inference from what the Gospels say about it in aggregate at a much later stage, will alone resonate helpfully with research into material culture. Inserting the urban Jesus of Luke directly into the agricultural context of Galilee described by Richard Horsley, for example, would produce a dissonance, which has more to do with the clumsiness of the investigator than with the impact of Jesus himself.

Recent work on Nazareth is well represented in Richard Horsley's study of economic life in Galilee.[1] He articulates a devastating critique of the facile assumption that Jewish communities there were simply swallowed up in the urban structures of the Hellenistic world. That assumption, built into John Dominic Crossan's portrait of Jesus as a Cynic philosopher in the mold of Diogenes, takes no account of the social isolation of small Galilean villages from Hellenistic towns such as Sepphoris nearby and their architectural distinctiveness. Nazareth was a tiny settlement of no more than a couple of hundred, housed in earthen sheds around courtyards for common cooking and milling, with a central facility for pressing wine and olives. No synagogue, no market, no baths, certainly no theater, in the manner of nearby Sepphoris.

Horsley puts especial emphasis on the discovery of hordes of coins in Galilee.[2] Repeatedly, these have been found in villages, but the remarkable feature is that the coins are mixed up—those in circulation and those not—and come from different areas. From this Horsley draws the conclusion that communities such as Nazareth did not ordinarily use currency, but practiced an exchange economy, in which custom regulated the production and distribution of goods and services.

There has often been a more than faintly Marxist cast to Horsley's Jesus, and a little caution is in order here. First, there have not been many finds of hordes; and whenever one is found, the possibility of disturbance—ancient or modern—must always be accounted for. Still, Horsley points out that the hordes are there, and they do not seem disturbed. But then there is another factor. We have tangible evidence of trade among Jewish villages, in the stone vessels used for purification and manufactured in Galilee itself.[3] Likewise, Josephus refers to the sale

---

[1]*Archaeology, History, and Society in Galilee: The Social Context of Jesus and the Rabbis* (Valley Forge, Pa.: Trinity Press International, 1996).

[2]See his *Galilee. History, Politics, People* (Valley Forge: Trinity Press International, 1995) 189-221.

[3]See James F. Strange, "First Century Galilee from Archaeology and from the Texts," *Archaeology and the Galilee. Texts and Contexts in the Graeco-Roman and Byzantine Periods:* South Florida Studies in the History of Judaism 143 (Atlanta: Scholars Press, 1997) 39-48.

by Galileans of their olive oil to Jews in Syria, even during the difficult conditions of the war with Rome (*Jewish War* 5 §§ 591-592).

So what we seem to have in Jewish Galilee is neither simply a Hellenistic urban economy imposed from without, nor a currency-free exchange economy among farmer/pastoralists, but a hybrid of local exchange among families and individuals and trade from village to village among communities, the latter implicitly involving at least some currency. Just that hybrid helps to explain how Jesus came, in Nazareth, to frame a classic picture of what he called the kingdom of God as evidenced in a saying from the source within the Gospels called "Q," probably to be dated to the year 35 C.E. (Matthew 8:11; Luke 13:28, 29):[4]

> Many shall come from east and west and recline in feasting with Abraam and Isaak and Iaqob....

There can be no doubt of the emphasis upon a future consummation in the saying, involving a particular (but unnamed) place, the actions and materials of festivity (including the luxurious custom of reclining, not sitting, at a banquet), and the incorporation of the many who shall rejoice in the company of the patriarchs.

Jesus' use of the imagery of feasting in order to refer to the kingdom of God, a characteristic of his message, is resonant both with early Judaic language of divine sovereignty and with his own activity. The picture of God offering a feast on Mount Zion "for all peoples," where death itself is swallow up, becomes an influential image from the time of Isaiah 25:6-8, and is developed later in an apocalytic key, for example in Isaiah 56 and Zechariah 14. Notably, the Targum of Isaiah refers to the divine disclosure on Mount Zion with the verbatim phrase "the kingdom of the LORD of hosts" (24:23);[5] that is, the Targum extends the reference to God's rule in the Hebrew text of Isaiah to a direct reference to the kingdom of God. As a result of such reference, the feast on Mount Zion had its place as part of the anticipation of divine judgment within the time of Jesus.[6] Sayings such as the one cited from "Q" invoke that imagery, and Jesus' practice of fellowship at meals with his disciples and

[4]On such sources, see Chilton, *Profiles of a Rabbi. Synoptic Opportunities in Reading about Jesus:* Brown Judaic Studies 177 (Atlanta: Scholars Press, 1989) and *A Feast of Meanings. Eucharistic Theologies from Jesus through Johannine Circles:* Supplements to *Novum Testamentum* 72 (Leiden: Brill, 1994).

[5]See Chilton, *The Isaiah Targum. Introduction, Translation, Apparatus, and Notes:* The Aramaic Bible 11 (Wilmington: Glazier and Edinburgh: Clark, 1987).

[6]See Chilton, *A Galilean Rabbi and His Bible. Jesus' Use of the Interpreted Scripture of His Time* (Wilmington: Glazier, 1984) also published with the subtitle, *Jesus' own interpretation of Isaiah* (London: SPCK, 1984).

many others amounted to a claim that the ultimate festivity had already begun.

Apart from its vivid imagery, the economics of this assertion are striking: the wealth that a Galilean can only imagine as achieved by means of trade, including symposial reclining, is to be enjoyed in the most fundamental medium of exchange—the festive communal meal. The transfer from what only trade can produce, complete with the couches of a Greco-Roman symposium, into what only the patriarchal exchange can consume makes this statement into a surreal promise in the context of Nazareth (as in the context of Galilee as a whole). In the setting of the periodic movements of rebellion, which broke in this region, such an economic transfer must have carried with it in the minds of some practitioners at least an implication that foreign wealth was to be appropriated.

As against this embrace of wealth within festal imagery, we have another well-known assertion; the simplicity of the words underscores their drama (Luke 6:20b-23), as well as the contrast with the promise asserted in rural Galilee:

> The poor are favored, because *yours* is the kingdom of God; Those who hunger now are favored, because you will be satisfied; Those who weep now are favored, because you will laugh; You are favored, when humanity hates you and when they exclude you and censure you and put out your name as evil on the one like the person's account. Rejoice in that day and skip, for look: your reward is great in the heaven; for their fathers did the same things to the prophets.

At first, it seems odd to find these words attributed to Jesus during his period in Capernaum. After all, here was a Jewish town – a real town, of a thousand rather than a few hundred—with a synagogue and genuine comfort: distinctive houses of basalt, with windows, stairs to upper stories, ornamental pebbles on the floors, and the relatively luxurious furnishings of ceramic lamps, plates, bowls and cups.[7] All quite unlike Nazareth, and potentially an image of just the sort of festivity Jesus had spoken of in the hill country of Galilee. And yet what had been praised as a metaphor is rejected when it becomes reality.

Confronted with wealth, he praises poverty, or so it might seem at first. But the situation is actually more complex. Capernaum lived off of its well developed port and fishing industry—a coordinated commerce involving those who caught fish, those who stored, those who salted and those who sold. Commerce that complex necessarily involved currency.

---

[7]See John J. Rousseau and Rami Arav, "Capernaum," *Jesus and His World* (Minneapolis: Fortress, 1995) 39-47.

From the year 19/20 C.E. (that is, his twenty-fourth regnal year) Herod Antipas had non-idolatrous coins struck for towns such as Capernaum at nearby Tiberius. Instead of bearing any image of an animal, an emperor, a god or a diadem, these coins sported palm trees, palm branches, dates, and reeds, all compatible with the commandment against idolatry. Discussion of coinage has filled out the picture of the economic structure of the town,[8] and has shown that the scholarly habit of referring to Jewish coins as "aniconic" is misleading. An inevitable byproduct of currency, however, is its absence, that is: the creation of poverty by the inability of some people to enter into trade. Josephus attests the existence of landless Galileans during this period, who were attracted not only to established towns such as Capernaum, but to the newly founded Tiberias, whose constructed on an old cemetery enraged local sentiment against it, but made for cheap land, and even free homesteads donated by Herod Antipas (*Antiquities* 18 §§ 36-38).

Jesus' well-known advice to a townsman is to reverse this progression, to give away his property and follow with the other disciples (Mark 10:17-31, cf. the analogous passages in Matthew 19:16-30 and Luke 18:18-30):

> He was proceeding out on a way and one ran up to him, and kneeling to him, interrogated him, Good teacher, what should I do so that I might inherit perpetual life? But Iesu said to him, Why do you say I am good? No one is good, except one: God! You know the decrees, Do not murder, do not commit adultery, do not steal, do not witness falsely, do not deprive, honor your father and mother. But he told him, Teacher, I have kept all these things from my youth. Yet Iesu look at him, loved him, and said to him, One thing is lacking you: depart, sell as much as you have and give to poor people, and you will have a store in heaven. And come on, follow me. But he was appalled at the word and went away grieving, because he had many effects. Iesu looked around and says to his students, With what labor will those who have effects enter the kingdom of God! But his students were astonished at his words; but Iesu replying again says to them, Children, what labor it is to enter the kingdom of God! It is easier for a camel to pass through a needle's hole than for a rich person to enter into the kingdom of God. But they were completely overwhelmed, saying to one another, So who can be saved? Iesu looked at them and says, Impossible with people, but not with God: because everything is possible with God. Rock began to say to him, Look: we left everything, and followed you. Iesu stated, Amen I say to you, there is no one who has left home or brothers or sisters or mother or father or children or lands for my sake and the sake of the message, except that shall receive a hundred times over—now in this

[8]See John W. Betlyon, "Coinage," *The Anchor Bible Dictionary* 1 (ed. D. N. Freedman; New York: Doubleday, 1992)1076-1089.

> time—homes and brothers and sisters and mothers and children and fields—with persecutions—and in the age that is coming perpetual life. But many first shall be last, and the last first.

The prominence of Peter is evocative of the apostolic community in Jerusalem which he headed, and in which communal possessions were the rule according to Acts (Acts 4:34-35). The ethos of that group is attested positively by its praise of Barnabas, who was willing (as the anonymous man who met Jesus was not) to sell up property and follow with the other disciples (Acts 4:36-37)). But there is also a negative—and far more dramatic — attestation of this ethos, when Ananias and his wife Saphira withhold from the value of property they claim to have turned the whole of over to the community, and are struck dead for lying against the holy spirit (Acts 5:1-11).

A policy of disposing of wealth in order to alleviate poverty is evident both here and elsewhere in the traditions of the New Testament, along with a claim that the reversion to an exchange economy by means of wealth so disposed will bring "a hundred times over—now in this time." Supported by the donations of others, and notably by contributions from an apostle named Paul, the community in Jerusalem attempted to implement this policy more than any other church known to us during the ancient period.

An obvious way forward now would be to claim that in this developmental movement from the ethos of Nazareth to the ethos of Capernaum, we see in Jesus not only change, but maturity. The old vision of the enjoyment of festal wealth is transformed by experience into a denial of the kind of wealth that produces poverty, and therefore a commendation of communal possessions. As we have seen, the circle of Peter appears to have taken just such a line in its overall evaluation of Jesus' position.

The vehemence of that point of view is evident in Matthew 17:24-27:

> Yet as they came into Kafarnaum, those who take the double drachma came forward to Rock and said, Your teacher does not pay the double drachma? He says, Yes. And when he came into the house, Iesu anticipated him saying, How does it seem to you, Simon? Who do the kings of the earth take customs or tax from? From their sons or from foreigners? Yet as he was saying, From the foreigners. Iesu stated to him, Therefore the sons are indeed free! But so that we will not cause them to falter, proceed to a sea, throw a fishhook, and take the first fish that comes up. Open its mouth, and you will find a stater: take that, give to them for me and you!

Here is a literal statement, to Peter of course, that those who want money for the Temple – which the tax of the double drachma was designed to collect – can literally go fish for it. Jesus refuses to confuse God and mammon, as he stated elsewhere, using the Aramaic term for money (Matthew 6:24; Luke 16:13), by introducing currency into the sanctuary.

The issue posed by Peter's interlocutors in v. 24 focuses on whether Jesus followed the normal custom. Peter's unqualified "yes" (v. 25a) would seem to put paid to the question, as well as to the tax. But Jesus' reaction (vv. 25b-27) makes his overall position appear ambivalent. Verses 25b-26 appear to constitute an emphatically negative response: since kings tax their subjects for the benefit of their sons, the sons are exempt. God does not tax his own people.

The sting in the tale of the parable in Matthew, of course, is that its attitude is developed in respect of the Temple, not Rome. Moreover, the "payment" is made in practice only in the sense that v. 27 refers to an action. Within the Matthean realm of meaning a miraculous event is probably implied, but—within its own terms of reference and its contemporary, Judaic context—the command Jesus gives Peter may well be taken as parabolic. Even on the supposition that v. 27 refers to the fishing as an actual event, the tax is not actually paid by Peter or Jesus in Matthew. What may at first sight appear an ambivalent response is in fact negative: the stater in the mouth of the fish is a sop, not a solution.[9]

Within the actual terms of conditions of Capernaum, of course, there was virtually no chance that such a policy could succeed among the general population. It is no coincidence that it is precisely to that town that Jesus says (Luke 10:15, cf. Matthew 11:23):

> And you, Kafarnaum, would you be exalted unto heaven? You will go down unto Hades'!

Currency here brings exactly the opposite of upward mobility.

But just as a neat policy seems to be emerging, and did finally emerge, fully developed in the *halakhah* of Petrine Christianity, we encounter a new economy, and a new attitude towards it. Jerusalem by the time Jesus entered the city during Sukkoth (probably in the year 31 C.E.) was going through an expansion, such that its population was around 50,000, including Roman soldiers, thousands of visitors, merchants from many lands, as well as residents, Jewish and otherwise. This was not merely a thriving place, but a magnet of commerce and

---

[9]For further discussion of the passage in its historical context and development, see Chilton, "A Coin of Three Realms: Matthew 17:24-27," *The Bible in Three Dimensions. Essays in celebration of forty years of Biblical Studies in the University of Sheffield:* Journal for the Study of the Old Testament, Supplement 87 (ed. D. J. A. Clines, S. E. Fowl, S. E. Porter; Sheffield: JSOT, 1990) 269-282, reprinted in Chilton and Craig A. Evans, *Jesus in Context. Temple, Purity and Restoration:* Arbeiten zur Geschichte des Antiken Judentums und des Urchristentums XXXIX (Leiden: Brill, 1997) 339-351.

capital; the building program of Herod the Great and his successors ensured an architectural development unparalleled at any time in the history of the city, and provided opportunities beyond the reckoning of any Galilean peasant, fisherman, or rabbi.[10]

So here would be a perfect occasion to decry wealth and everything to do with it, and in fact Jesus does object to vendors in the vicinity of the sanctuary (whose presence contradicted rabbinic practice as much as it did his own Galilean sensibilities). But when it comes to the crucial issue of what to do with the currency of Jerusalem, the most Romanized Jesus ever encountered, his *halakhah* apparently changes (see Mark 12:13-17, and the analogous passages in Matthew 22:15-22 and Luke 20:20-26):

> And they delegate to him some of the Farasayahs and Herodians, so they could catch him by speech. They came and say to him, Teacher, we know that you are truthful and no one concerns you, because you do not look to people's regard, but in truth you teach the way of God. Is it right to give Caesar tax or not? Shall we give or not give? But knowing their hypocrisy he said to them, Why do you press me to the limit? Bring me a denarius so I can see. Yet they did bring, and he says to them, Whose is this image and inscription? But they said to him, Caesar's.Yet Iesu said, Caesar's repay to Caesar, and God's to God. And they marveled over him.

And on most people's reckoning, that settles the matter: whatever Jesus recommended as a matter of personal policy (his own, his disciples', and potential disciples'), he left the question of money to worldly authority in the shape of Caesar. The only question then becomes that of the best authority for understanding that world, Plato or Aristotle, Karl Marx or Adam Smith.

But the neat secularism of leaving this world to Caesar and occupying one's truest life to God, serviceable though it has been to theologians and humanists alike, rests upon an anachronistic reading of Jesus' position. The assumption of much exegesis has been that Jesus is here addressing an issue of loyalties in the abstract: what belongs to Caesar, and what to God? That makes sense, provided no account is taken of the context of the dispute with the Pharisees and Herodians. Because a major aspect of their insidious question is that Jesus is standing, not on neutral ground where an abstract question about loyalties might be discussed, but precisely in the Temple he has just occupied in order to remove some of the commercial operations. They are asking about the relationship between the wealth that might be owned and the wealth that is to be sacrificed.

---

[10]See Philip J. King, "Jerusalem," *The Anchor Bible Dictionary* 3 (ed. D. N. Freedman and others; New York, Doubleday, 1992) 747-766.

Jesus' occupation of the Temple was itself no spontaneous act, but an enactment of the prophecy at the close of the book of Zechariah, where the elimination of merchants from the Temple is the climactic image. The purpose of that exclusion is not to exclude wealth as such, but to draw it in: to join in the governing image of people of all nations—Jews and non-Jews—offering sacrifice without mediation within the realization of God's sovereignty.[11] That economic action drives the prophetic realization. This is neither wealth dispensed nor accrued (as in Jesus' metaphor from his period in Nazareth), and it is far from a blanket rejection of wealth (as in his Capernaum period), but wealth here is focused in a sacrifice which provides for what sacrifice always provided for in Israel: distribution to humans as well as divine consumption. When it comes to ascertaining the reason for Jesus' apparent shifts in economic attitude, the answer lies not in Adam Smith nor Karl Marx, not in Aristotle nor Plato. It is not the economy, stupid, but Zechariah.

And if Zechariah, then the model of what drives the economic variability of Christian thought must change. Max Weber's picture of the rise of capitalism, as driven by the ability of Protestants to defer their rewards until the next world, has been rightly criticized for its inadequacy as an explanation of Catholic theology's penchant for capitalistic institutions.[12] But the problem with the picture is not only that its attempt to reduce the issue to Protestantism fails, but that it is too static in its picture of the transcendence that Christianity as a whole involves.

Jesus' perspective is not of one world and the next, but of one world becoming the next. As a result, elements of present experience become emblems of what is to come; a meal in Nazareth can prefigure festivity with Abraham, Isaac, and Jacob. At the same time, entire institutions can be resisted, when they appear to be in conflict with that vision, as when the poor are praised in Capernaum. Yet whether the attitude towards wealth and its creation appears to be acceptance, resistance—or, again, the sort of apparent compromise developed in Jerusalem—the operative principle is teleological, and therefore instrumental in its relationship to all the institutions of this world, including wealth and money.

---

[11]See Chilton, *The Temple of Jesus. His Sacrificial Program Within a Cultural History of Sacrifice* (University Park: The Pennsylvania State University Press, 1992).

[12]See *Protestantism and Capitalism. The Weber Thesis and Irs Critics* (ed. R. W. Green; Heath: Boston, 1959) and Ralph Schroeder, *Max Weber and the sociology of culture* (London: SAGE, 1992).

# 4

# Portraying the Temple in Stone and Text: The Arch of Titus and the Epistle to the Hebrews

Ellen Bradshaw Aitken
*Harvard Divinity School*

The Epistle to the Hebrews has attracted a variety of interpretive approaches, including readings that are predominantly structural, theological, literary, ethical, or sacramental. Seldom, however, does one find readings that explicitly explore Hebrews in political or ideological terms. This is due in part to the lack of easily identifiable historical references in the text.[1] It is also a result of the difficulty both of assigning anything but a fairly broad range of dates for the composition of Hebrews and of locating its geographical provenance. Thus Hebrews floats, as it were, unanchored in place and time, lending itself to readings that are less dependent upon place and time than are political and ideological approaches.[2]

[1]Hebrews seldom refers to the historical experience of its audience; an exception is Heb 10:32–34, "But recall those earlier days, when after you had been enlightened, you endured a hard struggle with sufferings, sometimes being publicly exposed to abuse and persecutions, and sometimes being partners with those so treated. For you had compassion for those who were in prison, and you cheerfully accepted the plundering of your possessions, knowing that you yourselves possessed something better and more lasting." On the relevance of this passage for the dating of Hebrews, see below.

[2]We might compare the development of political readings of parts of the Pauline corpus, which are facilitated by the relative precision possible in dating these letters. See, for example, Dieter Georgi, *Theocracy in Paul's Practice and Theology*

It is my contention in this essay, however, that it is possible to correlate certain aspects of the christology and community ethic found in Hebrews with events in Roman imperial rule, and particularly its expression in imperial propaganda, as it is manifested in monuments and ritual. This correlation invites an interpretation of Hebrews in political terms. In order to do so, however, it is necessary to provide the text with a provisional anchor in time and space, that is, by proceeding on the hypothesis that Hebrews was composed in the city of Rome in the 70s or early 80s of the first century C.E. Moreover, if the correlation is convincing, it can become the basis for establishing the plausibility of this hypothesis about the compositional date and provenance of Hebrews.

More specifically, I am arguing here that Hebrews should be read as one response to the imperial ideology expressed in the events and monuments surrounding the triumph of Vespasian and Titus, a triumph bestowed upon them by the Roman Senate for their victory in the First Jewish War and the destruction of Jerusalem in 70 C.E. To anticipate my conclusions, Hebrews makes use of some of the elements of the triumph—both the customary rites of the triumph and the key elements of the Flavian triumph—in order to articulate resistance to imperial rule and ideology. It does so by depicting to whom the "real" triumph belongs and where the "real" temple is. In addition, it does so by promoting an ethic for the community, its inscribed audience, an ethic that is consonant with the identity of the true triumphant ruler and which values solidarity with those who are perceived to be suffering under Flavian rule.

My presuppositions in making this argument include the following. First, Hebrews is a highly multivalent text that contains numerous

---

(trans. David E. Green; Minneapolis: Fortress, 1991); Helmut Koester, "From Paul's Eschatology to the Apocalyptic Schemata of 2 Thessalonians," in Raymond F. Collins, ed., *The Thessalonian Correspondence* (Louvain: Peeters, 1990) 441–58, reprinted as "Imperial Ideology and Paul's Eschatology in 1 Thessalonians," in Richard A. Horsley, ed., *Paul and Empire: Religion and Power in Roman Imperial Society* (Harrisburg, Penn.: Trinity Press International, 1997) 158–66; and Neil Elliott, *Liberating Paul: The Justice of God and the Politics of the Apostle* (Maryknoll, N.Y.: Orbis, 1994). David deSilva's recent commentary, *Perseverance in Gratitude: A Social-Rhetorical Commentary on the Epistle "to the Hebrews"* (Grand Rapids: Eerdmans, 2000), provides an explicitly *social* interpretation of Hebrews, in that he uses the categories of honor and shame as markers of social status. Although he speaks of the reproach, loss of honor, lowered economic status experienced by Hebrews' audience as a result of their refusal to participate in Roman religions and their rejection of their neighbors' values, he assumes this situation as common to all Christian groups and thus does not relate it to a historical, political situation specific to the audience of Hebrews.

interwoven ways of constructing and defining the identity and ethic of its audience, as is not uncommon in texts that are homiletical in character.[3] Thus, within a broad view, this is a reading that works together with others, for example, a recognition of the way in which the story of the journey through the wilderness toward the Jordan River is used to constitute the audience[4] or interpretations that emphasize the eschatological dimension of its worldview and theology.[5] Second, Hebrews is ultimately a parenetic text, aimed at shaping the community's way of life.[6] Third, I presuppose that there can be multiple rhetorical sites for developing political resistance, that such sites do not need to be explicitly political, and that a political ideology can be developed through scriptural interpretation, cultic reflection, allegory, hymnody, as well as through visual art, coinage, architecture, and religious festivals.

---

[3]On the homiletic character of Hebrews, see Lawrence Wills, "The Form of the Sermon in Hellenistic Judaism and Early Christianity," *HTR* 77 (1984) 280–83; C. Clifton Black, "The Rhetorical Form of the Hellenistic Jewish and Early Christian Sermon: A Response to Lawrence Wills [77:277–299 1984]" *HTR* 81 (1988) 1–18; Harold W. Attridge, "Paraenesis in a homily (λόγος παρακλήσεως)," *Semeia* 50 (1990) 211–26. See also George W. MacRae, "Heavenly Temple and Eschatology in the Letter to the Hebrews," *Semeia* 12 (1978) 179–99. Hebrews characterizes itself as a λόγος παρακλήσεως ("word of exhortation") at 13:22; see Attridge, *Hebrews*, 14, 408, who points out that this designation is used in Acts 13:15 for Paul's synagogue address in Psidian Antioch. More recently, David A. deSilva accepts the position that Hebrews is a sermon, but one that makes significant use of the conventions of hellenistic epideictic rhetoric; see deSilva, *Perseverance in Gratitude*, 58, 514.

[4]See Ernst Käsemann, *The Wandering People of God: An Investigation of the Epistle to the Hebrews* (trans. Roy A. Harrisville; Minneapolis: Augsburg, 1984); Ellen B. Aitken, "The Morphology of the Passion Narrative" (Th.D. diss., Harvard University, 1997) 165–213.

[5]See, for example, MacRae, "Heavenly Temple"; C. K. Barrett, "The Eschatology of the Epistle to the Hebrews," in W. D. Davies and D. Daube, eds., *The Background of the New Testament and Its Eschatology: C. H. Dodd Festschrift* (Cambridge: Cambridge University Press, 1954) 363–93; Jean Cambier, "Eschatologie ou hellénisme dans l'Épître aux Hébreux: Une étude sur μένειν et l'exhortation final de l'épître," *Salesianum* 11 (1949) 62–86.

[6]The alternation of exposition and exhortation in Hebrews is widely recognized and informs most attempts to outline the structure of Hebrews; see the discussion in Attridge, *Hebrews*, 14–21. Attridge also identifies (p. 21) the two types of exhortation found in the text, "let us hold fast" and "let us approach" (both found in Heb 4:14–16). On the pastoral dimension of Hebrews, see Otto Kuss, "Der Verfasser der Hebräerbrief als Seelsorger," *TThZ* 67 (1958) 1–12, 65–80.

## The Date and Provenance of Hebrews

A brief overview of the main arguments about the compositional date of Hebrews is in order. A date after 60 C.E. is supported by the indications that the audience have been believers for some time (5:12) and that they are dependent upon others who "heard the Lord" (2:3); earlier dates are generally tied to untenable hypotheses about Paul, Apollos, Aquila, or Priscilla as the author.[7] A date following the Neronian persecutions in Rome in 64 C.E. is suggested by the references to past persecution of the community (10:32–34, 12:4).[8] Arguments for a *terminus ad quem* of 96 C.E. depend upon a secure dating of *1 Clement*, with its use of the text of Hebrews, to 96 C.E. Harold Attridge, who does not accept such a certain date for *1 Clement*, posits the possibility that Hebrews could have been composed as late as 135 C.E., but more likely before 100 C.E., because of the reference to Timothy in the postscript of Hebrews (13:23). He thus concludes with a date range of 70–100 C.E., with the likelihood of a date in the 70s or 80s because of the theological and literary affinities with other Christian texts of this period.[9]

The destruction of the Jerusalem temple has occasionally been used in arguments about compositional date: the lack of any mention of the destruction of the temple in a text so concerned with the rituals of the temple, along with the use of the present tense for the temple activities, has been taken to indicate a date before 70 C.E.[10] Against this position, I agree with Attridge and Erich Grässer that Hebrews is concerned not

---

[7]For a summary of arguments about authorship, see Attridge, *Hebrews*, 1–6; Erich Grässer, *An die Hebräer* (3 vols.; EKK; Zürich: Benziger Verlag and Neukirchen-Vluyn: Neukirchener Verlag, 1990) 1. 19–22; Frederick Fyvie Bruce, "'To the Hebrews': A Document of Roman Christianity," *ANRW* 25.4:3496–99; deSilva, *Perseverance in Gratitude*, 23–39; Cynthia Briggs Kittredge, "Hebrews," in Elisabeth Schüssler Fiorenza, ed., *Searching the Scriptures*, vol. 2: *A Feminist Commentary* (New York: Crossroad, 1993) 430–34.

[8]See Attridge, *Hebrews*, 298–99, particularly on how the language of these verses recalls Tacitus's description (*Annales* 15.44) of the persecution of Christians in Rome under Nero in 64 C.E. The reference is admittedly ambiguous, however, and others, opting for an earlier date, have taken it as a reference to the expulsion of the Jews from Rome under Claudius in 49 C.E.; see William Manson, *The Epistle to the Hebrews: An Historical and Theological Reconsideration* (London: Hodder & Stoughton, 1951) 159ff.; Bruce, "'To the Hebrews,'" 3519.

[9]Attridge, *Hebrews*, 9. Grässer (*An die Hebräer*, 25), following the same lines of argumentation, prefers a date in the 80s or 90s, since he sees indications of increased pressure on the Christian community, a situation that he relates to the reign of Domitian (81–96 C.E.).

[10]See, for example, Bruce, "'To the Hebrews,'" 3514; Albert Vanhoye, *Situation du Christ: Épître aux Hébreux 1–2* (LD 58: Paris: Cerf, 1969) 50; August Strobel, *Der Brief an die Hebräer* (NTD; Göttingen, 1975) 83; and most recently, deSilva, *Perseverance in Gratitude*, 20–21.

with the Herodian temple per se, but with the desert tabernacle, and moreover uses the tabernacle cult as a foundation for the christology and parenesis of the text.[11] The destruction of the Herodian temple is thus not an expressed element in this exposition, and therefore cannot be determinative of the date of Hebrews. It is possible to observe, moreover, that this debate centers on the *destruction* or loss of the temple per se, rather than on the display and celebration of that destruction as part of the imperial propaganda of Vespasian, Titus, and Domitian.

The position that Hebrews was composed for an audience in Rome enjoys a broad consensus, and I shall not fully rehearse the arguments here.[12] I would note, however, that arguments that dissent from this view nonetheless connect Hebrews with Rome in some fashion, usually locating the author in a Roman context.[13] Any attempts to locate Hebrews geographically must contend with the phrase "those from Italy greet you" (ἀσπάζονται ὑμᾶς οἱ ἀπὸ τῆς Ἰταλίας, Heb 13:24), which may equally designate a group within Italy (including Rome) or a group abroad sending greetings back to their home community.[14]

The strong homiletical character of Hebrews also has implications for the discussion of the provenance and destination of the text. Even though Hebrews is unlikely to be a transcript of a sermon, it certainly uses considerable material from a homiletical context, material that may have developed within a Roman Christian environment. We might then

---

[11]Attridge, *Hebrews*, 8; Grässer, *An die Hebräer*, 25.

[12]Key elements in arguing for a Roman provenance for Hebrews include its use by 1 Clement, especially *1 Clem.* 36.2–6, but also elsewhere; see Attridge, *Hebrews*, 6–7; and Donald A. Hagner, *The Use of the Old and New Testaments in Clement of Rome* (NovTSup 34; Leiden: Brill, 1973). Peter Lampe is cautious about accepting Hebrews as a text of Roman Christianity and thus does not discuss it at any length in his study of earliest Christianity in Rome; see Peter Lampe, *Die stadtrömischen Christen in den ersten beiden Jahrhunderten: Untersuchungen zur Sozialgeschichte* (WUNT 2nd ser. 18; Tübingen: Mohr Siebeck, 1987) 60–61. F. F. Bruce, although dating Hebrews to the reign of Nero, takes it as a text written most probably to a community in Rome ("'To the Hebrews,'" 3517–19). The position that Hebrews was written to a Jewish Christian house-church in Rome was put forward a century ago by Theodor Zahn (*Einleitung in das Neue Testament* [2 vols.; Leipzig: Deichert, 1897–99) 2. 110ff.). Adolf von Harnack followed Zahn's arguments, arguing, however, not for a Jewish-Christian group as the addressees, but rather for the house-church associated with Priscilla and Aquila, and suggesting that Priscilla was the main author of Hebrews, with the help of Aquila; see Adolf von Harnack, "Probabilia über die Addresse und den Verfasser des Hebräerbrief," *ZNW* 1(1900) 16–41.

[13]Thus, Hugh William Montefiore (*The Epistle to the Hebrews* [New York: Harper, 1964] 11ff.) argues that Hebrews was written to the Corinthian church by Apollos, from Ephesus, but carrying the greetings of the Roman community after the death of Paul.

[14]See Attridge, *Hebrews*, 10.

reasonably suppose that this material was reworked into an elegant and coherent piece of rhetoric both for internal use and for sending to other communities. We should therefore expect ample resonance between the themes, motifs, and arguments of Hebrews and the experience of Christians in the city of Rome. Moreover, Hebrews lacks a thoroughgoing epistolary character, and we see little distance between the situation of the inscribed author or authors and the inscribed audience; both are located in much the same rhetorical context, a context that can be connected in a number of ways with Christianity in the city of Rome.[15] It is therefore appropriate to read Hebrews in the context of public life in the city of Rome, and provisionally, for the purposes of this argument, sometime in the 70s and 80s—that is, in during the reigns of Vespasian, Titus, and the early years of Domitian.

## The Flavian Triumph in Rome

The celebration of the Roman victory in Judea, culminating in the destruction of Jerusalem, has been characterized as the "Flavian Actium." In other words, just as the Battle of Actium in 31 B.C.E. provided one of the chief ideological foundations for Augustan rule, so too did the Flavians employ the Judean victory as the chief propagandistic tool for promoting their consolidation of imperial rule, following the civil wars of 69 C.E.—the year of the four emperors—as an assertion of imperial order out of factionalism.[16] The Judean war, of course, provided the political and military ground out of which the general Vespasian was acclaimed as *imperator* by the legions under his control in 69 and from which he began his cautious journey back to Rome in 70.[17] Following Titus's capture of Jerusalem and the Roman Senate's voting of a triumph for Vespasian and Titus in 71, the subjugation of Judea stood at the center of Flavian propaganda. That is,

---

[15]A consistent historical-rhetorical reading of Hebrews has yet to be done. Such a reading would evaluate the inscribed rhetorical situation (including the inscribed author and audience), before reconstructing the historical situation of the text. On such an approach, see Elisabeth Schüssler Fiorenza, *Rhetoric and Ethic: The Politics of Biblical Studies* (Minneapolis: Fortress, 1999) esp. 105–28.

[16]See G. C. Picard, *Les trophées romains. Contribution à l'histoire de la religion et de l'art triumphal de Rome* (Bibliothèque des écoles françaises d'Athènes et de Rome 187; Paris: Boccard, 1957) 343–44, 359–60, who argues that Jerusalem became the "Flavian Actium." See also Michael Pfanner, *Der Titusbogen* (Beiträge zur Erschließung hellenistischer und kaiserzeitlicher Skupltur und Architektur; Mainz: Phillip von Zabern, 1983) 101, on the use of this victory in Flavian propaganda and on the specific association of the triumph and the apotheosis of Titus.

[17]Fergus Millar, *The Roman Near East 31 BC—AD 337* (Cambridge, Mass.: Harvard University Press, 1993) 73–74.

the Flavian rulers exploited the one-time event of the triumph as the defining point for the public display of their rule.[18] Although the coin issues depicting *Judaea Capta* or *Judaea Devicta* would have spread across the empire,[19] most of the public display was in the city of Rome itself.[20] We may enumerate the chief ceremonial and monumental occasions of this display: in 71 the celebration of the triumph with prayers, procession, executions, and sacrifices; Vespasian's building of the Temple of Peace, dedicated in 75, next to the Roman Forum and in which were housed the spoils from the Jerusalem temple (Josephus *J.W.* 7.158–61); in 81 or shortly thereafter, following Titus's death,[21] the erection of the Arch of Titus at the highest point of the Via Sacra,[22] and it appears, another, earlier arch in the Circus Maximus, erected during

---

[18]On the increased political dimension of the triumph in the principate, see Michael McCormick, *Eternal Victory: Triumphal Rulership in Late Antiquity, Byzantium, and the Early Medieval West* (Cambridge: Cambridge University Press, 1986) 20. McCormick also points out (p. 21) that by such vehicles as monuments, vestments, coinage, titles, and religious rites, an emperor could amplify the victory celebrated in the triumph. On the relationship between triumphs and other Roman *pompae*, see Harriet I. Flower, *Ancestor Masks and Aristocratic Power in Roman Culture* (Oxford: Clarendon, 1996) 107–109. Flower (p. 109) argues that both the triumphal procession and the funeral procession were "overtly political in content, even and especially in representing relationships with the gods." In reading the triumphal rite as political, my work is also informed by that of Simon R. F. Price, *Rituals and Power: The Roman Imperial Cult in Asia Minor* (Cambridge: Cambridge University Press, 1984).

[19]See, among others, *British Museum Catalogue of Coins of the Roman Empire,* 2. 115–18. The first issue dates from 71 C.E., and appears to have been issued in preparation for the triumph; the coins continued through 73, and were revived in 77–78, as well as under Titus. See D. Barag, "The Palestinian *Judaea Capta* Coins of Vespasian and Titus and the Era on the Coins of Agrippa II Minted under the Flavians," *Numismatic Chronicle* 138 (1978) 14–23; C. M. Kraay, "The *Judaea Capta* sestertii of Vespasian," *Israel Numismatic Journal* 3 (1963) 45–46; H. Mattingly, *Coins of the Roman Empire in the British Museum* (2 vols.: London: The British Museum, 1923) 2. xlv–xlvi. E. Mary Smallwood, *The Jews under Roman Rule From Pompey to Diocletian* (Leiden: Brill, 1976) 330 n. 164; and McCormick, *Eternal Victory*, 26–27.

[20]Smallwood, *Jews under Roman Rule,* 329.

[21]Titus died in September 81; coins from 81/82 depict him as *divus* (see *British Museum Catalogue of Coins of the Roman Empire,* 2. plate 69, 9; and Peter N. Schulten, *Die Typologie der römischen Konsekrationsprägungen* [Frankfurt am Mainz: Numismatischer Verlag Schulten, 1979] 66–67), thus establishing a *terminus post quem* for the arch. Pfanner (*Der Titusbogen*, 91–92) argues for a date very early in the reign of Domitian as the most likely time for the erection of the arch.

[22]On the primary function of the triumphal arch, from the first century C.E. onwards, as an instrument of imperial propaganda, for advertising imperial events and honors, see Pfanner, *Der Titusbogen*, 97.

the lifetime of Titus, probably ca. 80,[23] which made explicit mention in its dedicatory inscription of Titus's conquest of Judea and Jerusalem, "following the precepts of his father."[24] The inscription on this earlier arch highlights an important dimension of the Flavian ideology, namely, the celebration of succession from victorious father to victorious son, precisely that dimension of rule which was missing in the Julian-Claudian period and most notably in the year of the four emperors (69 C.E.), during which the disputes over succession led to civil war.[25]

The Arch of Titus on the Via Sacra, as is well known, depicts the triumphal procession, including, on one of the large passageway reliefs (north), Titus and Vespasian in a four-horse chariot, accompanied by lictors, and on the facing relief (south), the weighty spoils from the Temple—a menorah (lampstand) and the table of the shewbread, to which are attached two vessels and two trumpets[26]—which are carried in the procession, along with depictions of the battles and signs with the names of the conquered cities and towns. The center of the arch's

---

[23]This arch has not been found, but may be one of at least four triumphal arches, known from coins, reliefs, and mosaics, in the Circus Maximus, and perhaps the triple arch depicted on the Forma Urbis Romae (the Marble Plan); on this hypothesis, see Pfanner, *Der Titusbogen*, 98. L. Richardson (*A Topographic Dictionary of Ancient Rome* [Baltimore: Johns Hopkins University Press, 1992] 30) accepts this location and suggests that it was most likely located at the rounded end of the Circus Maximus.

[24]*CIL* 6.944; and Hans Ulrich Instinsky, "Der Ruhm des Titus," *Philologus* 97 (1948) 370–71. The text of the inscription reads, "Senatus Populusque Romanus Imp. Tito Caesari Divi Vespasiani F. Vespanian(o) Augusto Pontif. Max. Trib. Pot. X Imp. XVII (C)os VIII PP Principi Suo quod praeceptis patr(is) consiliisq(ue) et auspiciis gentem Iudaeorum domuit et urbem Hierusolymam omnibus ante se ducibus regibus gentibus aut frustra petitam aut omnino intemptatam delevit." See Pfanner, *Der Titusbogen*, 98.

[25]This dimension is also apparent in the various literary descriptions of the triumph. Josephus (*J.W.* 7.121) remarks that although the Senate had voted a triumph each to Vespasian and Titus, they nonetheless decided to celebrate a common triumph. Suetonius (*Lives of the Caesars* 8.6) mentions that Titus shared in his father's triumph. Cassius Dio, writing around the beginning of the third century C.E., emphasizes the importance of the succession in his account of Vespasian's acclamation and the celebration of the triumph. According to Cassius Dio (*Roman History*, epitome of Book 65.12), upon his acclamation Vespasian is so overcome by emotion that he is able only to say, "My successor shall be my son or no one at all" (ἐμὲ μὲν υἱὸς διαδέξεται, ἢ οὐδεὶς ἄλλος).

[26]For a discussion specifically of the spoils from the Jerusalem temple, see Leon Yarden, *The Spoils of Jerusalem on the Arch of Titus: A Re-investigation* (Skrifter Utgivna av Svenska Institutet i Rom 8.16; Stockholm: Svenska Institutet i Rom, 1991).

coffered ceiling shows the apotheosis of Titus. This arch is the visual depiction of the triumph celebrated some ten years earlier.[27]

We have extensive knowledge about the celebration of this triumph, thanks to Josephus's detailed account of it in his *Jewish War* (7.123–162), combined with the relative conservatism of this aspect of Rome's ritual life.[28] It is possible to identify the key elements:[29] the triumph begins outside the city boundary of Rome, the *pomerium*, in the Campus Martius where the triumphators, Vespasian and Titus, had spent the night (*J.W.* 7.123); the triumphators are crowned with laurel, clad in purple, given the scepter to hold, and acclaimed (*J.W.* 7.124–26). Following prayers and breakfast, the triumphators and the procession enter the city through a gate, the Porta Triumphalis,[30] at which a sacrifice is made (*J.W.* 7.127–30). The lengthy procession customarily included the captives and the spoils taken in the war, as well as vignettes of the war (*J.W.* 7.139–47), with the triumphators, clothed as Jupiter Maximus Optimus, at the end,

---

[27]The dedicatory inscription on this arch is simpler than that on the arch in the Circus Maximus; it reads "Senatus Populusque Romanus Divo Tito Divi Vespasiani F. Vespasiano Augusto." Pfanner argues (*Der Titusbogen*) that the straightforward message of this inscription emphasizes the divinization of Titus over the celebration of the Judean victory per se, although the depiction of the triumph on the arch functions ideologically to support the Senate's divinization of the emperor.

[28]The fifth-century Christian historian Paulus Orosius provides a much shorter description of the same triumph in *Historiae* 7.9. His account is notable for his emphasis on the display of father and son as co-triumphators. "Vespasian and Titus, the emperors, entered the City celebrating a magnificent triumph over the Jews. This was a fair sight and one hitherto unknown to all mortals among the three hundred and twenty triumphs which had taken place from the founding of the City until that time, namely, father and son riding in one triumphal chariot, bringing back a most glorious victory over those who had offended the Father and the Son" (translation from Paulus Orosius, *The Seven Books of History against the Pagans* [trans. Roy J. Deferrari; Washington D.C.: Catholic University of America Press, 1964] 303). Josephus does not make mention of a single chariot, although his description is ambiguous on this point, "behind them Vespasian drove first, and Titus followed, but Domitian rode alongside" (μεθ' ἃ Οὐσεπασιανὸς ἤλαυνε πρῶτος καὶ Τίτος εἵπετο, Δομετιανὸς δὲ παρίππευεν; *J.W.* 7.152).

[29]A detailed discussion of the history and elements of the triumph, along with references to the relevant ancient testimonia, can be found in W. Ehlers, "Triumphus," *RE* 30 (1939) 493–511; see also H. S. Versnel, *Triumphus: An Inquiry into the Origin, Development, and Meaning of the Roman Triumph* (Leiden: Brill, 1970); and more recently Ernst Künzl, *Der römische Triumph: Siegesfeiern in antiken Rom* (Munich: Beck, 1988).

[30]On the importance of the *entry* into the city and its similarity to the Greek rite of εἰσέλασις, the privilege granted to Olympic victors of a triumphal return to their native town, see Versnel, *Triumphus*, 154–63.

followed by their freedpersons.[31] Prominent in the Flavian triumph were of course the sacred objects from the Jerusalem temple (*J.W.* 7.148–51), along with seven hundred "choice" prisoners of war, bound and in submission (*J.W.* 7.118, 137–38). The concluding phase of the triumph begins with the execution of the most prominent of the prisoners of war, in this case, the general Simon bar Giora (*J.W.* 7.153–55),[32] followed by the sacrifices and the dedication of the laurel crown to the Capitoline gods in the temple of Jupiter Capitolinus (*J.W.* 7.153, 156).[33] Although the procession was the most visible, public aspect of the triumph, historians of religion point out that the triumph was at its heart concerned with the return of the general or emperor to the temple of the Roman gods and with acclaiming the epiphany of the god in the person of the triumphator.[34] In other words, the apotheosis of Titus depicted on the ceiling of the Arch has already been displayed—in his lifetime—on the day of the triumph. The Arch celebrates his consecration.[35] We can recognize, in light of these monuments, that the

---

[31]Versnel, *Triumphus*, 95

[32]See also Otto Michel, "Studien zu Josephus: Simon Bar Giora," *NTS* 14 (1968) 407–408.

[33]See Inez Scott Ryberg, *Rites of the State Religion in Roman Art* (Memoirs of the American Academy in Rome 22; Rome: American Academy, 1955) 141. Ryberg's reading of the triumph attempts to find the "essential elements" of the triumph's significance; thus she identifies the sacrifices and the dedication of the crown as, to paraphrase, what really matters, even though other parts of the triumph may be more visible and memorable. I would eschew such an approach and recognize instead that the performance of the triumph as a whole matters; the Capitoline sacrifices may indeed be the culmination of the rites, but as such they participate with the elements within the patterns, structures, and sequences of the ritual.

[34]See Versnel, *Triumphus*, 83. Versnel's consideration of the triumph includes an examination of two opposing arguments, namely, whether the triumphator was seen as Jupiter or as an ancient Roman king; he concludes (p. 92) that the vesture of the triumphator with the *ornatus Iovis*, the *corona Etrusca*, and red lead, along with the acclamation *triumphe*, characterize the triumphator as the representative of Jupiter, but inasmuch as some of these aspects, notably the *ornatus Iovis*, were originally associated with the king, the royal and the divine are merged in the triumphator.

[35]Pfanner (*Der Titusbogen*, 99) stresses that the arch's iconographic program not only honors a divinized emperor, but also "grounds and demonstrates his divinity." The arch can thus be described as a "consecration monument" ("Konsekrationsmonument"). According to this reading, the lower registers depict Titus's earthly triumph as the foundation of his divine position, The ceiling coffer with the apotheosis of Titus is thus the heavenly consummation of this earthly triumph, supported by the portrayal of the guarantees of this status: the personified figures of the virtue, honor, and victory of the Augusti. Moreover, on the basis of a reference in Cassiodorus (*Variae* 10.30.1), it is possible that the arch was crowned with a pair of elephants or, more likely, a quadriga drawn by elephants; Pfanner interprets this feature as showing the heavenly

triumph was probably one of the most prominent features in the religio-political landscape of Flavian Rome.

## The Epistle to the Hebrews in Light of the Flavian Triumph

The depiction of the Son, Jesus, in the Epistle to the Hebrews, is expressed chiefly in the words of the psalms. Nevertheless it makes use of many of the motifs that we find in the Roman triumph, especially as it was celebrated by the Flavians. First, the principal themes of Hebrews 1 and 2 are the return of the Son, Jesus, to the heavenly realm, to his throne on the right hand of the Father, where he shares in the reign of the Father. The Son is said to have a scepter (1:5) and to be "crowned" with glory and honor (1:7). Moreover, all his enemies are "under his feet" (1:13) and all things are subject to him (2:7, ὑποτάσσω, precisely the word used for subjugated nations and prisoners). Through the use of Psalm 2, 9, and 110, Hebrews brings to the forefront of its depiction of Jesus issues of sonship, succession, and rule[36]—issues central to Flavian propaganda. Moreover, this depiction includes elements of the triumph: the crown, scepter, glory and honor,[37] the visible subjugation of enemies, and the triumphant journey of return to the temple (in this case the heavenly temple, as will become clear in Heb 9:11-12). Jesus is, in my view, depicted in Hebrews as the triumphator in procession to the temple. The text displays the apotheosis of Jesus, rather than the apotheosis of Titus, but both are portrayed as the son who rightfully rules alongside his father in victory.

Second, in Hebrews the Son is also the ultimate high priest (4:14–10), offering himself. We may recall that in the Roman triumph the triumphator is also the sacrificer, the priest of Jupiter Capitolinus, who

---

triumph of Titus, carried into heaven on the quadriga, and corresponding to the quadriga drawn by horses in his earthly triumph. See Pfanner, *Der Titusbogen*, 3, 99.

[36]On the importance to the triumph of holding the *imperium*, see Versnel, *Triumphus*, 185–94. On these themes in Hebrews, see Kenneth Schenck, "Keeping his Appointment: Creation and Enthronement in Hebrews," *JSNT* 66 (1997) 91–117, who argues that the focus of sonship in Hebrews is on the son's enthronement in heaven, where he fulfills his divine appointment.

[37]That the triumph and its associated monuments honor the emperors is without doubt. A more specific connection may be suggested by the presence of the figure of *Honos* (i.e., personified honor) accompanying Titus's chariot on the inner relief of the Arch of Titus. This figure, however, is also interpreted as the Genius of the Roman people; see Ryberg, *Rites of the State Religion*, 147; Pfanner (*Der Titusbogen*, 69–70) discusses the identification closely, concluding that the figure is more likely to be *Honos*. On the increased tendency to include allegorical and personified figures in monumental art at the end of the first century C.E., see Ryberg, *Rites of the State Religion*, 97.

makes the concluding sacrifice of the triumph.[38] Like Jesus in Hebrews, Titus was both son and priest, but Hebrews fills this image with allusions to a story of Jesus' death and his offering of himself (Heb 5:7–10; 9:12, 26, 10:1–18; 13:12–13).[39] I would suggest here that Hebrews is critiquing the ideology of divine rule expressed in the triumphal sacrifices, but doing so indirectly by means of typological reflection on the Yom Kippur rituals and the inadequacy of the high priests in the earthly sanctuary. Thus the typological argument about Levitical sacrifices becomes the rhetorical site for resistance to the Roman imperial ideology.

Third, the monumental and ritual expressions of the Flavian triumph all feature the spoils from the Jerusalem temple. These, as much as the glory of the son, become the vehicle of the ideology.[40] Josephus enumerates them as they were carried in procession: they "consisted of a golden table, many talents in weight, and a lampstand, likewise made of gold [he then depicts it in detail]. . .after these, and last of all the spoils, was carried a copy of the Jewish law" (*J.W.* 7.148–50). Hebrews 9:2–5 likewise goes into great detail about the furnishings of the sanctuary. Hebrews speaks of the "table," the "bread of the presence," the golden altar of incense, the ark of the covenant "overlaid on all sides with gold," the golden urn holding the manna, Aaron's rod, the tables of the

---

[38]Ryberg (*Rites of the State Religion*, 141) argues that at the heart of the triumph lies the repayment of vows made to Jupiter Capitolinus made prior to the general's departure on military campaign. Thus the concluding sacrifice, amid all the opportunities of display and glorification, is the performance of these vows, the returning to the gods of what was promised. Hebrews emphasizes that Jesus offers himself in accordance with God's will; by placing the quotation of Psalm 40:6–8 on the lips of Jesus, the author of Hebrews at 10:7 portrays Jesus as saying, "See, God, I have come to do your will, O God (in the scroll of the book, it is written of me)." Despite some differences, both the Roman triumph and Hebrews understand the sacrifice as fulfilling the demands of the relationship with the divine.

[39]On traditions of Jesus' passion in Hebrews, see Martin Dibelius, "Gethsemane," in Dibelius, *Botschaft und Geschichte*, vol. 1: *Zur Evangelienforschung* (ed. Günther Bornkamm; Tübingen: Mohr/Siebeck, 1953) 258–71; August Strobel, "Die Psalmengrundlage der Gethsemane-Parallele. Hebr 5:7ff.," *ZNW* 45 (1954) 256; Paul Andriessen, "Agonisse de la mort dans l'Épître aux Hébreux," *NRTh* 96 (1974) 2986–91; Helmut Koester, "'*Outside the Camp*': Hebrews 13:9–14," *HTR* 55 (1962) 300; Aitken, "Morphology of the Passion Narrative," 165–213.

[40]Ryberg (*Rites of the State Religion*, 146), surveying the iconography associated with triumphs, posits that the Arch of Titus is unusual in that it does not portray the triumphators sacrificing, a scene that might be expected as the companion relief to the triumphal procession. She suggests that the depiction of the golden objects from the Jerusalem temple was chosen instead because of the great interest that they attracted in Rome.

covenant, and the cherubim of glory overshadowing the mercy seat. It is important to note that Hebrews does not utilize these items in the following typological exposition; they are, as it were, extraneous to the immediate argument, but may serve some larger rhetorical purpose. Hebrews includes many more items than does Josephus and may draw upon a traditional list,[41] but all of the items on Josephus's list (table, lampstand, and copy of the law) are included, as are the lampstand and the table of the shewbread depicted on the Arch of Titus. There is, moreover, similarity in diction, not least the emphasis on gold. In view of other motifs of the triumph in Hebrews, I would suggest that the list of articles from the sanctuary are specifically included in Hebrews 9 because of the prominence of the temple spoils from Jerusalem in the display of Flavian ideology. Hebrews is thus rhetorically displaying the items within its own triumphal statement.

Like the Flavians, Hebrews makes use of the "sanctuary" of Israel to promote its message of true rule. Hebrews does so by turning to the wilderness tabernacle (perhaps precisely because the Jerusalem temple is no longer standing) and making it the earthly shadow of the heavenly realities, pointing out its inadequacies, and showing its abolition (12:9) through the self-offering of Jesus. We may thus be more precise and say that Hebrews makes use of both the earthly sanctuary and the heavenly sanctuary (the true one) to promote its message of true and proper rule, just as the Flavians made use of both the Jerusalem temple and the Capitoline temple to promote theirs.[42] Thus, one of the many strategies of Hebrews is to take the elements of the imperial triumph and place them in the service of its christology. This christology, following the opening chapters of Hebrews, is ultimately one of divine rule, in which the enthroned son shares in the reign of the father in the heaven, with his enemies subject to him (Heb 1:13). In the Roman triumph, the triumphator's freedpersons followed him in procession; so too in Hebrews, those whom Jesus has liberated from those held in slavery their whole lives by "the fear of death" (Heb 2:15) are to follow after Jesus in his victorious journey.[43] Thus Jesus in Hebrews is both "the one

---

[41]See the discussion in Attridge, *Hebrews*, 232–38.

[42]The transfer of the Jerusalem temple tax into the *fiscus Judaicus*, paid to the Capitoline temple and gods implies that, as a result of Roman victory, proper tribute is due not to the god of the Jerusalem temple, but instead to the Capitoline gods.

[43]Harold W. Attridge, "Liberating Death's Captives: Reconsideration of an Early Christian Myth," in James E. Goehring, et al., eds., *Gnosticism and the Early Christian World: In Honor of James M. Robinson* (Sonoma, Ca.: Polebridge, 1990) 103–115.

who leads the way" (ἀρχηγός, Heb 2:10; 12:2)[44] and "forerunner" (πρόδρομος, Heb 6:20) for the community of freedpersons, as they too enter "into his rest" (Heb 4:11) and into the heavenly realm.

The inscribed audience of Hebrews, moreover, is receiving a "kingdom that cannot be shaken" (βασιλεία ἀσάλευτος, 12:28). The explicit ethic for community is, in addition, one of solidarity with those who are exposed to abuse, torture, persecution, imprisonment, and dispossession of property. This ethic is first held up to the community as how they have indeed behaved in "those earlier days"; exposed to abuse and persecution, becoming partners (κοινωνοί) with those so treated, and "having compassion (συνεπαθήσατε) on those in prison" (10:32–34). They are, furthermore, explicitly exhorted to maintain that same ethical solidarity in the present, "Remember those who are in prison, as though you were in prison with them; those who are being tortured, as though you yourselves were being tortured" (Heb 13:3).[45] That is, the community that belongs to the reign of Jesus and is receiving an unshakable kingdom is here exhorted to be one with those in Rome (and presumably elsewhere) who are the objects of imperial persecution.[46] They are indeed to expose themselves to the same risks.

I would suggest that this ethic of solidarity may in part be a response to a perception of increased threat on the part of the Christian and Jewish communities in Rome[47]—a perception that may have been fueled by the

---

[44]On ἀρχηγός, see Paul-Gerhard Müller, *ΧΡΙΣΤΟΣ ΑΡΧΗΓΟΣ. Der religionsgeschichtliche und theologische Hintergrund einer neutestamentichen Christusprädikation* (Europäische Hochschulschriften ser. 23; Theologie 28; Frankfurt/Bern: Lang, 1973).

[45]I follow here the translation of the NRSV; the Greek emphasizes participation in the suffering of others: μιμνῄσκεσθε τῶν δεσμίων ὡς συνδεδεμένοι, τῶν κακουχουμένων ὡς καὶ αὐτοὶ ὄντες ἐν σώματι.

[46]In discussing Roman prisons and the practice of visiting prisoners, Craig A. Wansink suggests (*Chained in Christ: The Experience and Rhetoric of Paul's* Imprisonments [JSNTSup 130; Sheffied: Sheffield Academic Press, 1996] 80) that "association with the imprisoned drew suspicion to oneself, and this often led to one's death"; see, for example, Dio Chrysostom 58.3.7; 58.11.5–6; Philostratus *Life of Apollonius* 4.46; Tacitus *Annales* 6.5.9.

[47]A full consideration of the religious profile of Jewish and Christian groups in Rome in the second half of the first century is not possible here. Given the indications of a multiple synagogues and house churches in Rome in this period, along with the rich range of theological expression among Christians by the middle of the second century, it is reasonable to assume a great deal of diversity of practice and belief among Jews and Christians. We should not, moreover, assume sharp divisions between Jews and Christians in Rome; rather it is better to think of a variety of ways in which people may have identified their religious and social affiliations, including some groups who might be characterized, albeit imprecisely, as Jewish-Christian. Simon R. F. Price has recently discussed the question of pluralism and socio-religious identity in a lecture, "Religious

public display of *Judaea Capta,* as well as by the large number of Judean, Galilean, and Samaritan prisoners of war, slaves, in Rome following the war.[48] It is difficult to know how this display and this changing population affected Christians and Jews in Rome; there is little evidence, if any. Hebrews, however, may indeed contain some indications of the impact in its development of both an ideology of true divine rule held by the Father and Son and an ethic of solidarity with those who suffered under imperial rule. That is, in responding to a perception of increased threat and in resisting the public display of imperial rule expressed in the triumph, Hebrews develops its own triumphal scheme and writes its audience into the triumphal procession as the freedpersons of the victorious ruler, enthroned in heaven. Hebrews does not do so directly, but rather through the interpretation of scripture, particularly the psalms of divine rule, the story of the wilderness journey to the promised land, and the cultic prescriptions for worship in the wilderness tabernacle, through typology and allegory. It thus employs scriptural interpretation as a rhetorical site for developing a religio-political critique and the articulation of an ethic appropriate to that critique.

In conclusion, I would return to question of assigning a date for the composition of Hebrews. The argument presented here suggests that Hebrews fits well into the period when the ideology of the Flavian triumph flourished, not only in the ceremony of the triumph itself, but in its continued promulgation in the city of Rome through a series of monuments, that is, in the period between 71 and 81 C.E. A more precise date, namely, shortly after the death of Titus in 81 and the building of the Arch of Titus on the Via Sacra, celebrating his apotheosis, may be suggested by Hebrews' emphasis on the enthronement of the Son in heaven as the culmination of his triumph. This argument depends on the strength of the correlation between two distinct constructions of political theology, one preserved in the text of Hebrews, the other preserved in

---

Pluralism in the Roman World: Pagans, Jews, and Christians," at the Annual Meeting of the Society of Biblical Literature, Nashville, Tennessee, November 2000. Price argues for the importance of recognizing clusters of religious markers in any given case, rather than placing the evidence in impermeable categories of religious identity, e.g., Jewish *or* Christian; Isis *or* Mithras. On the Jewish and Christian communities in Rome, see, *inter alia,* George La Piana, *Foreign Groups in Rome During the First Centuries of the Empire* (Cambridge: Harvard University Press, 1927); Harry J. Leon, *The Jews of Ancient Rome* (Philadelphia: Jewish Publication Society, 1960); Lampe, *Die Stadtrömischen Christen;* Karl P. Donfried and Peter Richardson, eds., *Jews and Christians in First-Century Rome* (Grand Rapids: Eerdmans, 1998). Harnack's discussion of Hebrews in the context of multiple house-churches in Rome is also of interest in this regard; see Harnack, "Probabilia über die Addresse und den Verfasser des Hebräerbrief."

[48]See Smallwood, *Jews Under Roman Rule,* 519.

the rituals and monuments associated with the Flavian triumph. As a response to these articulations of the political theology of the Flavian emperors, as they were experienced in the city of Rome, Hebrews creates its own political theology out of the building materials available in its immediate civic context. The scriptures of Israel and the traditions available to this early Christian community then provide the means to fill out this depiction of Jesus as triumphator and divine ruler enthroned in heaven, but as triumphator whose journey is marked by suffering, struggle, and solidarity with those in need.

# 5

# Christianity: The Fourth Century Christian Basilica

James Riley Strange
*Emory University*

## The Problem of Origins

In its major cities across the Empire, beginning some time in the second century B.C.E.,[1] and up to the fourth century C.E., Rome constructed public buildings called "basilicas." These were civil or municipal structures, housing the tribunal court and accommodating both private and public business in their broad, open halls. They were also associated with the *genus* of the Emperor: many displayed his effigy,[2] and Suetonius reports that as Augustus' body was transported back to Rome, it lay in state in temples and basilicas along the way.[3] In the fourth century C.E. Christians also began to construct basilicas for their purposes, and very soon nearly all monumental church buildings in the Empire took that form.[4] Thus the appearance of the Christian basilica in

[1]J.B. Ward-Perkins, "Constantine and the Origins of the Christian Basilica," *Papers of the British School at Rome*, 22 (1954): 71.
[2]Richard Krautheimer, "The Beginning of Early Christian Architecture," in Krautheimer, *Studies in Early Christian, Medieval, and Renaissance Art* (New York: New York University Press; London: University of London Press, Ltd., 1969), 12; this article first appeared in *Review of Religion*, III (1939): 127-48; see also Krautheimer, "The Constantinian Basilica," *Dumbarton Oaks Papers*, No. 21 (Washington, DC: Dumbarton Oaks Center for Byzantine Studies, 1967), 123-4.
[3]*Vit. Caes.* II,100.
[4]For example, in his comprehensive work on Christian architecture in the first centuries C.E., Michael White treats all pre-fourth century church buildings—12 in all—that have been excavated or surveyed at various sites in the old Roman Empire (Europe, Greece, Asia Minor, Syria, Palestine, and North Africa). White

the fourth century presents a puzzle: for 500 years the Romans had been building basilicas; for the first three centuries of the common era Christians met in homes or small halls, but built no basilicas. During and after the fourth century, construction of civil basilicas appears virtually to have halted, while Christians began to build nearly all their monumental churches in that form. Thus the first public Christian buildings appeared suddenly and spread quickly, and Christianity rapidly took over the basilical architectural style.

The Christian basilica presents four problems. First, we have to explain how a secular building became a religious building. Before the fourth century, the civil basilica served no overtly religious purpose; its lofty halls and interior colonnades displayed the majesty of both Caesar and Rome, but the activities it housed were mundane in comparison. By contrast, as we see in the travel diary of the fourth century nun Egeria, Christian basilicas accommodated a solemn and elaborate liturgy. Christianity thus brought to the basilica a stately ritual that matched its regal architecture. Since the Christian basilica was the first public Christian building, we want to know why Christians chose a secular structure rather than some other, such as a temple, or one of their own invention.

Second, we must explain why Christians began erecting public buildings only in the fourth century. This is a problem because, with the advent of the Christian basilica, Christian worship was no longer conducted privately or in secret, admitting only the fully initiated and catechumens (potential converts), while excluding catechumens from the mass proper. The liturgy now was transformed into a public spectacle, accessible to all,[5] much as the worship of the Olympian pantheon had

---

demonstrates that none of these churches are basilicas; rather, all of them are some form of house church or small hall. Beginning in the late fourth century, however, basilicas were built over seven of these buildings, and I estimate that by the end of the fifth century there were over 100 basilicas across the Empire. Michael White, *The Social Origins of Christian Architecture*, Vol. II (Valley Forge: Trinity Press, Int'l., 1997); Richard Krautheimer *et al.*, *Corpus Basilicarum Christianarum Romae: The Early Christian Basilicas of Rome (IV-IX Cent.)*, Vols. I-V (Rome: Pontificio Instituto di Archeologia Christiana; New York: New York University Press, 1959); Asher Ovadiah, *Corpus of the Byzantine Churches in the Holy Land*, trans. Rose Kirson (Bonn: Peter Hanstein Verlag, 1970); Asher Ovadiah and Carla Gomez de Silva, "Supplementum to the Corpus of the Byzantine Churches in the Holy Land," *Levant* 13 (1981): 200-261, 14 (1982): 1222-70, 16 (1984): 129-65.

[5]Egeria makes no mention of two services in the Jerusalem churches, a fore-mass that admitted catechumens, and the mass proper, which excluded them. Rather, her language implies that an undifferentiated congregation of worshippers gathered at appointed times in the various churches. See discussion below.

been.[6] Thus in the fourth century, through its architecture and liturgy, Christianity recast itself as a public religion.

Third, we must explain why Christians continued to build their large, monumental churches only as basilicas rather than in a variety of architectural styles. That is, not only did Christians choose to build basilicas in the fourth century, but nearly all monumental churches built in the fourth through sixth centuries took basilical form.[7] Constantine erected the first in the Empire, so far as we know—Rome's basilica church of St. John the Lateran in 313—and soon other communities across the Empire began constructing their own.[8] We want to know why, when many different types of buildings could house large congregations, Christians built only one type of building.

Fourth, the floor plans of Constantine's basilicas all follow a standardized design.[9] We can identify Christian basilicas by a particular plan, common to all, that civil basilicas did not share. We may conclude, therefore, that Christian basilicas served a specific purpose, that they

---

[6]For the first 350 years of Christianity, worshipers gathered in homes or modest, privately owned structures—either houses or shops—that they converted for church use. The New Testament contains many references to Christians gathering in homes, some of which explicitly mention "the church in your house": Phil 1-2; Rom. 16:5; Col 4:15; see also Acts 2:46; 5:42; 12:12-16; 20:7-12, II Jn 10. Likewise, the *Didache*, Ignatius, Justin Martyr, Tertullian, and many other early Christian works contain references to Christians gathering in various "places," which we assume to refer to private homes. For a complete catalogue of these mentions, with original text and translation, see Michael White, *Christian Architecture*, vol. II, 33-120. In these cases, one could not distinguish a church by its façade: church buildings looked exactly like the other homes in the neighborhoods in which they stood. By contrast, the first Christian basilicas were massive, magnificently decorated edifices constructed by the State. The first public Christian buildings thus were some of the most prominent in their cities, for they took over the civil basilica's architectural style, its grand size, and ostentatious display. Eusebius does say that at the end of the third century, between 258 (Cyprian's death) and 303 (Diocletian's first edict), Christians built large churches (*eureas eis platos…ekklēsias*; *HE* VIII.1.5), but his language is vague, and the archaeological record has not yet revealed any substantial church buildings from this time.

[7]While many memorial churches were octagonal, cross-shaped, or circular (some of Constantine's basilicas incorporate these architectural features into their design; see the churches of the Holy Sepulcher and Holy Nativity, Figures 4 and 5 respectively), and many small churches were "chapels" or small halls, nearly all monumental churches took basilical form.

[8]For example, in Palestine alone, before the fourth century we have archaeological remains of only one church: the house church at Capernaum. By contrast, in 1970 Asher Ovadiah catalogued 45 fourth and fifth century Palestinian churches, 34 (76 percent) of them basilicas; Asher Ovadiah, *Corpus of the Byzantine Churches*, Table no. 1.

[9]We will unpack the features of this design more fully below.

symbolized a particular idea, or were meant to accommodate a particular behavior. For rather than reproducing the variety of basilicas that had existed before, Christians made only one type of basilica.[10] We want to know what happened in Christian basilicas—that did not happened in civil basilicas—that caused Christians to standardize their design.

Thus we naturally ask why the Christian basilica emerged. Given its abrupt appearance and immediate standardization, the Christian basilica appears to have been designed for a purpose. If this is so, what we want to know is, [1] what happened in Christian basilicas, [2] why Christians adopted the basilical style for their churches, and [3] why they standardized their design.

In this paper I propose a hypothesis to answer these questions. By looking at the design of Christian basilicas we ought to be able to infer some of the things that happened in them, much as we can do with the plans of Roman theaters. We can tell, for instance, that people entered through many vomitoria, and sat in curved and tiered rows, all facing toward a platform, apparently to observe what happened there. The first task, therefore, is to form a preliminary hypothesis that answers the question, What sort of movement did Christian basilicas accommodate? Answering that question should also suffice to answer why Christians adopted the basilical form, and why they standardized the design.

## The Data for the Present Study

The data for this paper is the floor plans of Constantine's five extant basilicas. I examine only these five—the Lateran and St. Peter's (both in Rome), Holy Sepulcher (Jerusalem), Holy Nativity (Bethlehem), and Eleona (Mt. of Olives)[11] for three reasons. Surveys and excavations in the 20th century have established that each of these churches is a basilica, which we will define below, and not some other type of structure. Furthermore, each was commissioned by the Emperor Constantine within 23 years of the others, between the construction of the Lateran in

---

[10]I do not claim that all Christian basilicas of the fourth century and following were identical, nor do I think that basilicas never deviated from the standard design that I claim they followed. Rather, I argue that Constantine's basilicas follow a design that subsequent basilicas emulate. Deviations from this design are infrequent enough for me to claim that they are exceptions to the rule.

[11]A sixth, Constantine's so-called basilica at Mamre near Hebron may not be a basilica at all; it is difficult to determine its specific floor plan; see A.E. Mader, "Les fouilles allemandes au Ramet El Khalil: la Mambré biblique de la tradition primitive," in *Revue Biblique* 39 (1930) 84: 115-7; Figs. 2, 5; Pls. 5, 7. A seventh, the basilica at Tyre, which Eusebius discusses, has not been discovered. Scholars dispute whether an eighth, Hagia Sophia in Constantinople, was begun under Constantine.

313 and the Holy Sepulcher in 335, two years before Constantine's death. Thus, if the Christian basilica was designed from the outset to accommodate a certain type of ritual movement, we expect to see that design in the earliest basilicas. Finally, it is possible that the builders of later Christian basilicas simply copy Constantine's without understanding the ethos behind the design.[12]

**Prior Solutions to the Problem of the Christian Basilica**

Before I announce my hypothesis, let me review previous work in the field of early Christian architecture. Two primary schools of thought aim to account for the emergence of the Christian basilica in the fourth century. The first (in the order in which we treat them, not the chronological order of their formulation) argues that church architecture develops in linear progression, beginning with the first century house church recorded in the New Testament and "naturally" evolving to the basilica in the fourth century. Michael White, who recently has written a two-volume comprehensive treatment of both archaeological and textual sources,[13] sees the predecessor of the basilica in the house *atria* and the elongated halls of the late third and early fourth century, such as the early church under San Crisogono in Rome (Fig. 1). White asserts that church architecture develops from the first century New Testament house church to the fourth century basilica incrementally, including as intermediate steps the modified *domus ecclesiae* (a house with enlarged interior space to facilitate Christian gatherings) and *aulus ecclesiae* (a former house or other building, completely taken over and modified as a church).

White solves the problem of the Christian basilica's origin by placing it at the end of an evolutionary process. Thus he does not ask why Christians chose to build churches as basilicas to begin with, or why they continued to build them for many centuries. These simply are not issues in White's evolutionary model, for he explains every step as "natural".[14] This is an odd formulation, for it characterizes deliberate human acts as natural events, or accidents. But this is not what happened at all in the development of church architecture: when, for example, when the house

---

[12]I do not think that this is so, however, for basilicas across the Empire do not reintroduce the variety of basilical plans found in the civil basilica. It seems to me that we cannot explain this fact by means of aesthetics alone.

[13]Michael L. White, *The Social Origins of Christian Architecture*, 2 vols. (Valley Forge, PA: Trinity Press International, 1990-7). Another well-known scholar of church architecture, J.W. Crowfoot, describes the architecture of specific churches without analyzing the data; he does not tell us what it means; J.W. Crowfoot, *Early Churches in Palestine* (College Park: McGrath Publishing Company, 1971).

[14]*Christian Architecture*, Vol. I, 128.

*Figure 1. Isometric reconstruction of early 4th century church under San Crisogono, Rome. After a drawing by Frankl.*

churches at Dura Europos and Capernaum no longer served the needs of growing congregations, they knocked down walls, and at Dura they installed a baptistry. In other places they built small churches from the ground up. These are not examples of "natural" evolution, but of humans adapting their environments.

White's solution, therefore, cannot adequately account for the appearance of the church basilica. First, as stated above, Christian basilicas emerge practically overnight with the construction of the Lateran and its subsequent continuators and copiers. White's model, on the other hand, cannot accommodate the sudden appearance of sophisticated new forms that have no precedent. Second, White's evolutionary model fails to account for how one species, and not many, filled an evolutionary niche. It cannot explain the development of the basilica when many other architectural styles could also accommodate large congregations. We are left, in our case, to ask why Constantine and other Christians built as basilicas if their sole need was to hold more people.

In contrast to White, other scholars, represented here by Richard Krautheimer and J.B. Ward-Perkins, see no reason to look further than the civil basilica for the model of the Christian basilica.[15] Both see that the basilica's imposing size could house large numbers of worshippers,

[15]Ward-Perkins, "Origins of the Christian Basilica," 85-7; Krautheimer, "Early Christian Architecture," 11ff.

and both note that the spectacular adornment of the interiors of Constantine's basilicas, as well as the clothing of the Bishop himself, borrow directly from state ceremony.[16]

Both scholars, however, stop short of accounting for why Constantine made the changes to the basilica form that he did. It is reasonable to assume that one of Constantine's goals was to admit large numbers of worshippers in a grand and ostentatious imperial style. While such a purpose might account for the structures' size, we are still at pains to understand why Constantine's monumental churches are *only* basilicas, and why they are all a *particular type* of basilica.

Thus we have the impetus for the present study: none of the three scholars surveyed contemplates how the design of the Christian basilica may accommodate the movement of people, and so none is able to explain adequately why Christians built basilicas in the first place, and why they built them the way that they did in the second. Turning now to the problem at hand, we will determine the architectural features that both make a basilica, and those that make a Christian basilica.

### Roman Civil Basilicas and Constantine's Basilicas

Krautheimer has suggested that the first church basilicas constructed in the fourth century C.E. were new creations, variations on the older theme of Rome's civil basilicas.[17] He lists the standard features of early Christian basilicas, and also makes note of those features that are unique to Constantine's. We register Krautheimer's observations and make some additions.

Constantine's churches are recognizable as basilicas by several regular features (Figs. 2-14). Both civil and church basilicas are elongated halls in which rows of interior columns partition a central mall or nave from two or more side aisles. A two-story high ceiling, often with exposed roof timbers (Figs. 7, 11), rises over the nave, while lower, single-story ceilings covers the aisles. Clerestories pierce the walls above the columns that line the nave, illuminating the nave and the opposite aisles. Both civil and Constantinian basilicas typically have at least one apse.

So Byzantine church basilicas are recognizable as basilicas because of several standardized features: a nave with side aisles, interior columniation, clerestory illumination, and the presence of an apse. On the other hand, Constantine's basilicas do not recapitulate the diversity of civil basilical forms. Rather, the differences between the two types of

---

[16]Krautheimer, "Early Christian Architecture," 11-2, and *Christian and Byzantine Architecture*, 40; Ward-Perkins, "Origins of the Christian Basilica," 87.
[17]Krautheimer, "Early Christian Architecture," 14-5.

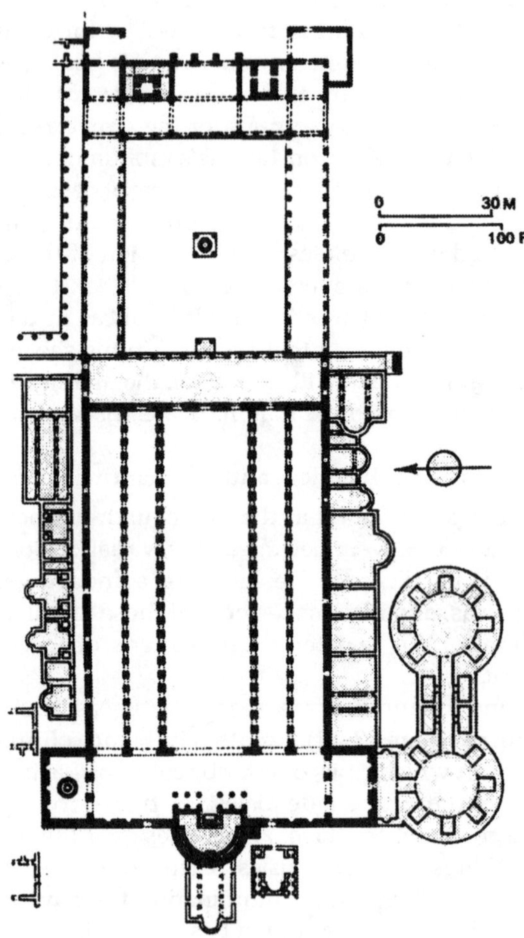


*Figure 2. Old St. Peter's, Rome, based on the work of Tibero Alfarano.*

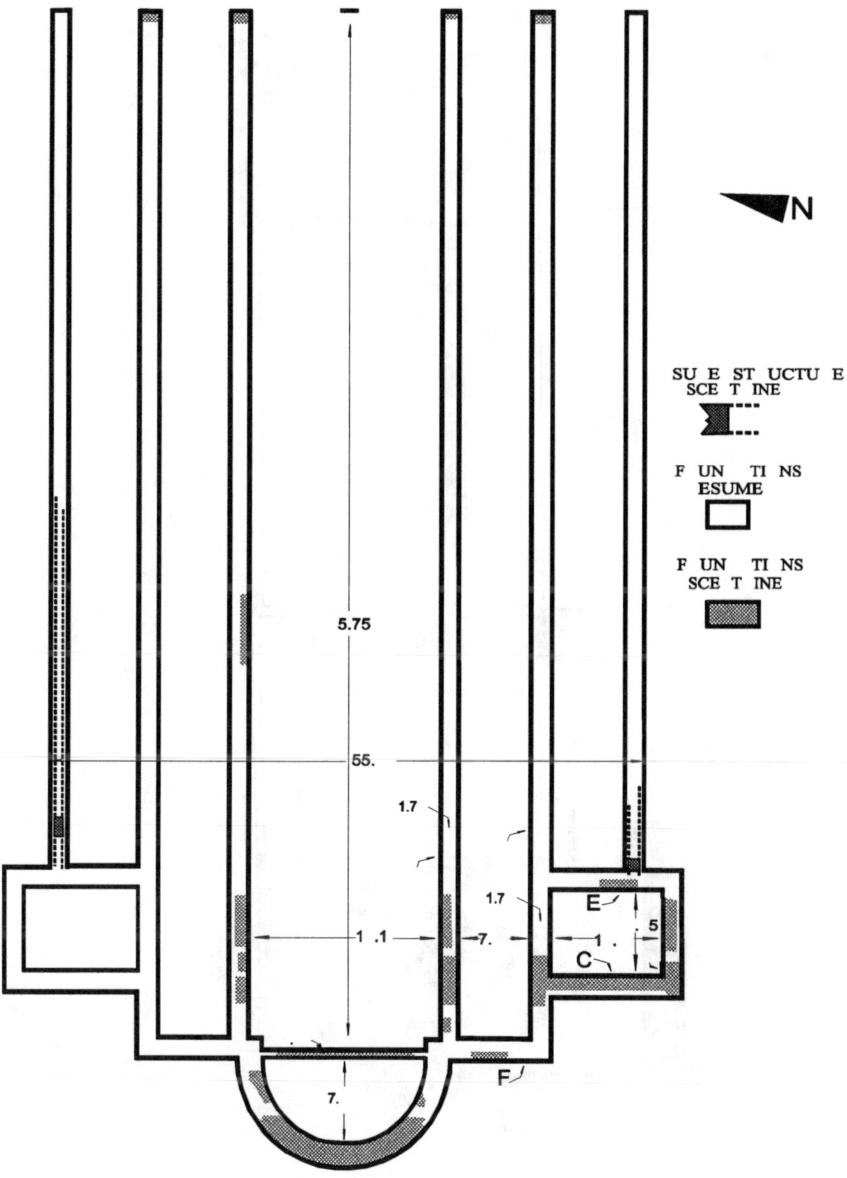


*Figure 3. Excavations at Constantine's Church of St. John the Lateran, Rome. After a drawing by Corbett.*

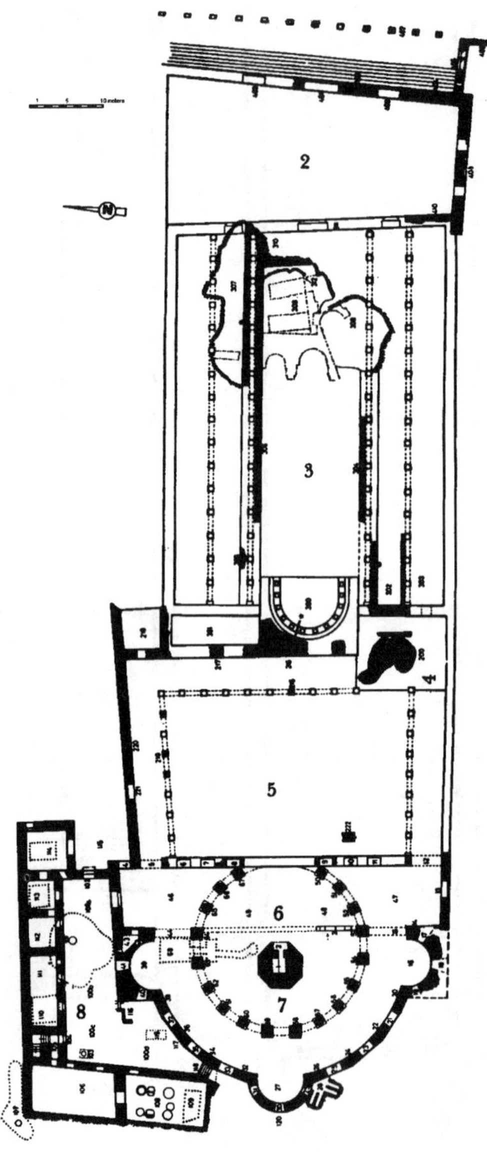


*Figure 4. Constantine's Church of the Holy Sepulcher, Jerusalem. Drawing by Corbo.*

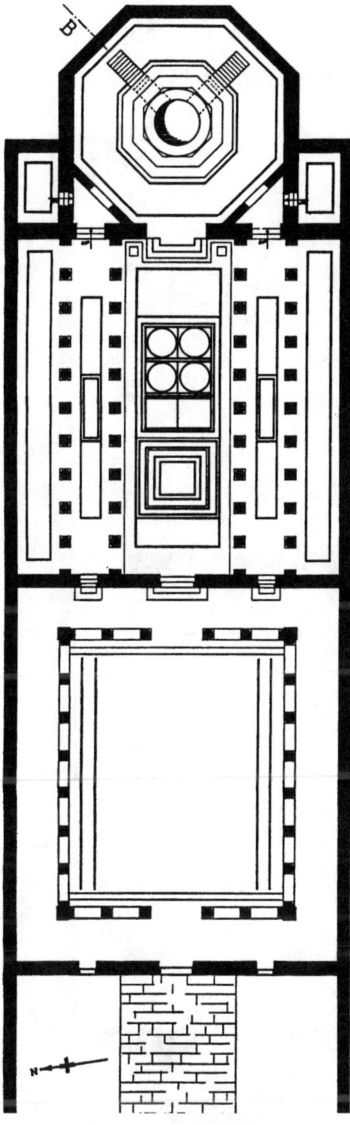

*Figure 5. Constantine's Church of the Holy Nativity, Bethlehem. Drawing by Richmond.*

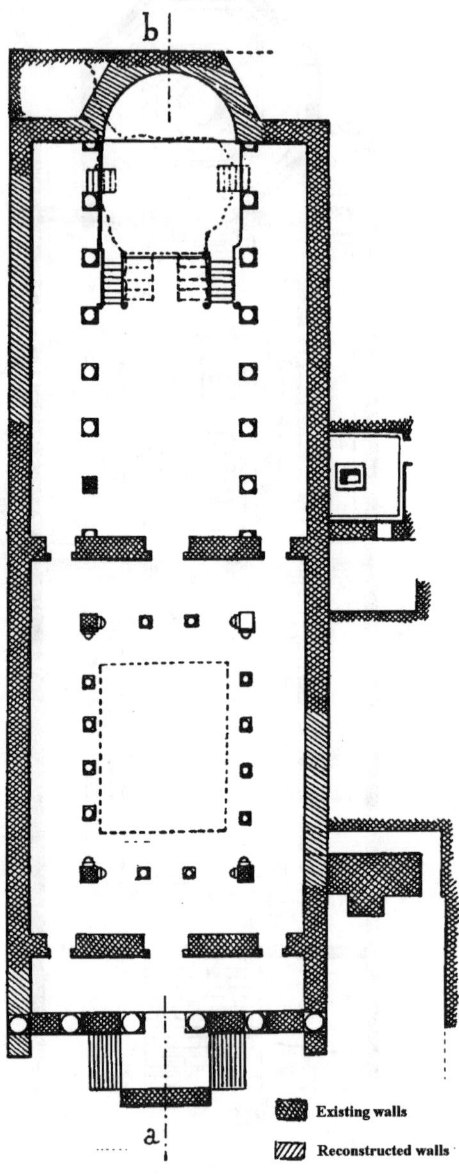


*Figure 6. Constantine's Eleona church, Mt. of Olives. Drawing by Vincent.*

*Figure 7. Fresco of the interior of the Lateran Basilica before 17th century.*

structures define a standardized style for later church basilicas that persists in spite of the variations—usually in size—that these basilicas begin to display.

1. Civil basilicas frequently stand adjacent to the forum, per Vitruvius' prescription that they accommodate the forum's commerce in inclement weather (see, for example, Fig. 13).[18] By contrast, only

[18]Vitruvius, *The Ten Books on Architecture,* trans. Morris Hicky Morgan (New York: Dover Publications, 1960) [originally published in 1914], 132.

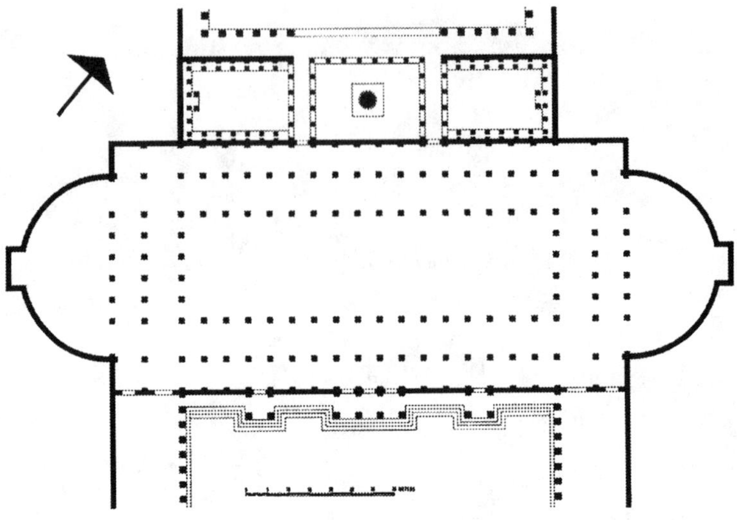

*Figure 8. Basilica Ulpia, Rome. Drawing by Macdonald.*

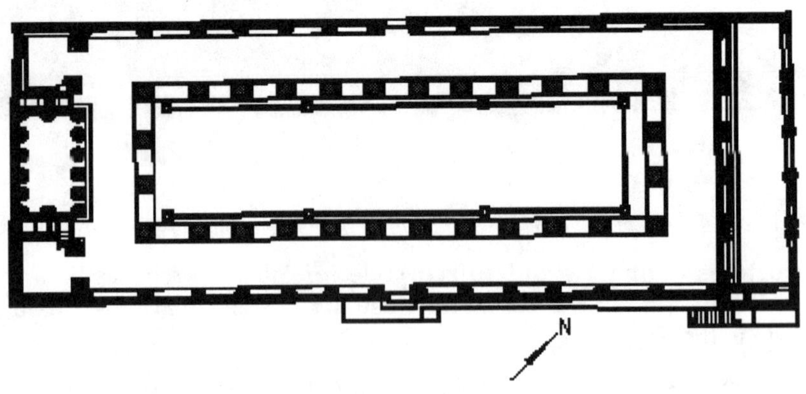


*Figure 9. Basilica at Pompeii. After a drawing by Durum.*

2. Constantine's Holy Sepulcher in Jerusalem stands near the forum,[19] although the proximity of the cave of the sepulcher to the market clearly is accidental.
3. Whereas civil basilicas could have an apse in both short walls (Figs. 8, 13), in one wall (Fig. 10), or no apse at all (Fig. 9), Constantine's basilicas uniformly have one apse, and they place it in the short wall opposite the main entrance. The sole exception to this rule is the church of the Holy Nativity in Bethlehem, which has no apse. In its place an entrance lets into the octagonal hall over the cave of the nativity (Fig. 5). Palestinian churches place their apses in the eastern wall, except for the Holy Sepulcher, which had its apse in the western wall toward the sepulcher (Fig. 4),[20] while the Roman churches have theirs in the western wall. In either case, nearly all later church basilicas across the Empire maintain this east-west orientation.

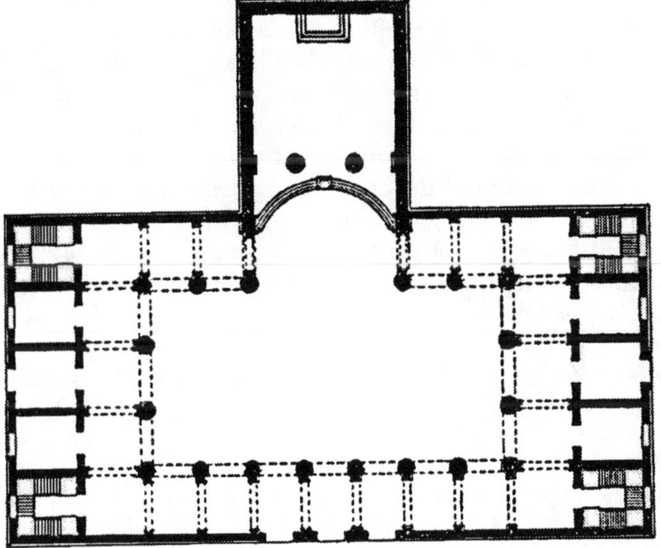

*Figure 10. Vitruvius' basilica at Fano.*

[19]Eusebius, *VC* III.39 (*PG* 20, 1100); cf. S. Siluae, *Pereg.* 43.7 (Geyer, 95).
[20]Vincent's plan and stone-by-stone drawing of the Eleona church provide no north arrow. I assume that this means that the apse is in the east; "L'église de l'Iléona," *Revue Biblique* 20 (1911): 259, Fig. 10 (Fig. 6 in this paper), Planche 1.

4. Similarly, whereas civil basilicas could have their main entrance in any wall, usually the long wall adjacent to the forum,[21] the primary entrance to Constantine's basilicas is always in the short wall opposite the apse and frequently is tri-portal.[22]
5. Constantine's basilicas uniformly have no aisles parallel to the short walls; the aisles run only parallel to the nave.
6. Constantine's basilicas have no shops or offices lining the aisles, nor second story offices above the aisles, as civil basilicas often do.[23]
7. I note with some caution the so-called "triumphal arch" at the terminus of the nave and the entrance to the apse, mentioned by Ward-Perkins in conjunction with the Lateran and St. Peter's.[24]

As mentioned in Chapter 1, all of these features that distinguish Constantine's basilicas from civil basilicas uniformly persist, with exceptions here and there, in church basilicas through the seventh century and even up to the present. Thus I claim that the plan of Constantine's churches is "standardized," and I suggest these churches were designed for a purpose. Both the uniformity and longevity of the design indicate that Constantinian basilicas are not simply aesthetic variations on the older theme of Roman architecture. Otherwise we might see later Christian basilicas returning to a "broad" type, or completely surrounding the nave with aisles, or placing the altar elsewhere than in front of the apse and opposite the entrance. The fact that the plan of Christian basilicas is standardized means that the need to accommodate large congregations cannot fully explain why Constantine's grand churches are only basilicas, and why the basilica immediately became the preferred architectural style for monumental churches.

How can we account for both the diversity of civil basilicas, and the uniformity of Constantinian basilicas? To answer that question, I

---

[21]Ward-Perkins argues that basilicas in the east typically are of the "long" type, with entrances in one short end opposite an apse or tribunal in the other, while in the west they are "broad," the entrance and apse/tribunal opposite each other in the long walls; "Origins of the Christian Basilica," 76-7.

[22]The 19th c. plan of Old St. Peter's shows a tri-portal entrance opening into the nave while two flanking entrances let into the adjacent aisles, making five entrances (Fig. 2); Corbo's plan of the Holy Sepulcher (Fig. 4), Richmond's of the Holy Nativity (Fig. 5), and Vincent's of Eleona (Fig.6) all reconstruct tri-portal entrances into the nave and side aisles.

[23]Krautheimer does say that the cornice of St. Peter's apparently supported a railing that allowed foot traffic on all four sides of the nave, but this is clearly not even a secondary area of traffic for the building; "Early Christian Architecture," 15; see Fig. 2, p. 377.

[24]"Origins of the Christian Basilica," 85.

suggest that these basilicas accommodate a behavior not found in, or not emphasized in, civil basilicas. It also is possible that Constantine's basilicas simulate another structure that already accommodated that kind of behavior.

*Figure 11. Interior of Sta. Sabina, Rome.*

What activities may we infer happened in Constantine's basilicas? Removing the aisles at the short ends, and placing the apse and altar at the short end opposite the entrance, implies that these buildings accommodate or encourage two-way traffic flow. Celebrants come in the main entrance and move straight ahead toward the altar in front of the apse opposite. To exit they reverse course, through the same doors by which they entered. Figures 11 and 12 illustrate how the standardized design of Constantine's basilicas encourages two-way traffic flow, which is uncommon in most civil basilicas, whose encircling aisles and surrounding shops seem to encourage movement in all directions, much like the forum itself. Although the tribunal and/or the apse provide a focal point in these structures, the architecture does not invite foot traffic to begin at one end of the building and terminate at the other.

Here we make special note of the large public peristyle building at Sepphoris, Israel, currently under excavation by J. F. Strange (Fig. 14). This two-story, 60 x 40 meter basilical structure, which takes up an entire city block, was constructed in the early first century and substantially remodeled in the late third or early fourth. Strange is inclined to interpret the last use of the building as a market because of the number of coins and the type of pottery and glass found on the floors and in the drains. On the white mosaic floors, black stripes apparently direct traffic, not down the nave, but around the sides where shops line the aisles.[25] Furthermore, although there are indications that a tri-portal entrance may offer access to the building from the courtyard to the east, in the long southern wall another large entrance (measuring 2.1 meters) lets into the southern aisle near the eastern wall that partitions the basilica from the portico. Four other smaller doors (1.77 meters wide) pierce this same wall to the west of the large entrance, and Strange has located at least one similar entrance in the long northern wall opposite.[26] Apparently the mosaic floor and location of the doors encourage explicitly what the architectural style itself invites implicitly: traffic around the periphery of the structure.

## The Roman Thoroughfare

Hence the architecture of civil basilicas appears to invite all-way or circular pedestrian traffic, between offices and shops, within and across the nave. In this way basilicas imitate the design of the porticoed forum, whose purpose they served in bad weather.[27] By the same token, the fact that Constantine's (and, to reiterate, nearly all subsequent Christian basilicas) standardize a basilical design with only longitudinal aisles parallel to the nave, and the main entrance in the short wall opposite the altar and apse, suggests that it is no longer all-way traffic that these structures accommodate, but two-way traffic.

Having reached this inference, it is striking that the grand Roman structure that accommodates large volumes of primarily two-way traffic also has a wide central avenue bounded on two sides by colonnaded porches or sidewalks. I am speaking of the thoroughfare street, such as the *cardo maximus*.[28] Figure 15 is a photo of the main avenue in

---

[25]James F. Strange, "The Eastern Basilical Building," in *Sepphoris in Galilee: Crosscurrents in Culture*, ed. Rebecca Nagy *et al.* (North Carolina Museum of Art, 1996), 117-121.

[26]James F. Strange, telephone conversation with the author (Tampa, FL, June, 1999).

[27]This fact may strengthen the argument that the name "basilica" (*basilikē*) originated as an adjective, as in the "royal porch" (*stoa basilikē*) in Athens. See Ward-Perkins, "Origins of the Christian Basilica," 70.

[28]The *cardo maximus* is the north-south "main street" that runs through the center of town, usually to the forum.

*Figure 12. Interior of Santa Maria Maggiore, Rome.*

Timgad,[29] while Figure 16 is the Arcadiané at Ephesus, and the parallels between them and a Christian basilica's floor plan are arresting.

Notice that the traffic on the thoroughfare falls into two different types. During the course of a normal day people travel both the paved street itself and the sidewalks to destinations within and without the city, and to the shops and offices lining the boulevard. Pedestrians may walk on the street, for they need not hurry to avoid the animal-drawn carts. On special occasions, however, pedestrians must confine themselves to the sidewalks to make way for processionals, primarily

[29]From William L. MacDonald, *The Architecture of the Roman Empire, Vol. II: An Urban Appraisal* (New Haven and London: Yale University Press, 1986), 28.

triumphal military parades and *adventi* of important state officials, which we will examine more fully below.

It is the latter pomp that concerns us here. As noted, it is striking that the thoroughfare, with its wide avenue, colonnaded sidewalks, and state parades finds its architectural match in the Constantinian basilica, with its wide nave, colonnaded side aisles, and—I presume—solemn processionals.

Table 1 compares the widths of major thoroughfares in cities across the Roman Empire with the widths of Constantine's basilicas.

**Table 1.**
**Comparison: Constantinian Basilicas (width of nave) with Roman Thoroughfares (width of street)**

| Constantinian Basilicas | | Roman Thoroughfares[30] | |
|---|---|---|---|
| Lateran | 25.1 m[31] | Antioch | 29 m |
| St. Peter's | apr. 23.5 m[32] | Gerasa | 22/24 m |
| | | Rome, *Via Flaminia* | 21 m |
| | | Apamea | 23 m |
| | | Ephesus, *Arkadiané* | 23 m |
| Holy Sepulcher | 14 m[33] | Augst, NW-SE | 14 m |
| | | Pompeii, NE-SW | 7/14 m |
| Holy Nativity | 10.4 m[34] | Ostia | 8/10 m |
| Eleona | 11 m[35] | | |

These data verify that Constantine's basilicas are neither too wide nor too narrow to be modeled after the thoroughfare. Rather, both the standardized style and the dimensions of Constantinian churches match the appearance and size of major Roman streets. This is the first piece of

[30]From MacDonald, *Architecture of the Roman Empire, Vol. II*, 41-2. Because MacDonald does not say, I assume that his dimensions are of the width of the street itself, not including the sidewalks.

[31]Richard Krautheimer, "The Constantinian Basilica of the Lateran," in *Early Christian, Medieval, and Renaissance Art* (New York: New York University Press, 1969), 22, Text fig. 5.

[32]Krautheimer, *Christian and Byzantine Architecture*, 55, Fig. 22.

[33]Virgilio C. Corbo, *Il Santo Sepolcro di Gerusalemme*, Parte II (Jerusalem: Franciscan Printing Press, 1981), Pl. 3.

[34]Asher Ovadiah, *Corpus of the Byzantine Churches in the Holy Land*, trans. Rose Kirson (Bonn: Peter Hanstein Verlag, 1970), 34.

[35]Ibid., 82.

concrete evidence that supports the hypothesis that Constantine's basilicas were designed to accommodate a processional.

The task of the remainder of the study is now clear. We have noted the architectural similarities between major thoroughfares and Constantinian basilicas, which we can plainly see, and their parallel functions, which we presume to exist. Hence we must answer the question, Did people move down the nave of fourth-century basilicas in the way described?

### The Processional

We have some evidence for supposing that whatever solemn ceremonies had embodied the liturgy before 313, now they were embellished and enlarged in much the same way as the church buildings were themselves. In fact, I argue that the church buildings were modified to accommodate the adapted liturgy. Specifically, I propose to show that it is reasonable to think that after 313 the liturgy began and ended with a grand processional that took on the solemnity and magnificence of imperial processionals and other state parades.

### The *Adventus* of the Emperor

I find a model for the Christian processional in the ceremony of the *adventus* of the Emperor or other state officials, which appeared in the first century C.E. and continued through the time of the Tetrarchs and on into the Byzantine centuries. MacCormack describes this occasion in his *Art and Ceremony in Late Antiquity*: a typical *adventus* was a solemn affair in which the population of a city came forth from the walls to greet an arriving Caesar and conducted him back to the forum. The ceremony included singing hymns to Caesar, dancing, playing instruments, and sometimes the delivery of two speeches written by a panegyrist, one outside the walls and one inside the city.[36] Often the visit was the occasion for the Emperor to grant special favors to the city, and this was sometimes depicted on coins or medallions minted to commemorate the event.[37]

One of the most famous *adventi* was Constantine's triumphal entry into Rome in 312, which is recorded on his arch. The scenes show Constantine in a carriage, entering Rome accompanied by foot soldiers and cavalry. No citizens come forth to meet the Emperor, but side panels on the arch show Constantine enthroned and surrounded by

---

[36]MacCormack, *Art and Ceremony*, 17-22.
[37]Ibid., Pls. 9, 10.

subjects in the forum: in a top panel he addresses the crowd, in the bottom he distributes gifts (Fig. 17).[38]

Upon his arrival in the forum, the panegyrists spoke of Caesar as *deus praesens*,[39] a deity within the very city who was available for its aid and protection. The language of the panegyrists reflected this apotheosis, as in this hymn reputedly sung to Demetrius Poliocretes as he entered Athens:

> Other gods indeed are a great distance away
> Or have no ears,
> Or they do not exist or take no notice of us.
> But you we see present,
> Not made of wood or stone, but truly.[40]

MacCormack claims that the pattern of the *adventus* formed the template for "the different types of arrivals of Christ and of arrivals of bishops and of relics,"[41] and for evidence he appeals to Egeria's description of the reenactment of Palm Sunday in Jerusalem and Chrysostom's account of the translation of St. Thomas' relics to his martyrium near Constantinople.[42] MacCormack's assertion is attractive because it appears to confirm the hypothesis presented here, but he supplies no evidence to support his claim. Thus we must make up the deficit, and review the data that links *adventus* with the liturgical procession. In order to do this, first we turn to the eighth century stational mass.

## The Stational Mass

As MacCormack describes it, the pattern of *adventus* finds a counterpart in Jungmann's description of Roman stational services in the seventh century,[43] which he derives from *Ordo Romanus I*.[44] Here the Bishop of Rome proceeds on horseback from the Lateran to the designated church. A "stately procession"[45] of the papal court accompanies him: acolytes and legal administrators afoot, deacons and chief dignitaries of the Apostolic Palace mounted. Upon the Pope's arrival at the church the gospel precedes him down the nave to the altar.

---

[38]Ibid., Pls. 12-5.
[39]Ibid., 22-33.
[40]Athenaeus, VI, 253 in Ibid., 23.
[41]Ibid., 64.
[42]Ibid., 64-5.
[43]Joseph A. Jungmann, *The Mass of The Roman Rite: Its Origins and Development*, 2 vols., trans. Francis A. Brunner (Benzinger Brothers, 1951 [Replica edition 1986 by Christian Classics]), I, 67-74.
[44]*PL* 78, 937-948.
[45]Jungmann, *Mass of the Roman Rite*, 67.

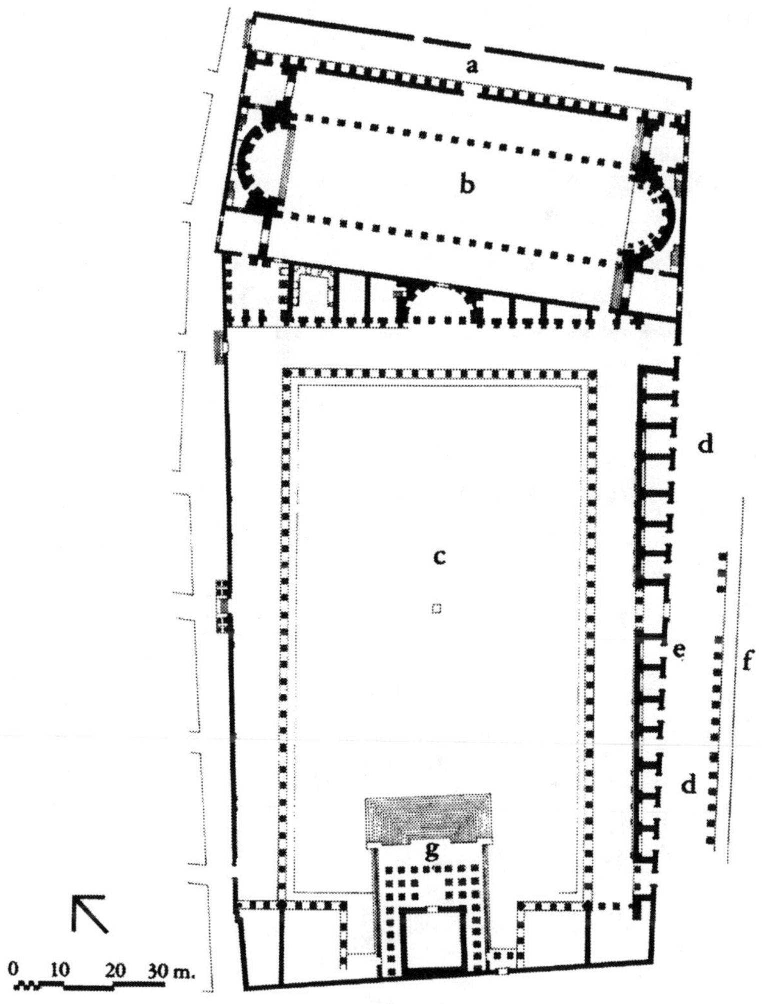


*Figure 13. Lepcis Magna, Severan forum with adjacent basilica. Drawing by Macdonald.*

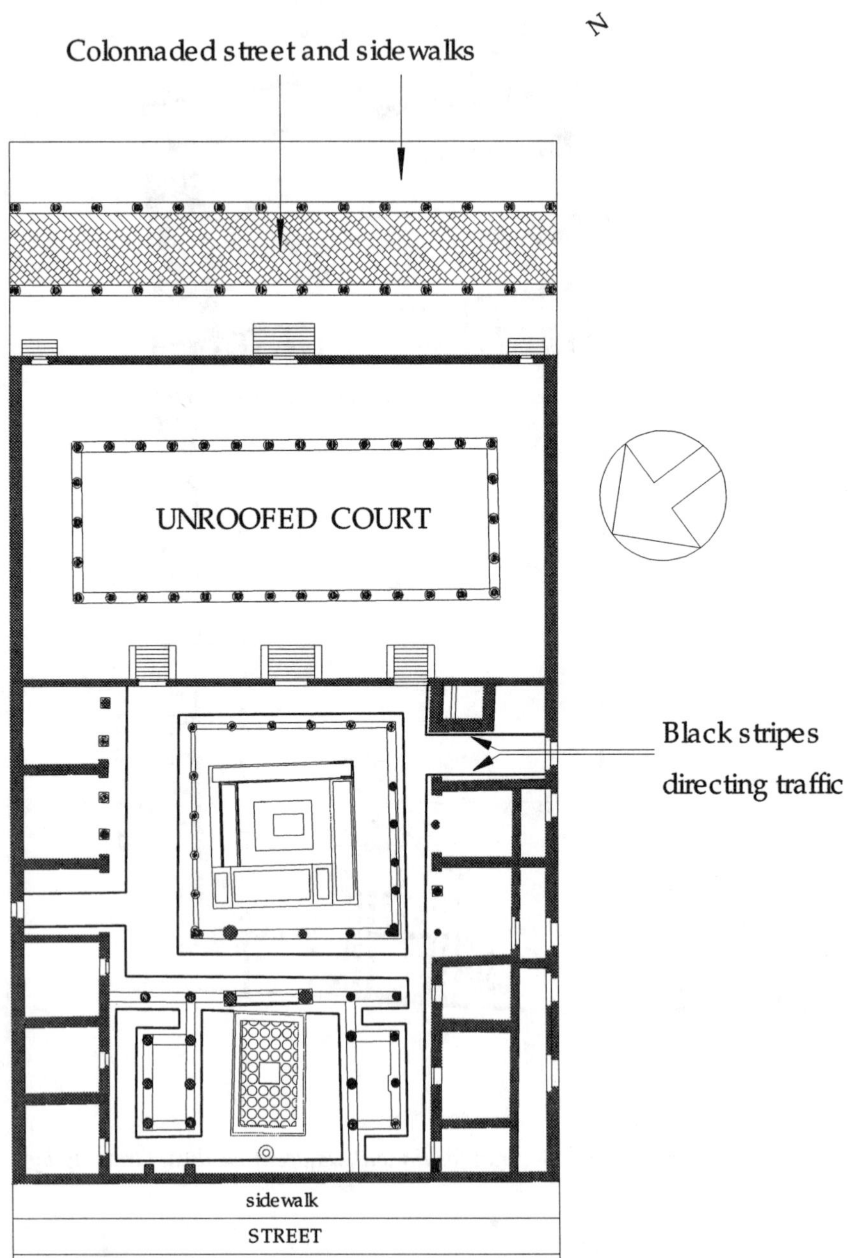


*Figure 14. Basilica at Sepphoris, Israel. Drawing by J. F. Strange.*

*Figure 15. Main east-west thoroughfare, looking west, Timgad.*

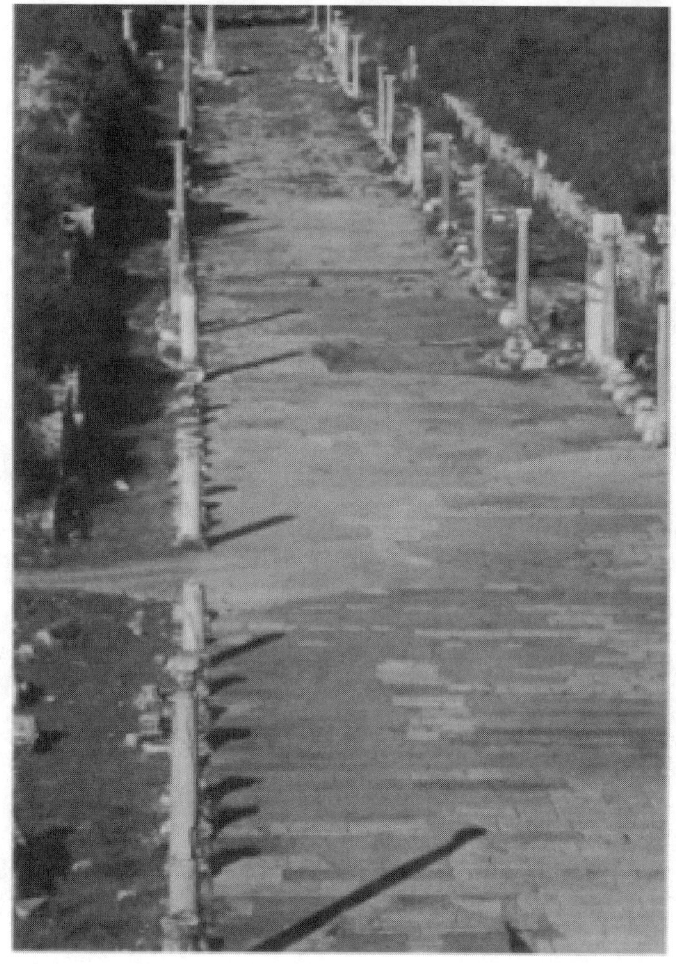

*Figure 16. Arcadiané, Ephesus.*

This procession is observed by the bishops and presbyters of the titular churches, who are already seated on their benches lining the apse, and by the crowds who have arrived in procession from the seven regions of Rome. When the Pope has been properly attired in the *secretarium* near the entrance, he too proceeds to his throne at the vertex of the apse accompanied by the tones of the introit. At the end of the service another procession returns the Pope to the *secretarium.*[46]

Jungmann makes several connections between this ceremony and "the ancient and originally oriental court ceremony"[47]: as the Pope processes to the altar clerics bring incense, seven acolytes bear torches in his honor, and two deacons kiss his hands as they conduct him down the nave. Jungmann thinks all these rituals hearken back to honors due to the Emperor and other state officials.[48] For our part, we may make a connection between the processional as Jungmann describes it, and what we see on Constantine's arch. In both, a processional conducts the honoree in "gorgeous pomp"[49] to a throne where, surrounded by officials and crowds, he presides over a solemn ceremony. Neither processional is made up of civilians or laypeople, but rather of clerics or soldiers, both on foot and in the saddle. The honoree himself is astride a horse, although in this case Constantine is in a carriage. Furthermore, three distinct symbols represent God's presence in the stational church, a counterpart to Caesar as *deus praesens* within the city: the Pope himself, the Gospel, and the elements of the Eucharist.[50]

I do not claim that a one-to-one correspondence links the two ceremonies, especially because the mass cannot compete with state parades in sheer size and grandeur, but the similarities do invite speculation. We may hypothesize that when the Church designed its stational processions, its template was the state pomp with which it was already familiar. Where we have difficulty is in claiming that the stational mass begins as early as the fourth century, when the earliest descriptions of these services come to us from the eighth century. We may conjecture that these masses existed before they were codified in *Ordo Romanus I*, but the evidence does not allow for us to claim that by the time any processional was officially recorded, it had already survived in some form for four hundred years. Thus the next step is to turn away from the *Ordo Romanus I* and toward earlier works to search for the origins of the processional.

---

[46]Ibid., 67-73.
[47]Ibid., 69.
[48]Ibid., 68-9, n. 7.
[49]Ibid., 73.
[50]Ibid., 446-7; MacCormack, *Art and Ceremony*, 18.

## Ancient Sources: The New Testament

Before proceeding with the sources that describe early Christian liturgy, however, we ought to take a look at the earliest Christian writings that depict anything that looks like a processional.

Paul's Epistle to the Colossians contains an ambiguous reference: "Wiping out the charge against us which was in decrees hostile to us, he has also removed it from us, by nailing it to the cross. He has divested himself of rule and authority and made a pubic example of them, triumphing over them by it."[51] Translators have chosen several ways to render *thriambeusas autous en autō*. The NASB says, "having triumphed over them through Him." On the other hand, Zerwick and Grosvenor[52] choose language that has implications for our hypothesis: according to them *thriambeusas...en autō* means "lead around (as, e.g., prisoners) in a triumphal procession...by it (the cross)." This language brings to mind Caesar's triumphal processionals, and the image of the cross certainly recalls later liturgical processions in which the cross is paraded through the congregation.

Paul's language, however, gives us no evidence to claim that he links Christ's triumph to Christian worship in any way. We may simply speculate that as early as Paul's writings Christians already pictured Christ as triumphant, and that Paul expressed that idea in language that recalled the triumphs of Caesar.[53]

The canonical gospels all describe Jesus' so-called "triumphal entry" into Jerusalem, and John's gospel in particular provides a familiar image:

> The next day, when the great throngs that had come to the festival heard that Jesus was coming to Jerusalem, they took branches of palm trees and went out to meet him, shouting, "Hosanna! Blessed is he who comes in the name of the Lord, the King of Israel!" Finding a young donkey, Jesus sat on it just as it is written: "Fear not, daughter of Zion. Look, your king is coming sitting on a donkey's colt."[54]

Here we see some elements that are to those from the *adventus* and the later stational mass: the citizens, hearing of Jesus' arrival, go out to meet him; they call him "King"; Jesus rides an equine beast; the people conduct him into the city. All of the elements are present for us to imagine an impromptu *adventus*.

The similarities between this New Testament event and state ceremony are difficult to ignore. In this case, it appears that the method

---

[51]Col 2:14-15.

[52]*A Grammatical Analysis of the Greek New Testament*, 5th revised ed. (Rome: Pontificio Istituto Biblico, 1996).

[53]See 2 Cor 2:14 for another instance of the same verb.

[54]Jn 12:12-15.

of Jesus' final entry into Jerusalem is not an accident, but designed either by himself or John's redactor to resemble an imperial *adventus*. Either when first century Jews greeted Jesus outside of Jerusalem, or when the authors of the next generation recorded the event, they gave it the structure of grand pomp with which they were familiar. We may thus argue that the model of the *adventus* was in place in Christian Scriptures as early as John's Gospel, and perhaps earlier in the canonical Gospels. What we must do now is show that beyond depicting Christ in royal tableaus, the Church acted out the triumph of Christ with some sort of liturgical pageantry in the fourth century or before.

**Ancient Sources: Justin Martyr**

Because no formal liturgical order tells us of grand or solemn pomp in the fourth century mass, we turn now to other Christian authors of late antiquity to search for mentions of a "processional." In the Greek authors we search for the verb *pompeuō* and its derivative noun *pompē*; in the Latin, for *procedo* and its derivatives. Other words in the same semantic field (*apantēsis*, *thriambuō*, *kōmazō*, and *semnoō* in Greek; *apparatus*, *commissatio*, *ostentatio*, and *triumphus* in Latin) do not appear to be technical liturgical terms in Christian authors.

One of the earliest possible mentions of the processional comes from the *First Apology* of Justin Martyr (d. 162-7 C.E.). While defending Christianity against the charge of atheism, Justin says,

> We have learned that the only offering worthy of Him is not to consume by fire those things He has brought into being for our sustenance, but to offer those things to ourselves and to the needy, and to conduct processions and hymns with thanksgiving to Him through speech ....[55]

Lampe's renders *pompas* as "solemnities" because Justin may refer to the entire Eucharistic service rather than its opening rite alone.[56] Leslie Barnard translates it the same way (*pompas...pempein* = "celebrating our solemnities"[57]), arguing that while the word usually means "a solemn procession," the text requires a less specific meaning because a procession would bring undue attention and therefore persecution to any congregation in Justin's day.[58] But presumably second century Christians conducted their Eucharistic worship out of sight in the

---

[55]Justin Martyr, *Apol. I*, 13 (*PG* 6, 315).

[56]G.W.H. Lampe, *A Patristic Greek Lexicon* (Oxford: Clarendon Press, 1961), 1120.A.

[57]*St. Justin Martyr, The First and Second Apologies*, trans. Leslie William Barnard (Mahwah, N.J.: Paulist Press, 1997), 30.

[58]Ibid., 115-6, n. 75.

privacy of their house churches. Also, in context *pempein* makes sense as "to conduct," connoting "to convoy" or "to escort"[59] rather than its more common meaning "to send" or Barnard's "celebrating." Furthermore, Justin mentions hymns accompanying the *pompas*, which sounds like what we know of the later introit, as described by Jungmann above.

Justin's example suggests that solemn—if not grand—processions were a part of Christian worship early on. Now we must link a grand and regal processional with Constantine's basilicas in the fourth century. For this we turn to the travel diary of Egeria.

## Ancient Sources: Egeria

The pilgrim nun Egeria probably visited Palestine between 381 and 384,[60] spending much of her time worshiping in the many churches in and around Jerusalem. The liturgy that she describes burgeons with references to the motion of the congregation and bishop, both within and between churches.

*Procedo* and its derivatives come up several times in Egeria's writing, most of them associated with two of Constantine's basilicas (the Holy Sepulcher and Eleona), and some with the church on Mt. Zion.[61] Michael Fraser is confident that when Egeria says *proceditur* she refers to the liturgical procession.[62] John Wilkinson, by contrast, never translates any instances of *procedo* as "the procession" or "they process," but always as "they assemble,"[63] although he does suppose that Egeria describes a processional[64] and translates one participle of *venio* as "their procession."[65] The text itself uses common verbs of motion, such as *ago*, *venio*, *ito*, *duco*, and *procedo* to describe worship that frequently moves worshipers and clergy from one church to another. When, on the other hand, she means to say that the people "gather" or "assemble" for worship in this or that church, she uses *colligo*, apparently in contrast to these verbs of motion.[66] In this context I favor *procedo* to connote motion

---

[59]*A Lexicon Abridged from Liddell and Scott's Greek-English Lexicon* (Oxford: Clarendon Press, 1963), 542.A.

[60]John Wilkinson, *Egeria's Travels* (London: S.P.C.K., 1971), 3; 237-9.

[61]Besides the attestations treated here, *procedo* appears in S. Siluiae, *Pereg*. 24.3, 27.3, 5, 6.

[62]See Fraser's translation at *Egeria and the Fourth Century Liturgy of Jerusalem* [hypertext version online] (University of Durham: Department of Theology, June 1994, accessed 30 July 1999); available from http://users.ox.ac.uk/~mikef/durham/egeria.html.

[63]Wilkinson, *Egeria's Travels*, 89-147.

[64]Ibid., 83.

[65]Ibid., 130; S. Siluiae, *Pereg*. 27.8 (Geyer, 79).

[66]See for example S. Siluiae, *Pereg*. 24.8, 43.3 (Geyer, 74, 94).

to or within a church, rather than gathering or assembling, as in the following example.

Describing regular Sunday worship, Egeria says,

> a. But at first light, because it is the Lord's day, they also process in [proceditur *in*] the great church, which Constantine built on Golgotha behind the Cross, and there they do all things according to the custom everywhere on the Lord's Day.[67]

If we maintain that *proceditur* connotes the movement of worshipers as a group rather than their gathering in one spot, then the use of *in* with the ablative rather than with the accusavive (or *ad* with the accusative) implies that Egeria describes movement within the church itself rather than into or toward it. This language suggests a liturgical processional of some sort, as with several other examples. One will suffice here.

> b. *Then* on the first [day of Easter], the day of the Lord itself, they process in [*proceditur in*] the great church (that is to the Martyrium)—also on the second and third days. Accordingly, having made the mass, they always go [*veniatur...ad*] from the Martyrium with hymns to the Anastasis. On the fourth day, however, they process in Eleona [*proceditur in*], on the fifth to the Anastasis, on the Sixth in Zion, on Saturday before the Cross; but on the Lord's day (that is on the eighth), once more in the great church (that is to the Martyrium).[68]

Based on these examples, apparently Egeria describes two different sorts of processionals, one that takes place within a church, and one between churches: thus "they process...*to* the Anastasis". If this is the case, then the movement between churches appears to be an intrinsic part of worship.

Why do I think that Egeria uses *procedo* in a technical sense? I have translated it as "they process," but Egeria may use it synonymously with other verbs of motion. What we need, therefore, is a context that clues us as to what Egeria means when she says *proceditur*. Besides these and other examples, Egeria uses a derivative of *procedo* twice more. One instance describes the rising of the sun:

> c. Then afterwards the mass is made from the Cross (before the sun rises [*procedat*]), and straightway the energetic ones go on to Zion to pray at the column at which the Lord was flogged.[69]

This example is significant because it suggests that Egeria uses *procedo* to connote motion rather than assembly, and in this case motion along a

---

[67]S. Siluiae, *Pereg.* 25.1 (Geyer, 74).
[68]Ibid., 39.2 (Geyer, 91). For other examples see ibid., 25.6 (Geyer, 75); 41 (Geyer, 93); 49.3 (Geyer, 101).
[69]Ibid., 37.1 (Geyer, 83).

fixed and regular course—that is, a ritual activity. I presume it is the same in the other cases as well.

It is the remaining iteration of *procedo* that appears to provide the particular technical usage for which we search:

> d. Indeed, the fortieth day of Epiphany is celebrated enthusiastically here with highest distinction. For the same day the procession [*processio*] is in the Anastasis; everyone processes and everything goes in order with greatest rejoicing just as during Easter.[70]

Here *processio* is a nominative noun, serving as the subject of the sentence, and it appears to function technically to mean a liturgical procession. These two examples, therefore, suggest that Egeria consistently uses *procedo* to refer to processionals that are regular parts of worship, both within the service and when worshipers and clergy move from one church to another.

Having established that it is plausible to think that Egeria describes several processionals, we now turn to other instances when she does not, so far as we can tell, use technical language, but does appear to mention ritual processionals. Because the text contains numerous examples, two will suffice to demonstrate what I mean. Moving to Egeria's description of Lenten services we read:

*Figure 17. Side panels on Arch of Constantine, depicting the Emperor addressing subjects in Rome's forum (top panel), and distributing gifts (bottom).*

[70]Ibid., 26.1 (Geyer, 77).

a. In Lent, as I said above, on the fourth day at nine, they process in [*poceditur in*] Zion in accordance with the custom the rest of the year....When, however, they have made the mass, the people lead [*deducet*] the bishop with hymns from there all the way to the Anastasis; in this way they come so that when they enter the Anastasis it is in time for Lucernare.[71]

And describing the end of Lent Egeria says:

b. So at the beginning of the seventh hour, everyone goes to the Lazarium, which is Bethany, perhaps in the second mile from the city. But on the way from Jerusalem into the Lazarium, perhaps fifty paces from the Lazarium, is a church on the pavement where Mary the sister of Lazarus met the Lord. When, therefore, the bishop has arrived, all the monks meet him and the people go in....But when they have come to the Lazarium, such a great crowd has gathered that not only that place itself, but also all the fields around are full of people.[72]

Although Egeria does not label these movements of the bishop, the language strongly suggests that they are formal, ritual processionals. First, the events are at appointed times. Second, the people lead the bishop from one church to the other, much as the army conducted Caesar from one city to the other in an *adventus* (and the people led him from the city gates into the forum), and as the clergy escorted the Pope from the Lateran to the appointed church in the later stational mass. Third, in example b. the bishop is met by waiting people twice, once by the clergy at the church by the road, and again by the assembled congregation at the Lazarium. This recalls both the populace gathering to receive Caesar, and the seven collected congregations assembled and awaiting the arrival of the Pope at the stational church. In another example from Egeria not treated here the people arrive first at the Anastasis and then send for the bishop, who arrives to find the congregation in place and ready for his service.[73]

Again we cannot go so far as to claim a one-to-one correspondence between *adventus*, the stational mass, and Egeria's processions, but the similarities invite speculation. All three examples of ritual movement share enough in common to allow us to make a plausible connection between them, to suppose that Egeria describes several processionals that resemble the *adventus*. Not only so, but in Egeria's diary these processionals seem to be the shank of worship, connecting the other elements, seamlessly joining mass in one place to mass in another. Thus

---

[71]Ibid., 27.6 (Geyer, 79).
[72]Ibid., 29.4-5 (Geyer, 82).
[73]Ibid., 24.3 (Geyer, 71-2).

motion defines the worship that Egeria describes—movement from one place to the next—and verbs of motion make up the bulk of the action.

## Basilical Synagogues

Having shown that very soon after their construction the liturgy in Constantine's Palestinian churches included solemn, ritualistic movement, the final step is to test the hypothesis by using a control group. Galilean synagogue basilicas provide an excellent test case for this task. Not only do these structures come on the scene roughly contemporary with the earliest church basilicas (the examples we will examine all come from the third through fifth centuries), but synagogue builders in the Galilee also almost uniformly constructed basilicas. What we wish to know is, did synagogue worship in these centuries include a grand processional, beginning at the entrance and proceeding down the axis of the nave? If it did, then we should expect to see a standardized design that accommodates this ritual, just as in Constantine's basilicas. If, on the other hand, synagogue worship had no processional comparable to that of Christian worship, then the opposite should be true: we not only should fail to find this design, but we should see another design that reflects the particular ethos of synagogue worship.

## Jewish Liturgy in the Formative Age

As with its Christian counterpart, the shape and content of Jewish liturgy in its formative age is largely conjecture, based on rabbinic sources that may have not have defined a widely-practiced norm until much later than the time of their writing. Additionally, the *Seder Rav Amram,* which represents the earliest "fixed" liturgy, dates to the middle of the ninth century. It is here that the *Shema' Yisra'el* and *Tefillah* become central to worship in most services in Europe and the Middle East, according to Lawrence Hoffman.[74] The *Seder Rav Amram,* however, presents the same difficulty as the *Ordo Romanus* of the Christian liturgy: we may surmise that the elements of Jewish worship codified in the *Seder* had existed for some time before they were written down, but we do not know for how long.

As with the Christian liturgy and other writings, the Jewish liturgy of Late Antiquity used titles that the Greco-Roman world had reserved for Caesar. Our question is Did the synagogue in Palestine ever appropriate state pomp in its liturgy? We find our answer in three examples from Jewish worship.

---

[74]Lawrence Hoffman, "Jewish Liturgy and Jewish Scholaship," in *Judaism in Late Antiquity,* Part I, *The Literary and Achaeological Sources*, ed. Jacob Neusner (Leiden: E.J. Brill, 1995), 249-50.

1. Two passages in the Mishnah appear to describe ritual processions, one associated with the festival of Sukkot, and another having to do with daily sacrifices in the temple. The passage from M. Sukkah 4.5 reads as follows:

   A. The religious requirement of the willow branch: How so?
   B. There was a place below Jerusalem, called Mosa. [People] go down there and gather young willow branches. They come and throw them along the sides of the altar, with their heads bent over the altar.
   C. They blew on the *shofar* a sustained, a quavering, and a sustained note.
   D. Every day they walk around the altar one time and say, "*Save now, we beseech thee, O Lord! We beseech thee, O Lord, send now prosperity* (Ps. 118:25)."
   E. R. Judah says, "[They say], '*Ani waho, save us we pray! Ani waho, save us we pray!*'"
   F. And on that day [the seventh day of the willow branch] they walk around the altar seven times.
   G. When they leave, what do they say?
   H. "Homage to you, O altar! Homage to you, O altar!"
   I. R. Eliezer says, "For the Lord and for you, O altar! For the Lord and for you, O altar!"[75]

Two difficulties tell us that this processional finds no match in Christian worship. First, none of its elements recall the *adventus* of the Emperor or the Christian rite: no honoree is paraded into the temple; rather, the honoree is the altar, which must remain stationary; the processional moves around the altar. Second, we cannot show that this temple processional was transferred to synagogue worship in the first through fourth centuries.

2. A second passage, Mishnah tractate *Tamid* 3:1, describes another temple processional:

   A. The superintendent said to them, "Come and cast lots [to determine] (1) who executes the act of slaughter, (2) who tosses the blood, (3) who removes the ashes of the inner altar, (4) who removes the ashes of the candlestick, (5) who carries up the limbs to the ramp:
   B. "(1) the head, (2) the [right] hind leg, (3) the two forelegs, (4) the rump, and (5) the [left] hind leg, (6) the breast, (7) the neck, (8) the two flanks, (9) the innards, (10) the fine flour, (11), the cakes, (12) the wine."
   C. They drew lots.
   D. Whoever won won.[76]

---

[75]*The Mishnah: A New Translation*, trans. Jacob Neusner (New Haven and London: Yale University Press, 1988), 287.
[76]Ibid., 865; cf. Yoma 2.

This processional appears to be the counterpart to the one that brought in the host in the Christian liturgy. The same problems apply here, however, as did with the earlier passage. Namely, on what basis may we suppose that this temple ritual was copied in the synagogue liturgy, which brought in no sacrifice? Furthermore, unlike the Christian processional, this processional could not have taken place through the midst of the congregation, for the pieces of the sacrificial victim might have contracted uncleanliness.

3. In later times a solemn processional does appear in Jewish worship, associated with the *simkhat torah* ("Joy of the Torah"), the last day of Sukkot. Here, however, the Torah scrolls were paraded around the bema, rather than in the entrance and down the axis of the nave.[77] This parade resembles the Great and Little Entrances in the Church liturgy more than the entrance processional of the bishop. Furthermore, although we can locate special readings assigned to this day in the Babylonian Talmud (Meg. 31a), we have no early references to the processional itself. Evidently, we cannot place this ceremony any earlier than the Middle Ages, and possibly must push it later than that.[78]

Thus the Mishnah and other texts do not lead us to infer the presence of processionals. The question now is, Do Galilean basilical synagogues look like Christian basilicas?

## Galilean Synagogues

Strange notes that some twenty synagogues in the Galilee share "one architectural feature that seems to be almost a constant; it is the habit of their builders to place a row of columns between the benches against the walls and the central worship space."[79] That is, like the Christian basilica, Galilean synagogues share a standardized design. Strange goes

---

[77]*Encyclopaedia Judaica*, s.v. "SIMHAT TORAH"; cf. Ismar Elbogen, *Jewish Liturgy: A Comprehensive History*, trans. Raymond P. Scheindlin (Philadelphia: The Jewish Publication Society, New York: The Jewish Theological Seminary of America, 1993 [German, 1913; Hebrew, 1972]), 160.

[78]In rather confusing language Elbogen says, "by the end of the Middle Ages we find [these processions] in every country," ibid., but he then admits, "no Medieval source mentions the processions on the Joy of the Torah," ibid., 429, n. 8.

[79]James F. Strange, "First Century Galilee from Archaeology and from the Texts," in Douglas Edwards and Thomas McCollough, eds., *Archaeology and the Galilee: Texts and Contexts in the Graeco-Roman and Byzantine Periods* (Atlanta: Scholars Press, 1997), 43-4. See also J.F. Strange's article, "The Archaeology of Religion at Capernaum: Synagogue and Church," Chapter 2 in this volume.

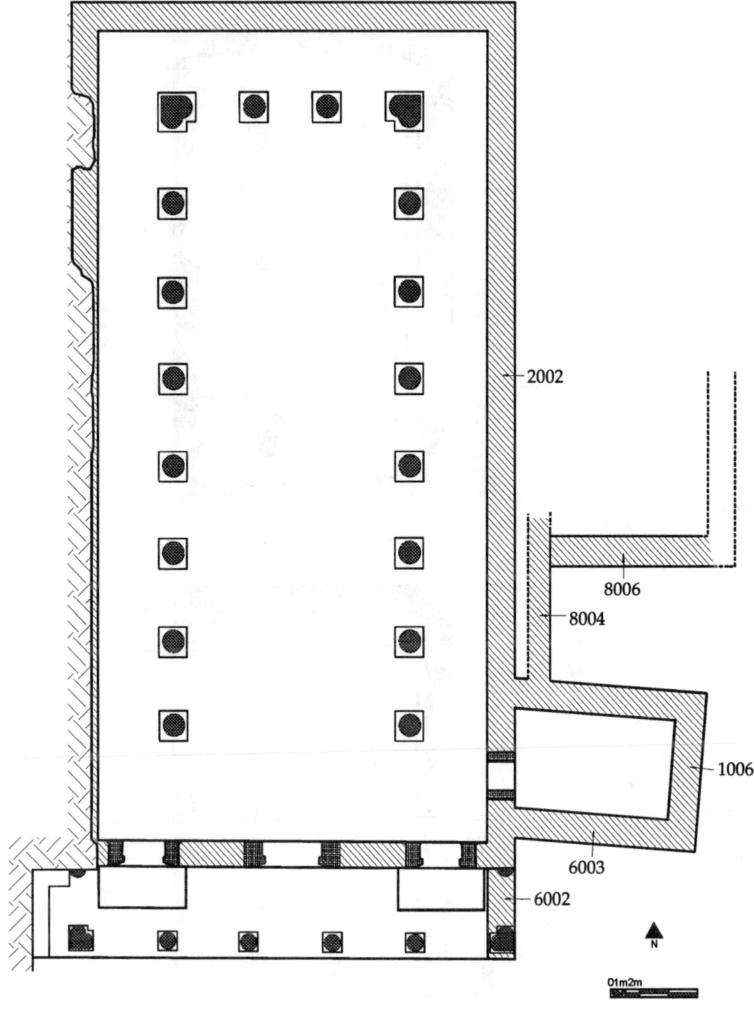


*Figure 18. Meiron synagogue. After a drawing by Larry Belkin*

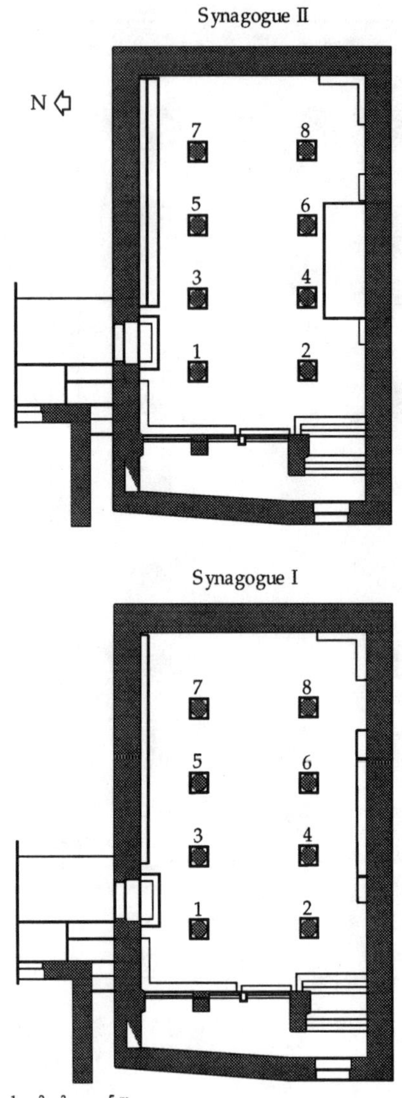


*Figure 19. Kh. Shema' synagogue. After a drawing by John Thompson.*

on to say, "This is a most peculiar arrangement, given the habit of the Romans to place rows of columns behind the backs of gathered spectators...."[80] This interior columniation creates a basilica that in many ways is indistinguishable from the many church basilicas that spring up in Palestine from the fourth through the seventh centuries. If this is so, how does one tell a Galilean synagogue from a church?

The chief method for archaeologists to distinguish a synagogue from an early Byzantine church is naturally through the decoration of the walls and floors and through inscriptions. But how might archaeologists conducting a surface survey tell these structures apart were they to encounter the foundations of one on the ground and in surrounding vegetation, where decorations and inscriptions were invisible? If we assume buildings of roughly the same size and surface pottery dating to the fourth or fifth century, at a site known to have housed both Jewish and Christian populations, what might distinguish a synagogue from a church? The simplest answer would be to count the rows of columns and to locate the entrances. As we have noted, we could be nearly certain that the church would have two rows of columns running the length of the building, east to west, and in the Galilee the main entrance would be in the short western wall opposite the apse in the east. Likewise, we could be almost equally certain that the Galilean synagogue would have three rows of columns arranged in a "horseshoe" around the nave. We might even call the presence of "heart-shaped" columns[81] an indicator of a synagogue versus a church.

In order to establish the regularity of these features, which we may also call a standardized design, I present three well-known Galilean synagogues as representatives of the genre.

1. The Meiron Synagogue (interior 28.4 m x 13.6 m; Fig. 18) was built in the late third century[82] in one of the four major villages of the Upper Galilee, of which Khirbet Shema' is another.[83] The structure is oriented north to south. A tri-portal entrance in the short south wall, which was still standing up to the lintels when the team began excavating in 1971,[84] offers access into the nave and two side aisles from a colonnaded porch. Thus, like church basilicas the building is

---

[80]Ibid., 43.

[81]"Heart-shaped" columns stand at the corners of rows, and when viewed in cross section from above, they have one "lobe" in line with one row, and another at right angles in line with the other row; see Figs. 18 and 20.

[82]The excavation's Stratum IV; Eric M. Meyers, James F. Strange, and Carol L. Meyers, *Excavations at Ancient Meiron* (Cambridge, MA: The American Schools of Oriental Research, 1981), xviii, 16.

[83]Ibid., 3.

[84]The eastern portal was reconstructed in 1950; ibid., 9.

oriented along the long axis. Unlike a church basilica, however, the building runs north-south, with a row of four columns across the back (i.e. north) wall. The two outer columns of this row are heart-shaped, forming the corners with the side colonnades. The columns thus form a horseshoe shape, with the open end facing south toward the entrance.

2. The synagogue at Kh. Shema' (interior apr. 12 m x 9.26 m[85]; Fig. 19) was first constructed in the mid to late third century[86] and reconstructed in the fourth.[87] The later synagogue was built upon the foundations and to the dimensions of the earlier synagogue. Both structures were oriented east-west and had two entrances: one in the long north wall offset west of center (letting into the north aisle between columns 1 and 2 of the north row), and another stepping down into the south aisle from an adjoining room to the west. Thus, although both buildings had only two rows of columns running longitudinally along the axis (no heart-shaped columns mark the corners[88]), there is nothing to indicate that these buildings were built to focus traffic down the length of the nave.[89] On the contrary, both synagogues had benches along the north and west walls, with a corner bench in the southeast. The earlier synagogue had a bench on the south wall as well, which the second synagogue mostly covered with a bema.[90] Apparently, therefore, the architecture focused attention into the center of the room and toward the long south wall closest to Jerusalem.

3. The date of the synagogue at Capernaum (interior 23.1 x 17.26 m[91]; Fig. 20) is disputed, although the evidence for a late fourth or early fifth century date seems irrefutable based on the pottery and thousands of coins found in two hoards beneath the floor.[92]

---

[85]These are my calculations from the stone-by stone ground plan in Eric M. Meyers, A. Thomas Kraabel, and James F. Strange, *Ancient Synagogue Excavations at Khirbet Shema'* (Durham, NC: Duke University Press, 1976), 40, Figure 3.4.
[86]The excavation's Stratum III; ibid., 31, 45-64.
[87]Stratum IV; ibid., 31, 64-81.
[88]Ibid., 61-63.
[89]See especially the isometric drawing of the synagogue with traffic patterns; ibid., 59, Fig. 3.10.
[90]Ibid., 54-5, 68-9, 71-3.
[91]These are my measurements of the plan—west wall north to south, and south wall east to west—in Virgilio C. Corbo, *Cafarnao*. Vol. I: Gli Edifici Della Citta (Jerusalem: Fraciscan Printing Press, 1975), 116.
[92]S. Loffreda, "The Late Chronology of the Synagogue of Capernaum," in Lee I. Levine ed., *Ancient Synagogues Revealed* (Jerusalem: Israel Exploration Society, 1981), 55-6.

Capernaum's synagogue floor plan looks much like Meiron's: three rows of interior columns form a horseshoe that is open on the south, and heart-shaped columns mark the northwest and northeast corners. In addition, the tri-portal entrance in the south wall opens into the nave and side aisles, while a smaller entrance in the long east wall offers access to a colonnaded porch on that side, and another in the northwest corner leads to a small room. Two-tiered benches run the length of the east and west walls. Again, these features indicate that the building is not designed to accommodate or encourage two-way traffic flow, but focuses worshippers' attention toward the center of the nave.

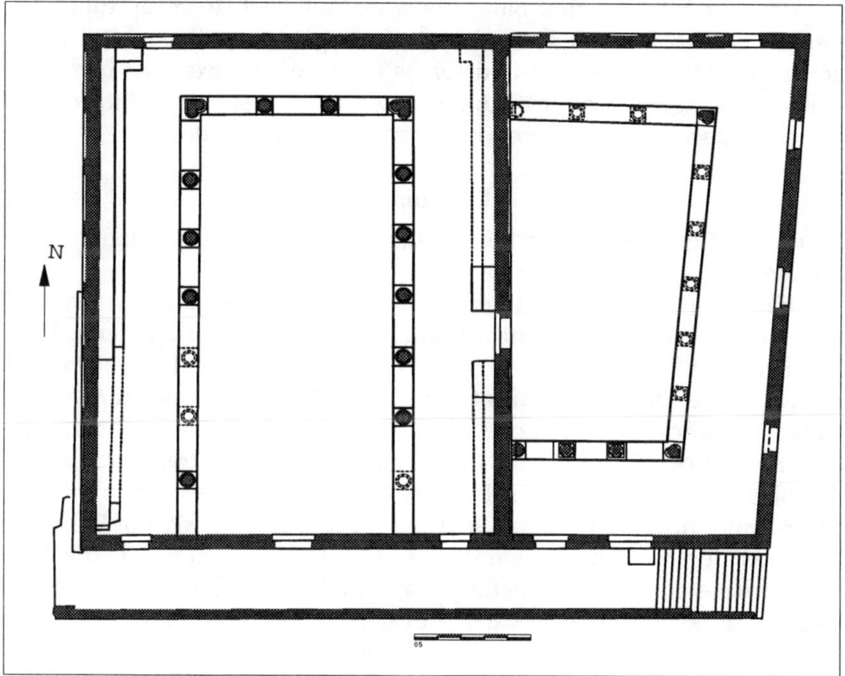


*Figure 20 Capernaum synagogue. After a drawing by Corbo.*

Drawing on this data, what can we conclude about the design of Galilean synagogues in late antiquity? We know that their standardized design makes no accommodation for a processional down the nave, but why, then, is the design standardized at all? Strange finds a simple explanation by appealing to Herod's Temple, and to the ethos of recreating its sacred space.[93] Just as in the temple one heard Torah read or watched the proceedings in the Court of Priests from the shade of the surrounding porticoes,[94] looking through columns in order to do so, so in the Galilean synagogue one peers through columns into the central worship space.

Strange presents a hypothesis that accounts for an architectural design that in so many words he says is "standardized" ("one architectural feature that seems to be almost a constant," cited above). The Galilean synagogue recreates the sacred space of the Jerusalem temple. Strange points out that this ethos also explains the absence of interior columniation in several Samaritan synagogues excavated in the environs of Mt. Gerizim: Samaritans do not wish to recapitulate the design of the Jerusalem temple.[95] Strange's hypothesis, therefore, accounts both for his data and for its absence; one explains both why Galilean synagogues place columns between the observer and the central worship space, and why Samaritan synagogues do not do so.

## Conclusion

Four questions regarding the development of the Christian basilica remain to be answered.

First, the hypothesis presented here does not explain the doubled aisles in four of Constantine's basilicas: the Lateran, St. Peter's, Holy Sepulcher, and Holy Nativity. One way to account for this feature is to appeal to the idea of grandiosity: doubling the aisles may simply make these churches all the more grand and monumental, befitting the commission of an Emperor.[96] In this case the high central nave flanked by columns still recapitulates the sense of a broad avenue.

Second, how do we know that the standardized design of Christian basilicas begins with Constantine's churches? Perhaps by the time Constantine began constructing his churches he simply took over a design "trend" that was already prevalent in the Empire. For example,

---

[93]J. F. Strange, "First Century Galilee," 43; cf. J. F. Strange, "Ancient Texts, Archaeology as Text, and the Problem of the First-Century Synagogue," in Howard Clark Kee and Lynn H. Cohick, eds. *Evolution of the Synagogue: Problems and Progress* (Harrisburg, PA: Trinity Press International, 1999), 27-45. Strange lays out this argument more completely in "The Synagogue as Metaphor," *Where We Stand*, vol. III, ed. Bruce D. Chilton, Alan J. Avery Peck, and Jacob Neusner (Leiden: Brill).

[94]See Strange's reconstruction of the Second Temple plan in ibid., 45, Figure 2.

[95]Ibid., 44.

[96]Doubling of colonnades is common in all types of basilicas, as in the Basilica Ulpia (Fig. 8), and in the famous reference from Tosefta Sukka 1:5 to the double colonnade of the Alexandrian basilica-synagogue.

the massive late third or early fourth century Basilica of Maxentius (interior dimensions of 82.40 x 62.70 m)—also called the Basilica of Constantine and Basilica Nova—is designed much like Constantine's church basilicas. It is laid out on a longitudinal axis, with only two side aisles running the length of the building, and with the tribunal apse in a short wall opposite a tri-portal entrance. It has some features, however, found in none of Constantine's other basilicas: four enormous piers partition the interior rather than colonnades, and cross vaults span the 25.30 meter-wide nave rather than roof timbers.[97] None of the basilicas that Constantine commissioned himself bear these rather significant architectural features which apparently reflect no enduring ethos but only a passing aesthetic for civil basilicas. For example, they do not appear in the basilica at Sepphoris, treated in Chapter 2.

Third, some find the origin of Constantine's basilicas in the design of the Domus Flavia basilical hall.[98] In this elongated room a main entrance pierces a short wall opposite an apse in the other. Colonnades flank the nave, but stand too close to the walls to form true aisles. Also, as MacDonald points out, the interior colonnades are "dubious modern restorations,"[99] and the one restored column is out of place and disproportionate to the rest of the structure.[100] The layout of this room is thus too conjectural for us to hypothesize that it provided a template for the Constantinian basilica.

Finally, it is possible that more than one type of symbol is in play here. For example, it is clear in Egeria that what we have called a "processional"—the ritual movement from church to church—may itself be a metaphor for pilgrimage. Once we have made this connection, it is arresting to note that two of Constantine's basilicas in Palestine incorporate into their designs centralized church plans, which become prominent in later memorial churches that define pilgrim routes. The Anastasis of the Church of the Holy Sepulcher surrounds the cave of the sepulcher with a circle of columns, and encloses these columns in a semicircular structure (Fig. 4). Likewise, the Church of the Holy Nativity encloses the cave of the nativity in an octagon (Fig. 5). The transept of St. Peter's in Rome, which houses the shrine to the saint, may be an example of cruciform architecture (Fig. 2). These centralized plans are typical of memorial churches built in the fifth century, such as the octagonal

---

[97]G.T. Rivoira, *Roman Architecture and Its Principles of Construction Under the Empire* (New York: Hacker Art Books, 1972), 212-4.

[98]MacDonald, *The Architecture of the Roman Empire,* I.53; see plan in Fig 6, B, p. 58 and Plates 40, 44.

[99]Ibid., 53.

[100]Ibid., Plate 39.

churches over Peter's house in Capernaum[101] and the church atop Mt. Gerizim. The Churches of the Sepulcher, Nativity, and St. Peter's are certainly over pilgrimage sites. It thus seems possible that if pilgrimage is a metaphor at play in the design of early Christian basilicas, then that metaphor continues in the later centralized churches that mark pilgrimage sites in Palestine and the rest of the Empire.[102]

## Conclusion

In spite of these lingering questions, however, we can now propose a hypothesis to explain both the standardized design of Constantine's basilicas, and the absence of that design in other basilicas. Furthermore, we can account for the Christian basilica's sudden appearance in the fourth century. Constantine's basilicas—the first erected—replicate the feel of a broad avenue that bears a ritual procession, which neither the civil basilicas that preceded nor the Jewish synagogue basilicas that followed attempt to do. Symbolism and metaphor, rather than aesthetics or function, account for religious behavior.

[101]See J.F. Strange, "The Archaeology of Religion," in this volume.

[102]See the discussion in Simon Coleman and John Elsner, "The Pilgrim's Progress: Art, Architecture, and Ritual Movement at Sinai," *World Archaeology* 26 No. 1 (June 1994): 73-89.

## Ancient Sources

Clement of Alexandria. *Paedagogus*. Patrologia cursus completus Series Graeca. Vol. 8.

Eusibius. *De vita Constantini imperatoris libri quatuor.* Patrologia cursus completus Series Graeca. Vol. 20.

———. *Ecclesiastical History*. Translated by C. F. Cruse. Peabody, MA: Hendrickson, 1998.

Fraser, Michael. *Egeria and the Fourth Century Liturgy of Jerusalem.* University of Durham Department of Thology, 1994. On-line hypertext version. Available from http://users.ox.ac.uk/~mikef/durham/egeria.html.

Justin Martyr. *Apologia primus pro Christianis.* Patrologia cursus completus Series Graeca. Vol. 6.

*Itinerarium Burdigalense.* Corpus scriptorum ecclesiasticorum latinorum. Vol. XXXVIIII. Itinera Hierosolymitana. Saeculi IIII - VIII. ed. P. Geyer. Vienna: F. Tempsky, 1898. 1-33.

*S. Siluiae, quae fertur, peregrinatio ad loca sancta.* Corpus scriptorum ecclesiasticorum latinorum. Vol. XXXVIIII. Itinera Hierosolymitana. Saeculi IIII - VIII. ed. P. Geyer. Vienna: F. Tempsky, 1898. 35-101.

Vitruvius. *On Architecture.* Ed. and Translated by Frank Granger. 2 Vols. Cambridge, MA: Harvard University Press and London: William Heinemann Ltd., 1983.

———. *The Ten Books on Architecture.* Translated by Morris H. Morgen. New York: Dover Publications, 1960 [Originally published by Harvard University Press in 1914].

Wilkinson, John. *Egeria's Travels.* London: S.P.C.K., 1971.

## Bibliography

Bradshaw, Paul F. *The Search for the Origins of Christian Worship: Sources and Methods for the Study of Early Liturgy*. New York: Oxford, 1992.

Cochrane, Charles Norris. *Christianity and Classical Culture: A Study of Thought and Action from Augustus to Augustine*. New York: Oxford University Press, 1957.

Coleman, Simon and John Elsner. "The Pilgrim's Progress: Art, Architecture and Ritual Movement at Sinai." *World Archaeology* 26 No. 1 (June 1994): 73-89.

Corbo, Virgilo C. *Il Santo Sepolcro di Gerusalemme: Aspetti archeologici dalle origini al periodo crociato*. Vol. II. Jerusalem: Fraciscan Printing Press, 1981.

Crowfoot, J. W. *Early Churches in Palestine*. College Park, MD: McGrath, 1971.

Davies, J. G. *The Origin and Development of Early Christian Church Architecture*. London: SCM Press Ltd., 1952.

Deissmann, Adolf. *Light from the Ancient East: The New Testament Illustrated by Recently Discovered Texts of the Graeco-Roman World*. Revised. Translated by Lionel R.M. Strachan. Grand Rapids: Baker Books House, 1980. German, 1909.

Dix, Gregory. *The Shape of the Liturgy*. London: Dacre Press, 1945. Reprint, 1964.

Elbogen, Ismar. *Jewish Liturgy: A Comprehensive History*. Translated by Raymond P. Scheindlin. Philadelphia: The Jewish Publication Society. New York: The Jewish Theological Seminary of America, 1993. German, 1913. Hebrew, 1972.

Goodenough, Erwin R. *Jewish Symbols in the Greco-Roman Period*. Vol. 1. *The Archaeological Evidence from Palestine*. Vol. 3. *Illustrations*. New York: Pantheon Books, 1953.

Gough, Michael. *The Origins of Christian Art*. New York: Praeger Publishers, 1973.

Grabar, André. *Early Christian Art: From the Rise of Christianity to the Death of Theodosius*. Translated by Stuart Gilbert and James Emmons. New York: Odyssey Press, 1968.

Hammond, Peter. *Liturgy and Architecture.* New York: Columbia University Press, 1961.

Hoffman, Lawrence A. *The Canonization of the Synagogue Service.* Notre Dame: University of Notre Dame Press, 1979.

———. "Jewish Liturgy and Jewish Scholarship." in Judaism in Late Antiquity. Part I, The Literary & Archaeological Sources. Ed. Jacob Neusner. Leiden: E.J. Brill, 1995. 239-66.

Jungmann, Joseph A. *The Mass of the Roman Rite: Its Origin and Development.* 2 Vols. Translated by Francis A. Brunner. Benzinger Brothers, 1951. Replica Edition 1986 by Christian Classics.

Kennedy, Roger G. *American Churches.* New York: Stewart, Tabori, and Chang, 1982.

Kohl, Heinrich and Carl Watzinger. *Antike Synagogen in Galilaea.* Jerusalem: Kedem Publishing, Ltd., 1973. Reprint of 1916 edition, Leipzig.

Krautheimer, Richard. "The Beginning of Early Christian Architecture." *Review of Religion.* III (1939): 127-48. Reprinted in *Studies in Early Christian, Medieval, and Renaissance Art.* New York: New York University Press. London: University of London Press Limited, 1969. 1-20.

———. "The Constantinian Basilica of the Lateran." *Antquity,* XXXIV (1960): 201-6. Reprinted in *Studies in Early Christian, Medieval, and Renaissance Art.* New York: New York University Press; London: University of London Press Limited, 1969. 21-5.

———. *Early Christian and Byzantine Architecture.* Baltimore: Penguine Books, 1965.

Krautheimer, Richard, Woflgang Frankl, and Spencer Corbett. *Corpus Basilicarum Christianarum Romae: The Early Christian Basilicas of Rome (IV-IX Cent.).* Vols I-V. Rome: Pontificio Instituto di Archeologia Christiana; New York: New York University Press, 1959.

Lietzmann, Hans. *Mass and Lord's Supper: A Study in the History of the Liturgy.* Leiden, Netherlands: Brill, 1979.

Loffreda, S. "The Late Chronology of the Synagogue of Capernaum." *Ancient Synagogues Revealed.* Ed. Lee I. Levine. Jerusalem: Israel Exploration Society, 1981, 52-7.

Macaulay, David. *City: A Story of Roman Planning and Construction.* Boston: Houton Mifflin, 1974.

MacCormack, Sabine G. *Art and Ceremony in Late Antiquity*. Berkeley, Los Angeles: University of California Press, 1981

MacDonald. William L. *The Architecture of the Roman Empire, Volume I: An Introductory Study*. New Haven: Yale University Press, 1965. *Volume II: An Urban Appraisal*. 1986.

———. *Early Byzantine and Christian Architecture*. New York: George Brasiller, 1982.

Mader, A.E. "Les fouilles allemandes au Ramet El Khalil: la Mambré biblique de la tradition primitive." *Revue Biblique* 39 (1930) 84: 115-7. Figs. 2, 5. Pls. 5, 7.

Mango, Cyril. *Byzantine Architecture*. New York: Harry N. Abrams, 1976.

Matthews, Thomas A. *The Clash of Gods: A Reinterpretation of Early Christian Art*. Revised. Princeton: Princeton University Press, 1993.

Meyers, Eric M., A. Thomas Kraabel, and James F. Strange. *Ancient Synagogue Excavations at Khirbet Shema', Upper Galilee, Israel 1970-1972*. The Annual of the American Schools of Oriental Research. Vol. XLII. Ed. David Noel Freedman. Durham, NC: Duke University Press, 1976.

Meyers, Eric M., James F. Strange, and Carol C. Meyers. *Excavations at Ancient Meiron, Upper Galilee, Israel 1971-72, 1974-75, 1977*. Cambridge, MA: The American Schools of Oriental Research, 1981.

Milburn, Robert. Early Christian Art and Architecture. Berkeley and Los Angeles: University of California Press, 1988.

Neusner, Jacob. *Symbol and Theology in Early Judaism*. Minneapolis: Fortress Press, 1991.

Ovadiah, Asher. *Corpus of the Byzantine Churches in the Holy Land*. Translated by Rose Kirson. Bonn: Peter Hanstein Verlag, 1970.

Ovadiah, Asher and Carla Gomez de Silva. "Supplementum to the Corpus of the Byzantine Churches in the Holy Land." *Levant* 13 (1981): 200-261. 14 (1982): 122-70. 16 (1984): 129-65.

Richardson, L. Jr. *Pompeii: An Architectural History*. Baltimore: The Johns Hopkins University Press, 1989.

Richmond, E.T. "Basilica of the Nativity: Discovery of the Remains of an Earlier Church." *Quarterly of the Department of Antiquities in Palestine* 5 (1936): 75-81. Pls. 27-48.

———. "The Church of the Nativity: The Plan of the Constantinian Church." *Quarterly of the Department of Antiquities in Palestine* 6 (1938): 63-72. Pls. 13-17.

Rivoira, G.T. *Roman Architecture and Its Principles of Construction Under the Empire.* New York: Hacker Art Books, 1972.

Schowalter, Daniel N. *The Emperor and the Gods: Images from the Time of Trajan.* Minneapolis: Fortress Press, 1993.

Sear, Frank. *Roman Architecture.* Ithaca: Cornell University Press, 1982.

Setton, Kenneth M. *Christian Attitude Towards the Emperor in the Fourth Century, Especially As Shown in Addresses to the Emperor.* New York: AMS Press, 1967.

Snyder, Graydon F. *Ante Pacem: Archaeological Evidence of Church Life Before Constantine.* Macon: Mercer University Press, 1991.

Strange, James F. "Ancient Texts, Archaeology as Text, and the Problem of the First Century Synagogue," in *Evolution of the Synagogue: Problems and Progress,* ed. Howard Clark Kee and Lynn H. Cohick. Harrisburg, PA: Trinity Press International, 1999, 27-45.

———. "First Century Galilee from Archaeology and from the Texts." in *Archaeology and the Galilee: Texts and Contexts in the Graeco-Roman and Byzantine Periods.* ed. Douglas R. Edwards and C. Thomas McCollough. Atlanta: Scholars Press, 1997, 39-48.

———. "The Eastern Basilical Building." In *Sepphoris in Galilee: Crosscurrents in Culture.* Ed. Rebecca Nagy *et al.* North Carolina Museum of Art, 1996, 117-121.

Taylor, Lily Ross. *The Divinity of the Roman Emperor.* Middletown, CT: American Philological Association, 1931.

Tsafrir, Yoram. *Ancient Churches Revealed.* Jerusalem: Israel Exploration Society, 1993.

Urman, Dan, and Paul V. M. Flesher, Eds. *Ancient Synagogues: Historical Analysis and Archaeological Discovery.* Vol. 2. Leiden: E. J. Brill, 1995.

Vincent, H. "L'église de l'éléona." *Revue Biblique* 20 (1911): 219-65. Pls. 1-10.

Ward-Perkins, J. B. "Constantine and the Origins of the Christian Basilica." *Papers of the British School at Rome* 22 (1954): 69-90.

———. *Roman Imperial Architecture.* Middlesex, England: Penguin Books, 1987.

Warren, F. E. *The Liturgy and Ritual of the Ante-Nicene Church.* 2nd Ed. Revised. New York: AMS Press, 1973.

White, James F. and Susan J. *Church Architecture: Building and Renovating for Christian Worship.* Nashville: Abingdon Press, 1988.

White, Michael L. *The Social Origins of Christian Architecture.* Vol. I, *Building God's House in the Roman World: Architectural Adaptation among Pagans, Jews and Christians.* Valley Forge, PA: Trinity Press International, 1990. Vol. II, *Texts and Monuments for the Christian Domus Ecclesiae in its Environment*, 1997.

———. *Jerusalem Pilgrims Before the Crusades.* Warminster, England: Aris & Phillips, 1977.

Zahavy, Tzvee. *Studies in Jewish Prayer.* Lanham, MD: University Press of America, 1990.

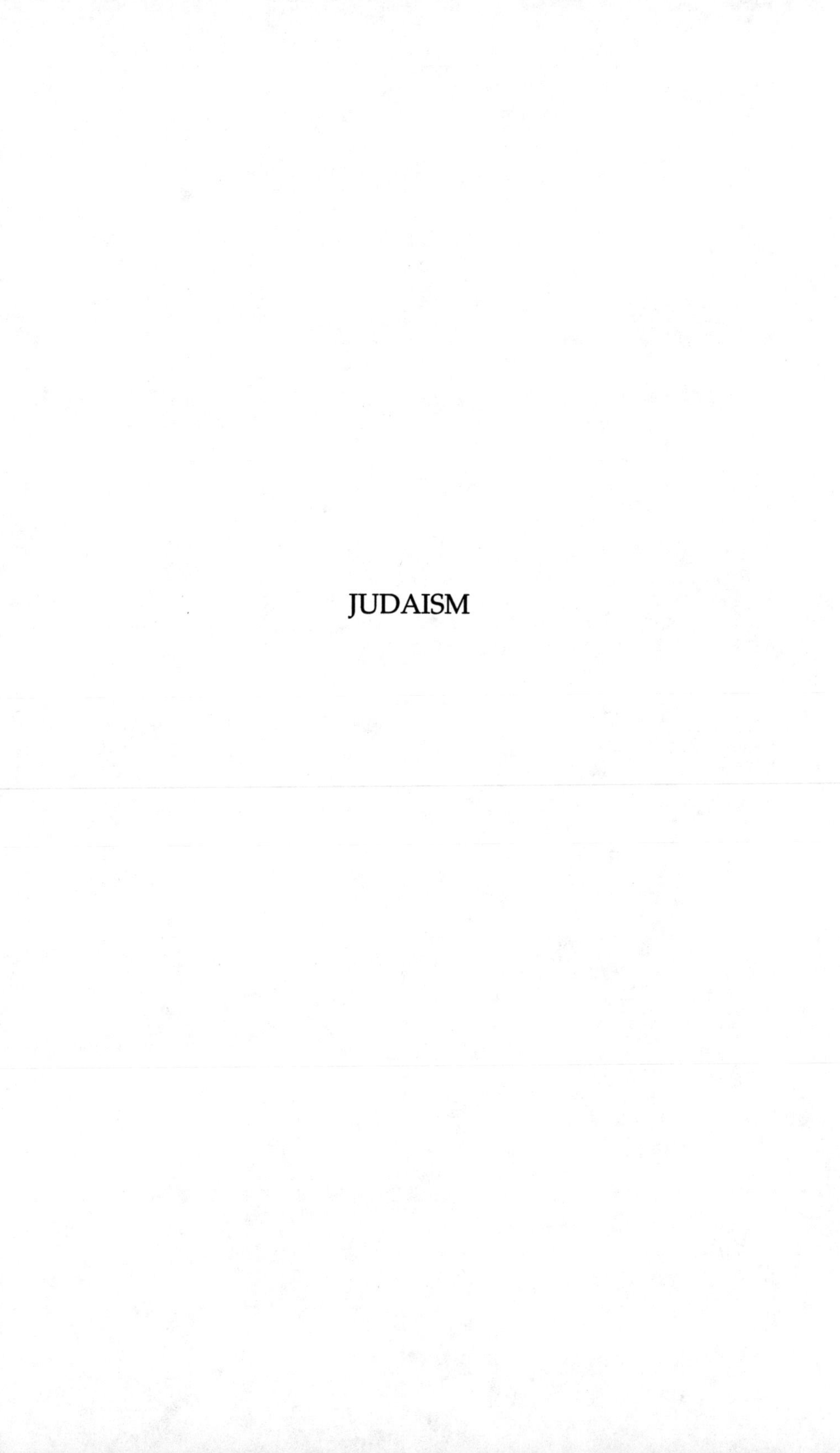

# JUDAISM

# 6

# It Takes a Village: Preliminary Reflections on Yodefat in the History of Judaism

William Scott Green
*University of Rochester*

Yodefat, called in Greek Jotopata, is a large village that sits in western lower Galilee. Within a few hours walking distance of Cana and Nazareth, Yodefat is 22 km SE of Akko and 9 km north of Sepphoris. The site is a small steep hill with a rocky crescent, and it is nestled together with other small hills that overlook the Beit Netofa Valley.

The Jewish general and historian Josephus accurately describes Yodefat as "almost entirely built on precipitous cliffs, being surrounded on three sides by ravines so deep that sight fails in the attempts to fathom the abyss. On the north side alone...it is accessible....Concealed by other mountains surrounding it, the town was quite invisible until one came right up to it."[1] Yodefat's role in history gives it a potential significance for the study of second Temple Judaism in the Land of Israel that belies its size.

Yodefat is important historically because it is the site at which Josephus, later known as Flavius Josephus for his Roman sponsors, surrendered to the Romans in the rebellion that ended with the destruction of the Jerusalem Temple in 70 A.D. Josephus claims that Yodefat was one of seventeen Galilean sites that he fortified to defend against the Roman assault on the Land of Israel. In *The Jewish War* he describes in vivid detail how the Romans besieged the village in a forty-

---

[1]Josephus, *The Jewish War,* H. St. J. Thackery, trans. (Cambridge, Mass., Harvard University Press, 1927) III: 158-160.

seven day struggle before destroying it on the first of the Hebrew month of Tammuz (roughly corresponding to July) in the year 67 A.D.

Yodefat is relevant to the history of second Temple Judaism because the site appears to have remained substantially uninhabited from the time of its destruction. Though there is evidence of settlement at its base in the late Roman and Byzantine periods, no one seems to have occupied the area of the village proper after the final battle with Rome. The latest coins and the surface pottery date to the early Roman period. "Coins and pottery that can be dated unequivocally to the end of the first century and the two subsequent centuries A.D. have not been found. This...shows that the town on the hill of Yodefat evidently ceased to exist not long after the early seventh decade of the first century A.D."[2] Hence, Yodefat offers extraordinary evidence of unadulterated remains of a first-century A.D. Galilean village. To learn what Galilean village life was like in the time of Jesus, Yodefat probably is the best place to start.

In this paper, I offer some preliminary observations of what the remains of Yodefat can tell us about the religion its inhabitants practiced, particularly at the time of its destruction. The questions to be considered are: What kinds of remains from Yodefat can testify about the religion of its inhabitants? What can the interpretation of those remains tell us about the interaction of texts and material culture for the reconstruction of Judaism in antiquity?[3]

Two primary sorts of evidence are directly relevant to the practice of Judaism at Yodefat: plastered stepped pools and hundreds of remnants of vessels made of stone. Let us consider each in order.

On the southeast side of the site, excavators uncovered two plastered stepped pools in the remains of two houses that are in close proximity to one another. The more southern of the two pools is totally cut into the bedrock and plastered. It has five steps. The other is a half-cut, half-built pool, well plastered, that contains three steps (Figure 1). Both pools can hold from 1.5 to 2 cubic meters of water. Each pool has enough space for an individual to enter and submerge in the water.

---

[2]David Adan-Bayewitz and Mordechai Aviam, "Iotopata, Josephus, and the siege of 67: preliminary report on the 1992-94 seasons," *Journal of Roman Archaeology* 10 (1997), pp. 131-165, p. 163. This article forms the basis of my description of the site and its artifacts.

[3]Though I participated in the excavation for various lengths of time Yodefat for nine seasons, I am not a professional archaeologist. The excavation is a joint project of the Israel Antiquities Authority and the University of Rochester. It is directed by Mordechai Aviam. The full archaeological details of the site will be described and analyzed in the excavation's final report, which is now in preparation. Here I write as an historian of ancient Judaism, studying Yodefat as

*Figure 1*

On the basis of their physical traits, it is possible to distinguish these pools from other kinds of water installations found at the site and at other comparable locations. These stepped pools were in individual homes and can be distinguished from cisterns, which are three to five meters deeper than the pools and have a narrow opening. They also can be differentiated from bathtubs proper, which are rectangular and shallow constructions with no room for submerging in the water. Gamla and Jerusalem contain sites in which a bathtub was constructed next to a stepped pool. These examples graphically illustrate the differences between the two installations and suggest that they served discrete purposes.[4]

The differences between the stepped pools and other water installations make it reasonable to suppose that Yodefat's pools are *miqva'ot,* Jewish ritual baths, installations built for the purpose of achieving ritual purity. At various places (Lev. 11:36; 15), the Hebrew

a small case study of how material culture contributes to our understanding of ancient Judaism.

[4]It is not controversial to assert that stepped pools were not bathtubs. See E.P. Sanders, *Judaism: Practice and Belief, 63* B.C.E.*-66* C.E. (Philadelphia: Trinity Press International, 1992), pp. 224-229, Adan-Bayewitz and Aviam, op.cit., p. 164, and the literature cited in note 51.

Bible suggests that immersion in water, usually in conjunction with the passage of an appropriate period of time, is part of the process of relieving impurity and achieving purification (for instance, after coming in contact with an unclean thing, after sexual intercourse, after a woman's menstrual period, after childbirth, etc.). Scripture nowhere mandates the construction of purification pools, but *miqva'ot* begin to appear in the Land of Israel during the Second Temple period, particularly in conjunction with the rise of the Hasmonean dynasty and the spread of Judaism outward from Jerusalem. The Israeli archaeologist Ronny Reich has identified at least 163 likely Second Temple period *miqva'ot* in the Land of Israel, [5] and his results do not include the finds at Yodefat. The Mishnah assumes the existence of *miqva'ot,* includes a tractate devoted to them and legislates about them extensively.

Because Yodefat was destroyed in 67 A.D., it is impossible to say for certain how the discovered *miqva'ot* were used. Second Temple period literary discussions of *miqva'ot* run from scant to nonexistent, and, without some compelling reason, it is anachronistic to suppose that the Mishnah, redacted nearly 130 years after Yodefat's destruction, can tell us how the village's inhabitants used their ritual baths. In this case, however, the Mishnah, despite its late date, may actually help us understand these *miqva'ot*.

It is tempting to suppose that the *miqva'ot* themselves indicate a concern for ritual purity throughout the village of Yodefat, but two considerations forestall that that conclusion. First, somewhat less than fifteen percent of the site has been excavated, so a broad conclusion about religious life throughout the village based on the *miqva'ot* alone would be ambitious. More important, the *miqva'ot* are located near an olive press. The press is outside the current city wall but very close to the houses that contain the *miqva'ot*.[6] This proximity may constrain our interpretation of the *miqva'ot* because it suggests that their use may have been specialized.

Leviticus 11:38 states that if the carcass of an unclean swarming land creature touches dry seed grain, the grain is clean. But "if water is put" on the seed grain and the carcass of an unclean swarming land creature touches it, the seed grain is unclean. The verse thus suggests that liquid makes the dry grain susceptible to impurity. Dry grain cannot contract uncleanness, but damp grain can. This principle is discussed in exquisite

---

[5]Ronny Reich, *Miqwa'ot (Jewish ritual immersion baths) in Eretz-Israel in the Second Temple and the Mishnah and Talmud Periods* (diss. Hebrew University, 1990).

[6]My colleague Mordechai Aviam, director of the Yodefat excavation, suggests that this part of the city wall was built in anticipation of the battle with Rome, and it thereby separated the olive press from the domestic residences. Initially, they probably were not separated by the wall.

detail in the Mishnah's tractate *Makshirin,* which treats the ways in which liquid can generate susceptibility to uncleanness. Mishnah Makshirin 6:4 lists olive oil as one of the seven liquids that can produce such susceptibility.

Yodefat is not the only location in which a *miqveh* was built close to an olive or wine press. Indeed, at Gamla, there is an instance of a *miqveh* dug within an olive press installation. Ronny Reich suggests that in these instances, the *miqveh* may serve a special purpose for workers to enable them to produce the oil or wine in a state of purity themselves. This reason also would apply if the oil or wine were meant to be consumed by priests.[7] Whether this interpretation fully applies to the evidence from Yodefat will depend on comparison of the Yodefat *miqva'ot* with other examples of *miqva'ot* in proximity to olive and wine presses.[8] But the suggestion that the *miqva'ot* at Yodefat may constitute early, pre-destruction material evidence for a concern and practice articulated in the Mishnah is not unreasonable.[9]

By themselves, Yodefat's *miqva'ot* cannot tell us how they were used or who used them or how often or for which purposes. They can, however, suggest how Judaism in first century Galilee may have related to the Judaism practiced in Jerusalem. Yodefat has no natural water supply. The site is pockmarked with cisterns, and the population lived from cisterns for much of the year. In such an environment, the decision to maintain a *miqveh,* whose water could not be consumed, suggests that something important was at stake. The *miqva'ot* testify to a concern about ritual purity—whether instrumental or sincere, we cannot say (and it may not matter). The concern for purity, in turn, indicates an interest in the cultic system of the Jerusalem Temple because it is one of the primary justifications for an interest in purity at all. As Jacob Neusner notes:

> In the Pentateuch uncleanness affects the conduct of three activities: eating, procreating, and attendance at the Temple. When the priests ate their priestly rations, they were to do so in a condition of cultic cleanness. Furthermore, all Israelites were to abstain from unclean foods and sexual relations during a woman's menstrual period or when affected by the cleanness of the sexual organs to

---

[7]Reich, op. cit., pp. 122-126.

[8]The examples that Reich lists of *miqva'ot* near olive or wine presses are Qalandiyeh, Jericho, Qedumim, Hurvat Hazan. This topic will be discussed at more length in the excavation's final report.

[9]Reich explains that the Mishnah requires a minimal volume of forty *se'ah* of water, which is less than one cubic meter, to effect purification. The two miqva'ot at Yodefat exceed that amount and therefore would have been deemed acceptable in Mishnaic practice.

> which Lev. 15 makes allusion. All Israelites also were to become clean to participate in the Temple cult, which would affect many at the time of the pilgrim festivals, Passover, Pentecost, and Tabernacles. In addition, among the Judaisms that flourished before 70 CE, when the Temple was destroyed, some groups, such as the Pharisees, the Essenes, and some represented by law codes found in the Dead Sea Scrolls, kept the rules of cultic purity in eating food at home, not in the Temple, a practice that did not characterize the bulk of the communities of Judaism.[10]

In ancient Judaism, while the Temple stood, at least, its cult was one of the ultimate grounds of the logic and urgency of purity—whether or not one subscribed to the management of the Temple as it stood. The *miqva'ot* at Yodefat supply additional evidence for the view that in first century Galilee, the practice of Judaism in principle need not have fallen outside of the range of—or been inherently hostile to—concerns and interests that defined the Temple-centered Judaism of Jerusalem.

Additional evidence for a concern with purity comes from a second sort of evidence found at Yodefat, vessels made from chalk (soft limestone). Excavations at the site uncovered 150 shards of stone vessels, most of them bowls and cups. These vessels are similar to those found in the priestly homes in the Herodian quarter of Jerusalem. One small, virtually complete, stone cup was found (Figure 2), and a rectangular stone container, most likely made to contain dough, also was uncovered. The stone container is the first uncovered in the Galilee and outside of Jerusalem. Stoneware is an important indicator of religious interests because in early Judaism it was deemed insusceptible to ritual impurity.[11] Like the *miqva'ot,* stoneware appears in the Land of Israel during the Second Temple period in conjunction with the rise of the Hasmonean dynasty. The stoneware industry appears to have declined sharply after the destruction of the Jerusalem Temple in 70 C.E.

At Yodefat, remains of stone vessels were found all over the site, but their presence in the residential areas on the southeast side—not connected to the area of the *miqva'ot*—is particularly interesting. The excavated residences on the southeast side of Yodefat are exceptionally modest. They are dug into the bedrock, and it appears that their inhabitants lived on packed earth floors. These were residences of people of limited means. Stoneware was more expensive to produce, and therefore to purchase, than were clay vessels, many of which likely

---

[10]Jacob Neusner, "Purity and Impurity in Judaism," in J. Neusner, A. Avery-Peck, and W.S. Green, eds, *The Encyclopedia of Judaism* (Continuum: New York, 1999), Vol III, pp. 1109-1124, pp. 1109-10.

[11]See Mishnah Kelim 10:1, Ohalot 5:5, Yadaim 1:2. Adan-Bayewitz and Aviam, op. cit., p. 164 lists additional references.

were produced in Yodefat's own kilns. That people of modest resources spent their funds on stoneware suggests that issues of ritual purity were of significant concern to them. This evidence, combined with that of the *miqva'ot,* makes it plausible to suppose that a meaningful sector of Yodefat's population took ritual purity quite seriously.

*Figure 2*

One final piece of evidence also contributes to a reconstruction of the Judaism practices at Yodefat. On the northern southeast side of the hill, the excavation uncovered the remains of a large villa or mansion that seems to have been a center of military activity during the rebellion. Partial frescoes of two walls of the villa were preserved and removed from the site for preservation (Figure 3). The partially excavated room has a frescoed floor, the first of its type found in a private house in the Land of Israel. A probe of the floor revealed that it contains a geometric design. The restored wall frescoes also contain no figurative art. Admittedly, the absence of evidence is not strong proof, but, if this pattern is maintained in the remainder of the building, it could suggest a sensitivity to the prohibition against images that is typical of Herod's designs at Masada.

*Figure 3*

The evidence collected so far makes it reasonable to suppose that Yodefat was a Jewish village and that at least a meaningful part of its population, from different economic strata, practiced a form a Judaism that observed the rituals of, and sought to maintain, cultic purity in domestic life. This, in turn, suggests a degree of interest in, and perhaps devotion to, Judaism's central religious institution, the Temple in Jerusalem. Such devotion might help to account for the decision of Yodefat's resident's to engage the Romans in what became the village's final battle.

How might we account for Yodefat's religious focus? The numismatic evidence from the site may supply the basic components of an answer. The preliminary report of the excavation suggests that there is a marked shift in the use of coinage in the late second century B.C.E. from Seleucid and Phoenician autonomous coins to those of the Hasmonean dynasty. "By the last decade of the 2nd c. B.C. there is virtually no numismatic evidence of contact between Yodefat and the cities of the Phoenician coast. From this period there are abundant Hasmonean coins, as plentiful as there had been Seleucid and Phoenician autonomous coins, beginning with those minted by Hyrcanus I."[12]

---

[12]Ibid, p. 160.

Yodefat's numismatic evidence is comparable to that of Gamla, which was part of the Hasmonean kingdom; but differs from that of non-Jewish locations in the Land of Israel, which did not use Hasmonean coins.

On the basis of the numismatic evidence, it is reasonable to suppose that Yodefat was part of the Hasmonean conquest of Galilee. The shift in coinage may suggest a shift in population, in which, following Alexander's model in creating Hellenistic cities, the Hasmoneans occupied territory they conquered with their own loyalists. This explanation can account for both the numismatic evidence and the *miqva'ot* and the stoneware. If this is correct, then we can understand Yodefat as initially a parochial Hasmonean colonial outpost, in which ancestral piety and loyalty to the traditional religious center could well have been paramount concerns. On this argument, Hasmonean loyalists brought their Jerusalem piety—including *miqva'ot* and the use of stoneware--to Galilee and maintained it in their village life until Yodefat was demolished in the final battle against Rome. The evidence of Yodefat should enhance our appreciation of the importance of Galilean Jewish villages in the development of ancient Judaism.

The interpretation of an archaeological site is a complex matter that requires comparison between and among multiple sites as well as an understanding of the interaction of the various sorts of material evidence found in the field. In addition, there is the interaction of the material evidence with the testimony of texts. In this initial probe into the religious life of Yodefat, the interplay of coins, stone vessels, *miqva'ot,* Josephhus's narrative, and biblical and rabbinic texts yields a plausible scenario for the origins and character of an important location in the history of Second Temple Judaism.[13]

---

[13]I am grateful to my colleague, Mordechai Aviam, for advice and encouragement in the preparation of this article and to Jacob Neusner and James Strange for including Yodefat among the examples of material culture to considered in the conference out of which this volume developed.

# 7

# The Synagogue in Law: What the Texts Lead Us to Expect to Find

Jacob Neusner
*Bard College*

## I
## The Halakhic Design of the Social Order of Holy Israel

Rabbinic Judaism, taking shape in the first six centuries of the common Era on the foundations of Israelite Scripture of the preceding millennium, sets forth through normative law, called Halakhah, norms of public, social behavior, an account of the Israel it wishes to bring into being. This law comes to us in codes and commentaries, in writing. The law is set forth in the Mishnah, a philosophical law code of the second century C.E., complemented by the Tosefta, a corpus of supplementary laws organized in relationship to the Mishnah, the two Talmuds, the Talmud of the Land of Israel, ca. 400 C.E., and the Talmud of Babylonia, ca. 600 C.E., commentaries to the Mishnah. Read as a coherent statement, these documents through their native category-formations lay out a social order to be realized by Israel, the holy people. They realize in concrete laws of conduct and relationship a large theory of holy Israel's social order. But whether, in the time that these laws were being recorded and expounded, the actualities of the Jews' societies corresponded certainly remains to be seen.

We cannot open the Mishnah and merely on the basis of what we read describe the material world of Jewish community life, the palpable culture characteristic of that community. All we can describe is the statement of the legal system on the topic at hand, all we can analyze is the coherence of that statement and its principal parts, and all we can interpret is the way in which, through its treatment of a given topic, the legal system makes its large and encompassing statement. How, then, are the legal sources to serve as a way of making sense of the artifacts of material culture, out of the ancient synagogues, that we have in hand?

Certainly, when we speak of the synagogue, we face the problem of relating the holy books and their account of the matter to the actualities of archaeological discovery. In general terms, on the basis of what the books say, we should anticipate that synagogues will contain only abstract art, but not concrete representations of persons and activities. But that is precisely what we find. In the century just passed, the contradiction between the second commandment as commonly understood to proscribe representational art and the discoveries of a rich and lively art of Judaism preoccupied learning. I need hardly review the dense debates on the matter, for instance, between Carl Kraeling and Erwin Goodenough on the interpretation of the Dura synagogue's art, to make the simple point at hand: what the books say and what the people do hardly match.

Rather, I wish to lay out an account of what the law leads us to anticipate in synagogue archaeology, to state in a systematic way precisely how the Halakhah of Rabbinic Judaism portrays the synagogue. What we shall see is that, in line with that portrait, we hardly need to anticipate digging up buildings especially designed for the requirements of synagogue rite and worship at all.

## II
## Sacred Space in Rabbinic Judaism: Is the Synagogue the Place of Worship?

The Halakhah knows two principal venues for Israel's meeting with God: Temple and the enlandised household, that is, the household that possesses real property in the Land of Israel. The first two are closely related and in many ways made to match and complement one another. The Temple forms the center of service, and the offerings for the Day of Atonement, Tabernacles, and Passover define a principal interest of the Halakhah in those occasions. The enlandised household defines the matching locus for the celebration of Passover and of Tabernacles. The Halakhah of Shabbat-Erubin explicitly takes shape around the binary opposites, Temple and household; what on the Sabbath (and, except for cooking, on festivals) one may do in the former location one may not do in the latter. And much of the Halakhah that defines how, in the enlandised household, the Israelite meets God concerns the householder's payment of God's share of the produce of the Land to God through his surrogates, the priests, Levites, and poor.

How about the village? Does it require a place for public worship? When it comes to crises of the public order, the location within particular, contained space hardly registers, in that, to conduct a public fast, the Torah is carried out into the marketplace of the town. The life of the village further is correlated with that of the Temple through the provision of the *ma'amadot* or delegations of local Israelites who accompany the priests to the Temple; and, more important, through the assignment of rites in the village meant to match those in the Temple when the local delegation goes up to the holy city. So viewed as a whole, the Halakhah identifies two locations for the encounter of God and Israel, the altar at the center, the households and villages arrayed round about. And that leads us to ask, where and how does the Halakhah find for the synagogue a place in its structure and system?

Since sages explicitly state that study of the Torah may take place anywhere, and since, we know full well, not only votive but obligatory prayer is offered wherever one is located at the time (excepting inappropriate places such as privies), what is left for the synagogue as a location, or, more to the point, the synagogue as an occasion (as the field or orchard present occasions for the encounter with God in possessing the Land, and as the household provides for meeting with God at meal-time, to take two obvious cases)? And what, within the framework of the Halakhah, can we possibly mean by "synagogue"? The answer is, the synagogue represents the occasion at which ten or more Israelite males assemble and so embody Israel, and provides for the declamation of the Torah to Israel: it is Sinai, no where in particular, to whom it may concern. It is a place made holy by Israel's presence and activity, anywhere Israel assembles, and the presence is for the activity of hearing the Torah proclaimed.

## III
## The Synagogue: A Place for Declaiming the Torah

In less extravagant terms, within the framework of the Halakhah of the Oral Torah, the one point at which Israel finds God in the synagogue in particular (if not uniquely) is in the declamation of the Torah. It is, specifically, in reference to the synagogue that the Halakhah provides its category-formation accommodating the rules for declaiming the Torah and—more to the point—it is in that context, and there alone, that the Halakhah further specifies *other* rules that govern the sanctity of the synagogue.[1] As we shall now see, in tractate Megillah, the Halakhah combines rules for declaiming the Megillah, the Scroll of Esther that must be recited at Purim, with rules for declaiming other obligatory passages of Scripture. These Israel must hear not only in community—that is, with other Israelites, e.g., in the marketplace of the village—but in the framework of a particular location, the synagogue and there alone. That is the premise of the Halakhah of the Oral Torah and accounts for its presentation first of the case, the public recitation in the synagogue of the Megillah, and then of the rule, the public declamation of other passages of the Torah.

Why choose the tractate devoted to Purim and the recitation of the Megillah for the occasion to present the Halakhah of the synagogue and the activities therein that make the synagogue important? It is because the occasion that is chosen in no way intersects with the activities of the Temple altar; no offerings at the altar are required for that occasion, for the obvious reason that, within the framework of the narrative, there was no altar at that time. And, furthermore, it is because sages find in the Halakhah of Purim as laid out in the Written Torah the requirement that a particular lection of the Torah be declaimed in the community of Israel. Without a Temple in view, therefore taking for granted that, for that purpose, the synagogue is meant, sages then find here the appropriate setting for the presentation of the Halakhah of the synagogue; here, above all, the Written Torah specifies an occasion where the synagogue, not the household and not the altar of the Temple, provides the self-evidently correct location for the meeting with God.

Why should sages have reached such a conclusion? The reason is that, when we come to the Halakhah of Megillah, we take up the only appointed season[2] in the Halakhah of the Oral Torah not commemorated at the altar. And yet, the declamation of the Megillah is a public occasion, so the household is excluded as a candidate for the principal venue. The marketplace cannot figure, being the setting for prayer and Torah-declamation only on the occasion of crisis, not celebration of redemption

---

[1]The other rules, in addition to the *Shema* and the Prayer, that are set forth in the setting of obligatory prayer concern conduct at the meal, the blessings recited before eating, the Grace after Meals, rules of cultic cleanness at the meal, and, at the end, other obligatory prayers, or blessings, and the occasions that entail them. Tractate Berakhot, the category-formation for prayer in the conventional sense of the word, scarcely hints that the synagogue is the particular venue for that activity, though the Halakhah accommodates public and communal prayer in the synagogue, as much as in the house of study or the fields, streets, marketplaces, and households.

[2]Hanukkah is no exception. While the Halakhah refers to Hanukkah, the Halakhah devotes no systematic presentation to the occasion in the way that it does to Purim.

from a crisis, as Ta'anit makes clear, and that leaves the synagogue. Then the Halakhah transforms the presentation of the holiday into the occasion for legislating about the declamation of the Torah in the synagogue; along the way, the Halakhah provides some further rules for the synagogue. I hardly need point out that Scripture provides nothing, knowing no such institution as a building devoted to public worship other than the Temple and its counterparts.

The Halakhah begins with the laws covering the declamation of the scroll of Esther, then proceeds to the more general topics of synagogue governance and the declamation of the Torah therein. I present only the normative Halakhah that pertains directly to the synagogue.

## The Laws of Synagogue Property and Liturgy

### A. The Disposition of Synagogue Property

**M. 4:1 [So Bavli; Mishnah: 3:1, and so throughout] Townspeople who sold [1] the town square may buy a synagogue with its proceeds; [2] a synagogue may buy an ark [with its proceeds]; [3] an ark may buy Torah wrappings [with its proceeds]; [4] Torah wrappings may buy scrolls [of Prophets or Hagiographa] [with its proceeds]; [5] scrolls may buy a Torah [with its proceeds]. But if they sold [1] a Torah, they may not buy scrolls [with its proceeds]; [2] scrolls, they may not buy [Torah] wrappings; [3] [Torah] wrappings, they may not buy an ark; [4] an ark, they may not buy a synagogue; [5] a synagogue, they may not buy the town square. And similarly with their left over funds.**

T. 2:12 R. Menahem b. R. Yosé says, "[If they sold] a synagogue, they should not buy a street" [M. Meg. 3:1J]. Said R. Judah, "Under what circumstances [is it so that if they collected funds for a matter of high sanctity, may they not make use of the surplus of the funds for a matter of lesser sanctity (M. Meg. 3:1K)]? When the charity-collectors of that town did not make a stipulation with them [that they may make use of the surplus for some other purpose]. But if the charity-collectors of that town did make such a stipulation, they may make use of the funds for any other purpose which they choose."

T. 2:13 He who makes an ark and coverings for a [holy] scroll, before one has made use of them for the Most High, an ordinary person is permitted to make use of them. Once one has made use of them for the Most High, an ordinary person is no longer permitted to make use of them. But one may lend a cloth for a scroll and go and take it back from him [to whom it was lent for such a purpose and then make use of it for a lesser purpose]. Clothes for covering a given set of scrolls they may use for different scrolls, but they may not make use of them for other purposes.

T. 2:14 He who makes a candelabrum or a lamp for a synagogue—before the name of the owner [who has donated it] is forgotten from these objects, one is not permitted to use them for some other purpose. Once the name of the owner [who donated them] is forgotten from them, one is permitted to make use of them for some other purpose.

T. 2:15 An individual who in his town pledged to give to charity gives it for the poor of his town. [If he pledged to give] in another town, he gives it to the poor of that other town. The charity-supervisors who in their town agreed to give charity must give it to the poor of their town. [If they promised it] in another town, they give it to the poor of that other town. He who pledges funds for charity, before the charity-supervisors have taken possession of [what he has pledged], is permitted to use the thing for some other purpose. Once the charity-supervisors have taken possession of [what he has pledged], he is not permitted to divert it for some other purpose, except with their knowledge and consent.

T. 2:16 A gentile who sanctified a beam for use in a synagogue, and on it is written, "For the Name"—they examine him. If he said, "I vowed it to the Holy Name," they store it away. But if he said, "I vowed it for the sake of a synagogue," they plane off the place of the Name and store [that chip] away and make use of what remains. Utensils [made for] the Most High—before they have been used for the Most High, an ordinary person may make use of them. Once they have been used for the Most High, an ordinary person may not make use of them. And utensils which to begin with were made for an ordinary person—they do not make use of them for the Most High [= T. Men. 9:21]. Stones and beams which one hewed to begin with for a synagogue—they do not make use of them for building on the Temple mount. Stones hewed for the sanctuary and the courts which were mutilated or damaged are not subject to redemption and must be stored away.

T. 2:17 Said R. Judah, "R. Eleazar b. R. Sadoq purchased the synagogue of the Alexandrians which was located in Jerusalem, and he did exactly as he wanted with it. They prohibited [using such a building for secular purposes] only if the original name still applies to it."

**M. 4:2 One may not sell something of the community to an individual, because one would [thereby] lower it from its [level of] sanctity, the words of R. Meir. They said to him: "If so, [things should not be sold] even from a large town to a small town."**

*Y. 3:2 I:1 Three members of a synagogue [who made an agreement in be half of the synagogue] are tantamount to the synagogue as a whole. And seven townsmen are tantamount to the town as a whole [to act in behalf of the synagogue or the town, respectively].*

**M. 4:3 One may not sell a synagogue unless on condition, that if they [i.e., the sellers] want, they [i.e., the buyers] will return it, the words of R. Meir. And the sages say: "One may sell it permanently, except for four things: a bath house, or a tannery, a [place of] ritual immersion, or a toilet." R. Judah says: "One can sell it as property, and the buyer can do [with it] what he wants."**

**M. 4:4 Moreover, said R. Judah, "A synagogue that has been destroyed: [1] one may not mourn in it; [2] and one may not spread out ropes in it; [3] and one may not spread traps in it; [4] and one may not spread fruit on its roof [to dry]; [5] and one may not use it as a shortcut, as is said, 'and I will destroy your sanctuaries' (Lev. 26:31) [meaning] their sanctity remains after they are destroyed. If [blades of] grass grew in it, one may not pluck them out, because of anguish."**

T. 2:18 Synagogues—they do not behave with them frivolously. One should not go into them on a hot day on account of the heat, or on a cold day because of the cold, or on a rainy day because of the rain. They do not eat or drink in them, nor do they sleep in them, nor do they take a stroll in them, nor do they derive benefit from them. But they read [Scripture] in them, repeat [Mishnah-traditions] in them, and expound [biblical lessons] in them. A public lamentation is made in them [vs. M. Meg. 3:3A]. Said R. Judah, "Under what circumstances? When they are in service. But when they are destroyed, they leave them be, and grow grass in them, because of the anguish" [M. Meg. 3:3H].

### B. Rules for Reading Scriptures in Synagogue Worship

**M. 4:5 [=M. 3:4] On the New Moon of [the Month of Adar] that falls on a Sabbath, one reads the Torah portion about sheqels [Ex 30:11-16]. If it [the New Moon] falls during the week, one advances it [the reading] to the one that passed [i.e., to the previous Sabbath] and interrupts [the cycle of special readings] until the next Sabbath [which will fall between one and two weeks after the New Moon]. On the second [special Sabbath, one reads] the Torah portion [beginning] "Remember" (Deut. 25:17-19). On the third [special Sabbath, one reads the Torah portion about] "a red heifer" (Num. 19:1 ff.). On the fourth [special Sabbath, one reads] the Torah portion [beginning] "This month is to you" (Ex. 12:1 ff.); On the fifth [Sabbath], one returns to their regular sequence. One interrupts [the regular sequence of Sabbath Torah readings] for all [special occasions]: On New Moons, on Hanukkah, and on Purim; on fasts, and on [special] prayer assemblies (*ma'amadot*), and on Yom Kippur.**

T. 3:1 On the new moon of Adar which coincided with the Sabbath they read the pericope of Sheqels (Ex. 30:16) [M. Meg. 3:4A-B], And for the prophetic lection joined to the pericope of Sheqels they conclude with the story of Jehoiada the priest (2 Kings 12). What is the first Sabbath? It is any in which the new moon of Adar happens to fall, even if it comes on Friday.

T. 3:2 On the second Sabbath [they read], "Remember" (Deut. 25:17-19) [M. Meg. 3:4D], And for the prophetic lection they read, "Thus says the Lord of hosts, I remember what Amalek did to Israel"` (I Sam. 15:2). What is the second Sabbath [just now referred to]? Any in which Purim happens to fall, even if it comes on Friday.

T. 3:3 On the third [they read] the pericope of the Red Cow (Num. 19:1ff.) [M. Meg. 3:4E]. And for the prophetic lection they read, "I will sprinkle clean water upon you, and you shall be clean from all your uncleannesses, and from all your idols I will cleanse you" (Ez. 36:25). What is the third Sabbath? Any which follows immediately after Purim.

T. 3:4 On the fourth [they read], "This month shall be unto you" (Ex. 12:2). And for the prophetic lection they read, "Thus says the Lord God: In the first month, on the first day of the month" (Ez. 45:18). What is the fourth Sabbath? Any in which the new moon of Nisan happens to fall, and even if it comes on Friday. [If] the pericope of Sheqels comes near the month of Adar, whether before or after it, they read it and go and read it a second time [vs. M. Meg. 3:4C], and so is the rule with the second, third and fourth [readings], and so is the rule as to Hanukkah and as to Purim.

**M. 4:6 [=M. 3:4-6] On Passover one reads the holiday portion of Leviticus [chapter 23]. On Pentecost, one reads, "Seven weeks..." (Deut. 16:9); On Rosh Hashanah, [one reads] "In the seventh month on the first of the month..." (Lev. 23:24 ff.) [cf. Num. 29:1]. Yom Kippur [one reads] "...after the death..." (Lev. 16). On the first day of the Festival [Sukkot], one reads the section about the holidays in Leviticus [chapter. 23]; and all the rest of the days of the Festival [Sukkot], [one reads] about the sacrifices of the Festival (Num. 29:12-34). On Hanukkah, [one reads the portion about] the princes [Num. 7]; [On] Purim [one reads] "And Amalek came" (Ex. 17:8 ff.); [On] New Moons [one reads] "And on your new moons..." (Num. 28:11 ff.); At prayer assemblies [one reads] about the act of creation; On fast days, [one reads] the blessings and curses. One may not interrupt during the curses, but rather one person reads them all. On the second and on the fifth [days of the week] and on the Sabbath at the afternoon service, one reads according to the [regular] order. And they [i.e., these last readings] do not count among the number [assigned to the weekly portion for the Sabbath]; as is said, "And Moses commanded the**

**holidays of the Lord to the Israelites" (Lev. 23:44), [meaning] their commandment is that they should read each and every one at its [appropriate] time.**

T. 3:5 They raise questions concerning the laws of Passover on the occasion of Passover, and the laws concerning Pentecost on the occasion of Pentecost, and the laws concerning the Festival on the occasion of the Festival. In the council they ask questions concerning the laws of Passover thirty days before Passover. Rabban Simeon b. Gamaliel says, "Two weeks." On the first festival day of Passover they read the pericope concerning the waving [of the 'omer] which is in the Priestly Torah [the book of Leviticus] [Lev. 23:4ff.]. And on all other days of Passover they skip around among the passages referring to Passover which are written in the Torah. On Pentecost they read, Seven Weeks (Deut. 16:9). [M. Meg. 3:5B]. And some say [that on Pentecost they read] In the third month (Ex. 19:1 ).

T. 3:6 On the New Year [they read], "Say to the people of Israel, In the seventh month, on the first day of the month, you shall observe a day of solemn test" (Lev. 23:24). And some say, "And the Lord remembered Sarah" (Gen. 21:1).

T. 3:7 On the Day of Atonement, they read, "After the death" (Lev. 16:1). And for the final lection they read, "On the tenth" (Num. 27:7), which is in the Book of Numbers.

T. 3:8 On the first festival day of the Festival [of Tabernacles] they read, "Say to the people of Israel, On the fifteenth day of this seventh month and for seven days in the feast of booths to the Lord" (Lev. 23:34); and on the second day, "On the second day" (Num. 29:17) on the third day, "And on the third day" (Num. 29.20) on the fourth day, "And on the fourth day" (Num. 29.23) on the fifth day, "And on the fifth day" (Num. 29 16) on the sixth day, "And on the sixth day" (Num. 29:29); on the seventh day, "And on the seventh day" (Num. 29.32) on the eighth day, "And on the eighth day" (Num. 29.35)

T. 3:9 On the New Moon which falls in Hanukkah [the first of Tebet] (Num. 28.11) [cf. M. Meg 3:6H] offer a burnt-offering to On the ninth of Ab—others say, "[They read], 'But if you will not hearken to me and will not do all these commandments' (Lev. 26:14)."

T. 3:10 At the place at which they stop reading [in the Torah] on the Sabbath morning at the morning service, there they begin at the afternoon [At the place at which they stop reading] at the afternoon service from there they begin on Monday. they begin at the place at which they stop reading] M [At the place at which they stop reading] on Thursday, from there they begin on the following Sabbath. R. Judah says, "At the place at which they stop reading on the Sabbath at the morning service, from there they begin reading on the following Sabbath.

## C. The Lections

**M. 3:1 [=M. 4:1 and so throughout] One who reads the Megillah may stand or sit. If one [person] read it, [or] if two [people] read it, they have fulfilled their obligation. In a place where it is customary to recite a blessing [in conjunction with the reading], one recites a blessing; and [in a place where it is customary] not to recite a blessing, one does not recite a blessing.**

**M. 3:2 On the second [day of the week] and [on] the fifth, and on the Sabbath at the afternoon service, three read in the Torah. One may neither reduce them nor augment them; and one does not conclude [with a reading] from a Prophet. The one who begins the Torah [reading] and the one who concludes [it] recites a blessing, [the former] before it and [the latter] after it.**

**M. 3:3 On New Moons and on the non-sacred days of a festival, four read [in the Torah]. One may neither reduce them nor augment them; and one does not conclude [with a reading] from a Prophet. The one who begins the Torah [reading] and the one who concludes [it] recites a blessing, [the former] before it and [the latter] after it.**

**M. 3:4 This is the generalization: Any [day] on which there is Musaf [i.e., either the additional service, or, in earlier times, an additional sacrifice] and is not a holiday, four read [in the Torah]: On a holiday, five. On Yom Kippur, six. On a Sabbath, seven. One may not reduce them, but one may augment them; and one concludes [with a reading] from a Prophet. The one who begins the Torah [reading] and the one who concludes [it] recites a blessing, [the former] before it and [the latter] after it.**

T. 3:11 On the festival day five are called to read the Torah on the Day of Atonement, six, on the Sabbath, seven [M. Meg. 4:2G-I]. "And if they wanted to call more [than these numbers], they may not call more," the words of R. Ishmael. R. Aqiba says, "On the festival day, five, on the Day of Atonement seven, on the Sabbath six. And if they wanted to call more, they do call more" [cf. M. Meg. 4:2J]. And all figure in the number of seven, even a woman, even a minor. They do not [however] bring a woman to read the Scripture in public.

T. 3:12 A synagogue which has only one person who can read—he stands and reads [in the Torah] and sits down, stands and reads and sits down, stands and reads and sits down, even seven times.

T. 3:13 A synagogue comprised of those who speak a foreign language [other than Hebrew]—if they have someone who can read in Hebrew, they begin in Hebrew and conclude in Hebrew [but read the shank in the vernacular]. If they have only one who can read, only one reads.

**M. 3:5 [=M. 4:3] [1] One does not conduct the recitation of the *Shema*; [2] and one does not pass before the ark; [3] and one does not raise his hands; [4] and one does not read in the Torah; [5] and one does not conclude from a Prophet; [6] and one does not stop and sit [after attending a funeral]; [7] and one does not recite the blessing for mourners or [8] consolations for mourners, or [9] the grooms' blessing;[10] and one does not invite [people to say the grace after a meal] in God's name among fewer than ten. [1] And regarding [the redemption of] land [that belongs to the Temple, a maximum of] nine [non-priests] and a priest, [2] and similarly regarding [the redemption of] a person.**

T. 3:14 They do not carry on the mourning rite of standing and sitting [en route home from accompanying a corpse to the grave] among less than ten people [M. Meg. 4:3F], and they do not carry on the rite of standing and sitting less than seven times. And they do not say the blessing for mourners among less than ten people [M. Meg. 4:3F]. And mourners do not count in the quorum of ten [for the above purpose]. They do not say the blessing for a wedding couple among less than ten people [M. Meg. 4:3G], and grooms count in the quorum. One says the blessing for the wedding couple both at the meal celebrating the betrothal and at the meal celebrating the marriage both on an ordinary day and on the Sabbath. R. Judah says, "If new people came, one says the blessing for grooms and if not, one does not say the blessing for grooms."

T. 3:15 When do they kindle beacon fires [to announce] the new moon? When it is at its proper time [on the thirtieth day of the outgoing month]. [If] it coincided with Friday and the Sabbath, they kindle beacon fires on its account at the end of the Sabbath [= T. R. 1:17]. Said R. Eleazar b. R. Sadoq, "Thus was the practice of the associations (haburot) that were in Jerusalem: Some were for celebration, some for mourning, some for a meal in celebration of a betrothal, some for a meal in celebration of a marriage, some for the celebration of the week of a son's birth, and some for the gathering of bones [of parents, for secondary burial]." [If one has to celebrate] the week of a son's birth and the occasion of gathering the bones of parents, the celebration of the week of a son's birth takes precedence over the gathering of the bones of parents. [If one has the occasion to join in] a house of celebration or a house of mourning, the house of celebration takes precedence over the house of mourning. R. Ishmael would give precedence to the house of mourning over all other occasions, since it is said, It is better to go to the house of mourning [then to go to the house of feasting, for this is the end of all men, and the living will lay it to heart] (Qoh. 7:2).

T. 3:16 R. Meir said in the name of R. Aqiba, "What is the meaning of the verse, And the living will lay it to heart (Qoh. 7:2)? [In Aramaic:] Do [for others], so they will do for you, accompany [others] to the grave, so they will accompany you, make a lamentation [for others], so they will make a lamentation for you, bury [others], so they will bury you" [= T. Ket. 7:6].

**M. 3:6 [=M. 4:4] One who reads from the Torah should not read less than three verses. And he should not read to the translator more than one verse [at a time], and from a Prophet, [no more than] three [verses]. If the three [verses of the prophetic book] were three paragraphs, one should read [them] one by one. One may skip [parts of the text] in a Prophet, but one may not skip in the Torah. How much may one skip? As long as the translator does not stop.**

T. 3:17 They do not read in the Torah less than three verses [M. Meg. 4:4A] in a single scroll. [If] it was a pericope of four [or] of five [verses], lo, this person should read the whole of it. [If] it was a pericope of five verses, and one read three and left out two, the one who comes up after him to read should read those two and three more in the next pericope. If it was a pericope of four verses or of five, lo, this one [who comes up afterwards] reads the whole of it.

T. 3:18 They do not read for the concluding prophetic lection more than three verses in a single scroll. If it was a pericope of four verses or of five verses, lo, this one should read the whole thing. One who cuts short [by reading only one verse at a time to the translator]—lo, this one is to be praised [cf. M. Meg. 4:4D]. Now if it was a brief pericope, for example, "Thus says the Lord, 'You have been sold for nothing'" (Is. 52:3), one reads it by itself. They leave over [on the Sabbath] at the end of a scroll only so much that seven will be able to read [the following week, thus twenty-one verses]. [If] one left over so much that seven will be able to read, and six read [the passage], let a seventh read in the next book [of the Pentateuch]. They leave over at the end of the Torah only a sufficient number of verses so that seven will read [twenty-one verses]. [If] one left over enough verses so that seven may read, but six read them all, one goes back to the beginning of the matter, and seven read them.

T. 3:19 They skip verses in the prophetic lections but not in the Torah lections [M. Meg. 4:4E]. And they do not skip one prophet to another prophet. But in one of the prophets of the Twelve [minor prophets] they do skip around, on condition that one not skip from the end of a scroll to the beginning of that same one.

T. 3:20 They put a Torah on top of a Torah, and Pentateuchs on top of Pentateuchs, Pentateuchs on top of scrolls of the prophets, but not scrolls of the prophets on top of the Torah or on top of Pentateuchs. They wrap a Torah with Torah-wrappings, and Pentateuchs with Pentateuch-wrappings, a Torah and Pentateuchs with wrappings for scrolls of the prophets, [but they do] not [wrap] scrolls of the prophets with wrappings used for a Torah or Pentateuchs [cf. M. Meg. 3:1]. One person reads in the Torah and one translates [into Aramaic]. One person should not read while two translate, nor should two read while one translates, nor should two read while two translate. One person reads in the prophetic lection and one translates, one reads and two translate, but two should not read while one translates, nor should two read while two translate. One reads in the Scroll of Esther while one translates, one reads while two translate, two read while one translates, two read while two translate [cf. M. Meg. 4:4].

T. 3:21 A minor translates in behalf of an adult, but it is not honorable for an adult to translate in behalf of a minor, since it says, "And Aaron your brother shall be your prophet. You shall speak all that I command you, and Aaron your brother shall tell Pharaoh" (Ex. 7:1). The minister of a synagogue should not read unless others tell him to. And so the head of a synagogue should not read unless others tell him to. For a person does not lower himself on his own initiative [and since the head of the synagogue supervises the reading, it is a diminution for him to read himself]. The minister of a synagogue who arises to read—someone stands and serves as minister [supervising the reading] in his behalf, until the time that he himself reads. How did the elders sit in session? It was facing the people, with their backs toward the sanctuary. And when they leave the ark [in the street on a fast-day], they face the people, with their backs toward the sanctuary. And when the priests raise their hands [in the priestly blessing], it is facing the people, with their backs toward the sanctuary. The minister of the synagogue faces the holy place, and all the people face the sanctuary, since it says, "And the congregation was assembled at the door of the tent of meeting" (Lev. 8:4).

T. 3:22 The doors of synagogues open only eastward, for so we find concerning the sanctuary that it was open eastward, since it says, "And those to encamp before the tabernacle on the east, before the tent of meeting toward the sunrise, were Moses and Aaron and his sons, having charge of the rites within the sanctuary" (Num. 3:38).

T. 3:23 They build them [synagogues] only on the highest place in town, since it says, "On the top of the walls she cries out" (Prov. 1:31).

T. 3:24 What is the sort of "rising" about which the Torah spoke, in saying, "You shall rise up before the hoary head land honor the face of an old man, and you shall fear your God" (Lev. 19:32)? One rises before him and asks after his welfare and answers while within four cubits [of the old man]. What is the sort of "honor" about which the Torah spoke in saying "And honor the face of an old man"? One does not stand in the place in which he usually stands, nor does one speak in his place, nor does one contradict what he says. One behaves toward him with fear and reverence, deals with him when he comes and goes in like manner, and [the elders] take precedence over everyone else, since it says, "And place such men over the people" (Ex. 18:21).

T. 3:25 He who goes forth to fight in an optional war goes back and squats down [to defecate], digs a hole and covers up [his excrement], since it says, "You shall dig a hole with it and turn back and cover up your excrement" (Deut. 23:13).

T. 3:26 He who covers his feet [to defecate] faces the people. And he who urinates turns his back toward the holy place. Said R. Yosé, "Under what circumstances? [When one is located] from Mount Scopus and inward [toward the Temple]. But from Mount Scopus and beyond, it is not necessary to do so."

**M. 3:7 [=M. 4:5-6] One who concludes from a Prophet conducts the recitation of the *Shema,* and passes before the ark, and raises his hands [for the priestly blessing]. And if he was a minor, his father or teacher passes [before the ark] next to him. A minor may read in the Torah or translate [it], but he may not conduct the recitation of the *Shema,* or raise his hands [in the priestly blessing], or pass before the ark. One who wears torn clothes may conduct the recitation of the *Shema* and translate [the biblical texts that are read], but he may not read from the Torah, and he may not pass before the ark, and may not raise his hands [for the priestly blessing]. A blind man may conduct the recitation of the *Shema* and translate [the biblical texts that are read]. R. Judah says: Anyone who never saw light throughout his lifetime may not conduct the recitation of the *Shema.***

T. 3:27 He who says the blessings before and after the *Shema'*, and he who says a blessing over fruit, and [he who says a blessing over] the doing of any of the commandments—lo, this person should not say, "Amen," after himself. And if he did respond in that way, lo, this is coarse behavior They do not respond, "Amen," either "as an orphan," [that is, if one has not actually heard the blessing], or "cut off," [that is, if one has not pronounced the entire word, Amen]. Ben 'Azzai says, "He who answers, 'Amen,' as an orphan—his children will be orphans. "[If he does so], 'Cut off,' his years will be cut off "[If he does so], by drawing out the word, 'Amen,' they will lengthen his days and his years." One who is wearing ragged clothing says the blessings before and after the *Shema'* and serves as the translator [M. Meg. 4 6C] Rabban Simeon b. Gamaliel says, "He should be careful about himself that [his flesh] not show through [the rags]"

T. 3:28 A blind person may say the blessings before and after the *Shema'* and serves as the translator. R. Judah says, "He who has never in his entire life seen the lights [of the firmament] should not recite the blessings before and after the *Shema*'' [M. Meg. 4:6D-E]. They said to him, "Many have expounded the vision of the Chariot [Ezekiel] who have never seen it."

**M. 3:8 [=M. 4:7] A priest who has blemishes on his hands may not raise his hands [i.e., may not participate in the priestly blessing]. R. Judah says: Even someone whose hands are dyed blue may not raise his hands [in the priestly blessing], because the people look at him [attentively].**

T. 3:29 A priest who has a blemish on his face, hands, or feet lo, this one should not raise his hands [in the priestly blessing], because the people will stare at him [M. Meg. 4:7A,C]. But if he was an associate of the town [and therefore well known], lo, this is permitted.

**M. 3:9 [M. 4:8-9] One who says "I will not pass before the ark [i.e., lead the recitation of the Prayer or Amidah] in colored clothes" may not pass [before the ark] even in white clothes. "...I will not pass [before the ark] in sandals" may not pass [before the ark] even barefoot. [If] one shapes his Tefillin round, it is a danger, and there is no [fulfillment of the] commandment through it. [If] he placed it [i.e., one of the Tefillin] on his forehead or on the palm of his hand, this is the manner of heresy. [If] he overlaid them with gold or placed it [i.e., the phylactery placed upon the arm or tefillin shel yad] on his sleeve, this is the way of outsiders.**

**M. 3:10 [If] one says [1] "May the good ones bless you,"—this is the way of heresy; [2] "May your mercies reach to the bird's nest, and may your name be mentioned for good";[or] "thank [you...], thank [you...]," we silence him. [If] one paraphrases the [biblical passages about] forbidden sexual relationships [cf. Lev. 18], we silence him. [If] one translates "and you shall not permit of your seed to pass to Molekh" (Lev. 18:21) as "Do not impregnate an Aramean woman," we silence him abruptly.**

T. 3:30 Lo, if one was cloaked in a short garment or in a traveling cloak, it is not appropriate that he read or translate or pass before the ark or raise up his hands in the priestly blessing [cf. M. Meg. 4:6C]. He who suspends his mezuzah in his doorway—it is a danger [when it is prohibited by law], and it does not partake of a doing a religious duty. [If] he put it on a staff and suspended it behind the door, it is a danger, and it does not partake of doing a religious duty. The members of the household of Mulbaz would do it this way in the shops [cf. M. Meg. 4:8C].

**M. 3:11 [M. 4:10] The story of Reuben [Gen. 35] is read and not translated. The story of Tamar [Gen. 38] is read and translated. The first story of the [golden] calf [Ex. 32:1-20] is read and translated; and**

**the second [Ex. 32:22-24] is read but not translated. The priestly blessing [Num. 6:22-27 and] the story of David and Amnon [cf. 2 Sam. 13] are read but not translated. One may not conclude [the Torah reading] with the [passage in Ezek. 1-3 about the divine] chariot, but R. Judah permits [it]. R. Eliezer says: One may not conclude [the Torah reading] with [the prophetic passage beginning] "Announce to Jerusalem" (Ezek. 13).**

T. 3:31 There are [passages of Scripture] which are read and translated, read and not translated, not read and not translated. The story of the works of Creation is read and translated. The story of Lot and his two daughters is read and translated. The story of Judah and Tamar is read and translated [M. Meg. 4:10B]. The first story of the golden calf is read and translated [M. Meg. 4:10C. The curses in the Torah are read and translated. One person should not begin, while a different one concludes [the reading of the curses of Lev. 28 and Deut. 28], but the one who begins is the one who concludes the reading of all of them. Verses referring to warning and to punishment in the Torah are read and translated.

T. 3:32 The story of Amnon and Tamar is read and translated [cf. M. Meg. 4:10E]. The story of Absalom and his father's concubine is read and translated.

T. 3:33 The story of the concubine of Gibeah is read and translated.

T. 3:34 Make known to Jerusalem her abominations (Ez. 16:2) is read and translated [vs. M. Meg. 4:10H].A certain party was reading before R. Eliezer, "Make known to Jerusalem her abominations." He said to him, "Go out and proclaim your mother's abominations" [cf. M. Meg. 4:10H]. The story of the Chariot do they read in public.

T. 3:35 The story of Reuben is read and not translated [M. Meg. 4:10A]. M'SH B: R. Hanina b. Gamaliel was reading in Kabul, "Reuben went and lay with Bilhah his father's concubine" (Gen. 35:22). "Now the sons of Jacob were twelve" (Lev. 35:22). And he said to the translator, "Translate only the latter [part of the verse, but not the former part]."

T. 3:36 The second story of the golden calf is read but not translated [M. Meg. 4:10D]. Now what is meant by the second story of the golden calf It is from, And Moses said to Aaron, What did this people do to you [that you brought a great sin upon them] (Ex. 32:21), to [And when Moses saw that the people had broken loose] for Aaron had let them break loose, to their shame among their enemies), then Moses stood in the gate of the camp" (Ex. 32:25). And one more verse, "And the Lord sent a plague upon the people, because they made the calf which Aaron made]" (Ex. 32:35).

T. 3:37 On this matter did R. Simeon b. Eleazar say, "A person has not got the right to give an excuse for a misdeed. For from the answer which Aaron gave to Moses, the heretics derived grounds for exposition [in support of their viewpoint]."

T. 3:38 The story of David and Bath Sheba is not read or translated [M. Meg. 4:10E]. But the teacher teaches it in the usual way.

T. 3:39 All Scriptures which were written by using disgraceful language do they read using praiseworthy language, for example: "You shall betroth a wife, and another man shall lie with her" (Deut. 28:30). Wherever it is written, "Will lie with her," they read, "will sleep with her."

T. 3:40 For example, "The Lord will smite you with the boils of Egypt and with the ulcers" (Deut. 28:27). Wherever it is written, "With the ulcers," they read, "With hemorrhoids." And for example, "And the fourth part of a qab of dove's dung for five shekels of silver" (2 Kings 6:25); "Has my master sent me to speak these words to your master and to you, and not to the men sitting on the wall, who are doomed with you to eat their own dung and to drink their own urine" (2 Kings 18:27); "And they demolished the pillar of Baal and demolished the house of Baal and made it a latrine to this day" (2 Kings 10:27]. R. Joshua b. Qorha says, "'And made it a latrine to this day' do they read just as it is written, for it is a disgrace to idolatry."

T. 3:41 A verse which is written in the singular they do not present in the plural, and one which is written in the plural they do not present in the singular. R. Judah says, "He who translates a verse just as it is presented in Scripture—lo, such a one is a deceiver. But the one who adds to what is written, lo, this person is a blasphemer." A translator who stands before a sage is not permitted either to leave anything out or to add anything or to change anything, except if [the translator] was his father or his master.

I see three divisions: rules for synagogue property, rules for declaiming the Torah, and the definition of the lections that are declaimed. Let me briefly reprise the Halakhah.

THE DISPOSITION OF SYNAGOGUE PROPERTY: Synagogues are treated as holy places. People not behave with them frivolously. But they read Scripture in them, repeat Mishnah-traditions in them, and expound biblical lessons in them.

RULES FOR READING SCRIPTURES IN SYNAGOGUE WORSHIP: In addition to the systematic, weekly reading of the Pentateuch, start to finish, there are special lections that correspond to seasonal requirements. Thus over the month prior to Passover, preparations for celebrating the holy season in the Temple involve readying the roads for the pilgrims, cleaning the Temple and removing corpse-uncleanness, and so on, not to mention taking note of Purim.

THE LECTIONS: One who reads from the Torah should not read less than three verses. They do not read for the concluding prophetic lection more than three verses in a single scroll While it is customary to declaim the Torah both in Hebrew and in the vernacular, certain lections are not translated. There are passages of Scripture which are read and translated, read and not translated, not read and not translated.

## IV
## The Synagogue in Law: Definition

It is that the declamation of Scripture takes place most suitably in the congregation gathered in a particular building erected and set aside for that purpose—not for prayer, not for sacrifice, not for study, but for Torah-declamation. That purpose defines within the Halakhah what the synagogue serves—that alone. And, as we have seen in the Halakhah, the synagogue is not at the apex of the ladder of sanctification, either of location or of activity.

To understand how the Halakhah defines the synagogue, we have to recall that, within the Halakhic system, the synagogue forms an anomaly. Scripture knows two foci of sanctification, meeting points for God and Israel, altar and village comprised by households or "tents." Only in the scroll of Esther is the Written Torah able to contribute to the exposition of the laws and life of the synagogue. It is only a single fact, the reading of the Esther scroll there. More broadly still, the written Torah contributes that there, in the synagogue, lections of the written Torah are declaimed. But that is a most limited claim indeed. Scripture does not permit the Halakhah to maintain that there uniquely or there better than anywhere else the Torah is set forth. Only by inference do we draw such a conclusion. That is to say, it is by the juxtaposition of what is explicitly required in Scripture—the reading of the Scroll of Esther—with synagogue-rules in general that yields the besought conclusion. What then defines the synagogue? Not its physical traits, but the particular functions performed in that location. It is not contained space of a particular character, e.g., a holy place, but the presence of the quorum of male Israelites assembled for the conduct of certain specific activities.

Strictly speaking, were the Halakhah to describe how things were, not only how sages wished them to be, archaeology should identify as synagogues in particular remarkably few contained spaces, e.g., buildings of a distinctive character. The Halakhah after all does not specify the traits that a building must exhibit to qualify for use as a synagogue, though it does recognize that a building certainly may be consecrated for synagogue-activities alone. But the Halakhah does indicate what is necessary for the conduct of the activities particular to a synagogue, and that is in terms of the presence of holy Israel, embodied in ten males, to repeat:

> Among fewer than ten (1) One does not conduct the recitation of the *Shema*; (2) and one does not pass before the ark to lead public worship; (3) and one does not raise his hands in the priestly benediction; (4) and one does not read in the Torah; (5) and one does not conclude from a Prophet; (6) and one does not stop and sit after attending a funeral; (7) and one does not recite the blessing for mourners or (8) consolations for mourners, or (9) the grooms' blessing; (10) and one does not invite people to say the grace after a meal in God's name.

Of the items on the list, some may be performed in private by an individual, e.g., Nos. 1 and 10; the others are conducted only within the required quorum. Some of the items on the list—the funeral cortege, for instance—clearly do not involve a particular contained space, a synagogue building, others may. But, we realize, since a quorum may assemble in any suitable space, a synagogue finds its definition in terms not of space but of circumstance. The synagogue, even when required for a particular holy deed, is embodied in the quorum, not in the building. But the building, once sanctified, is deemed holier than a contained (or open) space that has not been sanctified, as we shall see in a moment.

## V
## The Functional Definition of the Synagogue And Why Archaeology Should Find No Representations of the Synagogue

So the synagogue finds its definition in its function; it is not a place to which Israelites go to meet God, as the Temple is. Rather, it is utopian in the simplest sense:

> *anywhere where ten Israelite males conduct a specified activity, the public declamation of the Torah, the function of the synagogue is carried out.*

That is without regard to the location of the Israelites or the character of the dedicated space, if any, that contains them.

How does the synagogue compare with the Temple, on the one side, and the household, on the other—both places where the Halakhah identifies activities that engage God and Israel in specified occasions. Can we define those meeting places of God and Israel as anywhere where ten Israelite males conduct a specified activity? As a matter of fact, that is explicitly not the case when we define the two other venues where Israel and God meet, the Temple and the enlandised household, extending to the village, that is, the household in the Land of Israel possessed of a plot of land in the Land.

To state matters negatively,

[1] the Temple cannot be defined as the place where ten Israelites come together to kill a cow.

[2] The enlandised household cannot be set forth as a location where ten Israelites produce crops. It is only a plot of ground owned by an Israelite in the Land of Israel that produces crops.

The Temple is locative in that it can only be where it is and nowhere else, in Jerusalem, on the Temple mount. And, in positive terms, it is there and only there that the activities characteristic of the Temple can be carried out. Israelites may say their prayers anywhere, may gather to hear the Torah declaimed in any location. But to slaughter an animal designated for God, to collect its blood and toss the blood upon a stone altar, to burn up parts (or all) of the animal as an offering made by fire to God—these activities can take place only in one place.

The household, for its part, is utopian in the obvious sense that anywhere Israelites dwell, they constitute a household. But the household loses its utopian character in holy time, and then it becomes like the Temple, demarcated space with walls. For then, at sunset on the Sabbath, the Israelites attached to a given household situate themselves in space by reference to the location of that household and limit their activities to that particular space. On the Sabbath the household, moreover, situates itself in relationship to the Temple. The household then in holy time loses its utopian character. That is never the case for the synagogue: it is wherever the quorum undertakes the specified activities.

That synagogue in this context is anomalous and diminished. In the Oral Torah's Halakhic vision of where God and Israel intersect, the synagogue finds a merely subordinated place in the structure of laws that define Israel's relationship with God. Three considerations sustain that conclusion.

[1] First, as I have shown, the Halakhic requirements for the synagogue scarcely specify much of interest. The Halakhah differentiates categories that it values, and by that criterion, the synagogue enjoys a low priority. True, the location is to be treated with respect. But while (for example) acutely detailed laws define appropriate use of space for burying the dead, no counter-part rules of weight and substance, comparable to the ones on burial grounds, set forth the delineation of space for the synagogue; only a few make their appearance in the Mishnah,

> Tosefta, and two Talmuds. We know how large a burial plot must be, and how much space is allocated to individual kokhs; the Halakhah of the Oral Torah does not tell us how large the ark that contains the Torah must be, or how much space is allocated to individual scrolls.

And it goes without saying, the Halakhah devotes to the Temple, not only its activities but its space, a corpus of minute regulations with no counterpart for the synagogue. Nothing comparable to the tractate Middot, on the layout of the Temple, attends to synagogue-organization and construction.

The Halakhah, finally, in minute detail defines the priest, his responsibilities and rewards. But connecting the sage to the synagogue anachronizes. And in any event, even if the Rabbinic sage were deemed a synagogue counterpart to the Temple's priest, no comparable native-category devotes discussion to the sage and what he is to do. Tractate Abot, which provides random sayings on the topic, cannot be deemed a Halakhic treatise comparable to the tractates of the Mishnah and the Tosefta, nor does the Fathers According to Rabbi Nathan bear any resemblance to a Talmud's systematic analysis of a Mishnah- and Tosefta-tractate.

[2] Second, the Halakhah assigns to the provenience of the synagogue as consecrated space few critical activities of the life with God. The rhetoric of the Halakhah takes for granted that study of the Torah *may* take place anywhere, but *does* take place in the beth hammidrash or house of study.[3] In the Halakhic texts, that is a considerable fact. The synagogue is not identified with the house of study or with the activity of study in sages' sense; declaiming the Torah and reciting prayers in public do not compare.

What about individual and personal prayer—is this not an activity characteristic of the synagogue, as it is today and through time? As a matter of fact, it is not. While the Halakhah treats as established fact the provision (by sages) of an order of prayer, prayer takes place as much in the household and in the Temple as in the local synagogue. The Halakhah of Berakhot speaks of the *Shema*—the proclamation of God's unit—and the Prayer and the Grace after Meals, all the while taking for

[3]That leads me to wonder why archaeology has not identified a large number of sites that may be categorized as beth-hammidrash-buildings, by contrast to the numerous synagogue sites, not to mention miqva'ot! But what would have characterized a building erected for that particular purpose, and how would we know it, short of a plaque of some kind?

granted that the context for reciting these prayers is the household (and equivalent places, e.g., the fields and orchards where workers are at work). Individual obligatory prayers, the *Shema* and the Prayer, therefore take place wherever the Israelite is located; he need not enter sacred space. The Festivals of Tabernacles and Passover, we recall, encompass home-celebration and Temple activity, but what takes place in the synagogue on those occasions scarcely registers, and it goes without saying, the same is the case for Pentecost.

[3] Third, when it comes to *public* prayer, the Halakhah of the Mishnah assigns that activity to the venue of the Temple in the context of the Daily Whole Offering, so insists the Halakhah of Tamid. The account of prayer recited in public—as distinct from the preparation of the daily whole offering at the altar or prayer recited in private or in some other venue than the Temple—begins with the priests' recitation of the *Shema* after they have completed their labor of preparing and presenting the offering:

Q. All of them turned out to be standing in a row, and the limbs in their hands: (32B) (1) the first, with the head and a hind-leg, the head in his right hand, with its muzzle along his arm, and its horns in his fingers, and the place at which it was slaughtered turned upwards, and the fat set on top of it that place, and the right hind leg in his left hand, and the flayed end outermost; (2) the second, with the two forelegs, that of the right hand in his right hand, and that of the left in his left, with the flayed end outermost; (3) the third, with the rump and the other hind leg, the rump in his right hand, and the fat tail hanging down between his fingers, and the lobe of the liver and the two kidneys with it, the left hind leg in his left hand, with the flayed end outermost; (4) the fourth, with the breast and the neck, the breast in his right hand, and the neck in his left, and with its ribs between his fingers; (5) the fifth with the two flanks, that of the right in his right hand, that of the left in his left, with the flayed ends outwards; (6) the sixth, with the innards put in a dish, and the shanks on top of them, above; (7) the seventh, with the fine flour; (8) the eighth, with the baked cakes; (9) the ninth, with the wine.

R. They went and put them on the lower half of the ramp, on the west side of it.

S. And they salted them the limbs and meal offering.

T. Then they came down and came to the office of hewn stone to recite the *Shema*.

M. Tamid 4:3Q-T

Then the priests recite blessings and prayers:

A. The superintendent said to them, "Say one blessing."

B. They said a blessing, pronounced the Ten Commandments, the *Shema* (Hear 0 Israel (Dt. 6:4-9)), "And it shall come to pass if you shall hearken' (Dt. 11:13-21), and "And the Lord spoke to Moses' (Num. 15:37-41).

C. They blessed the people with three blessings: True and sure, Abodah, and the blessing of priests.

D. And on the Sabbath they add a blessing for the outgoing priestly watch.

M. Tamid 5:1

The upshot is, prayer—public or personal—in no way is linked by the Halakhah of the Oral Torah to the synagogue in particular, and the synagogue enjoys only a subordinate role in the everyday meeting with God that Israel undertakes.

The Halakhah, as always, states the main point best. In its scale of priorities, the synagogue ranks low, well below a Torah-scroll. The ascending hierarchy of holy places, objects, and activities tells the entire story:

Townspeople who sold
(1) the town square may buy a synagogue with its proceeds;
(2) a synagogue may buy an ark (with its proceeds;
(3) an ark may buy Torah wrappings (with its proceeds;
(4) Torah wrappings may buy scrolls of Prophets or Hagiographa with its proceeds;
(5) scrolls may buy a Torah with its proceeds.

But if they sold
(1) a Torah, they may not buy scrolls with its proceeds;
(2) scrolls, they may not buy Torah wrappings;
(3) Torah wrappings, they may not buy an ark;
(4) an ark, they may not buy a synagogue;
(5) a synagogue, they may not buy the town square. And similarly with their left over funds.

The upshot is simple. We should not expect to find elaborate buildings devoted to the rites and requirements of the synagogue. But we do. What conclusions we are to draw from that fact remain to be seen. The point is a simple one: the anomaly of the synagogue is not the art but the very existence of the building as a distinctive Judaic venue. Whatever for! The Halakhah has an answer to that question that hardly prepares us for the established fact that synagogues were imposing buildings, serving critical purposes, for those who built and supported them. Nothing in the Rabbinic Halakhic treatment of the subject explains why. That is the reason that, in interpreting the public art of the synagogues, the Rabbinic documents, the Mishnah through the Talmuds and associated Scripture-commentaries, hardly claim priority in the labor of interpretation.

# Neusner's Tannaitic Synagogue in the Light of Philology & Archaeology: Response to Jacob Neusner, "The Synagogue in Law"

Mayer I. Gruber
*Ben Gurion University of the Negev,*
*Beersheva, Israel*

Professor Neusner has demonstrated that in the world that the Mishnah seeks to create, the synagogue plays a very minor role. Moreover, he demonstrates that when the synagogue is mentioned in the laws of the Mishnah and Tosefta, primarily in Tractate Megillah, the synagogue is almost exclusively identified as a place where Scripture is read. In addition, Professor Neusner shows that the location of laws pertaining to synagogues in Tractate Megillah suggests that the paradigm for the reading of Scripture in the synagogue is the reading of the scroll of Esther on the Festival of Purim. It is this essential feature of the festival of Purim, which provides the framework for legislating in Mishnah Megillah 3 the cycle of reading from the Torah for the various festivals and for four special Sabbaths, which are associated with Purim, the arrival of the spring New Year on 1st of Nisan, and the celebration of Passover and in Tosefta Megillah 3 the cycle of readings from the 8 Prophetic Books, which are read at the conclusion (Heb. *Haftarah*) of the reading from the Torah on Sabbath and Festival mornings. Professor Neusner also points out that Mishnah and Tosefta frequently refer to another sacred space for public cultic activity apart from the not yet rebuilt Temple in Jerusalem, namely, the town square.

Prof. Neusner argues that the reason why the public reading of the Book of Esther on Purim is the paradigm adopted by Mishnah and consequently also by Tosefta for the cultic act of publicly reading Scripture on other occasions as well is as follows:

> because sages find in the Halakhah of Purim as laid out in the Written Torah the requirement that a particular lection of the Torah be declaimed in the community of Israel.[1]

In Bavli-tractate Megillah 7a the word 'book' in the clause "Write this as a reminder in a book" in Ex. 17:14 is taken to be a prophetic allusion to the Scroll of Esther in the Written Torah, i.e., the Pentateuch. Nevertheless, I would prefer both to adopt and to modify Prof. Neusner's observation that the sages of Mishnah found in the reading of the Scroll of Esther on Purim the paradigm for all other reading of Scripture in the synagogue. To begin with, when Rabbinic literature employs the term "Written Torah"[2] it refers to the Pentateuch. The rabbis, however, refer again and again to two other sources of authority. These are 1) the God-given Oral Torah,[3] which according to Mishnah Abot 1:1, Moses received at Sinai and handed down to the sages of the Mishnah by way of Joshua, the Elders, the Prophets and the Men of the Great Assembly;[4] and 2) "scribes' laws". [5] Individual articles belong to the category of "scribes laws" are called *taqqanot* 'human legislation',[6] and these laws are enacted under the authority granted to sages by their understanding of Deut. 17:9: "And you shall go to the Levitical priests or

---

[1]Jacob Neusner, "The Synagogue in Law: What the Texts Lead us to Expect to Find," pp. 4-5.

[2]See, e.g., Sifra at Lev. 24:46; Sifré Deuteronomy at Deut. 33:10; Bavli-tractate Shabbat 31a; Bavli-tractate Qiddushin 66a; see also the discussion in Mayer I. Gruber, "The Mishnah as Oral Torah: A Reconsideration," in Mayer I. Gruber, *The Motherhood of God and Other Studies,* South Florida Studies in the History of Judaism, no. 57 (Atlanta: Scholars Press, 1992), pp. 250-254.

[3]The classic exposition of this basic doctrine of Rabbinic Judaism is Jacob Neusner, "The Meaning of *Torah Shebe'al Peh* with Special Reference to *Kelim and Ohalot,*" *AJS Review* 1 (1976), pp. 151-170.

[4]See, e.g., Leo Jung, *Yoma Translated into English with Notes, Glossary and Indices,* The Babylonian Talmud, ed., I. Epstein (London: Soncino, 1938), p. 134, n. 7; quoted in Gruber, "The Mishnah as Oral Torah," p. 250, n. 5.

[5]See Mishnah-tractate Orlah 3:9; Mishnah-tractate Yebamot 2:4; 9:3; Mishnah-tractate Sanhedrin 11:3; Mishnah-tractate Parah 11:5, 6; Mishnah-tractate Tohorot 4:7, 11; Mishnah-tractate Yadayim 3:2; Tosefta-tractate Taanit 2:4; Tosefta-tractate Qiddushin 5:21; Tosefta-tractate Eduyyot l:1, 5; Tosefta-tractate Parah II:5; Tosefta-tractate Niddah 9:14; Tosefta-tractate Miqvaot 5:4; Tosefta-tractate Tebul Yom 1:10.

[6]See Martin S. Jaffee, "The Taqqanah in Tannaitic Literature: Jurisprudence and the Construction of Rabbinic Memory," *JJS* 41(1990), pp. 204-225.

to the non-priestly judge/official who will be in that time, and you shall inquire, and they shall tell you the law."[7]

On the basis of this authority, sages believed, Esther and Mordecai had the authority to create the festival of Purim and to insist that on this holiday 1) every Jew and Jewess present gifts to at least two indigent persons;[8] 2) every Jew and Jewess present some other Jew or Jewess with a gift consisting of two kinds of foods;[9] 3) every Jew and Jewess celebrate on the day of Purim a festive meal;[10] and 4) every Jew and Jewess hear the reading of the Scroll of Esther.[11]

There is a clear basis in the biblical Book of Esther 9:22 for three of these four precepts. There we read

> They were to observe them as days of feasting and merrymaking , and as an occasion for sending gifts to one another and presents to the poor.[12]

One of the four Purim obligations is missing from the list contained in Est. 9:22, namely, reading the Scroll of Esther. That this commandment is, of course, absent both from the Pentateuch or Written Torah and from the Scroll of Esther does not prevent the rabbis from believing that at the request of Esther the Scroll of Esther was written (Bavli-tractate Megillah 7a), that the Scroll of Esther is an inspired canonical work (there) and that postexilic prophets enjoined the public ceremonial reading of this scroll as an act of worship to be performed on Purim.

---

[7]See Bavli Berakhot. 19b; Bavli-tractate Shabbat 23a; Bavli-tractate Sukkah 46a.

[8]In Bavli-tractate Megillah 7a R. Joseph explains that when Scripture (Est. 9:22) states "gifts to indigent persons" (see also M. Megillah 1:3, 4; T. Megillah 1:4) employing the plural forms of both "gifts" and "indigent persons," Scripture implies that the precept is fulfilled by a person's presenting one gift to each of two indigent persons; so also Shulhan Arukh, Orah Hayyim 694:1.

[9]In Bavli-tractate Megillah 7a it is pointed out that in Est. 9:22 in the clause "sending gifts each one to another" the terms 'each one' and 'to another' are both singular while the term 'gifts' is plural. It is therefore explained there in Bavli-tractate Megillah that we are to conclude that each person fulfills the obligation by sending one gift consisting of two different comestibles to one other person; so also Shulhan Arukh, Orah Hayyim 695:4.

[10]According to Bavli-tractate Megillah 7a Raba derives from the expression "feasting and merrymaking" in Est. 9:22 the obligation to hold a feast on Purim Day; see Shulhan Arukh, Orah Hayyim 695:1.

[11]A *baraita* quoted in Bavli-tractate Arakhin 2b-3a states, "Everyone is obligated with respect to the reading of the Scroll of Esther." The Talmud asks, "To include what [is it stated in the *baraita* "everyone"]? [The Talmud answers]: "To include women, and it is in accord with the dictum of Rabbi Joshua b. Levi, for Rabbi Joshua b. Levi said, 'Women are obligated with respect to the reading of the Scroll of Esther....'" So also Shulhan Arukh, Orah Hayyim 689:1.

[12]Translation follows *Tanakh: A New Translation of the Holy Scriptures According to the Traditional Hebrew Text* (Philadelphia: Jewish Publication Society, 1985).

Moses Maimonides (1135-1204 C.E.) in his codification of Talmudic law, Mishneh Torah, Laws of Megillah and Hanukkah 1:1 writes as follows:

> The Reading of the Scroll of Esther at its appointed time is a positive precept from among scribes' laws, and it is known that it is an article of legislation enacted by the prophets.

It is but a small step from the assertion in the biblical Book of Esther that Mordecai and Esther instituted a new holiday to the belief that an integral part of the observance of that holiday is the public reading of the Book of Esther in the synagogue. It is but another small step to suggest that just as Mordecai and Esther exercised the legislative authority granted to sages in Deut. 17:9 so did Moses exercise that legislative authority in calling for the reading of the Torah every Sabbath and Festival Morning and so did Ezra in establishing the reading of the Torah every Monday and Thursday Morning and Sabbath Afternoon.[13]

What of the instances of Torah reading associated with the Temple service that have nothing to do with a synagogue?

There are two of these. The first of these is, indeed, provided for in the Written Torah in Deut. 31:10-13, which calls for reading the entire "Teaching" aloud in the presence of all Israel—men, women and infants—every seventh year during the Festival of Booths. The procedure for carrying out this commandment is found in M. Sotah 7:8, which assumes that everyone knows that this cultic reading from parts of Deuteronomy is called "the pericope of the king" because it is read by the king. The details concerning a similar cultic reading from Scripture probably modeled on "the pericope of the king" are found in M. Sotah 7:7 where this latter ceremony meant to take place on the Day of Atonement is called "the blessing of the high priest." This latter ceremony includes the reading from the Torah Scroll of the passages concerning the Day of Atonement found in Lev. 16 and Lev. 23 and the recitation from memory of the relevant passage from Num. 29. It is explained that the latter passage is read from memory so as not to burden the assembled persons while they roll the Torah Scroll from Leviticus 23 to Numbers 29!

It is in this passage—M. Sotah 7:7-8—that I find the explanation of two terms, which disturbed me as a philologist in Prof. Neusner's translation of T. Megillah 3:21. These terms are *ro'sh ha-kenesset,* which he translates 'head of a synagogue' and *hazzan ha-kenesset,* which he translates 'minister of a synagogue'. For me, at least, both of these are

---

[13]Yerushalmi-tractate Megillah 4:1; cf. Bavli-tractate Baba Qamma 82a; see also Shulhan Arukh, Orah Hayyim 1351:1 and commentaries *ad loc.*

most fortuitous mistranslations because they provided me with the inspiration to find in M. Sotah 7:7-8 and M. Yoma 7:1 the answer to a basic question, which the historians and archaeologists have been debating. Both passages in M. Sotah 7 and M. Yoma 7:1 as well as Tosefta Sukkah 4:6 indicate that the primary *Sitz im Leben* for both *ro'sh ha-kenesset* and *hazzan ha-kenesset* is a ceremonial reading of Scripture as an act of public worship. It may be concluded without question that the functional meaning of *kenesset* in all of these contexts is an assembly called together for the ceremonial reading of Scripture out of a scroll as an act of worship. Moreover the setting of both of these assemblies is the Temple court and not a synagogue. In all these contexts as well as in T. Megillah 3:21 *hazzan ha-kenesset* is 'an official of the assembly called together for the reading of Scripture' while *ro'sh ha-kenesset* is 'head of the assembly called together for the reading of Scripture'. We have thus accounted for the identical hierarchy reflected in M. Sotah 7:7 and in M. Sotah 7:8. In both of these texts the *hazzan ha-kenesset* is lowest in the chain of command and the *ro'sh ha-kenesset* is above him but below the assistant to the high priest.

Now, what then is a *bet kenesset?* The usage of *kenesset* attested in M. Sotah 7:7-8 and elsewhere indicates that a *bet kenesset* must be a building whose purpose is to host assemblies called together for the express purpose of cultic reading of Scripture texts apart from the two Scripture reading ceremonies, which M. Sotah 7:7-8 locates in the Temple Court. The paradigm for such a reading of Scripture in Mishnah's view, as demonstrated by Prof. Neusner, is the reading of the Scroll of Esther.

Prof. Neusner has demonstrated that in Mishnah and Tosefta *bet kenesset* is a primarily a place in which Scripture is read publicly as a cultic act. Philological method shows that that is precisely why such a place was indeed called *bet ha-kenesset* , i.e., a building which houses an assembly called together for the reading of Scripture out of a scroll as a cultic act. Such an assembly, we have seen, could take place also in the Temple court at two appointed times—every year on the Day of Atonement and once in seven years at the Feast of Booths. Many historians and archaeologists have suggested that in Tannaitic times the synagogue was a simple building built or adapted to house assemblies called together for the reading of Scripture as an act of worship.[14] They did not notice the philological proof found in M. Yoma and M. Sotah.

---

[14]See, e.g., Steven Fine, "From Meeting House to Sacred Realm," in *Sacred Realm: The Emergence of the Synagogue in the Ancient World*, edited by Steven Fine (Oxford: Oxford University Press/ New York: Yeshivah University Museum, 1996), p. 25 and the sources cited there; Pieter W. van der Horst, "Was the Synagogue a Place of Sabbath Worship Before 70 CE?" in *Jews, Christians and Polytheists in the Ancient Synagogue*, edited by Steven Fine (London: Routledge,

Two more activities which Mishnah refers to as taking place in synagogues can be directly accounted for on the basis of Neusner's demonstration that a synagogue was originally a place where Scripture was read as an act of worship. The first of these is what is called in T. Sotah 6:3 *miqra' hallel* , the singing of Psalms 113-118 as an act of worship. I am tempted to conclude from the rather consistent use of the verb *qara'* in Rabbinic Hebrew to refer to singing a biblical text from a scroll that the singing of Psalms 113-118 on Passover, Tabernacles, the Eighth Day of Solemn Assembly, Shabuot and Hanukkah involved the use of a scroll of Psalms and therefore took place in the synagogue, the building for assembling to read from Scripture. In fact, with reference to Mishnah's and Tosefta's desire that the singing of these psalms also be part of the home service on the Eve of Passover, T. Pesahim 10:8 suggests that families lacking an individual capable of singing these psalms should go to the synagogue and have them read the first of the sections of Hallel, i.e., Ps. 113 and then return home. Once again we see that *bet ha-kenesset* 'the synagogue' is a place where Scripture is read from a scroll and where you find people who have what we today call synagogue skills who can actually sing these texts out of the scroll. It was no small task in an era of nearly total illiteracy as attested in T. Megillah 3:12. Based on my explanation as to why Hallel would have taken place in the synagogue, I would account also for M. Sukkah 4:10, which calls for the waving of the *lulab* or palm frond to take place in the synagogue. Since the waving of the *lulab* is part of the ceremony of Hallel on the Festival of Sukkot, it would also have been brought into the synagogue, rather than carried out, let us say, in the town square.

---

1999), pp. 18-43 and the extensive literature cited there; and see Yoram Tasfrir, "Architecture of Galilean Synagogues," in *Ancient Synagogues: Historical Analysis and Archaeological Discovery*, edited by Dan Urman and Paul V. M. Flesher (2 vols.; Leiden: E. J. Brill, 1995), vol. 1, p. 79: "The archaeological finds known to us lead to a single conclusion, namely, prior to the third century synagogues did not exist as special structures, with external identifying signs, as in the third-century Galilean synagogues. The synagogues in which the *Tannaim* prayed in the second century and even those used by the early *Amoraim* were located in houses with the plan and facade of private homes. These buildings usually included one hall larger than the rest for study and prayer, and often had additional rooms which served the community. In terms later used to characterize the Christian community, one can say that this was a sort of 'religious community building'—*domus ecclesiae*." The semantic equivalent in Mishnaic Hebrew for Tsafrir's *domus ecclesiae.* is, strange to relate, *bet-ha-kenesset* . The origin of the *kenesset* itself, later housed in the *bet-ha-kenesset* was, at least in the imagination of the sages of Mishnah, in the septennial reading of the Torah in the Temple Court as prescribed in Deut. 31:10.

Finally, why should M. Rosh ha-Shanah 3:7 refer to the sounding of the *shofar* on the New Year as something which, like the reading of the Scroll of Esther on Purim, takes place in the synagogue? It is explained in Yerushalmi Rosh ha-Shanah 4:8 that the sounding of the shofar could well have been perceived by the Roman rulers as a call to war, as indeed the blowing of the shofar, frequently is in Hebrew Scripture.[15] Hence, the question is raised in M. Rosh ha-Shanah 3:7 as to whether one can fulfill one's obligation if the shofar is sounded "into a cistern, cellar or large jar."[16] Consequently, it is explained in Yerushalmi Rosh ha-Shanah that the blowing of the *shofar* was delayed from the Shaharit service to the Musaph service so that the Romans would see that it is part of a worship service that includes the reading from the Torah. It is reasonable to suggest, therefore, that the blowing of the shofar, which is a religious ceremony not connected with the reading of Scripture, was carried on in the synagogue to make it clear to the Romans that this was a cultic act rather than a political provocation.

Interestingly, archaeologists and historians tell us that the simple synagogues found in the land of Israel, which stem from the first Christian centuries, the era when Mishnah and Tosefta were composed, may have been converted domiciles. Moreover, they tell us that these simple buildings served initially for the reading of Scripture, not for elaborate religious services. It may even be significant that such simple buildings are precisely what Mishnah and Tosefta would have wanted. In this specific instance the gap between archaeology and ancient sacred texts surviving in late copies is not so great if only we get our chronology right and stop reading into either archaeological remains or ancient texts what we saw in another place from another time. To put it another way, with respect to the nature of the synagogue building what Mishnah seems to say that one should do and the archaeological evidence of what people actually did in the era of Mishnah seem, strangely enough, to coincide. What happened later on in the Byzantine era is, as we all know, another story for another time.

---

[15]See, e.g., 2 Sam. 18:16; 20:1; Jer 4:5, 19, 21; 51:27; Hos. 5:8; Am. 3:6.

[16]Jacob Neusner, *The Mishnah: A New Translation* (New Haven & London: Yale University Press, 1988).

# ISLAM

# 8

# Archaeological Evidence of the Early Mosque in Arabia

Donald Whitcomb
*University of Chicago*

"What we need are some simple, working 'methods,' that is, rules of thumb that guide the trip from text to material evidence and vice versa."

## Islamic city of Ayla (Aqaba)

Aqaba is the port of Jordan on the Red Sea, the modern country's maritime window to the world. The port achieved prominence in WWI when Lawrence of Arabia captured it (with the assistance of the Sharifan army of Mecca). He had visited Aqaba two and a half years earlier (in 1914), when conducting an archaeological survey; he discovered evidence of "an Arab settlement of some luxury in the early Middle Ages," which he located the site "a mile from the edge of the village" (Woolley and Lawrence 1914-15, 129).

This settlement was discovered in 1985, shortly before intended development as a hotel. Archaeological excavations began in 1986 and continued through 1995 (Whitcomb 1994a; fig. 1). One result of this research was the slow delineation of an early Islamic town, with typical features: gates, streets, houses. Aspects which proved most elusive were the central institutions of an urban settlement: the administrative (*dar al-imara*), economic (the suqs and khans), and religious (the mosques) structures. In 1993, the building known as the "large enclosure" was excavated and now seems to be the *jami'* or congregational mosque of Ayla (Whitcomb 1994b; fig. 2).

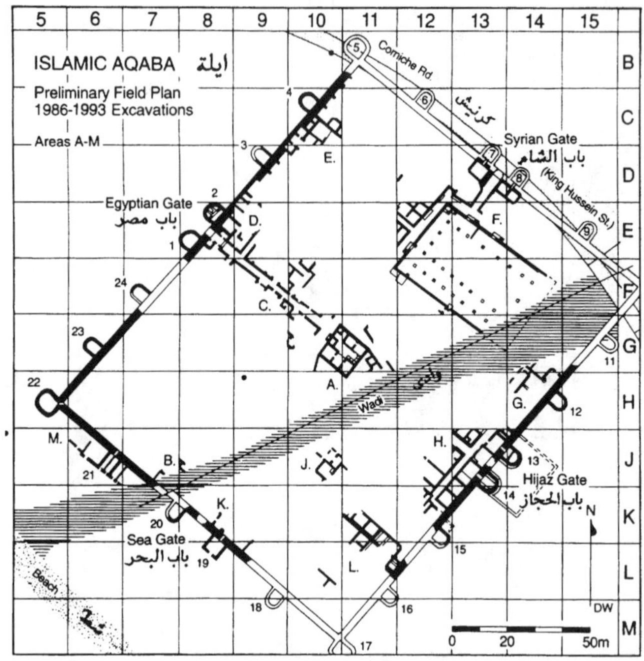


*Figure 1. General plan of the excavations on early Islamic Ayla (Aqaba; after Whitcomb 1994a, 11)*

*Figure 2. View of the mosque in Aqaba from the north, after conservation.*

## The Mosque of Ayla

The area had multiple layers of clean gravel floors just below the present ground surface (first suggesting a reservoir). We soon found walls and rows of columns indicating hypostyle arcades around an open court (*sahn*). Beneath the column foundations and gravel flooring was intentional fill containing only Umayyad artifacts (phase A, 650-750 A.D.). This fill was 3.5+m deep on the western side where it covered the original street line; elsewhere, the foundations were 1.5-2m deep, covering running foundations suggest an earlier building.

The resulting architectural features of the Large Enclosure seem consistent with early mosques (fig. 3a):

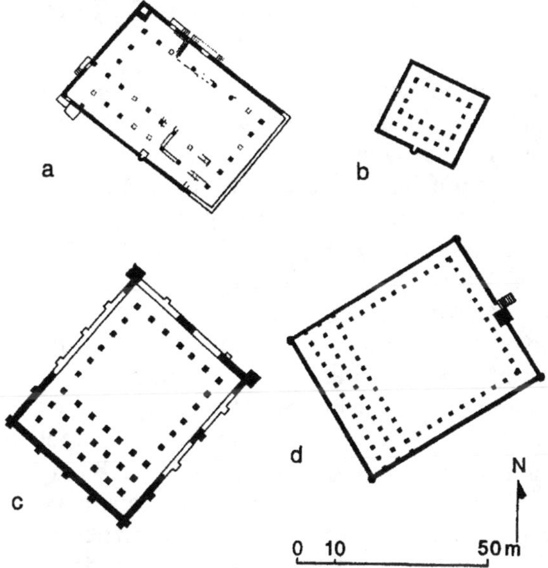


*Figure 3: Comparative plans of early mosques:*
*a. Ayla (Aqaba) mosque (after Whitcomb 1994a, 13)*
*b. Rabadha mosque (after al-Rashid 1986, 119)*
*c. Susa mosque (after Kervran and Rougeulle 1984, fig. 5)*
*d. Siraf I mosque (after Whitehouse 1980, fig. 3)*

1998 The size, 48m x 31m, is within the most common range for urban mosques.

1999 The building was a raised platform with at least three entrances, approached by platform stairways.

2000 In the north corner was a square structure which might have served as a tower (or *sauma'a*, an early minaret).

2001 The peristyle of columns has an additional row on the southwest side forming a covered area of two *riwaqs*, i.e., the sanctuary.

2002 The floor is composed of multiple layers (varves) of clean gravel without any artifacts.

2003 Numerous tesserae indicated that the inner face of the southwest wall was once covered with glass mosaics.

2004 Finally, there was a deep, semi-circular niche in the center of the south wall, its form very similar to early Islamic *mihrabs*.

Yet one might hesitate to label this structure the Congregational mosque (*masjid Jami'*) of early Islamic Ayla. The problem in this identification is the southwest orientation of the *qibla* wall; common *qibla* in southern Syria and Jordan is due south, and the actual direction of Mecca is slightly east of south. Early mosques are often oriented incorrectly; for instance, the mosque of Wasit was misplaced by some 34° (Safar 1945) or Qal'at 'Ana on the Euphrates, where the 9th century mosque was some 35° in error (Northedge, et al. 1988, 17). The *qibla* at Ayla was about 80° in error; for whatever reasons, this *qibla* seems to represent a variation to a strong Muslim tradition.

The operating hypothesis that this mosque was originally built by 'Uthman ibn 'Affan about 650 A.D., making this mosque the earliest discovered, is not sustainable. The sub-floor Umayyad artifacts and alteration of urban street design suggests construction in the early Abbasid period (phase B, 750-850 A.D.). This structure was part of the reconstruction of the city after the 748 earthquake. Nevertheless, a number of its features are decidedly *archaic* for the Abbasid period. These include: the broad mosque design, the platform stairways, even the hypostyle hall on an artificial platform. Add to these an early determination of the direction of *qibla*, and one may see this mosque as an Abbasid reconstruction of the original mosque of 'Uthman ibn 'Affan. The search for this original mosque—datable to only 20+ years after the death of the Prophet—relies on expectable patterns in architectural evidence. The point suggested here is that we must still determine the relevant features of a very early mosque.

## Early Arabian Mosques

A general description of the Arab mosque, provided with many caveats, is found in Hillenbrand (1994, 66). This architectural tradition, noted for both chronological precedence and an "absolute pre-eminence," is defined as a walled rectangular enclosure, an open courtyard, and a covered "sanctuary" near the *qibla* wall. The covered area and usually arcades around the courtyard are supported by columns prompting an epithet of "hypostyle" for this mosque type. This last term is used by Finster for early mosques (1994, 53-57), a study which focused on the mosques of Iran but which relies heavily on her acute observations of early mosques in Yemen. The following mosques from Arabia itself and peripheral regions exhibit features found in the Aqaba mosque:

1. *Rabadha.* The western mosque at Rabadha in the Hijaz has the same configuration (more broad than deep) as that of Ayla but is about one quarter its size (22.75 x 20.15m). This mosque is dated to late 8th. c., with some hesitation, and features two porticoes in sanctuary, single portico around *sahn,* and a projecting semi-circular *mihrab* (fig. 3b). "The floor was covered with gravel which was periodically renewed ... there is evidence that the walls were plastered with thick gypsum and decorated with paint...." (al-Rashid 1986, 22-23)
2. *al-Balid.* The mosque of *al-Balid* in southern Oman measures 46 x 38.5m and has a floor of thick gypsum laid on a bed of pebbles; this floor is a raised terrace about 1m above the *maydan,* approached by steps. Sounding I shows an earlier floor and column bases in differing placement, not thought to be separated by a long time; this duplication of construction is rather like the evidence at Ayla (Costa 1979, 135-38, fig. 25). The mosque is dated ca. 1100 (1979,146).
3. *Banbhore.* The mosque of Daibul in Pakistan measures ca. 38 x 38m and has a double arcade around *sahn* and a three bay sanctuary. There is a single platform stairway in the *qibla* wall of the mosque and it is thought to be early 8th c. (Ashfaque 1969; fig. 26).
4. *Susa.* La mosqué ancienne in southwestern Iran has no dating evidence, though an early 7th c. is suggested (fig. 3c). It rises on a mound, 48 x 37.7m, and has single arcade on three sides, and three bays on the sanctuary side (Kervran and Rougeulle 1984).
5. *Siraf.* The Congregational mosque on the Iranian coast begins in period 1 (early 9th c.) when it was 51 x 44m., standing on a platform 2m. high (fig. 3d). One should note that like Ayla, this mosque utilized ruined structures for the terracing, a feature not consistently observed in archaeological reports. The *sahn* had a single arcade and the sanctuary three bays deep. The *mihrab* was flat or contained in

the thickness of the wall; a salient niche was later added. The was one axial entrance, flanked by square minaret (Whitehouse 1980).

6. In addition there are two early mosques pertinent to the present study from Yemen: *Shibam* is located 40mi northwest of San'a' (Lewcock and Smith 1973) and posited to date to the 9th c. This mosque is 38 x 26m, with a square minaret in corner. The second is *Dhu Jiblah* mosque, located 50mi north of Ta'izz (Lewcock and Smith 1973). This mosque is 40 x 34m and is suggested to date to 1088 A.D.; the transverse plan of the sanctuary has been compared to that of Damascus (1973, 120).

## Answers from Yemen?

Another source of information on mosques in Yemen may be seen in manuscript illuminations found in the roof of the mosque of San'a'. Two of these depict hypostyle mosques on terraces with platform stairways (von Bothmer 1987). While there is some debate as to the age and identity of these depictions, they seem to represent early features of Umayyad mosques in Yemen.

These illuminations my corroborate an hypothesis that early mosques in Yemen have adopted features typical of pre-Islamic souith Arabian temples. Jung (1988) has noted concurrence in two types of temple: "the *court temples* enclosed by porches [which are] "...considered by several scholars as a precursor of the classic mosque (cf. e.g. the Jami' al-Kabir at Shibam-Kaukaban." Second are the "hypostyle temples" which may be antecedents for small hypostyle mosques in Yemen (Finster 1991, 1992). Characteristic elements in south Arabian temples (fig. 4) have been noted by Sedov and Batayi (1994):

1. platforms
2. flanking stairs, single and double
3. hypostyle hall
4. stone benches
5. four column propylon

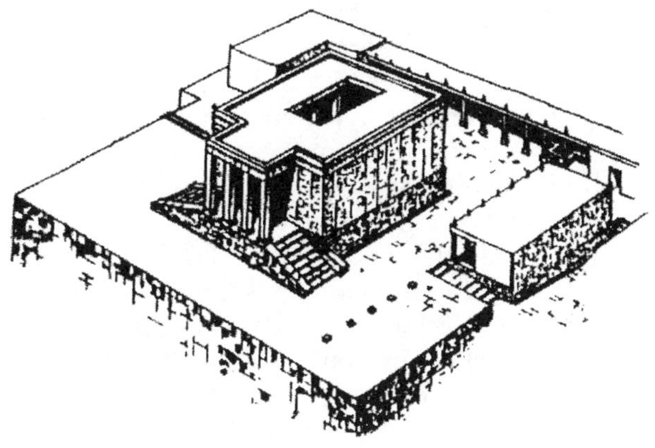

*Figure 4: Reconstruction of the Istar temple at Raybun (after Sedov 1997, 147)*

One should note the existence of Axumite parallels for this assemblage of features, especially the villa of Dungur in Axum itself (Anfray 1972). This structure was built on a terrace approached by double stairways; the structure appears to have been hypostyle, to judge from sub-floor structural elements (fig. 5). While originally characterized as a "villa", this building is now generally acknowledged as a temple or religious building. The features of this and other Axumite buildings confirms the interactions between this kingdom and South Arabia, especially in Late Antiquity.

*Figure 5: The "villa" of Dungur, Axum (photo credit: K. Bard)*

## Conclusions

The commonalities of architectural examples across the Red Sea suggests a strong tradition in religious architecture in pre-Islamic Arabia. The appearance of many of these features as essential elements in early mosques indicate an Arabian, and specifically a Yemeni origin for Islamic architecture. Distribution of these features further indicates an important cultural movement along the "commercial crescent" of the Indian Ocean. From Yemen, one may look to al-Balid, then the early mosque at Daibul in Pakistan and, of a similar date, that of Siraf. Siraf, on the southern coast of Iran (Whitehouse, 1980), evokes an even older antecedent, the hypostyle hall on a terrace, approached by platform stairways, the Appadana of Persepolis. In summation one may return to Aqaba with the observation that a curious number of Axumite features seem to be present in this Abbasid mosque.

The operating hypothesis suggested here is that a localized, formal conservatism reproduced features on the first congregational mosque, one possible constructed under 'Uthman ibn 'Affan. The Axumite elements are older South Arabian (and even old ideas for places of worship). The earliest mosque was associated with the house of the Prophet, but this was more of an enclosed communal center (see below). The area was mainly open with limited roofed area. Conversion from Judaism, Christianity, and presumably many pagan sects meant leaving enclosed religious structures, when joining this new community. Arabian architects selected certain elements from their heritage to ease this transition (or accommodate to more basic ideas of sacral space). They raised the enclosure upon a terrace or platform, approached by indirect, ceremonial stairways. They used continuous arcades before all interior walls. Further elements may also be elicited from archaeological research in Yemen and Arabia.

This mosque of Aqaba, like others in early Islamic times, was more than a place for religious services. The mosque was the scene of public meetings and political ceremonies, it was the place where the *qadi* held court, and the center of education in the religious and legal sciences. This last aspect was particularly important in Ayla. From the eighth through the ninth centuries, Ayla was a major center for *hadith* studies. A local Ayli school developed around al-Zuhri, particularly his students 'Uqayl ibn Khalid and Yunis ibn Yazid, the heads of two prominent scholarly families (Cobb 1995). Interestingly, these scholars also did periodic duty as police (or city-guards) in Madina. Needless to say, these men also emigrated to the great cities of Jerusalem, Damascus, Fustat (Cairo), and the port of Alexandria. The mosque of Ayla was rather like the Stoa of Athens, a place of study and discussion among the columns. And like

Athens, further archaeological research can only amplify our understanding of this social and intellectual milieu.

Archaeologists rely on assumptions based on typologies, in this case patterns in architectural remains. As Tim Insoll has recently suggested in his book on Islamic archaeology (1999), this reliance on art history has led to misunderstandings of Islamic culture. Rather, an archaeology of religion is necessary, in his view, to delineate the effect of Islam on a particular cultural tradition. His path seems to result in a static and tautological view of history, where theorizing in archaeology has become an end in itself. He would rather see contributions toward a socially aware archaeology, one in which historically situated communities may be known from contextual studies of their artifactual and environmental variables. Rather than an abstracted, post-processual archaeology with its own theoretical concerns, one might hope for an intermediate archaeology addressing specific cultural complexes, that is, historically situated communities known from contextual studies of their artifactual and environmental variables. One might argue that early Islam, represented in the architectural contexts at Aqaba and Yemeni sites, may be understood only through archaeological research.

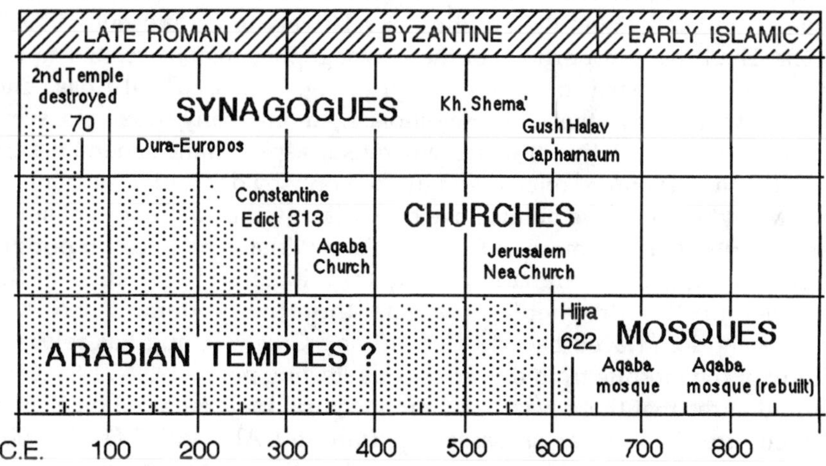


*Figure 6: Synoptic time-line of synagogues, churches, and mosques*

**Future Researach**

In the study of the beginnings of the mosque, an additional line of inquiry is the synagogues of late antiquity, particularly those which may be presumed to have existed in the Hijaz. Indeed, Aqaba was known to later geographers as a town of the Jews. It should be possible to find these synagogues but, for the archaeologist, this would be a matter of recognition—what would such a synagogue look like, and how would it differ from a mosque of church of the same time? Magness has recently noted that "...(monumental) synagogue bulding with a distinctive plan and clearly Jewish iconography of decoration (what I would call 'archaeologically identifiable synagogues') did not develop in Palestine until the fourth century, especially the later fourth century. It would be interesting to consider whether this may be related to (or in response to) the rise and development of churches" (2000, 90).

Tsafrir has excavated many Byzantine synagogues and notes: "The ... shape of the prayer hall approaches a square rather than the elongated rectangle characteristic of the church. ...The architect's intent was to promote closeness and attentiveness..., disdaining any hierarchy between the reader and worshipper. (An identical approach is found in Islam...which dictated the building of relatively broad mosques;" 1987, 152). The broad proportions of these synagogues may be related to the proportions of early mosques in Syria, e.g. Damascus, al-Aqsa, and Aqaba, with many others. These scholars, among many observers, seem to indicate a cumulative or better syncretistic aspect in the general design of religious structures, often distinguished only by decorative elements.

Many of the above points have been discussed in an important sutdy of the origins of the mosque (Johns 1999). Perhaps his most important contribution is an examination of the traditional understanding of the "house of the Prophet." He has thoroughly demolished this misconception, traced back to Caetani and Creswell, and has released study of the mosque from this erroneous starting point (1999, 71-80). We would agree that there was "...an architectural *koine* centered on Yemen which stretched as far as Sassanian Iran and Abyssinia" (1999, 100). Nevertheless, he seems too negative in conclusion that an immediate ancestor of the mosque may not be found. As the above discussion has attempted to indicate, this study remains a matter of recognition and more detailed observation of features and contexts for the archaeological remains of earliest mosques.

**References**

Anfray, F.
1972 L'archéologie d'Axoum en 1972, *Paideuma* 18, 60-78.

Ashfaque, S. M.
1969 The Great mosque of Banbhore, *Pakistan Archaeology* 6, 182-219.

Cobb, P. M.
1995 Scholars and society at early Islamic Ayla, *Journal of the Economic and Social History of the Orient* 38, 417-28.

Costa, P. M.
1979 The study of the city of Zafar (al-Balid), *Journal of Oman Studies* 5, 111-50.

Finster, B.
1979 Die Freitagsmoschee van Sibam-Kaukaban, *Baghdader Mitteilungen* 10, 193-228.
1991 Cubical Yemeni mosques, *Proceedings of the Seminar for Arabian Studies* 24, 49-68.
1992 An Outline of the history of Islamic religious architecture in Yemen, *Muqarnas* 9, 124-47.
1994 *Frühe iranische moscheen, vom Beginn des Islam bis zur Zeit saljuqischer Herrschaft.* Berlin, Archaeologische Mitteilungen aus Iran, erganzband. 19.

Hillenbrand, R.
1994 *Islamic architecture: Form, function and meaning.* New York, Columbia University.

Insoll, T.
1999 *The Archaeology of Islam.* Oxford, Blackwell, 1999.

Johns, J.
1999 The "House of the Prophet" and the concept of the mosque, *Bayt al-Maqdis: Jerusalem and early Islam.* J. Johns, ed. Oxford, Oxford Studies in Islamic art 9, pt. 2. 59-112.

Jung, M.
1988 The Religious monuments of ancient southern Arabia, a preliminary typological classification, *Annali dell'Istituto Orientale di Napoli* 48, 177-218.

Lewcock, R., and G. R. Smith
1974 Two early mosques in the Yemen: A Preliminary report, *Art & Archaeology Research Papers* (London) 4, 117-32.

Kervran, M., and A. Rougeulle
1984 Recherche sur les niveaux islamiques de la Ville des Artisans, *Cahiers de la Délégation archéologique française en Iran* 14, 7-120.

Magness, J.
2000 The Question of the synagogue: The Problem of typology, *Judaism in Late Antiquity: Where we stand, part three.* J. Neusner and A Avery-Peck, eds. Leiden, Brill. 1-48.

Northedge, A., A. Bamber, and M. Roaf
1988 *Excavations at 'Ana, Qal'a island.* Warminster, Aris & Phillips.

Al-Rashid, S.A.
1986 *al-Rabadhah: Portrait of early Islamic civilisation in Saudi Arabia.* Harlow, Longman.

Safar, F.
1945 *Wasit: The sixth season's excavations.* Cairo, Institut français d'archéologie orientale.

Scerrato, U.
1985 Archaeological activities in the Yemen Arab Republic, 1985: Islamic Period, *East and West* 35, 375-95.

Sedov, A. V.
1997 Raybun, *Yemen, au pays de la reine de Saba'.* Paris, Institut du Monde arabe.

Sedov, A. V., and A. Batayi'
1994 Temples of ancient Hadramawt, *Proceedings for the Seminar of Arabian Studies* 24, 183-96.

Schmidt, J.
1982 Zur altsüdarabischen Tempelarchitektur, *Archäologische Berichte aus dem Yemen* 1, 161-69.

Tsafrir, Y.
1987 The Byzantine setting and its influence on ancient synagogues, in L. I. Levine (ed.), *The Synagogue in Late Antiquity.* Philadelphia, American Schools of Oriental Research. 147-57.

von Bothmer, H. G.

1987 *Architekturbilder im Koran. Eine Prachthandschrift der Umayyadenzeit aus dem Yemen,* Bruckmanns Pantheon 45, 4-20.

Whitcomb, D.

1994a *Ayla: Art and Industry in the Islamic port of Aqaba.* Chicago, The Oriental Institute.

1994b The Ayla mosque: Early Islamic remains in Aqaba, Jordan, *Fondation Max van Berchem Bulletin* 8, 3-6.

1996 Urbanism in Arabia, *Arabian Archaeology and Epigraphy* 7, 38-51.

2005 Out of Arabia: Early Islamic Aqaba in its regional context, *Colloque inter-national d'archéologie islamique.* R-P. Gayraud, ed. Cairo, Institut français d'archéologie orientale. 403-418.

Whitehouse, D.

1980 *Siraf III: The congregational mosque, and other mosques from the ninth to the twelfth centuries.* London, British Institute of Persian Studies, n.d. [1980]

Woolley, C.L., and T.E. Lawrence

1914-15 *The Wilderness of Zin.* London, Palestine Exploration Fund Annual.

# 9

# Towards Islamic Archaeology

Katherine Strange
*Oriental Institute, Chicago, Illinois*

"What is Islamic Archaeology?" It is appropriate to ask this question given the purpose of this conference to discuss how texts intersect with material contexts to tell us something about ancient religions. For, as the name implies, Islamic Archaeology must have something to do with the religion of Islam. It is the aim of this conference to determine the ways in which archaeology can illuminate religion. But how? What is the relationship between the archaeology of Islam and Islam? How can Islamic Archaeology, along with historical texts, be employed to understand the religion of Islam?

Before we can determine the relationship between archaeology and Islam, we will need to define terms. For instance, what is Islam? Or more precisely, what is Islam as an object of inquiry? Is 'Islamic' an adequate modifier for the archaeology that is practiced under the rubric of Islamic Archaeology? How does one even find Islam in the material remains, so that one can in turn interpret what one finds to illuminate the practice of religion?

Islamic archaeology is unusual in being archaeology defined by a religion, although certainly all archaeologists must deal with religion. We may draw comparisons, however, with Syro-Palestinian archaeology, often still referred to as Biblical archaeology. This discipline studies ancient cultures in the Near East that are important to both the Jewish and Christian faiths, and seeks to illuminate the world of the Bible and the lives of early practitioners of these faiths. The Qur'an, which in contrast to the Bible is not rich in narratives, benefits from archaeology in a similar way. Those who study the early periods of Islam and immediately pre-Islam can seek to understand the world in which the Qur'an was written, collected and compiled. Islamic archaeologists go far beyond that, however, and study the cultures throughout the world that have been either ruled by Muslims or made up of a majority Muslim population.

In this way Islamic archaeology faces the problem that Christian archaeology would face, if it were practiced in its broadest sense.[1] That is, it is too broad. Temporally, it can refer to any time from 622 (the year of Muhammad's *Hijra* from Mecca to Medina) to the present. Geographically, it can occur anywhere there have been practicing Muslims, or where the government has claimed to be Muslim. Thus although it traditionally has been concentrated in the lands of early Islam, it is studied from what is now Spain to Southeast Asia (and even parts of modern China), and in parts of Africa. Because of this breadth it is important that the scholar that engage in its study Studies' be able to explicate the assumptions about Islam that informs his or her approach.

At least since the middle of the twentieth century, scholars in various disciplines of the humanities and social sciences who studied some aspect of Islam as a culture or religion have made attempts at answering the question "What is Islam?" in order to justify their own exploration of the topic. Fields such as Islamic Anthropology, Islamic Art and Islamic History must approach the idea of "Islam" in a similar way. Used as a modifier of things such as history or art, and certainly anthropology, the word "Islamic" connotes something more cultural than religious. How do the practitioners of these fields deal with Islam in its religious and cultural meanings? We will briefly review some of the more recent attempts at definition here, to get an idea of current approaches to 'Islam' in Islamic archaeology and its companion fields. We will see that many are the same, or very similar:

Richard Ettinghausen and Oleg Grabar, when applying the adjective 'Islamic' to 'Art' write

> It refers to those people who have grown and lived under rulers who professed the faith of Islam or in cultures and societies which have been strongly influenced by the modes of life and thought characteristic of Islam. But 'Islamic' unlike 'Christian', refers not only to a faith but also to a whole culture, since—at least in theory—the separation of the realm of Caesar from that of God is not applicable to Islam.[2]

---

[1]Christian archaeology was in fact once the name for what is now called Byzantine archaeology, and some scholars still use the older name. It was conceived of primarily as the archaeological study of early Christianity and a branch of classical archaeology. (Saradi 1997): 396.

[2](Ettinghausen and Grabar 1994): 17. They are referring to the notion that Islam was originally conceived as a religion and a political system together, which

Many other art historians use the same basic definition of Islam as a culture as well as a religion, careful to include art made by non-Muslim artists, and at times even art made by Muslims in non-Muslim lands.[3] We see that this is a particularly broad definition of 'a' culture, but we see the same concept in the study of history:

The historian Marshall Hodgson explored these ideas in the 1970s, in the first volume of his classic series *The Venture of Islam: Conscience and History in a World Civilization.* Hodgson terms both the religion and its attendant cultural and social manifestations 'Islam.'[4] He sees cultural continuity among Muslims that goes beyond the level of religion.[5] This is the overarching 'Islam' that was carried from one culture to another by means of 'high culture,' that is, literature of all sorts, especially religious.[6] Thus even though Islam as a religion and a force that forms cultural traditions has varied enormously from one place and time to another, many people from different regions can be grouped together and studied as a whole, as those who make up 'Islamdom.'[7]

Another contribution of Hodgson's was to offer very precise terminology for use of those studying Islamic topics. He suggested 'Islamdom' as the collective referent to "the various peoples among whom Islam has been predominant and which have shared in the cultural traditions distinctively associated with it." 'Islamicate' is the term for the distinctive civilization of Islamdom and its cultural traditions, to distinguish it from 'Islamic,' which would only refer to religious art or literature within the traditions of the Islamic faith, for instance. 'Islamicate' has a more indirect relationship to Islam than does 'Islamic.' Hodgson is not strict about these uses, simply pointing out that this distinction may be helpful at times. "Some term for the civilization

---

makes it unique among the major world religions: "Whereas the Muslims did not spread their faith through the sword, it is, nevertheless, true that Islam insisted on the assumption of political power since it regarded itself as the repository of the Will of God, which had to be worked on earth through a political order." (Rahman 1966, 1979): 2.

[3]See, for example (Hillenbrand 1994): 8; (Bloom and Blair 1997): 5; (Irwin 1997): 12.

[4]"Not only what may be called the religion proper, then, but the whole social and cultural complex associated with it—indeed, at the most extreme extension, the totality of all the lifeways accepted among any Muslims anywhere—may be looked on as Islam and seen as a self-contained whole, a total context within which daily life has proceeded in all its ramifications. All can, in some sense, be derived as consequent upon the initial posture of *islâm*, of personal submission to God." (Hodgson 1974): 75.

[5]Ibid.: 87.

[6]Ibid.: 92.

[7]Ibid.: 79, 94.

that refers to Islam is still preferred over 'Perso-Arabic civilization,' for instance, because of the pre-eminent role played by Islam and by Muslims."[8]

Not all scholars accept this terminology. The art historian Robert Hillenbrand's position on the term 'Islamic,' is similar to Hodgson's, but he does not find any use for new terms:

> The advantage of the word 'Islamic' is that it refers as much to a culture—a culture as self-contained as that of Western Europe—as to a faith. As a descriptive term it is therefore a good deal more useful and expressive than 'Christian', even if the pictures it most readily evokes may smack of cliché. Thus there is no need to complicate the issue with such neologisms as 'Islamicate' or 'Islamdom.'[9]

Hillenbrand also points out that the regional variations in material culture (he is speaking specifically of architecture) between Muslim countries is as great as between any European regions. His justification for using the term 'Islamic architecture' is based on its utility. He argues that it is similar to the term 'European architecture,' which is an acceptable, if general, term for architecture that is distinctly of that region.'[10]

Alistair Northedge agrees with Hodgson and Hillenbrand insofar as Islam can be seen as a cultural force. In his recent article "Archaeology and Islam," Northedge closely links archaeology to history and defines it as follows: "The archaeology of Islam is not the archaeology of a religion, but rather of a *single world culture* in the same way as Roman archaeology. However, Islam is a much more diffuse culture combining many different geographical regions in a single civilization."[11] He includes architecture, styles of art and even patterns of living in the package of Islam. These made up the 'cultural baggage' that Islam brought with it from the Middle East, and took to India as well as Spain, for example. That is why, according to Northedege, it is possible to compare architectural styles in the two regions.[12]

The archaeologist Timothy Insoll, like Hodgson and Northedge, is content to define Islam as a single, definable entity, carrying with it certain cultural practices. In his recent book exploring some of these very issues, he writes:

---

[8]Ibid.: 95.
[9](Hillenbrand 1994): 8.
[10]Ibid.: 8.
[11](Northedge 1999): 1101 (emphasis mine).
[12]Ibid. In.: 1101.

> Islam, the religion, exists as a definable, cross-culturally applicable entity: a set of religious beliefs which have been adapted and interpreted across the world depending on cultural context. In other words, we can see Islam as a uniform superstructure composed of the fundamentals of belief, with a diverse substructure of practices, cultures and their material manifestations below.[13]

While recognizing the existence of regional traditions, he would prefer to see them as one flexible Islam.[14]

Although he speaks of a single civilization "of which Islam was the dominant religion, and which expressed itself mainly in Arabic, Persian and Turkish," Albert Hourani critiques the culture-religious approach to history espoused by Hodgson and others. It is precisely this approach, he says, that allows even the most 'secular' aspects of life to be seen as Islamic: the 'Islamic city,' 'Islamic countryside' and 'Islamic governments or armies.'[15] Nevertheless he is of the opinion that 'Islamic history,' despite the problems inherent in grouping such a vast geography and time-span together, is still a useful phrase. If it is dispensed with altogether, one must confront "the danger of looking at the world in which Islam was the dominant religion as having no reality of its own, and having to be explained in terms of something other than itself."[16]

These approaches in the main seek to justify the investigation of many different societies and cultures that have a government that is at least 'Islamic' in name, and populations that include Muslims. They include the assertion that Islam itself is a carrier of cultural traditions, including human behavior. An implication of this is that Islam can be interpreted as a single, monolithic entity, or that even if one recognizes some variation in tradition (such as the broad *shi'a—sunni* division) or in material culture, there must be an essential 'Islam,' a core of belief and practice that is the same everywhere, that allows for gross comparisons to be made.

Talal Asad explored this issue in his 1986 article "The Idea of an Anthropology of Islam" and in his 1993 book *Genealogies of Religion: Discipline and Reasons of Power in Christianity and Islam*. He vigorously critiques the essentialization of Islam that is at the root of three main theoretical approaches he identifies in modern anthropology. These either deny Islam as a definable theoretical object of study, conceive of it as a completely heterogeneous collection of items each of which is labeled 'Islamic' by the anthropological informant, or conceive of Islam

---

13(Insoll 1999): 1.
14Ibid.: 10-11.
15(Hourani 1976): 113.
16Ibid. In.: 115.

as a blueprint for social order.[17] Regarding the last approach especially, Asad writes that one must not attribute an individual's behavior solely to 'Islam,' but to the individual. "...It is not the literal scope of the *shari'a* which matters here but the degree to which it informs and regulates social practices, and it is clear that there has never been any Muslim society in which the religious law of Islam has governed more than a fragment of social life."[18] Asad reminds us that rather, Islam is a wide-ranging tradition that contains a multiplicity of forms. By 'tradition,' he means oriented to the past, not necessarily traceable to the past. Islam as an object of anthropological study should be approached as a discursive tradition, not a static.[19] Similarly we must recognize that Islam, as a religion, is not separate from power, a concept which is the norm in the West. Assad reminds us that religion has no separate essence of its own, and the risk we take when thus defining it is to make it "a transhistorical and transcultural phenomenon" rather than something with historically specific elements and relationships. Even an attempt to give it a universal definition, will fail, as it can only be a product of our own history..[20]

This critique, while aimed specifically at anthropologists, can offer a caution to archaeologists and others who are too willing to make broad comparisons of architectural style, for example, across the Islamic world and across history.[21] The caution is to investigate cross-cultural contacts rather than to assume them based on a common religion. While historical sources may indicate inter-regional contacts, or relationships resulting from paying taxes to a common government, for example, which can be investigated by archaeology, so archaeology may point to contacts that are absent from the literature. Therefore the point is not to avoid comparison, but to rework the conceptual framework that leads one to make comparisons. As obvious as it seems, we must remember that Islam was and is a religion carried by people, and it is the people who brought with them various cultural practices. Thus one can only conceive of 'Islam' as a carrier of culture in the specific sense of Muslim peoples from a particular region moving to another region and bringing with them certain practices. Not all of the practices they brought with them were directly related to religion.

---

[17](Asad 1986): 1.
[18]Ibid.: 13.
[19]Ibid.: 7.
[20](Asad 1993): 28-29. This may seem a rather obvious idea, but it is precisely the opposite of Hourani's approach. The universalization and essentialization of Islam still occurs in scholarly and non-scholarly writing.
[21](Hillenbrand 1994): 8.

For the purposes of discussion, then, let us use the definition of Islam that we have seen is used by most scholars working in the field, and regard Islam as a religion that does have recognizable cultural manifestations, even if we may not be able to name all of them. We can use "Muslim" to refer to something specifically religious, and "Islamic" to refer to something cultural that comes from being Muslim. If we accept this we must ask, "What things does Islam, as a culture, spread? How does Islam show itself in the archaeological record?" In other words, we want to look for ways in which ancient people show themselves to be Muslims in the remains they left behind. Timothy Insoll is perhaps the only person to have addressed this question directly. His book is dedicated to examining categories of evidence and how they might ideally be Islamic. These are the mosque, the domestic environment, Muslim life, art, trade and ideas, death and burial, and the community environment. What makes this investigation difficult is that in any given Muslim society, "all aspects of life, from birth in the domestic environment to death and burial, can be structured according to religious, and the resultant social, codes."[22] Nevertheless discussion and exploration of what might comprise concrete evidence for religion in the record is useful. An example from his study will serve to illustrate this approach and its difficulties.

Insoll's argument is as follows: There are as many "Islamic houses" as there are countries in which there are Muslims, and more. This is because Islam, although it sets guidelines for how one should build one's house, offers no specific prescription, and, unlike a mosque which exists because of the requirement for prayer (and the particular blessedness of communal prayer according to tradition),[23] a house exists for the physical and social needs of human beings. As an artifact of a family, which is the smallest social unit of a society, a house reflects normative social conditions and customs. It must therefore reflect the social customs prescribed by or resultant from religion. Insoll asserts that therefore there is an Islamic domestic architecture.[24] We observe that the first weakness in his approach is the reductionist argument that leads us to accept there is such a thing as Islamic domestic architecture before we have seen the evidence. Examination of some physical evidence reveals additional problems:

Although the forms of Islamic houses are culturally diverse, according to Insoll there are two major social concerns that seem to be

---

22(Insoll 1999): 228.

23Ibid.: 90; (Waines 1995): 90; (Campo 1991): 34. (Found in Bukhari's *Sahih* and *Salah*, in and Muslim b. al-Hajjaj's *Sahih* and *Masajid*.).

24(Insoll 1999): 61.

universal in the Muslim domestic situation: the concern for privacy and the corresponding seclusion and protection of women.[25] These two social concerns are universal in Islam not because they are so easily discerned in the archaeological record, but because they are elaborated in the Qur'an and in hadith.[26] On the contrary, because privacy and the protection of women are found in rules governing the house, we expect to find evidence in house remains, but the difficulty lies in identifying features that might be in compliance with these rules. House forms may in many cases be identical with the pre-Islamic houses in that area, or with contemporary houses occupied by non-Muslims, but they may deal with the issues of privacy or the division of space into men's and women's areas in ways that do not survive in the record.[27]

The continuity of house forms, and the difficulty in distinguishing Muslim houses from those of non-Muslims is well illustrated by Yizhar Hirschfeld in his study of Palestinian houses.[28] His goal is to show the continuity of house forms from the Roman-Byzantine period in Palestine to the recent present, and to use the modern homes to illustrate how ancient people may have used similar space. Although he does not address the specific question of the religious affiliation of house occupants (except in some of the modern houses in Hebron), it is possible that his medieval examples are Muslim households, and it is certain that most of his modern examples are.

At the site of Gerasa a group of rooms that Hirschfeld interprets as an Umayyad apartment house was excavated in the 1930s.[29] It is

[25]Ibid.: 62; 64; 85 Although as Insoll points out (page 66), Muslims have never had a monopoly on issues of privacy or seclusion of women, which further complicates the interpretation of domestic remains. Also see (Goitein 1983): 63.

[26](Insoll 1999): 62. Regarding protection for the persons of women, see Qur'an 33:59 concerning women wearing concealing garments when out-of-doors. Also see Qur'an 33:53, which enjoins believers to keep a screen between themselves and Muhammad's wives when invited to a meal at his home. Leila Ahmed discusses these verses and some associated traditions in relation to the seclusion of women in (Ahmed 1992): 53-56.

[27]Curtains for the division of interior space, for example, are much less likely to survive in the record than walls.

[28]Hirschfeld, Y., *The Palestinian dwelling in the Roman-Byzantine period*. Jerusalem, 1995.

[29]See Kraeling, C. H. (editor) 1938 *Gerasa: City of the Decapolis*. American Schools of Oriental Research, New Haven, Connecticut.: 271-284, plates LV-LVI and plan XLV for the original publication of the excavations by Yale University, The British School of Archaeology in Jerusalem, and the American Schools of Oriental Research in the years 1928-34. The excavators dated the structure to the sixth century, and the remains of rooms and an alley below to the third and fourth centuries. They called this conglomeration of rooms the "Clergy House," based on a historical document describing the location of the bishop's house.

comprised of five or six dwellings sharing a central courtyard of irregular shape.[30] Most of the dwellings have a plan similar to a simple house, comprising only one or two rooms. (Hirschfeld suggests that the back room was used for sleeping and the front for daily living.) The apartment house was located between streets, with three shops along the main street forming part of the façade of the building.[31]

There are elements of the house at Gerasa that may be interpreted as protecting privacy, the most obvious of which are the entrances. Rather than opening directly onto the street, the front entrance of the house leads through a passage to the street on which the shops are located. This passage is a sort of "buffer zone" between the public area of the street and the semi-private (because of its use by more than one family) domestic space of the courtyard, as are the shops that line the street. Although there may be other reasons for constructing the entrances in this manner, such as restrictions of size due to already existing structures or streets, they nevertheless serve the purpose of providing an intermediary between public and private domains.

Because the house at Gerasa is described as an apartment house, we must look at the ways in which a family might preserve its privacy and the protection of its women while sharing a courtyard with several other families. Although from both archaeological and ethnographic evidence we know that courtyards were used for a variety of domestic activities such as laundry, food preparation, dining and entertaining guests, it may be that the front room of the house acted as a sort of extension of the courtyard.[32] As such it would provide a place for some of these domestic activities so that the women of one household would not risk being under constant observation by the men of another. On the other hand, there is the possibility that of the two rooms of each house, the one towards the back was reserved for the use of women and the front by men, at least on the occasion of entertaining visitors. We would not expect the ideal of women's seclusion to be practiced in poor households, or to be visible architecturally, but there may have been some attempt to accommodate it.[33] It is impossible, of course, to make

---

These rooms are located between buildings they identified as the Church of St. Theodore and the Baths of Placcus.

[30]The courtyard's irregularity is because of its opportunistic use of pre-existing (Roman) walls.

[31](Hirschfeld 1995): 49-50

[32]Ibid.: 139.

[33]See Ahmed, L. 1992 *Women and Gender in Islam: Historical Roots of a Modern Debate.* Yale Univeristy Press, New Haven & London: 60-62, 79-80 and 117 for discussion of the ideal of women's seclusion beginning under the Rashidun caliphs. She points out that it is likely only the houses of the middle classes and

much of this analysis given no contextual information on this structure. If the information on artifact positioning within each house were available, we could attempt to confirm this hypothesis, although even then it would be difficult to confirm a strict gender-based division.

We may attempt one more analysis of the house at Gerasa in regards to Muslim domestic architecture. Insoll reminds us that a house may reveal something about familial structure. Keeping in mind historical and ethnographic data that the ideal Muslim family is extended, patrilineal and patrilocal, we can look for ways in which the archaeological evidence might support this ideal. This might be shown in the unfinished quality of a building, which is ready to be built on as the family expands.[34] This is not the case in the Gerasa house, in which each two-room dwelling unit is complete. It may be, however, that although this building is described as an apartment house, it was meant to hold several related families, or a very large extended family. On the other hand, from ethnographic evidence we can guess that even small one-room houses may hold sixteen members of an extended family.[35] Although we do not know the personal space requirements of seventh-century inhabitants of Palestine, we can at least suggest the possibility that each of the units at Gerasa housed an extended family. Again, however, we face the possibility that other religious groups living in the same region would have similar ideal family domestic situations.

It is obvious that given only a ground plan and description, it is impossible to identify the building at Gerasa as Muslim, or even as a house. We require the contextual data from inside and outside the house, which may not help us to positively identify the religion of its occupants in any case. For example, if the occupants were observing the *halal* dietary requirements, one would expect not to find pig bones in the associated refuse.[36] On the other hand, Muslims were not the only ancient Near Eastern religious group that followed dietary restrictions forbidding pork, so the identification cannot be positive. Wine is also *haram* (forbidden) for Muslims, and so we might suggest we would expect to find no wine jars in an observant household.[37] However, Donald Whitcomb has noticed that some of the modern Muslim inhabitants of Hadir, a small town in Syria, reuse discarded wine bottles

---

wealthier people will show any architectural evidence of female seclusion. She has no archaeological examples, of course, but relies on the historical and anecdotal works of S. D. Goitein and Edward Lane.

[34](Insoll 1999): 78.

[35](Hirschfeld 1995): 135.

[36](Insoll 1999): 95-107.

[37]Ibid.: 99.

after washing them seven times.[38] We should not put such ingenuity past ancient and medieval Muslims, who may also have found ways to reuse ceramic wine jars and thus thwart the modern archaeologist's attempt at identifying them as Muslims. Perhaps the most difficult hindrance to archaeological interpretation of houses is the reuse of previously existing buildings. Buildings begin as shops, become houses, and revert to shops, or vice-versa. In their lives as houses they may be used successively by people of different religious confessions. Although buildings are often adapted quite well to new uses, we have seen that there is no architectural feature of a house that would help us to identify it as used by Muslims. Without clear indications such as inscriptions, documents or identifiable religious artwork, identification of any domestic remains as Muslim is impossible.[39]

It is apparent that Insoll's desire to identify Muslim people in the archaeological record will often be impossible for the archaeologist. If we cannot positively identify Muslims in the record, how then can archaeology illuminate Islam? The most obvious answer is to use evidence from specifically religious contexts, or to make observations with a religious artifact in mind. Perhaps the most important artifact is the mosque. Because it is the topic of another paper in this volume, here I will only suggest some questions that would be interesting to explore.

Beginning with the building itself, one first asks how a mosque is identified. One might ask questions about the general plan of many mosques (hypostyle), the existence of something to indicate direction of prayer, such as niche (*mihrab*), whether there are provisions made for people to sit or stand, the location of the entrances, whether they are built on raised or level ground, the existence of water installations inside or nearby, and the existence of architectural decorations and if so the nature of those decorations. One could note the relationships between the structures and elements of mosques and those of synagogues and churches. There are several similarities, including the use of a basilical plan and a specific orientation. One might also note the great diversity of mosque structures, from a simple line of stones in the sand to an

---

[38]Donald Whitcomb, personal communication June 1999.

[39]Whereas there is known iconography for Christianity and Judaism that is sometimes found on houses and religious buildings, there is no such evidence (that I am aware of) for early Islam. It may yet be found, however. Juan Campo has done some very interesting work on modern houses in Egypt, Libya, Syria and Israel-Palestine that have depictions of the *Hajj* pilgrimage painted on their façades. (This is done on the occasion of one of the occupants of the house making the *hajj*.) Historical sources indicate this may have been done at least as early as the 8th/14th century in Cairo and certainly by the 16th century A.D. in Cairo. (Campo 1991): 139-181.

imposing monument such as the great mosque of Samarra. Moving beyond the building, we note where it stands in relation to other buildings in a town, such as the governor's residence and markets. We ask whether there was a limit on the number of mosques that could be built in a town, or if they were simply built to accommodate the population. We would notice that mosques are both free standing, and sometimes a part of other structures. Inside towns, especially in the later periods, we notice their inclusions in complexes that might comprise a hospital, a *madrasa* and a mausoleum for the founder of the complex. Outside of towns, we observe the mosque's inclusion in caravanserais and country estates. All of these observations or questions about mosques will lead one to conclusions about Islam, beyond how it was practiced to how the practice ties into Islam's conception of itself.

There are other ways to try to understand Islam apart from mosques, however. Inge Demant Mortensen's study of the tombstones of a group of nomads in Luristan is illustrative of an interdisciplinary approach to Islamic history, combining archaeology and ethnography. The end result is not only an interpretation of tombstone art, but also the illustration of the religious beliefs of the ancestors of a group of people who are losing their cohesion and identity in modern Luristan. Her conclusions are a stepping-stone for us to inquire about one aspect of Islam.

Mortensen studied the tombstones of the Lur, a mostly illiterate nomadic group living in the westernmost part of Iran. The graveyards, located along the Lur's migratory route, were dated roughly from the late 18th century to the mid-20th century. The tombstones usually included pictorial information as well as epigraphic. These were scenes or objects of both secular and religious use, divided along gender lines. Most of the depictions were of objects such as combs or prayer beads that look the same as those used by the modern Lur. Some of the images were not so easily interpreted, however. Although Mortensen interviewed many people she concluded that forcible settlement of the Lur in the 1920s and '30s had resulted not only in the partial cessation of their migration but had caused a social and economic breakdown such that the modern people were unable to interpret the images on the tombs of their ancestors.[40]

One image on men's tombs was particularly puzzling. It depicted a riderless horse, tethered at the head and hind leg, with weapons (presumably of the deceased) strapped to its saddle. Three women stood nearby with their arms on each other's shoulders. This scene may be interpreted as a reference to an ancient custom found in Roman times

[40](Mortensen 1991): 81.

and before, of either burying a warrior's horse with him, or tethering it to his gravesite for use in the afterlife. Mortensen developed an alternative hypothesis tying into the religion of the region, using ethnographic evidence.[41]

Mortensen discovered that the modern nomads are known to occasionally put on elaborate shows of the *Muharram* procession, part of the shi'ite passion play called the *Ta'ziyeh* that depicts the martyrdom of the Prophet's grandson Hussein at Kerbala in 680. Performance of this play probably originated in the 10th century in Baghdad, but is still common in shi'ite populations, as participation in the event is believed to secure Hussein's intercession for the individual on Judgement Day. The funeral procession includes Hussein's riderless and bloodstained horse, followed by mourners and flagellants. Mortensen suggests that the tombstones are depicting this religious event, either to focus the observer's attention on the afterlife or to indicate the deceased's piety.[42]

What does the physical evidence on its own and as interpreted by Mortensen tell us about Islam? While any single case will be too specific to offer insight into Islam in general, we may find out something about the Islam that the Lur practice. If we accept the interpretations of some of the depicted objects as prayer beads, prayer stones and ewers for ritual ablution, we notice that these are devout people, or at least people who want to be depicted as devout after their death.[43] Because of the existence of tombstones, with both words and pictures on them for the literate and the illiterate, we might postulate a custom of visiting gravesites. This is especially interesting in the light of religious literature on the subject of treatment of the dead. Although the Qur'an is virtually silent on this subject, there is a verse that has been used as an injunction against mourning the dead as the unbelievers do.[44] There are also numerous *ahadith* that explicitly forbid against all manner of mourning practices, and that dictate expedient and simple burial: Without ceremony the body was to be wrapped in three plain white pieces of Egyptian cloth, buried quickly, and the site left level with the ground and unmarked.[45] In fact, gravestones and mausolea are the norm in Islam despite the orthodox position on burial, and probably have been

---

[41]Ibid. In.: 84.
[42]Ibid. In.: 85-86.
[43]Ibid. In.: 80.
[44]See Qur'an 60:13, "O ye who believe! Turn not (for friendship) to people on whom is the Wrath of Allah. Of the Hereafter they are already in despair, just as the Unbelievers are in despair about those (buried) in graves."
[45](Hillenbrand 1994): 253.

since at least the eighth century.[46] Thus we have illustrated here the distinction between the Islamic orthodoxy of the learned, and the practice of ordinary people. Yet the erection of gravestones is not defiance of religion, but an expression of it. The commonness of mausolea (including those built by Muslim rulers) and tombstones throughout the centuries indicates that remembrance of the dead is part of Islam whether it was considered orthodox or not. In marking the graves of their loved ones believers expressed their hope in the afterlife, and maintained a connection with their dead in anticipation of the resurrection of all believers on the Last Day.

The issue of aversion to images of living beings can also be discussed in connection with the Lur tombstones, especially those containing the scene that Mortensen has interpreted as the *Muharram* procession. Despite Islam's old reputation among scholars as a religion that forbids making images of living beings, the example of the Lur gravestones can be added to numerous examples of objects and architecture from all periods, including objects commissioned by the various dynasties of Islam, that include images of human beings and animals. In fact the Qur'an says only that it is forbidden to make idols.[47] This discussion was taken a bit farther in religious literature in the twelfth and thirteenth centuries, but only became significant in the twentieth century.[48] The ordinary practice, again, defines the Islam of this period.

The Lur tombstones illustrate the importance of using archaeology in conjunction with religious texts to define the religion of Islam. Without the material evidence, we might believe that no Muslim erected tombstones or performed any rite to remember the dead, since it is so explicitly forbidden in religious literature. Without the twentieth century religious debate regarding depiction of images, we might never be aware the images on the tombstones dated from the eighteenth to the mid-twentieth centuries might have been seen as somewhat controversial to Islamic scholars.

We should also reiterate the point that without the existence of other evidence both for tombstones and depictions of living beings, we would not be able to say anything about greater 'Islam'. Archaeologists should not be too quick to make pronouncements about 'Islam' from the evidence of one site, rather should be content to illuminate the local religious practices. The gradual accumulation of contextualized pieces of

---

[46]It is recorded that the Abbasids desecrated the graves of the Umayyads. If this is true, the tombs must have been marked. Ibid.: 254. See Robert Hillenbrand's discussion of mausolea and funeral stele and their role in Islam in Ibid.: 253-268.
[47]See Qur'an 5:90 and 6:145.
[48](Grabar 1977): 145. Also read (Crone 1980).

evidence will help us understand Islam in each area and time period, not extrapolation from a few sites to the entire Muslim world. Islam, as all other religions studied by archaeologists and scholars of religion, was and is too dynamic to be defined in this way.

The archaeology of Islam seeks to illuminate all aspects of Islamic civilizations and Islamic societies, from the seventh century through the recent past. Its aims are the recovery and preservation of history, which can be used to understand the development of Islam as a religion. Yet without clear graphic or epigraphic information, the religious affiliation of those who left the remains we excavate cannot often be determined. This seeming absence of evidence may indicate, however, the many similarities of material life between Muslims, Christians, Jews and others.[49] Clearly religious information (such as that having to do with mosques or *madrasas*, for example) also can be used by archaeologists or religious studies scholars to piece together the history of the practice of the religion of Islam, in its various manifestations. This aspect is especially useful given the paucity of historical and religious written material from the first few centuries of Islam. In the later periods, there is a wealth of historical and literary information giving clues as to the nature and practice of Islam, but this can be augmented by the material record. For example, the proliferation of *madrasas*, structures built for the purpose of Islamic education, after the mid-eleventh century gives us a clue to the missionary nature of Islam, especially in its *shi'ite* form.[50] Also, the foundation of mosques by people other than the ruler indicates that under most medieval Muslim regimes Islam was not a state religion in the sense of being totally state-funded or mandated. Documentary and physical evidence of substantial Christian and Jewish communities living under Muslim rule, along with legislated protection of *dhimmis* and the special status of the *Ahl al-Kitab* in the Qur'an all point to Islam's sense of genealogy regarding the history of religions, and its acknowledgement of kinship to Christianity and Judaism. No doubt there are many other issues and aspects of religion that will benefit from careful excavation and publication of Islamic remains, and the cooperation of archaeologists, historians, and religious studies scholars.

---

[49]This is supported by documentary information of the Egyptian Jewish community from the Cairo Geniza for the ninth through thirteenth centuries. See Goitein, S. D. 1960; 1967-1993a; 1967-1993b; 1971; 1978a; 1978b; 1983

[50](See Hillenbrand 1994): 173-251 for an introduction to *madrasas*.

## Bibliography

Ahmed, L.

1992 *Women and Gender in Islam: Historical Roots of a Modern Debate.* Yale Univeristy Press, New Haven & London.

Asad, T.

1986 The Idea of an Anthropology of Islam. *Occasional Papers Series. Center for Contemporary Arab Studies Georgetown University*:22.

—

1993 *Genealogies of Religion: Discipline and Reasons of Power in Christianity and Islam.* Johns Hopkins University Press, Baltimore.

Bloom, J. M. and S. Blair

1997 *Islamic Arts.* Art & Ideas. Phaidon Press, Ltd., London.

Campo, J. E.

1991 *The Other Sides of Paradise: Explorations into the Religious Meanings of Domestic Space in Islam.* University of South Carolina Press, Columbia, SC.

Goitein, S. D.

1960 Minority Selfrule and Government Control in Islam. *Studia Islamica* 9:101-116.

—

1967-1993a *The Community.* A Mediterranean Society: The Jewish Communities of the Arab World as Portrayed in the Documents of the Cairo Geniza 2. 5 vols. University of California Press, Berkely.

—

1967-1993b *Economic Foundations.* A Mediterranean Society: The Jewish Communities of the Arab World as Portrayed in the Documents of the Cairo Geniza 1. 5 vols. University of California Press, Berkely.

—

1971 *The Community*. A Mediterranean Society: The Jewish Communities of the Arab World as Portrayed in the Documents of the Cairo Geniza 2. 5 vols. University of California Press, Berkely.

—

1978a *The Family*. A Mediterranean Society: The Jewish Communities of the Arab World as Portrayed in the Documents of the Cairo Geniza 3. 5 vols. University of California Press, Berkely.

—

1978b Urban Housing in Fatimid and Ayyubid Times (As Illustrated by the Cairo Geniza Documents). *Studia Islamica* 47:5-23.

—

1983 *Daily Life*. A Mediterranean Society: The Jewish Communities of the Arab World as Portrayed in the Documents of the Cairo Geniza 4. 5 vols. University of California Press, Berkely.

Grabar, O.

1977 Islam and Iconoclasm. In *Iconoclasm*, edited by A. Bryer and J. Herrin, pp. 45-52. University of Birmingham, Birmingham.

Hillenbrand, R.

1994 *Islamic Architecture. Form, function and meaning.* 1 vols. Edinburgh University Press, Edinburgh.

Hirschfeld, Y.

1995 *The Palestinian dwelling in the Roman-Byzantine period*, Jerusalem.

Hodgson, M. G. S.

1974 *The Classical Age of Islam*. The Venture of Islam: Conscience and History in a World Civilization 1. 3 vols. University of Chicago Press, Chicago
London.

Hourani, A.

1976 History. In *The Study of the Middle East: Research and Scholarship in the Humanities and Social Sciences*, edited by L. Binder, pp. 97-136. John Wiley & Sons, New York.

Insoll, T.
1999 *The Archaeology of Islam*. First ed. Social Archaeology. 1 vols. Blackwell Publishers, Oxford
Malden, Massachusetts.

Irwin, R.
1997 *Islamic Art in Context: Art, Architecture, and the Literary World*. Perspectives. Calmann & King, Ltd., New York.

Kraeling, C. H. (editor)
1938 *Gerasa: City of the Decapolis*. American Schools of Oriental Research, New Haven, Connecticut.

Mortensen, I. D.
1991 From Ritual Action to Symbolic Communication. In *Sacred and Profane: Proceedings of a Conference on Archaeology, Ritual and Religion. Oxford, 1989*, edited by P. Garwood, D. Jennings, R. Skeates and J. Toms, pp. 80-87. vol. 32. Oxford University Committee for Archaeology, Oxford.

Northedge, A.
1999 Archaeology and Islam. In *Companion Encyclopedia of Archaeology*, edited by G. Barker, pp. 1077-1107. vol. 2, London.

Rahman, F.
1966, 1979 *Islam*. Second ed. University of Chicago Press, Chicago and London.

Saradi, H.
1997 Byzantine Empire. In *The Oxford Encyclopedia of Archaeology in the Near East*, edited by E. M. Meyers, pp. 394-398. The Oxford Encyclopedia of Archaeology in the Near East. vol. 1, E. M. Meyers, general editor. 5 vols. Oxford University Press, Oxford.

Waines, D.
1995 *An Introduction to Islam*. Cambridge University Press, Cambridge.

# ASIAN RELIGIONS/HINDUISM

# 10

# Lighting Lamps of Ghee: Inscriptions and the Reconstruction of Medieval Hinduism

Richard H. Davis
*Bard College*

When I was living in Thanjavur to do research on medieval Hindu ritual texts for my dissertation, my landlord coaxed me out of my medieval world one day to attend a Hindu wedding. South Indian middle-class weddings are wonderful, festive, colorful affairs. Families rent out large wedding halls and deck them with paper streamers and multicolored flashing lights. Women wear their brightest silk sarees. Children run riot, snatching food on the run. Insistent film music blares over loudspeakers. And the food is rich, delicious, and abundant.

At the wedding I found my own attention drawn to the brahmin priests seated on a small raised dais. Throughout the tumult of Thanjavur society "meeting and greeting" (as the Indian- English phrase has it), the brahmins tended their fires, ladled out ghee onto them, and unperturbedly recited mantras. Then at one moment, they became the center of all attention when the bride and groom entered the pavilion and were led around the fire–the ritual moment at which the couple become wife and husband. Everyone turned towards the platform, and cameras flashed. Then the crowd drifted off into more meetings and greetings, and on soon to the feast. Meanwhile the brahmins continued their ministrations around the fire.

My landlord, a local civil servant, afterwards pronounced the wedding a great success. I first imagined he meant by this that the brahmins had successfully united a couple in marriage with no egregious ritual errors. But this was not at all how he judged the ceremony. It was a success, he indicated, because of the number of people attending, including several prominent local landholders and politicians, and the quantity of rich food served. For him, the really important ghee was not the ghee brahmins poured as oblations onto the sacred fire, but the ghee cooks poured onto the suitably rich rice.

In evaluating an event, all depends on the eyes through which we see it, the voices to which we attend. If I had spoken with the brahmins about the wedding, they might well have judged it a success because they had correctly recited the Vedic texts on which they based their performance. They would have pointed me to the continuity of a text-based ritual tradition that goes back more than three thousand years, or in their view perhaps to the beginning of the cosmos. For my landlord, on the other hand, the wedding had to do with social relations and status in the present, with wealth and with public generosity, with constituting and recreating a community and articulating claims about status within that social sphere.

In reconstructing a historical event or period or religious tradition, likewise, much depends on the voices to which we choose to listen. Sometimes these choices are governed by present concerns, as my attention at the wedding was drawn by the brahmin ritualists due to my then-current research in ritual texts. For the historian, it is also a matter of what voices from the past have left, or been able to leave, records of themselves. The capacity to record and transmit ideas and facts in permanent form, in most times and places, has been a privilege restricted to those with claims to intellectual, political, or economic authority.

In this essay I wish to pose the question of voice in the historical construction of medieval Hinduism. Scholars have based the historical study of Hinduism overwhelmingly on religious texts–hymns, narratives of gods and their doings, epic poems of legendary heroes, devotional songs, ritual guidebooks, and the like–that convey the views and concerns of religious specialists, such as brahmin priests, renunciatory philosophers, and devotional poet-saints. While such voices have undoubtedly been crucial to the ongoing articulation of Hinduism as a way of thought and practice, religion is never the exclusive domain of specialists. What if we could attend also to medieval voices much like those of my practical, status-conscious Thanjavur landlord when writing the history of Hinduism? In fact, such voices were recorded extensively in medieval South India, in the form of myriad epigraphs inscribed on copper plates and the stone walls of temples. My aim in this paper is to consider, in a very preliminary manner, how the use of archeological inscriptions as historical sources might enable us to reconstruct the history of medieval Hinduism.

## Textual Hinduism and Other Possible Hinduisms

The historical study of Hinduism as a Western scholarly discipline–a branch of "Indology," the logos of India–grows directly out of the "discovery" of ancient Sanskrit texts by British and other European scholars in the late eighteenth century. ("Discovery" is placed in quotations here because this was a discovery only to Western scholars; Indian custodians of these textual traditions already knew the texts well and many collaborated actively with Western scholars from the start of the early Indological project.) The circle of Orientalists based in Calcutta, led by William Jones and patronized by the British Governor-General Warren Hastings, assiduously began the enterprise of collecting, translating, and disseminating these old texts of India. Jones publicized the idea that the Sanskrit language was directly related to Greek and Latin, and with the postulation of an "Indo-European" family of languages came an excited search for the beginnings of civilization itself. The new discoveries of the Orientalists provoked great intellectual excitement in Europe, like a second "Oriental Renaissance," in Raymond Schwab's evocative phrase.[1]

The subsequent history of this scholarly enterprise is too complex to relate here, but for my purposes in this essay several ramifications of this origin story are important. For British colonial officials of the eighteenth century and later, this recovery of Indian texts was not simply a matter of disinterested intellectual curiosity. They also sought to utilize these texts to acquire mastery over the newly-colonized Indian territories. For example, Jones and his cohorts set out to administer law in eighteenth century colonial Bengal on the basis of the oldest legal texts they could find, the *dharmasastras* composed in the early centuries C.E.[2] In so doing, they repeatedly privileged the ancient, as being aboriginal, formative, and therefore essential, over the modern, which they considered to be an inferior residue of that earlier legal formulation. Likewise they privileged knowledge gained from texts over that acquired from any other source, such as contemporary practice. For the Orientalists, India's old texts held the key to the true essence of Indian civilization, and the Indian reality they saw around them they judged a sad deterioration from ancient greatness.

---

[1]The Orientalists' story had been told often. For its positive effects in European intellectual life, Raymond Schwab's *The Oriental Renaissance: Europe's Rediscovery of India and the East, 1680-1880* (1984) provides a rich and far-reaching account.

[2]Edward Said's Orientalism (1978) remains the seminal critique of the integral connection between knowledge and power in the colonized East. Bernard Cohn's essays collected in *Colonialism and Its Forms of Knowledge* (1996) explore this relationship within the Indian colonial situation specifically.

From the corpus of key texts they privileged, Western scholars derived certain strong and persistent characterizations of Hinduism, characterizations that continue to reappear with discursive regularity in most modern textbook accounts of Hinduism. As Ronald Inden has argued, scholarship has recurrently figured Hinduism "as exemplifying a mentality which privileges the 'imagination' and the 'passions' rather than 'reason' and the 'will' (1990: 89)." In contrast to European systems of thought, Hinduism and India lack a "world-ordering rationality." This is reflected in the Hindu emphasis on, or obsession with, *moksa*, the attainment of personal liberation from worldly bondage. Rather than order their world, we are told, Hindus seek to escape it. Accordingly, the most authoritative philosophical viewpoint, following this perspective, is that of monistic Vedanta, grounded in the oldest Hindu texts, which advances an idealist or illusory pantheism.[3]

The early Orientalists of Calcutta were also aware of and interested in types of evidence about India's past other than texts, especially in archeological inscriptions. In the first volume of *Asiatick Researches* in 1788, the Sanskritist Charles Wilkins published several translations of inscriptions, and William Jones commented on Wilkins' contributions. Over the next several decades, other Orientalists like Henry Colebrooke made important disciplinary contributions to the beginnings of Indian epigraphy, while in another part of India Colin Mackenzie made the first systematic collection of inscriptions as primary source material for the study of the Indian past. He amassed over 8000 inscriptions in the course of his survey of southern India.[4] Later in the nineteenth century, the British established institutions that systematically collected epigraphical sources, most notably the Archaeological Survey of India, and publication series that disseminated epigraphical research, such as *Indian Antiquary* (from 1872), *Corpus Inscriptionum Indicarum* (1877), *Epigraphia Indica* (1888), and *South Indian Inscriptions* (1890).[5]

The results of this enterprise of recovery are enormous. By D.C. Sircar's estimate, as of 1977, some 90,000 inscriptions had been collected or copied, and thousands more have appeared in the two plus decades since Sircar made his estimate. They come from every part of India, and

---

[3]Ronald Inden provides a detailed critical overview of Hinduism as an object of Indological discourse, in *Imagining India,* chapter 3, "Hinduism: The Mind of India" (1990: 85-130).
[4]Richard Salomon, *Indian Epigraphy* (1998: 199-225), gives a succinct review of the history of Indian epigraphy, focusing especially on the early pioneers of the field.
[5]Cohn 1992. For a narrative history of early archeology in India, see Roy 1953.

range in time from the 3rd century B.C.E. up to the 19th century C.E.[6] These inscriptions may be brief records of donors' names, or lengthy detailed records inscribed on copper plates or the stone walls of temples. Overall, this immense corpus of archeological remains provides a tremendous source for reconstructing the history of Hinduism. Or at least it should do so.

The great majority of Indian inscriptions concern matters of religious practice. They record donations to Buddhist stupas, for instance, or royal land grants to maintain communities of brahmin priests. Thousands of inscriptions outline provisions made for Hindu temple worship. Yet, strangely, this great resource has never figured centrally in the historiography of Indian religions.[7] Somehow, inscriptions have become the specialized preserve first of all of the epigraphists themselves, then of dynastic historians like K. A. Nilakanta Sastri, and more recently of social historians such as Burton Stein.[8] Indeed, inscriptional evidence has been fundamental for reconstructing a more or less reliable "dates and dynasties" historical chronology for India. Sircar estimated that something like 80% of what we know of early Indian political history has come from inscriptional sources. Scholars have constructed the early history of Indian religions, by contrast, almost entirely on the basis of textual evidence.

The question I pose in this paper grows out of this scholarly imbalance. How would the history of Hinduism look if we based it more centrally on inscriptional sources? How would it change our depiction of Indian religious history to listen more attentively to the voices that speak to us not through texts but through words carved on copper and stone? Would a different Hinduism present itself to us?

Gregory Schopen has posed himself a similar question in the field of Indian Buddhist studies, and he answers that it differs substantially. In "Archeology and Protestant Presuppositions in the Study of Indian Buddhism," Schopen begins by observing that the modern scholarly study of Indian Buddhist history has been "decidedly peculiar," due to "a curious and unargued preference for a certain kind of source

---

[6]D. C. Sircar, *Early Indian Numismatics and Epigraphical Studies* (1977). Sircar was the most distinguished epigraphist of the post-Independence period in India. See also Sircar 1965 and Salomon 1998.

[7]Of course, some historians of Hinduism have used inscriptions extensively. Notable examples include D. C. Sircar himself (1971), David Lorenzen (1972), and V. S. Pathak (1960). Salomon gives a brief overview in *Indian Epigraphy* (1998: 238-241). Two recent studies of Cola inscriptions in relation to religion, each exemplary in a different way, are those of Leslie Orr (1999) and Daud Ali (2000).

[8]K. A. Nilakanta Sastri, The Colas (1955) and Burton Stein, *Peasant State and Society in Medieval South India* (1980).

material," namely literary texts.[9] He distinguishes two types of materials available for study: archeological material and literary material. Archeological sources, he comments, can be reasonably well located in time and space, and reflects what Buddhist monks and lay-followers actually practiced and believed. Literary texts, on the other hand, often cannot be dated, and record what a small, atypical part of the Buddhist community wanted that community to believe or practice. Yet here too, Buddhologists early on made a choice to privilege these literary sources, and have followed that preference ever since.

Working consciously against that grain, Schopen has focused on epigraphical sources in his historical work, and on that basis he suggests many areas in which the standard depiction of Indian Buddhist history needs to be substantially altered. For example, his work has called into question the coherence and dating of the Mahayana school, widely portrayed in the text-based literature as a new form of Buddhism arising in the early centuries C.E. He has also raised serious questions concerning the normative Buddhological distinction between monastic and lay practices. In practice, Schopen's inscription-based studies have shown, monks and laity are not always so different as the texts would lead us to believe.

Schopen bases his major revisions of Buddhist history on a long-term, detailed, comprehensive study of early Indian Buddhist epigraphical sources. My aims in this essay are much more modest. Working with a few select inscriptions from the Cola period in southern India, I will outline some of the kinds of economic, social, and political information Cola inscriptions provide. Lurking behind this information, I believe, is a Hindu religious world that differs significantly from the Hinduism of our textbooks and scholarly summaries. This essay, then, is a preliminary inquiry into how the study of archeological inscriptions might broaden and alter our understanding of medieval Hinduism, to rematerialize Hinduism as a religious formation deeply engaged in its economic, social, and political world.

## The Economics of Temple Lamp Lighting

I base this inquiry around one of the simplest and most common practices recorded in inscriptions of the Cola period–the act of lighting a ghee-lamp. And I will focus primarily on a few inscriptions from one ancient town, Melpadi, situated in northern Tamilnad.

---

[9]Schopen 1991: 1. This is Schopen's broadest critique of Buddhology and his clearest statement of method. This essay and eleven others are conveniently collected in Schopen 1997.

On the north wall of the now-abandoned Colesvara temple to the god Siva, in Melpadi, the following epigraph is engraved in beautiful florid Tamil characters:

> Hail! Prosperity! In the 29th year of the glorious king Rajaraja I..., I, the cultivator Aruva-Kilal Muttigandan of Maruda-nadu in Venkunra-kottam, gave one perpetual lamp (*tiruananda-vilakku*) to the god Mahadeva [Siva] of the holy Arinjisvara [Colesvara] temple...and assigned to this lamp ninety-six full-grown ewes (*atu*), which must neither die nor grow old.
>
> Having received these ewes, I, the shepherd Eni Gangadharan of Rajasrayapuram [Melpadi], shall pour out daily, as long as the sun and moon shall endure, one *ulakku* of ghee, measured by the *Rajakesari*.[10]

The reigning king when this brief text was carved was Rajaraja I, who ruled from 985 to 1014 C.E., and since this inscription specifies the 29th regnal year, it was composed in 1014, his final year of rule. The two portions I have elided refer to King Rajaraja, and I will return to these later in this paper.

In 1014, then, a local cultivator presented to the Siva temple in Melpadi a lampstand, and also a donation of goats to ensure the temple would receive a regular supply of ghee sufficient to keep the lamp flame burning "perpetually." Throughout southern India, devotees light such ghee-lamps to please the deity, whom they consider to be physically present and embodied in the icon or image at the center of the temple. Hindu deities evidently enjoy the light. And, not incidentally, in those days before electricity was employed to light Hindu shrines, the multiplicity of perpetually burning ghee lamps provided the illumination by which human priests ministered to the deities inside the dark, windowless inner sanctums of temples.

As common and important as it is, the act of lamp-lighting is not the sort of topic one finds in histories of Hinduism. The practice seems too simple, too elementary, too quotidian. Lighting a temple lamp is a basic and perhaps unchanging activity that appears to subsist beneath the range of historigraphical radar, outside the major ritual and ideological shifts that occupy those who trace Hinduism as a changing historical religious formation.[11] Yet in this practice, and in the myriad inscriptions

---

[10]The inscription was collected in 1889 by the Government Epigraphist, E. Hultzsch, and was published with translation in *South Indian Inscriptions* vol. 3, no. 17 (1899: 26-27). I use Hultzsch's translation here, with elisions I will discuss later in this paper. For further information on the temple, see Balasubrahmanyam 1971: 213-217.

[11]One notable exception to this is C. J. Fuller (1992), in his overview of ethnographic studies of modern Hinduism. Fuller treats the act of lighting camphor, which give a brief intense flash of light, as a paradigmatic act of Hindu

that outline provisions to sustain the practice throughout the temples of southern India during the Cola period, one may begin to glimpse the fabric of economic, social, and political relations centered around these temples.

According to this inscription, it takes one *ulakku* (or about 12.5 cubic inches) of ghee to maintain a lamp burning continuously. Not surprisingly, this measure never varies from inscription to inscription, since the physics of oil-flames presumably remains constant. However, other Cola inscriptions do mention other categories of lamps that burned less than continuously and therefore required less ghee: day-lamps requiring one-half the amount of a perpetual lamp, night-lamps also needing one-half *ulakku*, and lamps intended for one worship- period a day (most often sunrise or sunset), which require one-tenth of an *ulakku*. We also learn of other types of lamps altogether, such as the "lamp-garland" (*tipamalai*), a lamp-stand allowing for multiple flames, providing a "garland" of illumination for the deity, and consequently needing a much larger regular supply of ghee (*SII* 23, no. 227).

The ghee for the lamps comes from the milk of female goats, and we learn from this inscription that a herd of 96 goats can produce this amount of ghee. This amount, too, is fairly constant. The number fluctuates from ninety to one-hundred, while in Rajaraja's time the rate seems fixed at ninety-six goats per perpetual lamp. Other milk-producing livestock besides goats, such as cows and she-buffaloes, could also supply ghee. These larger animals naturally produced greater amounts of milk, and so it took only 48 cows or 16 she-buffaloes to produce the necessary ghee for a lamp. As in our inscription, goats are by far the most common ghee- producers for Cola temple lamps, but in Brhadisvara, the great imperial temple Rajaraja built in his capital of Thanjavur, the king assigned a herd of 2832 cows, 1644 goats, and 30 she-buffalos to 366 cowherders, who were required to supply 60 *ulakkus* of ghee per day (*SII* 2, no. 63).

In the Melpadi inscription, the cultivator Aruva-Kilal Muttigandan presents the lamp and also assigns (*vaitta*) a herd of 96 goats directly to the Colesvara temple. However, we learn from other inscriptions that there were other methods of making donations for lamps as well. The donor might give gold or money to the temple, and the temple could then make direct cash purchase of goats. The inscriptions of Brhadisvara temple specify the purchase price as 3 goats for one *kasu*, and so a gift to the temple of 30 to 33 *kasus* would allow the temple to maintain one perpetual lamp.

---

devotional practice, one he considers so important that he names his book *The Camphor Flame*.

More often, though, temples of the Cola period appear to have followed more long-range economic strategies in handling donations, and these strategies involved the religious institutions in economic roles within their surrounding communities reaching far beyond the conduct of worship. Acting as banks, they might lend out money donated, for repayment in cash. To take one example among many, an inscription of the Siva Adhipurisvara temple of Tiruvorriyur, dated to 942, records that King Parantaka's eldest son Rajaditya deposited 60 *kalanju* of pure gold, weighed against the village stone, to furnish two perpetual lamps in the temple (*SII* 3, no. 105). The *kalanju*, a measure of weight used for gold and other precious metals, was equal to about 80 grains or 1/72 lb. Troy, so Rajaditya's gift was a bit less that 1 pound troy weight of gold. From this donation, residents of the village Vellivayil borrowed 30 *kalanju*, and agreed to pay interest on the loan at the annual rate of 15% or 4 1/2 *kalanju* per year, collected at two times each year. The villagers also hospitably agreed to provide two meals everyday to the persons who came to collect the interest. Failure to feed them would result in a fine.

Temples might also use donated money to purchase land, let it out to a cultivator, and collect rent in the form of ghee. For example, on the wall of Somanathesvara temple in Melpadi, an inscription of Rajaraja's time records:

> ...we, the assembly (*sabhaiyor*) of Tiruvallam...have received 15 *kalanju* of gold, weighed by the balance of charitable edicts, from Irayiravan Pallavarayan [a royal official]. For these 15 *kalanju* of gold, we assigned one thousand *kuli*, measured by the rod of Chidambaram, of land...to the god Mahadeva [Siva] of the Solendrasimha-Isvara [Somanathesvara] temple at Rajasrayapuram [Melpadi] in Tuynadu, for burning one perpetual lamp as long as the sun and the moon endure. These one thousand *kuli* of land we, the assembly, made over to Kandan Maravan...in order to supply to this perpetual lamp one *ulakku* of ghee daily.[12]

A prominent royal officer here makes a donation to the Somanathesvara temple, of gold sufficient to establish and maintain one perpetual lamp for the deity. But the members of the town assembly (the *sabha*) take the money, and in exchange assign land to the temple. The *kuli* is a measure of land that has varied historically from 144 square feet to 576 square

---

[12]*SII* 3 no. 19. The inscription is dated to Rajaraja's 14th regnal year, or 999 C.E. I have left out the opening royal eulogy, which I will discuss later in the paper, and detailed identifying information of the donor, the land, and the recipient of the land. The Somanathesvara temple of Melpadi, originally constructed in brick by Cola king Parantaka I, was rebuilt in stone probably during the reign of Rajaraja I. It is still in service, and is larger than the nearby Colesvara temple. For information, see Balasubrahmanyam 1971: 213-17.

feet. Acting on behalf of the temple, the assemblymen then let out the land to a local cultivator, Kandan Maravan, who is expected to remit the necessary amount of ghee to the temple each day.

Finally, temples might utilize cash donations to support reclamation of unused land, in effect acting as speculative developers of agricultural production. For instance, one inscription at the Siva Ghrtasthanesvara temple at Tillasthanam records how two wealthy persons gave 25 *kalanju* of gold each, to support two perpetual lamps (*SII* 3, no. 113). With this money, a certain amount of land "was cleared of its borders and mounds and converted into a wet field." The inscription goes on to specify the borders of the land. Receiving from the temple the ten *sey* of cultivated rice-producing land, the local assembly then agrees to burn the two lamps in the temple as long as the moon and the sun endure. The *sey* is a field measure used primarily for wet land, equal to 76,176 square feet, or roughly 1 3/4 acres, so the local assembly received 17 1/2 acres of rice land. Other arrangements that must have also been involved here, this inscription does not bother to specify. How was the gold used to clear the land? Did the assembly hire laborers? Who supplied the ghee? Did the village assembly use the rice from the new cultivated fields to purchase a herd of goats and to feed a goatherder. These more contingent specifications, evidently, were beyond the range of what was considered most important to record in stone.[13]

At the other end of these arrangements, goatherders like Eni Gangadharan and Kandan Maravan also became part of the network of temple supply. In receiving ninety-six goats from the Colesvara temple, Eni Gangadharan (and presumably his immediate family) assume responsibility for tending the goat herd, milking the goats, churning the milk, refining the butter into ghee, and supplying ghee to the temple daily at the specified rate. He agrees to maintain the herd at its present number; this is what the inscription means in speaking of full-grown ewes "which must neither die nor grow old." For his labors, the goatherd could no doubt retain any additional ghee over the assigned quantity, and likewise enjoy the surplus mutton if the herd were to grow. At the same time, goatherders place themselves in contractual relationship with the temple and its deity "as long as the sun and moon shall endure." There are fines for those who fail in supplying the ghee.

---

[13]In his early work on South Indian temples, the social historian Burton Stein focused on exactly these economic functions of temples. See "Economic Function of a Medieval South Indian Temple" (1960). Others have also discussed the multiple economic roles of temples in medieval South India, starting with Nilakanta Sastri 1932.

Moreover, it appears that this responsibility rested not with the individual goatherder, but with the local herder community. So in another Melpadi inscription dated a few years later, Eni Gangadharan is one of ten herders who act as surety when another of their group, Eran Sattan, receives his herd of ninety goats from the Colesvara temple.

> ...we, all the following shepherds of this village: Kalli Kulterna, Punnai Singan, Eni Gangadharan, Vanan Somadan, Tandan Anai, Nambi Sadevan, Ayidi Kadadi, Nambi Tinaiyan, Nambi Panri, and Vanan Puliyan, agreed to become security for Eran Sattan, a shepherd of this village, who had received ninety ewes of this temple, in order to supply ghee for burning one perpetual lamp.
>
> We shall cause the shepherd Eran Sattan to supply daily to one perpetual lamp one *ulakku* of ghee, measured by the Rajakesari.
>
> If he dies, absconds, or gets into prison, fetters or chains, we, all these aforesaid persons, are bound to supply ghee for burning the holy lamp as long as the moon and the sun shall endure.[14]

The collective responsibility the herders take here points to the dangerous possibility of individual default, and also to the strong social pressure that Eran Sattan must have felt from his own birth-group (*jati*) to comply with the agreement.

Such economic arrangements extended the relations of these temples outward, into the local community and often still further afield into regions beyond the immediate locale. A big temple might well enjoy the revenues from lands throughout Tamilnad. Even the simple act of lighting a perpetual lamp leads us to see a host of economic relationships between temple and society. Through active reinvestment of the wealth of gold, land, and other materials given to them, temples played significant economic roles within Cola society. By looking at these relations of exchange and their changes over time, religious historians could begin to reconstruct the economy of temple Hinduism.

## The Social Texture of Devotion

It would be a mistake, however, to view these arrangements simply as impersonal relations of a religious institution with the surrounding population. To understand the social texture of these relations, we need to look more closely at the persons involved in these transactions. For each gift of devotion, inscriptions specify a recipient, one or more donors, and others who also become involved in the transaction. Once again, the basic act of lighting a lamp provides an excellent point of departure.

---

[14]*SII* 3 no. 18, of the 9th regnal year of Rajendra I, or 1021 C.E.

Who receives the pious gifts intended to provide for perpetual lamps? The initial inscription from Melpadi answers clearly: the donor gives the lamp "to the god Mahadeva [Siva] of the holy Arinjisvara temple." In a medieval South Indian Saiva temple, Siva manifests himself physically in an icon, the Siva-linga, that serves as the primary focus of all worship within the temple.[15] His devotees consider Siva to be a transcendent divine Absolute, yet at the same time Siva takes on a specific, immanent, local form to become present within a particular temple. This is not understood as symbol or abstraction; the Siva-linga of the Arinjisvara temple is a living personality imbued with Siva's divine presence. And, in this local and personal form, Siva is the lord (*svamin*) of the temple, recipient of all gifts to the temple, and owner of all the property that thereby pertains to it.[16]

Scholars have often observed the close homology in medieval India between the king in his palace and the divine icon in its temple. It begins with terms that refer equally to both: the Tamil *koyil* signifies both royal palace and divine temple, and terms like *svamin* are used interchangeably for both human and divine lords. The homology extends to the parallel daily palace routines of earthly kings and temple liturgies of the iconic deities. And so too, temple deities like human rulers have "courts" of attendants, officials, servants, and hangers-on. Like any lord, Siva as lord of a temple does not deign to perform all his tasks directly. Other agents devote themselves to carrying out the lord's economic will. So we observe, looking more closely at the second Melpadi inscription quoted above, that the members of the village assembly take it upon themselves to transform a gift of gold into usable ghee, on behalf of the temple icon. It may be helpful to separate out the parts of the transaction that this inscription specifies:

(1) the royal official Irayiravan Pallavarayan gives 15 *kalanju* gold to the god Mahadeva, Siva of the Somanathesvara temple;

(2) the local assembly receives this gold from Mahadeva, and in return assigns 1000 *kuli* of land to Siva; and

---

[15]The theology of divine presence here has been widely discussed. For my own account, see *Lives of Indian Images,* chapter 1, (1997: 15-50), and the more detailed ritual account, based on Saiva Siddhanta ritual texts, in *Ritual in an Oscillating Universe: Worshiping Siva in Medieval India,* especially chapter 4 (1991: 112-136).

[16]The consequences and problematic of God's legal proprietorship is discussed at length in Hindu legal literature, the *dharmasastras.* Sontheimer 1964 provides an authoritative treatment. For a similar notion in Indian Buddhist institutions, see Schopen 1990. Finally, for a recent application of this medieval notion in a modern British court, see Davis, *Lives of Indian Images,* chapter 7 (1997: 222-259).

(3) the local assembly then leases the temple land to a cultivator, Kandan Maravan, who agrees to supply the ghee needed to burn one perpetual lamp.

Since temples in medieval South India came to control considerable resources in gold, money, land, and produce, roles of serving the god's interests in a temple could involve significant local power and prestige. The most common phrase for temple management is "to carry out the holy duties" (*srikarya-cey*). Such administrative roles were formulated, first of all, as devotional in nature. Indeed, in many Cola inscriptions, we find the primary managerial role occupied by a figure who is identified as "the primary servant (*adidasa*) of the highest Lord (*paramasvamin*)"–Candesvara. For example, an undated inscription on the Kailasanatha temple in Kanchipuram specifies:

> In the 3rd year of Ko-Rajakesarivarman, we, the villagers of Menalur...made the following written agreement. We have received from *Adidasa* Candesvara in the holy stone-temple at Kanchipuram eighteen *kalanjus*, three *manjadis* and one *kunri* of gold. From the interest of [this gold], we shall pour out daily, as long as the moon and the sun exist, for one perpetual lamp, one *ulakku* of ghee with an *ulakku* measure, which is equal to a quarter according to the standard of the authorities of this village. As the villagers...told me, I, Alappadi, the headman of the village, wrote this document. This is my signature (*SII* 1, no. 84).

Here Candesvara, not the village assembly, acts most directly on behalf of the lord of the temple, to insure that gold given to the temple is converted to ghee for a lamp. However, Candesvara differs from the assemblymen of Melpadi in one fundamental respect. Like Siva, Candesvara is an animated icon who has "graciously taken his seat" in the temple precincts.

In Cola times, Candesvara or Candan was remembered as a legendary devotee of Siva, whose hagiography Cekkilar related in the eleventh century epic poem *Periya Puranam*, a Tamil narrative of the lives of sixty-three Saiva devotional saints (*nayanmars*) who had lived mainly in the seventh and eighth centuries. Briefly, Cekkilar tells how a young cowherd boy of the brahmin class, Vicarasarman, used to take the village herd to the fields, and occupy his time there fashioning Siva-lingas in the sand and honoring them with ablutions of milk. The elders soon realized that the young cowherd was redirecting the cow milk meant for their Vedic rites to other purposes, and Vicarasarman's father went out to put a stop to the boy's misbehavior. But Vicarasarman refused to forego his honoring of Siva, and when his father tried physically to prevent him, Vicarasarman took his small axe and cut off his father's feet. At this moment of high excitement, Siva appeared and declared that henceforward Vicarasarman would be known as "leader" (*talaivan*) among his devotees (*tontar*). This is when he received the name Candesvara or Candan, the "hot-tempered one."[17]

Perhaps as a result of Siva's declaration, Candan also appears as a member of Siva's divine entourage in temples of the Cola period. He "graciously took his seat" in an icon, most often located in a separate small shrine immediately northeast of the main sanctum. As an enshrined divine person, Candan received his own tribute during the daily temple liturgy, and occasionally gifts would be presented directly to Candan's subordinate shrine.[18] In Cola period inscriptions, though, Candan appears most often as Siva's primary agent. He receives offerings made to the temple, lends out temple money, and witnesses agreements involving temple property. Presumably much of the business of the temple was transacted at the Candan shrine, where Candan himself stood as iconic agent of his lord Siva's economic interests.

Even with Candan serving as primary mediator, human agencies were also directly involved in the administration of temple affairs. In the inscriptions we have looked at so far, the main human administrators have been members of the local village or town assembly (*sabhaiyor*). Temples were, in one sense, local institutions, and local worthies and deliberative bodies often exercised considerable authority within them. Yet with a temple (or more precisely, Siva as proprietor of the temple) often the most substantial repository of wealth and the controller of most extensive land rights within a particular locality, the authority to manage temple resources could become hotly contested. Interests from outside the local region might, and often did, seek to insert themselves into positions of control. Such battles over temple property control, however, go beyond the scope of this paper.

Inscriptions specify donors, as well as the recipient, of gifts to temples. To give gold or property to Siva as embodied in a temple was a pious act of devotion, for which the donor received intangible merit or favor. However, we do not learn much about the motivations of donors, nor the rewards they hoped to receive, from inscriptions of the Cola period. By and large, Cola inscriptions present the act of giving as a

---

[17]T. N. Ramachandran, trans., *St. Sekkizhar's Periya Puranam* (1990).

[18]For a brief account of Canda-puja as a final part of the daily temple liturgy, see *Ritual in an Oscillating Universe*, pp. 156-57. Eric af Edholm investigates the relation of Canda the Tamil nayanmar and the temple figure, in "Canda and the Sacrificial Remains" (1984). For an example of a gift to the Canda shrine at the Brhadisvara temple in Thanjavur, see *SII* 2 no. 60.

simple, taken-for-granted action. At least we do learn the identities of the donors, and occasionally the circumstances of their gifts.

In our first inscription from Melpadi, the lamp donor identifies himself as a "cultivator" (*vellalan*) from the surrounding area of Marutanatu. In south Indian society of Cola times, the *vellalans* constituted a dominant class of peasant cultivators, enjoying a high social status in the agrarian society prevalent throughout Tamilnad. In the second Melpadi inscription, by contrast, the donor was designated by name only, Irayiravan Pallavarayan, known from other inscriptions to have been a prominent royal officer under Cola king Rajaraja I. Thus, from these two examples we see already that temples received donations both from local worthies and from members of the royal entourage based outside the area.

One could make a detailed study of temple donors, in terms of social statue, gender, proximity to the recipient temple, and other variables. A religious historian could investigate whether the patterns of temple donation change over time during the Cola period. For my purposes here, a few preliminary comments based on a small sample of inscriptions will have to suffice.

Not surprisingly, the greatest number of lamps were sponsored by Cola royalty and those close to the royal family. We learn of donations by Cola kings, the kings' wives and sisters, and high royal officials related to the Colas through marriage allinace. The king Rajaraja I makes the single most extensive provision for ghee lamps, as part of his foundation of Brhadisvara temple in the capital of Thanjavur. In a single inscription he records the donation of almost 3000 cows, 1600 goats, and water-buffalo as well. This is only appropriate, since the imperial temple was built on an altogether different scale than any other Cola period temple up to that point, like a cathedral compared to village churches, in the analogy of art historian Percy Brown (quoted in Nilakanta Sastri 1955: 710). Intended to serve as an overpowering symbol of royal accomplishment, as well as a grand palace for the lord Siva, it was necessary that provisions for this temple also outstrip all others.

Cola royalty, however, also engaged in providing for lamps in temples far away from the capital. Royal officeholders both major and minor frequently made lamp donations to temples throughout the Cola dominions. What were the intentions of these royal emissaries in endowing lamps so far afield?

## Lamps, Temples, and Political Integration

We have seen, through light shed by ghee lamps, some of the economic relationships established around temples, and the social networks built around donative acts. To fill in the political picture, I need to return to Melpadi and restore to the initial inscriptions a portion I previously omitted. Here is the text, with the restored portion in italics:

> Hail! Prosperity! In the 29th year of the glorious king Rajaraja I *who, in his life of growing strength, during which, in the belief that, as well as the goddess of fortune, the goddess of the great earth had become his wife,–he was pleased to destroy the ships at Kandalur-Salai and conquered by his army, which was victorious in great battles, Vengai-nadu, Ganga-padi, Nulumba-padi, Tadiga-padi, Kudumalai-nadu, Kollam, Kalingam, Ila-mandalam, the conquest of which made him famous in the eight directions, and the seven and a half lakshas of Iratta-padi,–deprived the Seliyas of their splendour at the very moment when Udagai, which is worshipped everywhere, was most resplendent*, I, the cultivator Aruva-Kilal Muttigandan of Maruda-nadu in Venkunra-kottam, gave one perpetual lamp to the god Mahadeva [Siva] of the holy Arinjisvara [Colesvara] temple . . . and assigned to this lamp ninety-six full-grown ewes, which must neither die nor grow old.
>
> Having received these ewes, I, the shepard Eni Gangadharan of Rajasrayapuram [Melpadi], shall pour out daily, as long as the sun and moon shall endure, one *ulakku* of ghee, measured by the *Rajakesari.*

Grammatically, the entire portion in italics is a lengthy relative clause modifying the glorious king Rajaraja I. The Melpadi inscription, then, contains two main elements: the provisions for the ghee-lamp sponsored by the cultivator Aruva-Kilal Muttigandan, and a lengthy account of the deeds of the reigning king, who is this case has nothing to do with the temple transaction.

The royal panegyric, known by the Sanskrit term as *prasasti,* is a common feature of donative inscriptions throughout Indian history. *Prasastis* typically trace the genealogy of the ruling house, in ornate Sanskrit verse, and praise the virtues and accomplishments of the reigning king and his predecessors. Such eulogies both reflected and sought to extend the *kirti,* or fame, of the royal person issuing the grant (Sircar 1965: 3). The Tamil term for such panegyrics, *meykkirtti* ("true-fame"), points directly to this concern for fame and reputation. The dynastic lineages that epigraphical *prasastis* contain have provided vital primary information for dynastic historians of India.

Rajaraja I, however, initiated a new kind of *prasasti* in many of his temple inscriptions, including this one, and subsequent Cola rulers followed and expanded upon his innovation. Rajaraja's Cola *prasastis* differ in three primary respects from most other medieval inscriptional panegyrics. First, he used the local vernacular language, Tamil, rather than the pan-Indian language of Sanskrit preferred by most rulers of the period. This no doubt reflects a desire to make this eulogy accessible to a broader local audience. Second, his Tamil *prasastis* focus only on the present ruler, with no mention of his Cola forebears. And third, he adopted a single, standardized *prasasti* text, repeated in all his temple inscriptions. Rajaraja began this practice early in his twenty-nine year regin, and added new accomplishments to his *prasasti* sequentially, so that the Melpadi inscription of his twenty-ninth regnal year contains the lengthiest list of his achievements. Rajaraja's cumulative listing of royal conquests, growing regnal year by year, has enabled dynastic historians of the Colas, most notably K. A. Nilakanta Sastri, to retrace his annual military campaigns quite precisely.[19] Our interest here, however, is not primarily with the military affairs of the Colas, except as they affect Hindu temples. The more basic question is, what is a poem detailing the king's conquests doing here, inserted into an inscriptional text that recounts a temple donation having nothing to do with the king or anyone close to him?

As we have seen, the medieval Indian ruler was considered to offer a homology with the Highest God as divine ruler. Yet a Hindu king did not portray himself solely as earthly counterpart to a heavenly divinity. Since the Hindu deities make themselves physically present on earth, in the form of iconic incarnations, the human ruler also enters into a direct devotional relationship with those divine persons. This dual relationship of homologous sovereignty and devotional subordination is spelled out clearly in two of the most common honorific names (*biruda*) adopted by the Cola king Rajaraja. Most commonly, "Rajaraja" refers to him as "king over other kings," just as the common epithet of Siva, "Devadeva," denotes his dominion over the other gods. But Rajaraja also adopted the name Sivapadasekhara, "he whose crown bows at the feet of Siva."

Rajaraja and his royal family certainly acted as Siva's most lavish hosts on earth. Rajaraja's supreme act of devotional largess undoubtedly was his building of the great imperial temple he called Rajarajesvara, more commonly known as Brhadisvara, the "big temple," in the capital of Thanjavur. Construction began in 1003 C.E., and when it was completed six years later it stood as the largest and wealthiest edifice in the subcontinent. In lengthy inscriptions covering the walls of the temple, Rajaraja had his extensive donations to the temple recorded in detail. In addition to material gifts of gold, silver, jewelry, and livestock, Rajaraja required that other villages and temples throughout the

[19]K. A. Nilakanta Sastri, *The Colas,* pp. 168-193 on Rajaraja I. Subsequent Cola rulers expanded upon Rajaraja's relatively austere listing of conquests, and developed fuller, more vivid narratives of their royal activities. For a short treatment of Cola *prasastis* as literary texts depicting the landscapes of war and peace, see Davis, "Cola meykkirttis as literary texts."

kingdom supply personnel to his temple. Some four hundred dancers were brought in, and forty-eight musicians came to accompany the regular recitation of Tamil devotional songs. One inscription mentions eight persons whose sole responsibility was to light the multitude of ghee lamps in the temple.[20] Rajaraja's temple had good claim to be, as he called it, the Daksinameru, or "World-Mountain of the South."

Other members of the royal family, especially the royal women, built and patronized still other temples. Most prolific was the queen Sembiyan Mahadevi, wife of Gandaraditya (r. 949- 957) and mother of Uttama Cola (r. 969-985). She constructed or reconstructed at least eleven temples in the regions around Thanjavur, as well as making donations to many others. Rajaraja's sister Kundavai, his sister Lokamahadevi, and still other women of the royal court also employed their royal wealth in acts of temple sponsorship (Venkataraman 1976). At the center of the Cola rule, then, the patronage of Saiva temples and participation in devotional activities at major religious centers must have served compelling royal interests.

Most historians writing about medieval Hinduism, myself included, have based characterizations of royal religious activity around major Hindu centers and prominent kings.[21] However, the view from a smaller, more peripheral temple might well differ. In the persuasive view of social historian Burton Stein, agrarian peasant communities of early medieval southern India enjoyed considerable autonomy. The Cola state was not a centralized, highly integrated polity, Stein argued, but rather a military elite of relatively limited instrumental power seeking to gain some measure of political integration through acts of "ritual sovereignty."[22] Stein's view suggests that material acts of Hindu devotion, from building a temple to providing for a ghee- lamp, may be seen as important means by which a ruler could extend his presence more broadly within the predominantly rural, agricultural society under his tenuous control.

The example of Melpadi and its two old temples seems to bear out Stein's hypothesis. But more than this, a closer look at the history of Melpadi suggests that it held a special political significance for the Cola rulers.

---

[20]See Nilakanta Sastri 1932 for an overview of the economic provisions for Brhadisvara.

[21]For example, Davis 1991: 4-9, where Rajaraja and Brhadisvara are used to introduce temple Hinduism, in a study of medieval temple ritual texts.

[22]Stein 1980 contains his most comprehensive statement of this position. Stein articulated his depiction of Cola society as a revision of the earlier "bureaucratic" description in K. A. Nilakanta Sastri 1955.

Melpadi is located in northern Tamilnad, almost 200 miles from the Cola center of power in the Kaveri River delta around Thanjavur. In medieval times it occupied an important strategic position, along a main trade route between Tamilnad and Karnataka. In the ninth and early tenth centuries the area was controlled primarily by the Banas, whose capital was at nearby Tiruvallam, and the surrounding regions came to be known as Perumbanapadi, "Big Bana Country." By the middle of the tenth century, however, the Colas under Parantaka I (r. 907-955) expanded their kingdom at the expense of lesser powers like the Banas, and Melpadi evidently came under Cola control. Melpadi was given a new name, Viranarayanapuram, based on one of Parantaka's surnames. Parantaka also sponsored the Colendrasimhesvara temple, later renamed Somanathesvara, in Melpadi (Balasubrahmanyam 1971: 213-17). During Parantaka's reign, the Colas became the dominant power throughout the Tamil region. However, in 953 the Colas suffered a devastating military defeat at the hands of a still more potent ruling dynasty, the Rastrakutas of Manyakheta, who controlled virtually all of the Deccan.[23] The Banas got their revenge by allying with the Rastrakutas against their old Cola foes. After defeating the Cola armies at Takkolam, not far from Melpadi, the Rastrakuta forces moved southward into Tamilnad, and used Melpadi as one of their camps. So the Rastrakuta king Krishna III announces in one of his inscriptions:

> Be it known to you that, while my glorious and victorious army is encamped at Melpadi for the purpose of creating livings out of the provinces in the southern region for my dependents, of taking up possession of the whole property of the lords of provinces, and of erecting temples of Kalapriya, Gandamartanda, Krishnesvara, etc....

And Krishna III goes on to grant a village to a Saiva ascetic.[24]

Following the defeat by the Rastrakutas and the Rastrakuta occupation of the northern Tamilnadu areas they had formerly conquered, the Colas went through several decades of curtailed power and conflict over dynastic succession. They sought sporadically to retake the northern regions they had lost, and by the time Rajaraja took the throne in 985, the Colas had probably controlled the Melpadi area once again. It was only with Rajaraja's extensive conquests in every direction–a veritable *digvijaya*, or "conquest of the quarters"–that the

---

[23]On the Rastrakutas as the dominant "imperial formation" of India during the eighth through tenth centuries, see Inden, *Imagining India*, ch. 6 (1990: 213-262).

[24]R. G. Bhandarkar, "Karhad Plates of Krishna III; Saka Samvat 880," *Epigraphia Indica* 4 (1896-97): 278-290, beginning line 56. These three temples of Kaveripakkam no longer exist, but two other temples in Tamilnad date from the Rastrakuta occupation. See Meister and Dhaky 1983: 219-221.

Colas were fully restored as a dominant South Indian power. Among Rajaraja's conquests were the areas around Melpadi and further north in the Andhra and Karnataka regions, identified in his *prasastis* as Vengai-nadu, Ganga-padi, Nulumba-padi, Tadiga-padi, and Kudumalai-nadu. Moreover, Rajaraja claimed to have taken the former territories of the Rastrakutas, the "seven and a half lakshas of Iratta-padi." This is something of an exaggeration, since the Rastrakutas had already been overthrown by another Karnataka-based dynasty, the Calukyas of Kalyani.

On account of its former Bana and Rastrakuta connections, Melpadi was singled out for special royal reappropriation by the Cola king. The town received a new name, Rajasrayapuram, incorporating one of Rajaraja's surnames. Two streets of the town likewise gained royal names, Mummadi-Cola High Street and Arumolideva High Street, based on still other common names of the king. Most importantly, Rajaraja sponsored the building of the Colesvara or Arinjigai-Isvara temple. At this point we need to restore one final portion to our initial inscription. Once again, the restored part is italicized.

> Hail! Prosperity! In the 29th year of the glorious king Rajaraja I, who, in his life of growing strength, during which, in the belief that, as well as the goddess of fortune, the goddess of the great earth had become his wife,–he was pleased to destroy the ships at Kandalur-Salai and conquered by his army, which was victorious in great battles, Vengai- nadu, Ganga-padi, Nulumba-padi, Tadiga-padi, Kudumalai-nadu, Kollam, Kalingam, Ila- mandalam, the conquest of which made him famous in the eight directions, and the seven and a half lakshas of Iratta-padi,–deprived the Seliyas of their splendour at the very moment when Udagai, which is worshipped everywhere, was most resplendent, I, the cultivator Aruva-Kilal Muttigandan of Maruda-nadu in Venkunra-kottam, gave one perpetual lamp to the god Mahadeva [Siva] of the holy Arinjisvara [Colesvara] temple–*which the lord Sri Rajarajadeva had been pleased to build as a resting-place* (pallipadai) *for the king who fell asleep at Arrur, in Melpadi, alias Rajasrayapuram, a city in Tunadu, a subdivision of Perumbanapadi, in Jayankonda-Cola mandalam*--and assigned to this lamp ninety-six full-grown ewes, which must neither die nor grow old.
>
> Having received these ewes, I, the shepard Eni Gangadharan of Rajasrayapuram [Melpadi], shall pour out daily, as long as the sun and moon shall endure, one *ulakku* of ghee, measured by the *Rajakesari.*[25]

[25]The same phrase for the temple is also employed in *SII* 3, nos. 15 and 16. Balasubrahmanyam (1971: 214) observes that *pallipadai* denotes a memorial sepulchral temple.

The "king who fell asleep at Arrur" was Rajaraja's own grandfather, Arinjaya (r. 956-967), who enjoyed a brief period of kingship during the troubled period after the Rastrakuta victory and evidently died in the Melpadi area during Cola efforts to recover the region from Rastrakuta occupation. In addition to this memorial temple for his grandfather, Rajaraja also rebuilt in stone the Colendrasimhesvara (later Somananthesvara) temple, formerly constructed in brick by his great grandfather Parantaka.

In effect Rajaraja did three things at Melpadi. He symbolically reappropriated the town from earlier rulers by renaming it. He commemorated his grandfather, who had died trying to accomplish the territorial recovery that Rajaraja would complete. And he enacted his devotion to Siva through establishment of a new temple. These acts of "ritual sovereignty" demonstrate how a Hindu ruler might combine the dual roles of king-of-kings and royal devotee. Rajaraja decisively integrated Melpadi, associated with past Bana and Rastrakuta rulers, into Cola dominion, while the new temples he established for Siva created a new devotional center for the town, where both local cultivators like Aruva-Kilal Muttigandan and royal officials like Irayiravan Pallavrayan could light lamps for the deity.

## Conclusion

Historians of Indian religions, following Indian traditional accounts, depict early medieval South India as the birthplace of devotionalism, or the "bhakti movement." During this period, poet-saints known as *nayanmars* devoted to the god Siva wandered throughout the Tamil region, from shrine to shrine, singing the praises of the god they encountered in each place. Their songs conveyed the direct emotional engagement with Siva they passionately sought and, sometimes, achieved. Their songs were repeated and compiled, according to tradition, at the behest of the Cola ruler Rajaraja. During the Cola period the singing of *nayanmar* poetry was incorporated into temple liturgy as a regular part of worship (Peterson 1990).

Cola inscriptions are certainly not devotional texts, in the way *nayanmar* poetry is. They avoid any description of emotion towards the deity. There is no discussion of motivation, nor of the merits to be gained through acts of devotion. By and large they record matter-of-fact transactions, a great majority of which center around Hindu temples. They may be wonderfully detailed in their tracing of land boundaries or in listing the many parties involved in economic transactions, but they remain frustratingly oblique when it comes to a description of the mentalities involved in these transactions.

In this paper I have looked at a very small sample of the enormous corpus of Cola inscriptions, drawn primarily from one town. I have focused on one of the most elementary of all ritual acts, the lighting of a ghee lamp. Yet even this restricted sample, I believe, illuminates another side of the devotional world than that of the poetry of the Saiva saints. Through inscriptions we can begin to reconstruct the economic exchanges that established and maintained regular services of worship at Saiva temples like those at Melpadi. We can glimpse the social structure of the Cola period, and the varying ways people of differing social status became involved in the devotional network whose center was the temple. And we can begin to see royal participation in the Saiva temple cult, as both a conspicuous display of devotion and a strategy of political integration. South Indian inscriptions have long remained the preserve of archeologists and dynastic and social historians, but they need not remain so. Those of us who wish to reconstruct the history of Hinduism need to listen seriously to the practical voices inscribed in the stone walls of the Hindu temples of Tamilnad.

## Bibliography

### Inscriptional Sources

*Epigraphia Indica*

Vol. 4. 1896-97. See Bhandarkar.

*South Indian Inscriptions*

Vol. 1. 1892. E. Hultzsch, ed. Madras: Government Press.

Vol. 2. 1891-1917. E. Hultzsch, V. Venkayya, and H. Krishna Sastri, eds. Madras: Government Press.

Vol. 3. 1899-1929. E. Hultzsch and H. Krishna Sastri, eds. Madras: Government Press.

Vol. 23. 1979. G. V. Srinivasa Rao, ed. Madras: Thomson and Company,

### Secondary sources

Ali, D. 2000. Royal Eulogy as World History: Rethinking Copper-Plate Inscriptions in Cola India. In *Querying the Medieval: The History of Practice in South Asia*, ed. R. Inden, 165-229. New York: Oxford University Press.

Balasubrahmanyam, S. R. 1971. *Early Chola Temples: Parantaka I to Rajaraja I, A. D. 907-985*. Bombay: Orient Longman.

Bhandarkar, R. G. 1896-97. Karhad Plates of Krishna III; Saka-Samvat 880. *Epigraphia Indica*, 4:278-90.

Cohn, B. S. 1992. The Transformation of Objects into Artifacts, Antiquities and Art in Nineteenth Century India. In *The Powers of Art: Patronage in Indian Culture*, ed. B. S. Miller, 301-29. Delhi: Oxford University Press.

———. 1996. *Colonialism and Its Forms of Knowledge*. Princeton: Princeton University Press.

Davis, R. H. 1985. Cola meykkirttis as literary texts. *Tamil Civilization*, 3(2-3):1-5.

———. 1991. *Ritual in an Oscillating Universe: Worshiping Siva in Medieval India*. Princeton: Princeton University Press.

———. 1997. *Lives of Indian Images*. Princeton: Princeton University Press.

Edholm, E. a. 1984. Canda and the Sacrificial Remains: A Contribution to Indian Gastrotheology. *Indologica Taurinensia,* 12:75-91.

Fuller, C. J. 1992. *The camphor flame: popular Hinduism and society in India.* Princeton: Princeton University Press.

Inden, R. 1990. *Imagining India.* Oxford: Basil Blackwell.

Lorenzen, D. N. 1972. *The Kapalikas and Kalamukhas: Two Lost Saivite Sects.* Australian National University Centre of Oriental Studies Oriental Monograph Series, vol. 12. New Delhi: Thomson Press (India) Limited.

Meister, M. W., and M. A. Dhaky. 1983. *Encyclopaedia of Indian Temple Architecture: South India, Lower Dravidadesa, 200 B.C.-A.D. 1324.* New Delhi: American Institute of Indian Studies.

NIlakanta Sastri, K. A. 1932. The Economy of a South Indian Temple in the Cola Period. In *Malaviya Commemoration Volume,* ed. A. B. Dhruva, 305-19.

———. 1955. *The Colas.* 2d ed. Madras: University of Madras.

Orr, L. C. 2000. *Donors, Devotees, and Daughters of God: Temple Women in Medieval Tamilnadu.* South Asia Research. New York: Oxford University Press.

Pathak, V. S. 1960. *History of Saiva cults in northern India from inscriptions (700 A.D. to 1200 A.D.).* Varanasi: Ram Naresh Varma.

Peterson, I. V., tr. 1989. *Poems to Siva: The Hymns of the Tamil Saints.* Princeton Library of Asian Translations. Princeton: Princeton University Press.

Ramachandran, T. N., tr. 1990. *St. Sekkizhar's Periya Puranam.* Thanjavur: Tamil University.

Roy, S. 1953. Indian Archaeology from Jones to Marshall (1784-1902). *Ancient India,* 9:4-28.

Said, E. W. 1978. *Orientalism.* New York: Pantheon Books.

Salomon, R. 1998. *Indian Epigraphy: A Guide to the Study of Inscriptions in Sanskrit, Prakrit, and the Other Indo-Aryan Languages.* South Asia Research. New York: Oxford University Press.

Schopen, G. 1990. The Buddha as Owner of Property and Permanent Resident in Medieval Indian Monasteries. *Journal of Indian Philosophy,* 18:181-217.

———. 1991. Archeology and Protestant Presuppositions in the Study of Indian Buddhism. *History of Religions*, 31(1):1-23.

———. 1997. *Bones, Stones, and Buddhist Monks: Collected Papers on the Archaeology, Epigraphy, and Texts of Monastic Buddhism in India.* Studies in the Buddhist Traditions. Honolulu: University of Hawaii Press.

Schwab, R. 1984. *The Oriental Renaissance: Europe's Rediscovery of India and the East, 1680-1880.* Trans. G. Patterson-Black and V. Reinking. New York: Columbia University Press.

Sircar, D. C. 1965. *Indian Epigraphy.* Delhi: Motilal Banarsidass.

———. 1971. *Studies in the Religious Life of Ancient and Medieval India.* Delhi: Motilal Banarsidass.

———. 1977. *Early Indian Numismatic and Epigraphical Studies.* Calcutta: Indian Museum.

Sontheimer, G.-D. 1964. Religious Endowments in India: The Juristic Personality of Hindu Deities. *Zeitschrift Für Vergleichende Rechtswissenschaft*, 67:45-100.

Stein, B. 1960. The Economic Function of a Medieval South Indian Temple. *Journal of Asian Studies*, 19(2):163-76.

———. 1980. *Peasant State and Society in Medieval South India.* Delhi: Oxford University Press.

Venkataraman, B. 1976. *Temple Art under the Chola Queens.* Faridabad: Thomson Press Limited.

# Response to Richard Davis' "Lighting Lamps of Ghee: Inscriptions and the Reconstruction of Medieval Hinduism"

Bob Easton-Waller
*Saint Leo University*

The purpose of Richard Davis' "Lighting Lamps of Ghee," as suggested in its subtitle, is to reconstruct medieval Hinduism through an analysis of inscriptions found in medieval Hindu temples. More specifically, Davis focuses on inscriptions that record and detail various economic transactions between Cola temples and their donors, borrowers, and subcontractors. His central claim is that these inscriptional sources lead to a different image of medieval Tamil Hinduism than the one that is usually derived from analyses of medieval Tamil religious texts. Davis' goal is to reconstruct medieval Tamil Hinduism by first deconstructing its textually-informed image then re-imaging it with inscriptional data taken into consideration.

His basic argument is as follows: Western scholars have constructed an image of Hinduism as irrational. This image was made possible by privileging scriptural sources over other types of sources. Many Hindu religious texts, such as the Upanishads, emphasize the concept of *moksha*, or liberation from the mundane world of birth, suffering, death, and rebirth. Others, such as the poems of the medieval Tamil Nayanmars, emphasize theistic devotion and espouse "an aesthetic of personal experience and feeling," to use the words of Indira Peterson.[1] Such

[1]Peterson, Indira Viswanathan, *Poems to Siva: The Hymns of the Tamil Saints* (Princeton, NJ: Princeton University Press, 1989), p. 31.

scriptural sources allowed the eighteenth-century Orientalists and subsequent western scholars to depict Hinduism as escapist, emotionalistic, and, ultimately, irrational. However, inscriptions taken from Cola temples reveal a side of medieval Hinduism that is devotional and rationalistic at the same time. While the Orientalists asserted that Hindus seek to escape the world rather than rationally order it, Cola inscriptions reveal a highly rationalized world order with complex web of economic relationships and an equally complex correlation of the social order with its king and court to the cosmic order with its god and temple.

Davis' basic enterprise is an important one. The efficacy of scriptures in reconstructing religions has been overestimated for far too long, and we would certainly be remiss if our attempts to understand medieval Hinduism neglected to take material culture into account. Furthermore, I believe Davis is correct in his suggestion that inscriptional sources shed new light on the world-ordering rationale of Cola temple-based Hinduism. The old Orientalist notion that Hindus prefer escaping the world to ordering it is patently absurd in light of the inscriptional evidence that Davis uncovers. The medieval Tamil Saivites of Davis' inquiry willingly entered economic contracts that affirmed a world order in which kings are associated with gods, temples are places of mediation between humanity and divinity, and the world of ordinary, material existence is, thereby, sacralized. In short, the most appropriate reaction to the world depicted in Cola temple inscriptions is not emotional escape but rational participation.

While Davis' basic argument is compelling, a few of his lesser propositions raise questions that the author neglects to answer. For example, in his analysis of the inscription detailing the contract between the cultivator Aruva-Kilal Muttigandan and the shepherd Eni Gangadharan, Davis asks the poignant question, "(W)hat is a poem detailing the king's conquests doing here, inserted in an inscriptional text that recounts a temple donation having nothing to do with the king or anyone close to him?" Unfortunately, Davis never answers this question. Instead, he explains that Melpadi, the region in which Muttigandan and Gangadharan entered their contract, had been hotly contested for centuries and only recently reclaimed from the Rastrakutas by the Cola king Rajaraja. Davis aptly points out that eulogizing Rajaraja in this particular inscription (and others like it) extended the king's presence "within the predominantly rural, agricultural society under his tenous control." But he still does not answer the question of why the eulogy appears in the inscription. Did Rajaraja mandate that all Tamil temple inscriptions include a list of his accomplishments? Did temple officials mandate the eulogy on the grounds that support for Rajaraja was an affirmation of Tamil religiosity? Was the inclusion of this eulogy simply a matter of custom, spawned by a growing Tamil nationalism? Did the cultivator and the shepherd include it voluntarily, out of admiration for the great culture hero?

"Lighting Lamps of Ghee" does little to explicate the motives of the various parties involved in the transactions that are detailed in Cola temple inscriptions. In fairness, this confusion is better attributed to the inscriptions themselves than to Davis. Davis openly acknowledges that "we do not learn much about the motivations of donors, nor the rewards they hoped to receive, from the inscriptions of the Cola period. By and large, Cola inscriptions present the act of giving as a simple, taken-for-granted action." Unfortunately, the problem of unknown motivations may be greater than Davis seems to recognize. If we do not know why donors such as Muttigandan and Rajaraja himself gave their gifts to the Tamil temples, how can we say for certain that their giving is an act of devotion, as Davis suggests when he writes that "royal participation in the Saiva temple cult" was "but a conspicuous display of devotion"? Are there not other reasons that Hindus might make donations to temples? Could Muttigandan's donation have been an act of penance, for example? Could he have been motivated by a desire to accrue karmic merit? Perhaps his donation was merely a way of publicly asserting his social worth.

In fairness, I should admit that I think Davis is probably right in his suggestion that the act of giving goats and cash to Cola-era temples was conceived by donors and recipients as an act of devotion. This explanation seems more plausible than any of the ones I imply in the questions above. The problem is that my suspicion about Davis being right is only a hunch. The inscriptions themselves, at least as they are presented in "Lighting Lamps of Ghee," are not sufficient to explain decisively the motivations of donors. On the one hand, this problem of unknown motivations does little if anything to undermine Davis' greater argument. Even if donations to Cola temples were not acts of devotion, they still reveal a world-affirming rationale that stands in contrast to the Orientalists' scripturally-informed image of Hinduism as world-negating and irrational. On the other hand, the problem of unknown motivations raises some unanswered questions that are important to the general study of material culture. If the record of a temple donation does not tell us explicitly why a donor made her/his donation, how can we know anything for certain about the religious motivations that inspired the donation? Does that record tell us anything about religion other than its economic dimension? Finally, to state the question more generally, when an object of material culture is not explicit about the religious intentions of its creator(s), how reasonable is it to it make inferences about those intentions based on what we know about the general religious milieu in which the object was created?

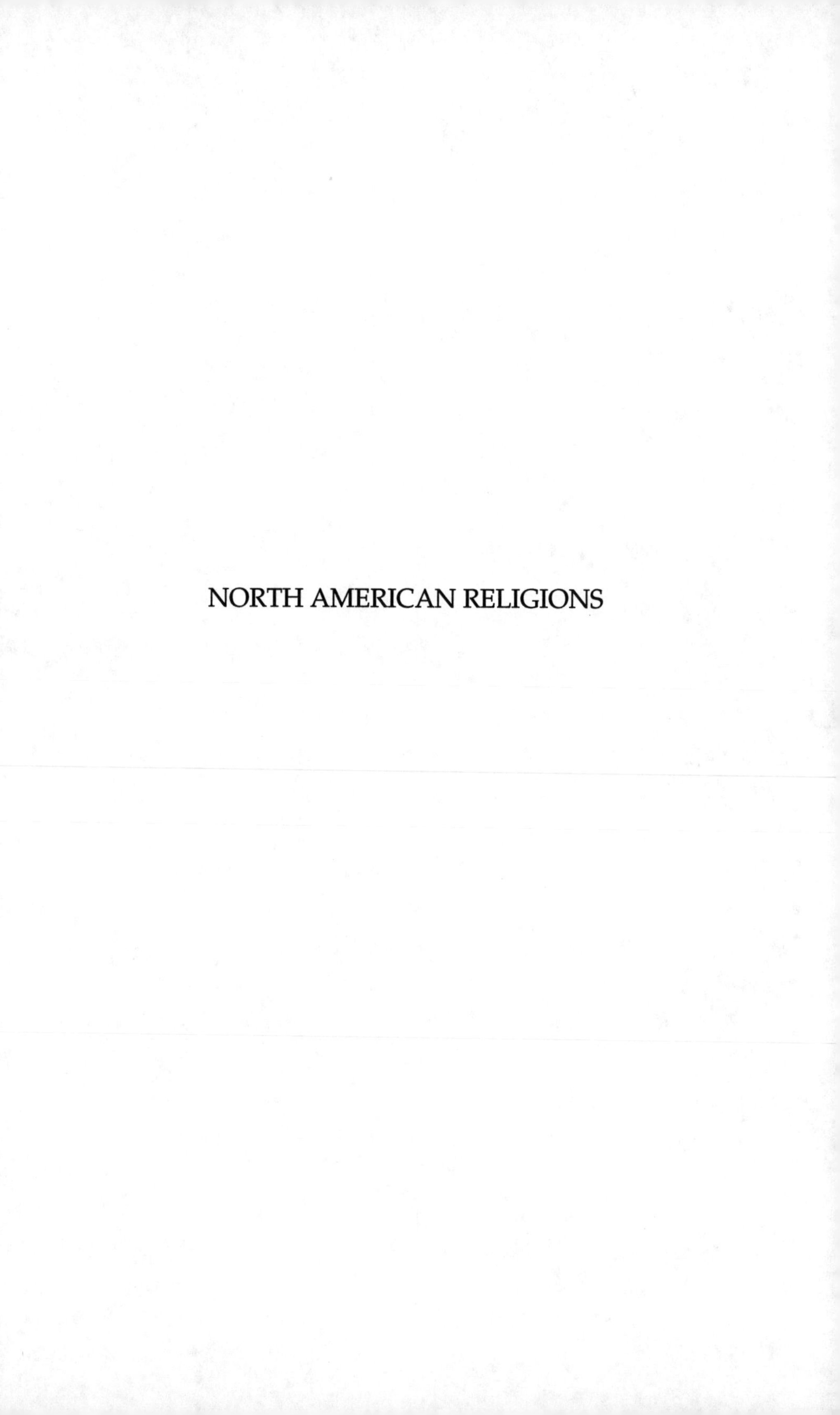

NORTH AMERICAN RELIGIONS

# 11

# Ancient Maya Religious Practices: Textual and Archaeological Voices

Traci Ardren
*Florida State University*

Fantastic advances in the understanding of ancient Maya texts have allowed scholars of ancient Maya religion a new lens through which to reconstruct ritual practices and beliefs. These decipherments have also allowed more subtle interpretations of traditional archaeological data, such as burials and architecture, although by no means do the texts resolve all questions of interpretation that the archaeological record provides (Houston 2000). In fact, the "new" textual evidence available to Mesoamerican scholars has opened a chasm in the scholarly study of ancient religious life between those who see the texts as meaningful records of ancient belief and those who see them as largely a distraction from the goal of archaeological investigation.

This chasm may be due in part to the nature of Maya textual data, although certainly the arrival of an enormous body of information, which contradicts at times the conventional wisdom of archaeological models, is also responsible. Ancient Maya texts, by some estimates still only 75% readable, are concerned to a very large degree with the lives and beliefs of ancient rulers, especially those who lived during the Classic period (200 C.E.-900 C.E.) in the lowlands of the Yucatan peninsula of Mexico, Belize, and Guatemala. In contrast to many other ancient cultures of the world, the ancient Maya did not use their sophisticated writing system for any form of economic or legal records. The subject matter is exclusively the lives and accomplishments of rulers, some of whom paid particular attention to their ritual obligations while others felt it more important to record accomplishments in war. As a whole, the Maya textual corpus reflects upon only a small percentage of the ancient Maya population; the elite segment commissioned, produced, and were likely the only ones to read these texts. Thus the chasm has arisen about how to bridge the anthropological goal of understanding ancient cultures, in their entirety, with textual evidence from a small, and not necessarily representative, sector of the population. This paper will show that the bridge need not be an elaborate argument about the meaningfulness of elite beliefs to their governed population or a complex maneuver by which elite propaganda can de doubly deciphered for its relevance to the lives of ancient peasants. Archaeological data recovered from small structures at cities that were not heavily dependent upon the use of texts to justify or legitimate royal claims to power nevertheless demonstrate the material remains of ritual practices described over and over in the textual corpus. Thus a continuum exists between elite portrayals of cosmological principles in texts and the manifestations of these principles in material evidence.

## Maya Hieroglyphic Inscriptions

The ancient Maya recorded texts by either carving or painting them onto wood, stone, ceramic pots, precious materials like jadeite and alabaster, and paper made from bark. The majority of preserved texts are found carved on limestone panels that stand upright, called stelae, or on architectural components, such as a lintel. Stelae, which usually depicted a portrait of a ruler were often paired with altars and provided a location for offerings. Lintels often showed a ruler and his family engaged in ritual activities, which took place in the room in which the lintel was placed. The hieroglyphic texts on these monuments complement the figural representation, or in some cases, stand alone.

Current research suggests that the scribes in Classic Maya culture were high-ranking members of a royal family who lived in and around the royal compounds. In some cases scribes even signed the texts they produced, using the phrase *u tz'ib*, 'his painting'. While ceramic pots only have a single scribal signature, stone monuments like stelea sometimes have as many as eight signatures (Houston 1989:31). The cooperative nature of stone carving is reflected in some monuments which demonstrate different 'styles' of writing on a single piece. There are very few depictions of scribes or artists in Maya art, and while the status of a scribe may have been relatively high, their lives were not celebrated in art or text.

Epigraphers working with ancient Maya inscriptions estimate there may be as many as 800 different glyphs, although only about 200-300 were in use at any given time (Harris and Stearns 1997:3). This large number of glyphs derives in part from the fact that the Maya scribe had

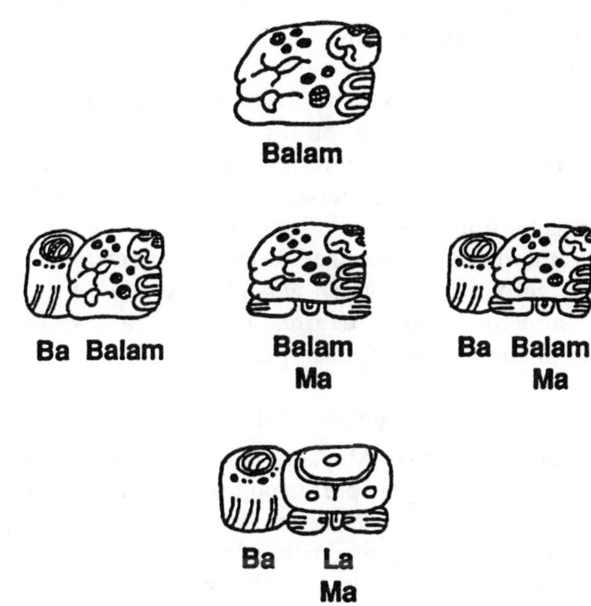


*Figure 1. Often several glyphs can stand for the same logograph or phoneme; these are all representations of* balam. *(After Harris & Sterns 1997).*

many ways in which to write a single word. Figure 1 shows that the word jaguar or *balam* in Maya, could be written one of five ways during the Classic period. It could be written as a pictograph; an actual representation of the jaguar. The next three examples show a combination of the pictograph with one or two phonetic complements, demonstrating that the writing system could also combine representational and abstract writing. The final example shows a purely phonetic form of *balam*. The current syllabary of phonetic elements in ancient Maya includes around 175 distinct glyphs and at any time a scribe could usually choose from a number of options for each individual phonetic sound. In addition to these choices, the ancient Maya were fond of homonyms, and would often substitute one glyph for another when two words sounded alike. Thus the Maya words for 'four' and 'snake' sound alike and in some cases a snake's head would be used for the number 4, rather than the normal bar and dot numerical system (Harris and Stearns 1997:6).

Numbers are some of the easiest hieroglyphs to recognize, and were extremely standardized across the Maya world. Since many texts concerned events in the life of a ruler, the accurate recording of time was very important, and more than half of the text on most stelea concerns calendrical information. The Maya used a bar and dot system of notation where a bar has the value of 5 and a dot the value of 1. In addition to the bar and dot system, numbers can be represented by a homonym, as discussed above, or for the numbers 1-19, by a head variant, a distinctive representation of a creature (usually incorporating both human and animal characteristics) associated with the number. Finally, these same numbers can also be represented by a full figure of the creature, rather than just the head. Maya mathematicians had use of the concept of 'zero' or null, which was represented by its own glyph, head variant, and full figure creature. It seems to have connoted the concept of 'completion' rather than emptiness.

### The Content of the Texts

The argument that ancient Maya texts were not read by the majority of the population stems in large part from the complexities of the writing system, as outlined above. Certainly one does not have to be fully literate to recognize the use of written language or to appreciate its ability to convey information. In fact, the use of written language in a largely non-literate society can be an extremely powerful way to demonstrate control. But the location of most texts also underscores the fact that these messages were highly specialized and intended for a small segment of the population. Stelea, altars, and lintels are all found primarily in the central or downtown areas of most Maya cities, and portable objects with hieroglyphic texts are even more limited in distribution. Clearly this was a royal writing system and what the royals chose to write about was largely their religious accomplishments. Within the context of Maya culture however, religious accomplishments could include not only rituals of dedication or offerings to the Gods, but also accession to the throne, successful capture of prisoners of war, and the creation of ancestors. One of the most interesting recent accomplishments of Maya epigraphers, is the recognition of how many texts formerly thought to concern primarily dynastic history now can be read with a deeper level of meaning that reflects the actions of priest-kings who were re-enacting mythological principles of creation.

Linda Schele was responsible for much of the new decipherment of cosmological principles in the texts. An important example of the deliberate conflation of history and mythological principles can be found in the texts of Palenque, in the Mexican state of Chiapas. In one section of the site center, a group of three small temples known as the Cross Group contain important textual panels at the back of each temple. The panels frame a central image of the ruler who commissioned all three works, and in all three the left panel text is mythological, while the right panel text is historical (Schele 1990:143). The mythological events concern the births of the mother and father of the Gods, and the births of the three patron Gods of Palenque (Schele 1990:143). The historical events are the major accomplishments of the ruler Chan Bahlum II, including his birth, accession to the throne, and his dedication of these temples (Schele 1990:143). The texts deliberately compare the dedication of these small but beautiful temples with events from the cosmic origin myth in order to demonstrate the power of Chan Bahlum II to derive order from the universe just as originally done by the Gods. Figure 2 shows the texts in translation from one of these temples.

*Figure 2. Altar 5, Tikal (after Jones and Satterthwaite 1982: fig. 23).*

The central act by which Chan Bahlum II aligned himself with the Gods is a ritual dedication he performed over a four-day period (Schele 1990:145). The dates of this ritual dedication are mentioned in the texts of all three temples, they are linked to his accession on one panel, and to the birth of the patron Gods of Palenque on another with some indication of a causal link between these two events (Schele 1990:145). The ritual began on July 23, 690 because the planets Jupiter and Saturn were conjunct in the sky and would remain so for the next 40 days. The text describes that the next day the temples were dedicated as the *ma k'ina bahlum k'uk' na* or 'house of the lineage founder Bahlum', and on the third day Chan Bahlum II let blood to activate the temple and converse with his ancestors (Schele and Freidel 1990:255). Although not mentioned explicitly in the texts, part of the dedication ritual probably included the deposition of ceramic vessels beneath the floor of the temples. Many elaborate vessels were found beneath the floors during excavation (Garcia Moll 1985:180-226). These ceramics, mostly large plates, recall images of Maya palace interiors where similar vessels hold strips of paper onto which a person has let blood. The bark paper offerings may have been burnt as part of the dedication ceremony or buried intact.

A recent study of ancient ritual texts by the accomplished epigrapher David Stuart concludes that dedication texts, like the panels from Palenque, constitute the main focus of most inscriptions from the Classic period (Stuart 1998). In Stuart's view the lengthy statements of dynastic legitimation serve only to underscore or contextualize the action taken by an individual, which commonly appears toward the end of an inscription. Focus upon the initial historical phrases of a text may lead to a biased interpretation that misses the point of the inscription. Verbal phrases have been some of the more difficult hieroglyphs to decipher, and Mayanists have paid closer attention to the more straightforward calendrical and historical events. But given the ancient Maya concern with preparation, activation, and termination of physical space, as demonstrated in the architectural record, Stuart's suggestion that dedication events were central and highly important ritual actions makes sense.

Dedicatory rituals often took place in and around new architectural features, and Stuart is able to identify several architectural forms which are mentioned repeatedly in the texts as sacred loci: *nah* or 'structure' as opposed to *otot* or 'dwelling', *eb* or 'stairway', *way ib* or 'dormitory', *pib nah* or 'sweatbath', and a ballcourt glyph that has been identified but not deciphered. Giving a monument or structure a proper name was an essential component of the dedication ritual, as seen in the example from Palenque where Chan Bahlum's house was named, *ma k'ina bahlum k'uk' na* or 'house of the lineage founder Bahlum'. Other examples include *chahuk nah* or 'lightning house' the home of a king from the site of Piedras Negras, and *et nah* or 'companion house' found on the hieroglyphic stairway of the palace at Palenque (Stuart 1998).

The observation of many naming events in the inscriptions adds a significant new dimension to the study of ancient architecture. First, the appearance of naming events in the inscriptions demonstrates how important these ritual actions were to the rulers who commissioned the monuments. The dedication and naming of a new temple or palace was as significant, in many cases, as accession to the throne or successful military campaigns. This in turn, suggests that the considerable investments of labor and resources noted by archaeologists as we excavate large pyramids and palace compounds were not just the result of a need to demonstrate political power to a subjugated populace, but were in fact a source of pride or even a requirement for a life lived in accordance with cultural mores. Second, the action of giving an architectural feature a proper name highlights for archaeologists the degree to which ancient Maya saw structures as much more than functional settings for daily life or administration. Bestowing names on houses continues as a cultural practice today in Mesoamerica, where it is part of 'feeding' or dedicating a new residence and filling it with spirit (Vogt 1976). Apparently naming in prehistory derived from a similar conception of ensoullment, the correct execution of which would result in the animation of a structure. This act conveyed an essential quality to the space that was subject to the same risks as any other life; the archaeological record is full of termination deposits as well—ritual actions that could extinguish the life force present in a space in either a hostile or reverential manner (Ardren 1999).

Stuart has identified a number of textual phrases that describe specific elements of the architectural dedication ceremony especially those that concern the controlled use of fire (Stuart 1998). At Palenque and elsewhere Stuart and other epigraphers have identified a glyphic phrase which reads *och k'ak' ta-y-otot* or 'the fire enters into his house'. A related phrase describes the ritual action of *el-nah* or 'house censing'. Both phrases occupy the same position in textual passages, usually at the end of a long passage of calendrical and dynastic information. Stuart suggests that both phrases may refer to the same ceremony, or to closely related rituals that both serve as the main elements of architectural dedication. The glyph for house censing resembles the common ceramic censers found in many caches at Maya sites. The *och k'ak' ta-y-otot* and *el-nah* events may have consisted of carrying censers filled with smoking copal resin throughout a structure in order to purify the space, just as incense is used in many other religious traditions or to feed the spirit of the house, as copal resin is used by modern Maya (McGee1990:44). The fire dedication rites may also have included the kindling of a hearth fire within the structure in order to feed or animate the space. Given textual evidence for an animate view of architectural space, the use of ceremonial fire must have nourished the ensoulled house even further.

There is even evidence that the construction and dedication of houses took on cosmological significance. What is known of ancient Maya mythology indicates that the "First Hearth Place" was the origin of

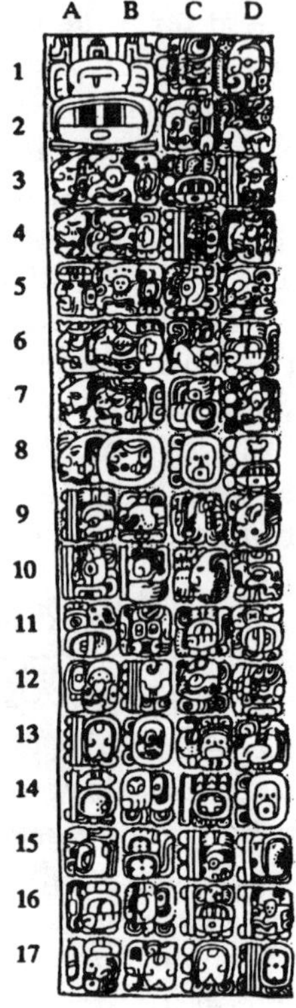


On November 8, 2360 B.C.
when the eighth Lord of the Night ruled,
it was ten days after the moon was born,
5 moons had ended,
X was its name and it had 30 days.
It was 14 months and 19 days
after God K set the west quadrant.[1]
It was the third birth and GII was born. [A1–D2]

34 years, 14 months after GII, the *matawil*, had been born
and then 2 baktuns (800 years) ended
on February 16, 2325 B.C.
On that day Lady Beastie, Divine Lord of *Matawil*,
manifested a divinity through bloodletting. [C3–D11]

It had come to pass
on *Yax -Hal Witznal*
in the shell place
at the *Na-Te-Kan*[2]
on November 8, 2360 B.C.
2,947 years, 3 months, 16 days later[3] . . . [C12–D17]

[1] The scribe made an error here by adding rather than subtracting the Distance Number. The correct station is 1.18.4.7.1 1 Imix 19 Pax with red and east.
[2] These three locations refer to the Mountain Monster under Chan-Bahlum's feet, the shell under Pacal's feet, and the Foliated Cross in the center of the panel (See Figure 6:12).
[3] The Distance Number should be 7.14.13.1.16.

*Figure 3. Text from Tablet of the Foliated Cross. Palenque. (After Schele & Freidel 1990).*

**. . . on July 23, 690, GII and GIII were in conjunction.**
**[L1–M4]**

**On the next day,**
**the Mah-Kina-Bahlum-Kuk Building was dedicated**
**in the house of Lord Chan-Bahlum,**
**Divine Palenque Lord. [L6–L9]**

**On the third day Lord Chan-Bahlum, Divine Palenque Lord,**
**he let blood with an obsidian blade;**
**he took the bundle**
**after it had come to pass**
**at the Waterlily Place.**
**Wac-Chan-Chac Ox-Waxac-Chac acted there. [L10–L17]**

**49 years, 6 months, 4 days after he had been born**
**and then he crowned himself,**
**Lord Chan-Bahlum, Divine Palenque Lord**
**on January 10, 692. [M17–P5]**

**6 years, 11 months, 6 days after he had been seated as *ahau***
**and then GI, GII, GIII and their companion gods**
**came into conjunction.**
**Lord Chan-Bahlum enacted a ritual.**

**In 1 year, 12 months, 4 days it will happen,**
**the end of the 13th katun on March 17, 692.**
**And then it came to pass July 23, 690**
**and then they were in conjunction**
**the gods, who are the cherished-ones of,**
**Lord Chan-Bahlum, Divine Palenque Lord.**

all life on earth, and that the universe itself was described in symbolic terms derived from the common household (Freidel, Schele, and Parker 1993). Rulers took pains to obscure the disjunctions between their opulent lives and the lives of the common farmers who supported them, and one way this goal was achieved was by rituals that represented royals as living in the same conceptual universe as commoners, a place where homes were built and dedicated with fire, and where everyone planted corn and was dependent upon its growth for their existence. Within this cosmology the household provided the universal cognitive map of how space was experienced. Archaeologists have known for years that most palaces of Maya elite did not differ in any great detail from the modest living structures of the farmer. Palaces were elevated slightly above ground level in many cases, but besides elaborate decoration on the exterior of palace structures, the interior dimensions, amenities, and densities appear nearly identical to those of the rest of the population. The textual evidence now helps us to understand that the model for elite structures was not determined solely by lack of innovation or resources, but perhaps by an ideological need to mirror (in amplified form) the lifestyle of agriculturalists who provided the foundation of the society.

The *och k'ak'* or 'fire enters' verb is also found in association with tombs in certain textual passages (Stuart 1998:396). In an example from the site of Tonina, Stuart reads a passage that commemorates the anniversary of the death of the ruler portrayed on the monument. The hieroglyphics describe a fire dedication event at a location owned by the dead ruler, the *muk nal* or 'buried place' (Stuart 1998:397). A similar passage from Seibal notes a fire enters the tomb ceremony held 300 years after the ruler was interred. Figure 3 shows Altar 5 from Tikal, which depicts this ritual in process accompanied by a textual passage that describes the tomb firing ceremony. The text states that on a date 8 years after her death, the bones and skull of a royal woman were opened from her tomb at the Nine Lord House, and a fire ceremony was performed (Stuart 1998:407).

This important decipherment helps clarify a situation that has puzzled archaeologists for many years. There is ample evidence from many different Maya sites that tombs were regularly re-entered for ritual activities. At Tikal, Copan, and Yaxuna, tombs were opened, burned, and re-sealed. In some cases this act can be interpreted as reverential and had little impact on the burial itself. Such was the case in burial 23 from Yaxuna where we excavated the royal tomb of a middle-aged king. The tomb had been reopened in antiquity and a small, contained fire burned on a rock adjacent to the body (Suhler 1996). Evidence that the fire was post-depositional and not part of the original funeral ritual was found in a series of rocks placed throughout the tomb to enable a person to move from one end to the other without touching the body or floor. The rocks could not have come from the tomb ceiling or walls, and were evenly spread around the body like stepping-stones.

In other cases like burial 37-8 from Copan and burial 25 from Yaxuna, bones were scattered and removed as part of a burning ritual, which does not appear to have been reverential. The individual in burial 25 was a middle aged elite woman who died during a time of relative peace at Yaxuna. She was buried in a crypt under the floor of an elaborate structure that we have interpreted as a *popol nah* or government council house. Perhaps 100 years later, Yaxuna was under siege from its expansionist neighbors and this burial was re-opened and burned. The patch of plaster that covered her interment was removed, and the skeletal remains from the upper half of her body were removed, leaving only a few tiny jade beads and hematite mirror fragments (Ambrosino 1996). Fire was burned inside the crypt and debris from the destruction of the *popol nah* was left on top of her remains. Further application of textual data to burial assemblages from other parts of the Maya area should eventually produce a useful distinction between different types of tomb firing ceremonies.

## The Material Record of Ritual Life

Where does an archaeologist recover evidence of the important rituals now known from the ancient Maya textual record? As discussed briefly above, research at Yaxuna recovered a number of examples of ritual behavior, which can now be more fully interpreted through analogy to rituals described in the textual corpus. The texts themselves do not mention many details about specific material objects that might form part of the permanent archaeological record, although clearly architecture, bones, and burning activities are all important components in the textual descriptions and also materials that might be detected by the archaeologist. In addition, ceramic vessels that might have played a role in dedication offerings and ceramic censers that might have been used in tomb firing or house censing rituals are commonly found. Let us examine some of these deposits before considering their possible connection to ritual activity as described in the texts.

At the Classic Maya site of Yaxuna where the Selz Foundation Yaxuna Archaeological Project conducted research from 1986-1996, a number of significant caches were found which might be the material remains of architectural dedication rituals. The term cache is used by Mayanists to refer to any deposit that does not contain human bone, especially one which appears to have been ritualized. Common materials recovered from caches include ceramic vessels, lithic tools and/or fragments, marine shell, jade jewelry, and decayed organic material.

One very beautiful cache from Yaxuna was found under the floor of a small but very important Preclassic structure. Structure 6E-120, also known as the Dance Platforms, was a nondescript 3 meter high mound that when excavated revealed itself to be a labyrinth of terraced platforms surrounding an inner sanctum (Suhler, Freidel, and Ardren 1998). At different terrace levels small staircases led up to what must have been a perishable superstructure, perhaps through the use of trap doors. This unusual structure was clearly not the small house mound we expected it to be, and seems to have been a performance space, perhaps for rituals of accession. The cache found beneath the floor in the southern corner of 6E-120 confirms its royal status. In a large ceramic 'bucket', 3 centimeters of dense organic debris surrounded a small greenstone axe and mirror, which were stylistically much earlier than the structure. Resting on top of the two jade jewels was a limestone sphere. Karl Taube has argued these spheres are symbolic tools that represent the hearthstones of creation (Taube 1994). Because the jade mirror and axe are representative of the God of rulership, the stone sphere recalls the primordial hearth place, and the cache was found in an unusual labyrinthine structure, we are confident that the ritual process responsible for this cache re-created elements of cosmological myth in order to animate the Dance Platforms structure.

The category of cache is not always as easy to identify as it might seem, and some archaeological projects have discovered a significant number of what are termed 'problematic deposits' because they combine traditional materials found in caches with human or animal remains. Furthermore, burials can often be found in unusual places which closely resemble the pattern established for caches. The bundled body of an individual, probably a captive, was buried on the centerline of a stairway at Yaxuna, in association with the bones of seven different small animals, and a ceramic censer (Suhler 1996). In this case the burial seems to have been about much more than just disposal of the dead, and careful interpretation must consider multiple levels of meaning.

Based upon 20 years of archaeological research at Tikal, Marshall Becker has suggested a useful way to conceptualize caches, problematic deposits, and burials. Becker considers all three to be part of a continuum of "earth offerings", where an elaborate ceramic vessel, precious material like jade, or even a human body could be used as an offering (Becker 1992:186). Noting that the archaeological materials may not be sufficient to reveal whether the intention of the actors was to 'offer' or 'bury', Becker argues for careful attention to the context of the offering as a clue to its meaning. For example, in cases where architectural building is integral to the offering and seals the burial or cache, the deposit may be considered dedicatory to the structure. In cases where a burial or cache intrudes into a pre-existing structure which is then patched so that the former structure may continue in use, the offering may be considered non- dedicatory. At Tikal, all structures with dedicatory burials (as defined above) were non-residential, usually small shrines located on the eastern side of a residential group (Becker 1992:189). Using archaeological and iconographic data, Clemency Coggins suggested that burials that intruded into an earlier structure may have been seen as 'impregnations' which re-created the act of planting maize in the earth or re-creating new life (Coggins 1988). These perspectives on 'earth offerings' are certainly consistent with the conception of structures as animate objects, as suggested by textual evidence.

An example of a deposit on the continuum between cache and burial is feature 1 from the Xkanha acropolis at Yaxuna. Discovered in the construction fill of a small tower or lookout platform, feature 1 consists of fragments of a human skull, a small shell bead, a shell ear flare, and three ceramic vessels (Ardren 1994). Two of the pots probably held the skull and beads, but the context of the construction fill damaged the bowls before excavation uncovered the deposit. While a single skull hardly qualifies as a 'burial', clearly human remains were involved and thus the term cache does not seem completely accurate. When initially discovered, it appeared that this might represent a sacrificial head placed into the construction fill of the tower. This interpretation is still accurate, but with analogy to rituals described in the texts, feature 1 may represent a dedication rite, meant to activate or ensoul the new tower. Certainly the tower was not built as a monument to the individual whose head was so callously placed in boulder fill—rather it seems that the structure required a dedication offering before it was considered complete.

Another dedicatory cache from Yaxuna may reflect the actions related to the *el nah* or house censing ritual as known from the texts. While whole ceramic censors are relatively rare in archaeological contexts, fragments of censers with associated charcoal or ash are more common. At the Maya version of Pompeii, the site of Ceren in El Salvador, archaeologist Payson Sheets has documented that fragments of ceramic vessels were being used as commonly if not more commonly than whole vessels, and for the same purposes (Sheets 1993). Thus the discovery of a censer fragment in an archaeological deposit may reflect burning or censing as clearly as an entire censer.

Structure 6F-9 is one of the later buildings in central Yaxuna, dating to the time after the wars of the Terminal Classic period. It is part of an entire quadrangle of buildings erected by those who conquered the site. Excavation at 6F-9 revealed a dedicatory cache of an obsidian blade fragment, an obsidian projectile point fragment, and a large piece of a ceramic censer in the northeastern corner of the room (Suhler and Freidel 1993). The cache was placed into a plastered pit next to the wall and covered with two plastered stones, then the original floor of 6F-9 was completed. The contents of the 6F-9 cache are completely consistent with dedicatory rituals as described in the texts, and demonstrate evidence of two main dedicatory ritual components—censing and bloodletting. Without the textual evidence the contents of this cache would be interesting, and certainly significant, but not necessarily coherent elements of a ritual cycle.

Another cache from the same time period demonstrates the patterning evident in the material record. At the summit of the tallest structure on the Xkanha acropolis, excavation revealed an unusual shrine in the middle of the floor of the summit structure. As part of clearing the floor of the structure, we discovered an alignment of re-used construction stones lain directly on the floor and adjacent to the back wall of the structure (Ardren 1994). The alignment was roughly u-shaped, and enclosed a small square area roughly 1.5 m on a side. Outside the alignment of stones that defined the shrine we found a single jade bead and two concentrations of ceramic sherds on the floor. Both concentrations of ceramic material represented fragments of whole vessels that had been smashed and then burned. Inside the shrine area we recovered 3 large stone slabs that covered a dedicatory cache of 4 obsidian blade fragments and a single large ceramic sherd. The sherd does not appear to be from a censer, but rather a large jar. While the entire deposit seems to combine elements of a dedicatory cache and a termination ritual (smashed and burned pottery is characteristic of termination), the elements inside the shrine area are consistent with the ritual actions of bloodletting and dedication.

A final archaeological example will be presented in more detail in order to evaluate its possible meaning in light of textual rituals. My current research is centered at the Classic Maya city of Chunchucmil, where control of a nearby salt source provided citizens with a means by which they could live in an area hostile to intensive agriculture. Since 1998 excavations at Chunchucmil have focused on the composition of this ancient trading city, looking at residential areas for clues to the ethnic composition of the population, and at monumental architecture for information about how trade may have contributed to the negotiation of power and status. The large settlement (16 $km^2$) supported a dense population, many of whom seem to have been engaged in craft manufacture and/or modification of the raw materials that flowed

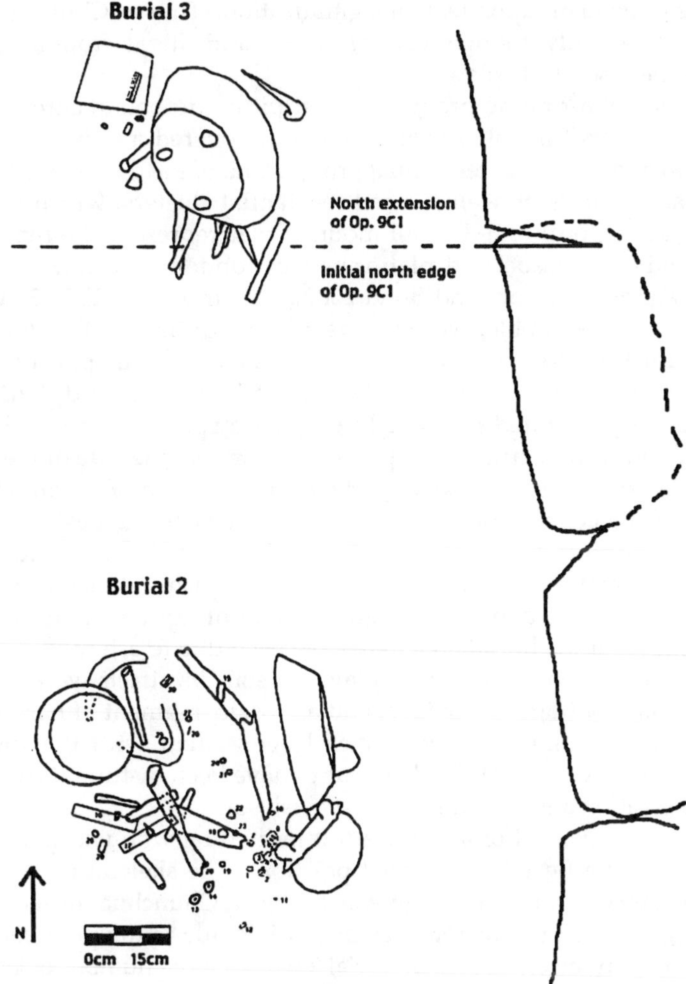


*Figure 4. Chunchucmil burials2&3 (after Hudson 2000).*

through the city in exchange for salt. Thus while poor in foodstuffs, the population of Chunchucmil was rich in material objects like obsidian, marine shell, and ceramics. The northern Maya lowlands have fewer hieroglyphic texts and authority was expressed in other ways or at least was less dependent upon textual legitimization. Thus at Chunchucmil to date we have only a single textual phrase and this is from a portable object to be discussed below.

As part of a routine program of test pitting to obtain chronological information, staff member Scott Hutson discovered a pair of very rich burials in a very simple residential group. One of the distinctive features of Chunchucmil is its well-defined residential clusters, which we have defined as a group of 3-4 small mounds that represent the remains of households and associated platforms surrounded by a low boundary wall (Magnoni, Hutson, and Bond 2000). At structure S2E2-23, a low 2 meter mound of rubble, we recovered a pair of burials that had been placed into an low platform (Hutson 2000). This platform was approximately 40 cm above the ground surface and had been deliberately penetrated in order to prepare a space for the burials. A construction wall of crudely shaped stones formed one side of the burial pit, while two stone slabs covered the burials. A gap of 50 cm between the top of the construction wall and the stone slabs suggested that the crypt was not intact, or had been modified after its initial manufacture. Beneath the stone slabs was a 40 cm layer of grayish soil that covered the burials. The soil above the slabs was light brown, and the gray discoloration of the burial area may have been due to ash mixed into the natural matrix. Within this 40 cm layer of soil, 3 artifacts were found; a shell pendant, a fragment of jade, and a mosaic fragment of hard brown stone. These artifacts are very clearly consistent with the funerary materials from the burials, and appear to have been disturbed from their original position and mixed into the grayish soil.

Burial 2 consisted of a single adult individual who was placed into the ground in a flexed or bundled position. The skeletal material was poorly preserved due to the high water table at Chunchucmil, estimation of sex, age, and health factors was impossible due to the poor condition of the bone. In the chest area of Burial 2 were a large number of jade and marine shell beads which probably represent the royal jewels of this individual. In association with the skeletal material were three whole ceramic vessels, including a large plate, a jar, and a spherical bowl elaborately carved with a dedicatory phrase and two images of the Maize god (shown in Figure 4). The texts describe the vessel as 'the corn gruel drinking vessel of Lord ?' (whose name cannot be deciphered) (R. Krochock and D. Stuart personal communication: 2000). The carved vessel had an oversized lid with five tinklers arranged in a quincunx patter, and both vessel and lid appear to date to the Early Classic period.

Approximately 50 cm to the north, we recovered the body of burial 3. The skeletal material from burial 3 was also poorly preserved and even less complete than burial 2. Fragments of adult long bones and a scapula were found inside a large plate, very similar to the one found with burial 2. The highly disarticulated and fragmentary nature of these bones made it very clear that burial 3 was placed into the ground as part of a bundle. In addition to the skeletal material, 2 other whole vessels were recovered, and a significant number of jade and marine shell beads, a long obsidian blade, and two carved jade pendants indicative of royal status. The plate from burial 3 had been broken in antiquity but curated or kept as an heirloom until deposition in this burial. Ground specular hematite, which has a deep red color favored by the Maya for its similarity to blood, was found in both burials.

Further excavation by Hutson in this location during the 2000 field season documented the fact that a 1.5 meter high square platform was built over burials 2 and 3, probably at the same time that they were deposited, sealing the burials into construction fill (Hutson 2001). A series of stone compartments (1.75m x 1.3m) were attached to the southern side of the platform, each resting on a plaster floor and each plastered on the interior area of the compartment. One of these compartments contained a fine ceramic vessel and fragments of hematite and jade. Below this dedication offering a circular cist carved into bedrock was found. The cist contained fine soil and charcoal that are currently under analysis for possible organic remains. One of the other compartments contained two ceramic vessels, one a bowl that held a fragment of bone and the other a 15 cm tall vase. Across the compartment from these vessels was a large jade bead. The compartments were filled in with construction matrix that was probably coeval with the ceramic offerings. Clearly structure S2E2-23 has at least three dedicatory events associated with architectural construction. One is the placement of burials 2 and 3 while the main platform was being built. The other two are both related to the modification of the compartments into a large platform area.

Excavation in the vicinity of structure S2E2-23 produced a very high concentration of obsidian fragments—up to 128 pieces from 1.1 cubic m of trash debris. These fragments were concentrated in areas to the north and south of the main platform. Also to the south of S2E2-23 a small residential mound was excavated which was unremarkable in most respects except for the discovery of a large obsidian core outside the structure.

Standard archaeological interpretations of the A'ak group where structure S2E2-23 located suggest a modest residential function for these buildings based on their small size, arrangement around a central courtyard area, and lack of major architecture. Clearly the remains found in burials 2 and 3 challenge this interpretation, and suggest that structure 23 may have been an ancestral shrine for the residential group. The high concentration of obsidian fragments might suggest that this was the household compound of a craftsperson, perhaps someone who worked with wood or other perishable material. The modest 1.5 meter high platform defies easy interpretation, as it does not conform to the very standardized design of Maya residential structures, nor to the usual pyramidal form of an ancestral monument. Platforms, which may or may not have had a perishable superstructure, are usually associated with production activities or performance areas in the Maya area. The material evidence from structure 23 suggests the former interpretation.

When textual evidence is used in conjunction with the material evidence, a more complex explanation of this structure is possible. The platform may be modest, but it contains the remains of a highly significant ritual act, a dedicatory burial which may contain the bundled remains of ancestors who have been either dis-interred from some other location and then placed in structure 23 as part of the ritual dedication, or perhaps re-opened and re-visited on multiple occasions at structure 23. Although this small group lacks carved stone monuments which might describe the individual responsible for the naming and dedication of the platform, as we saw on Tikal altar 5 (figure 2), the act is no less significant because all the ritual components of an architectural dedication are present. Ceramic vessels as depicted in scenes of blood sacrifice were placed with both burial 2 and 3, in association with a long obsidian blade. Human bone which had been dis-interred or curated for some time was present, as were royal jewels indicating the high status of the individuals and their connection to the deities of rulership. The text of the carved bowl clearly follows the pattern of ritual dedications found in cities more dependent upon textual communication and demonstrates the inhabitants of ancient Chunchucmil were conversant in the same ritual practices and worldview as Maya from sites that have a fully developed textual corpus. Evidence of burning or the *och k'ak' t-u-muk-il* or 'fire enters his tomb' event may be present in the ashy soil above the burials while the burial area itself was stained with powdered hematite the color of blood, where the soul was believed to reside. Finally, the evidence of construction activity in concert with the deposition of burials 2 and 3 strongly suggests that they were dedicatory to the main platform that was constructed. Textual evidence would further suggest that the burials were not only dedicatory, but were in fact a necessary step in the ensoullment or animation of this structure, and a significant accomplishment for whomever commissioned the event.

Because the ancient Maya were obsessed with the recording of time, we know from textual inscriptions that certain ritual structures were used for centuries, and that significant ritual events could be commissioned centuries after the original construction and dedication of a structure which would recall and commemorate its original ceremonial inauguration. This too is consistent with the archaeological or material record that shows that certain structures were maintained and used for long periods of time while others were abandoned. In the case of structure S2E2-23, we clearly see evidence for a continuity of purpose in the later dedications when the compartments were converted to a platform. The second platform may have served a similar purpose to the first, perhaps as performance area or ancestral shrine, and the best evidence for this supposition is the presence of similar dedicatory offerings in the construction fill of the second platform. Clearly the new platform was also ensoulled or animated with ceramics, jade, and bone when a second platform was needed in the group. Given that this architectural expansion could have happened in any direction, it is significant that the compartments were chosen for modification. In the absence of dramatic terminations of this area, one might assume a relative continuity of purpose or function when the compartments were converted to the second platform. A textual perspective might suggest that this was done on the anniversary of the original platform dedication or to commemorate the ritual action taken by the person who commissioned the first platform and burials 2 and 3.

## Final Considerations

This paper has emphasized the relative degree of agreement between the ancient Maya textual evidence and the material record. But in what ways do these two sets of data fail to intersect? In what ways are they distinct? The claim has been made that inaccuracies exist in the hieroglyphic record, that elites manipulated chronological records to suit their needs, and thus that epigraphic data are suspect (Henderson and Sabloff 1993). Certainly there are inaccuracies in the hieroglyphic corpus; modern software programs can detect minute mistakes in the record keeping of ancient scribes. But for the most part, scribal errors are to be expected in an ancient literary corpus, and throughout prehistory when writing systems were controlled by a small group of elites, distortions or political exaggerations were commonplace.

The more fundamental disjunction between the archaeological record and the material contexts of ancient Maya culture comes from the unequal segments of ancient life they address. Archaeological data is recovered from a much greater range of activities than are discussed in the ancient texts, and thus large areas of ancient social life are not treated from a textual perspective. For example, isotopic analyses of human bone material have greatly advanced our understanding of ancient Maya health patterns in the last five years (White 1999). But as opposed to ancient Egyptologists, or even prehistorians working in central Mexico, we have no ancient medical texts, recipes, or even indications of how disease was perceived. This means our study of ancient health patterns proceeds largely without the inclusion of the native perspective, and researchers interested in how declining health may have affected the collapse of ancient society must work in relative isolation from textual assistance.

A more fundamental disjunction is the almost total absence of any textual evidence concerning ancient economic relations in the Maya area. This is a real handicap, for there is ample archaeological evidence to suggest that movement of prestige goods as well as basic household materials was relatively constant. Ceramicists who look at the appearance and disappearance of ceramic groups through the entire Maya area, are beginning to discuss the role political alliances between ancient dynasties (for which there is ample textual evidence) may have played in the movement of ceramics, one of the fundamental cultural currencies in Mesoamerica. The ubiquitous problem of central Mexico's degree of influence within the Maya area would be greatly redressed if hieroglyphic texts were discovered that concerned who controlled the movement of obsidian from central Mexico into the Maya area at certain periods of time, or what characterized the nature of alliances between Teotihuacan and large Maya cities. For now, epigraphers and iconographers work at this problem by looking at the appearance of central Mexican iconography in the art, while archaeologists study the sources of raw materials and determine which artifacts are imports or local copies; again, two groups working largely in isolation from one another on nearly identical questions.

In should be obvious then that the character of Maya texts has driven a wedge between the archaeological communities. Those archaeologists who are interested in what the texts have to offer have been led to conduct research that predominantly addresses ritual behavior or elite levels of society. Prehistorians who are interested in health, economics, or the environment, have seen little of use in the inscriptions and continue to work largely in isolation from the recent decipherments. Their interpretations of archaeological data are often driven by statistical analyses of large bodies of data and result in publications that describe sweeping changes within Maya society. In contrast, archaeologists working in conjunction with epigraphers often present a more historical interpretation of the material record, and focus on the achievements of a specific individual or city.

The old-fashioned claim that Maya textual evidence is not applicable to anyone who lived outside a palace compound is not supported however. There is a very large body of archaeological data to demonstrate that all levels of ancient Maya society were deeply concerned with religious practices and conducted rituals that may have varied in scale but were essentially consistent in intention. Because at the ordinary household level these ritual actions are sometimes hard to detect, the overemphasis of the texts on ritual activities has had a positive and productive effect on interpretation. The accumulation of evidence about elite ritual life has forced the recognition of material patterns that can now be observed throughout ancient Maya society.

## References

Ambrosino, James

1996 "Excavations at Structures 6F-4, 6F-68, and 6F-72" In *The Selz Foundation Yaxuna Project Final Report of the 1995 Field Season.* Department of Anthropology, Southern Methodist University: Dallas.

Ardren, Traci

1994 "Section 1:Xkanha" In *The Selz Foundation Yaxuna Project Final Report of the 1993 Field Season.* Department of Anthropology, Southern Methodist University: Dallas.

1997 *The Politics of Place: Architecture and Cultural Change at the Xkanha Group, Yaxuna, Yucatan, Mexico.* PhD dissertation, Yale University: New Haven.

1999 "Palace Termination Rituals at Yaxuna, Yucatan, Mexico" In *Land of the Turkey and the Deer,* R. Gubler ed.:25-36. Labyrinthos: Lancaster, California.

Becker, Marshall

1992 "Burials as Caches; Caches as Burials: A New Interpretation of the Meaning of Ritual Deposits Among the Classic Period Lowland Maya" In *New Theories on the Ancient Maya,* E. Danien and R. Sharer eds.:185-196. University of Pennsylvania Press: Philadelphia.

Coggins, Clemency

1988 "Classic Maya Metaphors of Death and Life" *RES (Anthropology and Aesthetics)* 16:65-84.

Freidel, David and L. Schele, J. Parker

1992 *Maya Cosmos: Three Thousand Years on the Shaman's Path.* William Morrow: NY.

Garcia Moll, Roberto

1985 *Palenque 1926-1945.* Instituto Nacional de Antropologia e Historia: Mexico, D.F.

Harris, John F. and S. Stearns

1997 *Understanding Maya Inscriptions: A Hieroglyphic Handbook.* University of Pennsylvania Press: Philadelphia.

Henderson, John and J. Sabloff

1993 "Reconceptualizing the Maya Cultural Tradition: Programmatic Comments" In *Lowland Maya Civilization in the Eighth Century A.D.*, J. Sabloff and J. Henderson eds.:445-475. Dumbarton Oaks: Washington D.C.

Houston, Stephen D.

1989 *Reading the Past: Maya Glyphs.* British Museum Publications: London.

2000 "Into the Minds of the Ancients: Advances in Maya Glyph Studies" *Journal of World Prehistory* 14(2):121-201.

Hutson, Scott

2000 "Excavations at Residential Groups A'ak and Chiwo'ol" In *Chunchucmil Regional Economy Program Report of the 1999 Field Season,* T. Ardren ed.:24-30. Department of Anthropology, Florida State University: Tallahassee.

2001 "Excavations at the A'ak Group" In *Pakbe Regional Economy Program Report of the 2000 Field Season,* T. Stanton ed.:18-45. Social Science and Business Division, Jamestown Community College: Jamestown, NY.

McGee, R. Jon

1990 *Life, Ritual, and Religion Among the Lacandon Maya.* Wadsworth: Belmont, California.

Magnoni, Aline and S. Hutson, T. Bond

2000 "The Peculiar Cultural Landscape of Chunchucmil" Paper presented at the annual meeting of the American Anthropological Association, San Francisco.

Schele, Linda

1990 "House Names and Dedication Rituals at Palenque" In *Vision and Revision in Maya Studies,* F. Clancy and P. Harrison eds.:143-158. University of New Mexico Press: Albuquerque.

Schele, Linda and D. Freidel

1990 *A Forest of Kings: The Untold Story of the Ancient Maya.* William Morrow and Company: NY.

Sheets, Payson

1993 Introduction to the 1993 Research Season, Ceren, El Salvador" In *Preliminary Report of the Ceren Research Project, 1993 Season*, P. Sheets, ed.:1-23. Department of Anthropology, University of Colorado: Boulder.

Suhler, Charles

1996 *Excavations at the North Acropolis Yaxuna, Yucatan, Mexico.* PhD dissertation, Southern Methodist University: Dallas.

Suhler, Charles and D. Freidel

1993 *Selz Foundation Final Report of the 1992 Field Season.* Department of Anthropology, Southern Methodist University: Dallas.

Suhler, Charles and D. Freidel, T. Ardren

1997 "Northern Maya Architecture, Ritual, and Cosmology" In *Anatomia de una Civilizacion*, A.Ciudad R. et al eds.:253-274. Sociedad Espanola de Estudios Maya: Madrid.

Stuart, David

1998 "The Fire Enters His House: Architecture and Ritual in Classic Maya Texts" In *Function and Meaning in Classic Maya Architecture*, S. Houston ed:373-426. Dumbarton Oaks: Washington D.C.

Taube, Karl

1994 "The Jade Hearth". Manuscript in possession of the author.

Vogt, Evon Z.

1976 *Tortillas For The Gods: A Symbolic Analysis of Zinacanteco Rituals.* Harvard University Press: Cambridge.

White, Christine

1999 *Reconstructing Ancient Maya Diet.* University of Utah Press: Salt Lake City.

# 12

# Violent Stones and the Great Aztec Temple: The Imagination of Matter in the City of Sacrifice

David Carrasco
*Princeton University*

"As if it were the realization of a dream, archaeology guides us now in finding, in the reality of the stones, what remains of the splendid temple with which we were already familiar from descriptions in the codices, the Nahuatl texts and the eyewitness accounts of the Spanish conquerors."

Miguel Leon Portilla
"The Ethnohistorical Record for the Huey Teocalli of Tenochtitlan" p. 91

When the Spaniards arrived in the Valley of Mexico and saw the Aztec capital of Tenochtitlan in 1519, they were startled by both its architectural wonders and ritual violence. Bernal Díaz del Castillo, a sergeant in Cortés's troop, has left us this memorable first impression of the Aztec capital.

> During the morning we arrived at a broad causeway and continued our march towards Iztapalapa and when we saw so many cities and villages built in the water and other great towns on dry land and that straight and level causeway going towards Mexico, we were amazed and said that it was like the enchantments they tell of in the legend of Amadis, on account of the great towers and cues and buildings rising from the water, and all built of masonry. And some of the soldiers even asked whether the things that we saw were not a dream. Gazing on such wonderful sights, we did not know what to say . . . and the lake itself was crowded with canoes and in the causeway there were many bridges at intervals and in front of us stood the great City of Mexico . . . and the paths full of

> roses and flowers and the many fruit trees and the native roses and the pond of fresh water... and all was cemented and very splendid with many kinds of stone (monuments) with pictures on them, which gave much to think about.[1]

Compare that reverie with one of the last impressions the Spaniards had of the Aztec city before the military conquest of Tenochtitlan. During the ferocious Spanish siege of Tenochtitlan, the Aztecs made a desperate sacrifice of captive Spaniards to their sun and war god Huitzilopochtli whose shrine sat on top of the Great Temple, the Templo Mayor, located in the heart of the ceremonial center.

> When we retreated near to our quarters and had already crossed a great opening where there was much water, the arrows, javelins and stones could no longer reach us. Sandoval, Francisco de Lugo and Andreas de Tapia were standing with Pedro de Alvarado each one relating what had happened to him and what Cortés had ordered, when again there was sounded the dismal drum of Huichilobos and many other shells and horns and things like trumpets and the sound of them all was terrifying, and we all looked towards the lofty Pyramid where they were being sounded, and saw that our comrades whom they had captured when they defeated Cortés were being carried by force up the steps, and they were taking them to be sacrificed. When they got them up to a small square in front of the oratory, where their accursed idols are kept, we saw them place plumes on the heads of many of them and with things like fans in their hands they forced them to dance before Huichilobos and after they had danced they immediately placed them on their backs on some rather narrow stones which had been prepared as places for sacrifice, and with some knives they sawed open their chests and drew out their palpitating hearts and offered them to the idols that were there, and they kicked the bodies down the steps, and the Indian butchers who were waiting below cut off the arms and feet and flayed the skin off the faces, and prepared it afterwards like glove leather with the beards on, and kept those for the festivals when they celebrated drunken orgies and the flesh they ate in *chilmole*.[2]

These radically different impressions of Aztec life and religion, one emphasizing the peaceful order and architectural wonders of a capital city, the other lamenting the gruesome human sacrifices at the Great Temple, reflect the incongruous and enigmatic image of Aztec life which has troubled modern readers for centuries.[3] The Aztec image which

---

[1]Bernal Díaz del Castillo, *The Discovery and Conquest of Mexico* (New York: Farrar, Straus, and Giroux 1956), p. 191.

[2]Ibid, p. 436.

[3]See Benjamin Keen's expansive *The Aztec Image in Western Thought* (New Brunswick: Rutgers University, 1971) for an entertaining and thorough outline of the ways that modern scholars and artists have responded to the Aztec enigma.

glares at us through these passages is an image of startling juxtaposition of Flowers, Songs/Blood, Cut! We begin with a written text, composed by a foreigner, written many years after the fact, which alludes to the supreme sacred building and most powerful religious ritual in the Aztec world, i.e. the Templo Mayor called Coatepec (Serpent Mountain) by the Aztecs and the rites of *nextlahualtin* ( the debt payments), what we call human sacrifice. For students concerned with the various ways that the "interplay of textual and material evidence presents problems of interpretation" (J. Neusner on "The Topic and Problem" of this conference), this fractured image raises difficult questions. Just the second passage leads to such questions as "Did the Aztecs really carry out large scale human sacrifices" and "Just how lofty was this pyramid? Was it as big as the pyramids of Egypt?" and "What is the symbolic meaning of Spaniards going up and down the steps of the temple pyramid?" and "Why skin people?" And most importantly for our conference, "How are we to know, to find out?" As Inga Clendinnen asked about finding out about Maya peoples, "Is it possible to discover anything of the views and experiences of a people whose voices were hushed to a murmur more than 400 years ago?" Especially when these voices come to us, in part, through the Spanish word, perspective and bias. The Spaniards saw what they saw well but their records are to be tentatively used because on the one hand they tended to stereotype and project a "narrowly instrumental perspective, and one entailing distortion" while on the other hand they were often competing *with each other* to gain an interpretive upper hand for political and economic purposes. Clendinnen summarizes well the task at hand in this essay on the imagination of matter of the Great Aztec Temple.

> "Therefore the trick is to strip away the cocoon of Spanish interpretation to uncover the sequences of Indian actions, and then try to discern the pattern in those actions, as a way of inferring the shared understanding which sustains them."[4]

The problem of understanding this sacred place and ritual is particularly relevant at the present moment. While the Great Temple had been blown apart, dismantled and used as the foundation for colonial houses by the time Diaz del Castillo wrote his twilight memories, nevertheless the entire foundation of the temple has been excavated just within the last 20 years and new discoveries are taking place as we meet. This excavation as Leon Portilla's quote above states, has brought religious texts (codices, pictorials and eyewitness accounts) and material contexts into profound interaction and altered the formulation of

---

[4]Inga Clendinnen, *Ambivalent Conquests: Maya and Spaniard in Yucatan, 1517-1570* (Cambridge, Cambridge University Press, 1987) p. 132.

knowledge about the axis mundi of the Aztec empire. Because of the 20 year progress of this excavation I will both summarize how archaeology has already stimulated new questions and discoveries and raise several questions still to be explored in the interplay of religious texts and material contexts.

The most popular question is still "did the Aztecs really carry out human sacrifices?" Once we realize that the answer is yes, another more profound question arises which is "what did the Aztecs think they were up to (Clendinnen's "shared understanding") in building and using their main temple as the site for these kinds of ritual human sacrifices." As a way of getting at this second question about cosmovision, violent stones and the imagination of matter through the propinquity of text and material context I will focus on three passages in Diaz del Castillo's reminiscence (while not a "religious" text, it describes a religious place and rite). These passages are a) The "lofty pyramid where...we saw them place plumes on the heads of many of them and... b) "forced them to dance before Huicholobos...drew out their palpitating hearts and offered them to the idols...kicking the bodies down the steps" and c) "they flayed the skin off the faces, and prepared it afterwards like glove leather with the beards on". The first passage refers to height of the great temple pyramid that Eduardo Matos Moctezuma has been excavating continually since 1979. The second passage refers to the Aztec god Huitzilopochtli and the ritual of heart sacrifice and rolling sacrificial bodies down the stairways. As we shall see this emphasis on Huitzilopochtli shows no awareness of one of the most significant female goddesses associated with the Great Temple (and this rite) and uncovered in the excavation, namely the Coyolxauhqui stone. The third passage tells of the flaying of warriors and reflects one of the great Aztec ceremonies, Tlacaxipeualiztli, or the Feast of the Flaying of Men depicted in both pre-Hispanic pictorial ceremonies and 16th century research carried out by Spanish priests. Using these passages as cues, I will utilize both indigenous "sacred texts" and archaeology to tentatively illustrate how questions and answers evolve as we move our way along an ensemble of sources-from Spanish eyewitness accounts to the royal song/myth about the Great Temple to the material context of Proyecto Templo Mayor. (1978-01). Inserting my own interests into this process I will explore how three general questions, "how lofty was the pyramid", "why sacrifices to Huitzilopochtli" and "why skin people", are re-directed, in part, by archaeology and become

1) What is the nature of Aztec monumentality?
2) What is at the bottom of the sacrificial steps?

3) What is the meaning of Aztec sacrificial exchanges with the gods?

In what follows I will favor the archaeological evidence from Proyecto Templo Mayor and argue that a skillful interplay of an **ensemble of texts** and their material contexts will enable us to "find out" some of what the Aztecs thought they were up to in dragging those Spaniards up and down the steps of the Great Temple, taking out their hearts and flaying their skins. My own search for the patterns in these actions will be aided by reference to two central Nahuatl metaphors of ritual space and action. First, the metaphor of the *altepetl* or Water Mountain and secondly the metaphor of the *teotl ixiptla* the living image of the god. In this way I hope to reflect on the imagination of matter reflected in all types of evidence. By imagination of matter[5] I mean a) the ways that material forms in the Aztec world such as hills, stones, water, animals *and* humans impact human thought and b) ways that the Aztec imagination reshaped and reworked these material forms into sacred buildings, religious texts, offerings and meanings.

## The Aztec Ensemble

In focusing our questions on the Templo Mayor, we enter into the "Aztec ensemble of evidence." I stress the ensemble because the growing consensus in Mesoamerican studies is that rather than depending on one or even two types of evidence for interpretation, collaboration between multiple types of evidence and disciplines is essential. Leon-Portilla refers to the value of working with this ensemble above when he lists archaeology, pictorial manuscripts, Nahuatl poetry and Spanish eyewitness accounts as primary sources. We can add three other kinds of sources useful for understanding Aztec religion, i.e. Spanish priestly accounts, usually the result of interviews and conversations with Mexica survivors of the wars of conquest, colonial documents by Spaniards and mestizo authors, and contemporary ethnography.[6] Unlike the majority of texts available to us about the Aztecs, which were painted or written

[5] I borrow this term from Charles H. Long.

[6] It's important to say that a hermeneutics of suspicion is helpful in using these sources. Remember that the contact with native American peoples has never been fair or neutral but rather characterized by tremendous violence and greed. This fact affects the appraisal of Mesoamerican realities. As I have written elsewhere, "Between us and the pre-Columbian...symbols stand not just time and wear, distance and cultural diversity, and renewal with a tradition of wisdom, but also the conquest and the invention of the American Indian." In *Quetzalcoatl and the Irony of Empire: Myths and Prophecies in the Aztec Tradition,* (Niwot, University Press of Colorado, 2001) p. 6-7.

during the conquest or colonial period, and which reflect that crisis situation,[7] the Templo Mayor is a pre-Columbian expression and it can be viewed as an Aztec statement of their world view. My strategy now is to move from Diaz del Castillo to an overtly "religious text" the indigenous royal sacred song about the birth of Huitzilopochtli (a "religious text") and then to the archaeology of the Templo Mayor to explore the questions.

## Part 1
## What is the Nature of Aztec Monumentality?
## "the lofty pyramid where we saw them"

The central religious "text" associated with the Great Aztec Temple was collected and written down for the first time by a Spanish Franciscan friar in the middle of the 16th century, centuries before archaeological work contextualized it in a profoundly meaningful way. Even before Diaz del Castillo wrote down his dramatic recollections, Bernardino de Sahagun utilized the "round table agreement method" of Q and A with Aztec elders and younger scribes to reconstruct an encyclopedic view of Aztec life[8] that included extensive cosmological episodes. During one of his interviews, the Aztec elders recited a "teocuicatl" or divine song about the birth of their great god Huitzilopochtli at a place called Serpent Mountain.

This text can be summarized as follows.

On Coatepec (Serpent Mountain), the mother of the gods, Coatlicue (Lady of the Serpent Skirt) was sweeping out the temple.[9] A ball of feathers "descended upon her" and she placed it in her bosom. Later she discovered it had disappeared and immediately realized that she was pregnant. When the *centzon huitznahua* (the four hundred southerners, her children) heard that their mother had become pregnant at a holy place, they were outraged. Led by their sister Coyolxauhqui who was

[7]The nature of pre-Columbian primary sources present a distinct set of problems for the scholar interested in working with Mesoamerican materials. For a sampling of these problems and helpful approaches to them see, Donald Robertson, *Mexican Manuscript Painting of the Early Colonial Period: The Metropolitan Schools* (New Haven: Yale University Press, 1959); Charles Gibson, "A Survey of Middle American Prose Manuscripts in the Native Historical Tradition," *Handbook*, 15:311-21 and David Carrasco, "City as Symbol in Aztec Thought: Some Clues from the Codex Mendoza" in *City of Sacrifice*, (Boston, Beacon Press, 1999).

[8]See David Carrasco's discussion of Sahagun's method of research in *Quetzalcoatl and the Irony of Empire: Myths and Prophecies of the Aztec Empire*, (Niwot, University Press of Colorado, 2001) pp. 44-50.

[9]Bernardino de Sahagún's *Florentine Codex* III: 1-4 has the official Aztec version of this myth.

furious "as if bursting her heart," and who said, "My brothers she has dishonored us, we must kill our mother..."they prepare for the journey to Coatepec where they plan to attack their mother. Coyolxauhqui, "greatly excited and aroused the siblings to prepare for war." They "dressed themselves in war array with paper crowns, nettles, painted pipe streams and bells" and marched in military order to attack their mother. One member of the attacking troop, snuck out of camp at night, rushed to the mountain and delivered a warning of the attack to his mother. Coatlicue was frightened for her life but a voice spoke to her from her womb, "Have no fear, already I know what I must do." After a long journey of many days and nights the army, led by Coyolxauhqui in full fury, rushed up to the top of Serpent Mountain to kill Coatlicue. Just at the moment of attack, she gave birth to the god Huitzilopochtli who sprang from his mother's womb full grown. He dressed himself as a warrior and engaged his brothers and sisters in combat. He grabbed a serpent of fire, charged the leader Coyolxauhqui in a rage, and decapitated her in one swipe. The text reads,

> her body went falling below and it went crashing to pieces in various places, her arms, her legs, her body kept falling.

Huitzilopochtli then turned to the others, "he drove them away, he humbled them, he destroyed them, he annihilated them." In an act of symbolic possession he strips his sibling enemies of their symbols of military rank and "introduced them into his destiny, made them his own insignia."

In an important epilogue verse, we are told that since ancient times the Aztecs venerated Huitzilopochtli and "made sacrifices to him" at Serpent Mountain. Templo Mayor scholarship based primarily on written and pictorial sources (prior to the excavations which began in 1978) show that while it was generally understood that this myth served as a model of some kind for the Aztec shrine, very little was understood about the extent or specifics of this relationship. Archaeology has revealed that this song was a "mythic structure" for the Great Temple but also that the Great Temple became the architectural mythic structure par excellence of ritual life.[10]

There are several layers of meaning to this influential story. At one level Huitzilopochtli's birth and victorious battle against the four hundred siblings represents the solar dimension of Aztec religion. It represents the daily sunrise out of the earth and above the sacred

---

[10]For a cogent description and use of "mythic structure" see Jacob Neusner's *The Way of Torah: An Introduction to Judaism,* (Belmont, California, Wadsworth Publishing, 1993) pp. 78-93

mountain and the disappearance of the moon (Coyolxauhqui) and the stars (*centzon huitznahua).* Secondly this daily experience of nature is viewed by the bellicose Mexicas as a celestial conflict, war and sacrifice. The natural order is a violent order. The days are renewed through ritual combat at the sacred mountain. A third meaning is found in the historical chronicles of Diego Durán and Alvarado Tezozomoc. Their versions, collected from survivors of the Spanish attacks emphasize historical conflicts and battles between competing social groups. The leader of one group, Huitzilopochtli defeats the warriors of a woman leader, Coyolxauhqui, and tears open their breasts and eats their hearts at a mountain called Coatepec. Both historical versions tell of the origin of human sacrifice at the sacred place, Coatepec, during the rise of the Aztec nation and at the foundation of Tenochtitlan.[11]

It is important to focus on the meaning of the term Coatepec in the drama. Coatepec or Serpent Mountain was the name which Aztec peoples gave, not only to various hills but to their largest temple located in the center of their capital city which was the imperial center of an empire which integrated more than 400 cities and towns into its realm. According to several colonial pictorials, the Great Temple consisted of a massive platform supporting a pyramid whose facade supported two stairways rising to the two shrines; one dedicated to the sun god Huitzilopochtli and the other to Tlaloc the rain god. While the written and pictorial evidence refer to its monumentality and loftiness, it is only when we turn to the archaeology of the last 20 years that we begin to understand the Aztec commitment to a myth of monumentality.

*The Question of Monumentality and Proyecto Templo Mayor*

> "Another important contribution of the 1978-89 explorations was the discovery of several stages of construction of the Templo Mayor that were not known to either the Indians or the Spanish conquerors who lived in Tenochtitlan at the beginning of the sixtieth century. It was found that the Huey Teocalli was amplified on at least seven occasions on all four sides and that there were five more additions o the western facade." Leonardo Lopez Lujan, 1994, p. 64

In spite of the many colonial written references to the Templo Mayor, no one was certain as to its exact location under the streets and buildings of Mexico City. Was it beneath the National Cathedral, the Presidential Palace or off to one side? The excavation settled this question decisively. Also, there had been serious confusion about the orientation of the great temple precinct. Did it face East/West as several 16th century chronicles argued or North/South as many scholars insisted? The excavation

[11]Broda, "Aztec Ideology and Human Sacrifice," pp. 24-7.

clarified that it had been astronomically aligned on east-west orientation, lined up on the spring equinox.

But the "loftiness" of the pyramid that so impressed the Spaniards includes the following characteristics. First, as Lopez Lujan's quote above shows, the Great Aztec Temple was rebuilt and expanded seven complete times in a 200-year period with 4 extra facades added to its western sides. Correlation of this data with ethnohistorical analysis reveals that each Tlatoani (Chief Speaker) or Ruler was required to launch a war of conquest AND rebuild the temple as part of his inauguration festivities. This means that as the empire expanded in its control over more and more towns and territories, the Great Temple also grew in width and height until it reached the measurements of 84 meters East to West, 77 meters North to South and approximately 45 meters high. This size emphasized an impressively vertical image. To compare, the massive pyramid of the Moon in Teotihuacan was twice this size *at its base* but was the same height. To imagine the superior image of this structure it is important to remember that the entire city of Tenochtitlan was built on the swamps of the lake and the capital became a compact settlement of over 200,000 people. Secondly, the monumentality hinted at in Diaz del Castillo (and Cortes' eyewitness reports) has been expanded by the discovery of 30 other small and large temples and ritual structures immediately adjacent to the main temple. While we knew from Sahagun's research that 78 buildings were located within the larger (400 by 400 meters square) enclosed sacred precinct, the excavations have revealed stunning details about the symbolism, purpose, orientation, decorations and cult uses of these temples. In this sense, monumentality means abundance of cults at the heart of the empire. Also, these adjacent temples reveal a profound historical/ancestral vision of the Aztecs barely alluded to in the written sources. For instance, one structure is clearly a copy of temple architecture in Teotihuacan (the site popularly known as "the pyramids" near Mexico City), the greatest ancestral civilization of Mesoamerica that existed and collapsed over 700 years prior to the Mexica arrival in the Valley of Mexico. Another temple carries the symbolism of Tula, the great 10th century capital of the Feathered Serpent, revered for being the place of origin of the calendar, agriculture, astronomy and the arts. Archaeology has shown us in material terms, in color and shape that the Aztec sense of their "loftiness" included the claim that their sacred lineage reached back to the heights of urbanized culture. The Spaniards never knew they walked among and were sacrificed in the symbolic landscape of central Mesoamerican history linking the Mexicas with the legitimizing capitals of Teotihuacan and Tula. And while the Aztec claim to great lineages is slightly available in other parts of the documentary ensemble, nothing in those colorful glyphs or encyclopedic accounts approaches the lithic imagination of cosmology and monumentality evident in these many temples.

The excavation also illuminates two other types of monumentality important to the Aztec community: the abundance of human sacrifice and the abundance of buried offerings. It is not that the excavators found scores of human remains at the Templo Mayor but rather they found sacrificial victims and sacrificial ritual objects and symbols. In one case, Ofrenda 48, they found collected together in one cache the remains of 42 children between the ages of 2 and 7 who had been sacrificed and ritually decorated beneath the floor on the Rain God's side of the temple. Archaeologists have been able to combine information from this dig and ethnohistorical sources to reconstruct significant parts and meanings of this particular mass sacrifice of children. And as we shall discuss in the next section on the significance of the sacred stairs, excavators found over 7000 ritual objects, most from distant communities collected *into the great container* that was the Great Temple.

## Part 2:
## What is at the bottom of the sacrificial steps?
## "Huitzilopochtli...down the steps"

We have known from a few 16th century written sources that the symbolism of Huitzilopochtli's birth at Coatepec and the defeat of his siblings was *somehow* incorporated into the sculpture and architecture of the Great Aztec Temple.[12] But these texts favored the prominence of the male god Huitzilopochtli and never mentioned the most astonishing single piece of sculpture found in the Americas since 1790, the 11-foot circular stone of Coyolxauhqui. Every element of this stone is remarkable including its symbolic location, gender and imagery.

In February of 1978 electrical workers excavating a pit beneath the street behind the National Cathedral uncovered a massive oval stone more than ten feet in diameter with the mint condition image of an Aztec goddess carved on it. The image consisted of a decapitated and dismembered female goddess whose blood streams were connected to jewels meaning this was divine blood. Her striated head cloth, stomach, arms and legs were circled by serpents. A skull served as her belt buckle. She had earth monster faces on her knees, elbows and ankles. Her sandals reveal a royal figure and the iconography shows that this is

[12]Miguel Leon Portilla "Ethnohistorical Record for the Huey Teocalli of Tenochtitlan", in Elizabeth Boone, *The Aztec Templo Mayor,* (Washington D.C., Dumbarton Oaks, 1987) pp. 71-95.

the Aztec moon goddess Coyolxauhqui.[13] As a result of this incredible discovery, Proyecto Templo Mayor was initiated to excavate the foundation of the entire structure. Initial excavations uncovered another, older Coyolxauhqui stone beneath alongside several impressive "Ofrendas" or what appeared to be Aztec offerings to gods.

In order to understand further how archeology stimulates new questions and answers about the *teocuicatl* of Huitzilopochtli's birth we recall that a handful of written sources suggested that the Templo Mayor was the architectural replica of the song. The Templo Mayor excavation uncovered the seven complete rebuildings of the temple (with five extra facades) but we did not previously mention that each rebuilding consisted of replicas of the dual stairways leading from the general platform up to the two shrines at the top. It is estimated that what the Spaniards saw were the two grand stairways of over 120 steps leading up to the shrines. A major archaeological clue to the significance of sacrificed Spaniards being thrown down the steps in Diaz del Castillo's account and Coyolxauhqui being thrown down the hill in the song comes from where the great stone was discovered in relation to the temple. The circular monolith was found directly at the base of the stairway leading up to Huitzilopochtli's temple. On both sides of the stairway's base completing the bottom of the stairway's sides, were two large grinning serpent heads. Many serpent heads jutted out from at least two sides of the outer wall of the Great Temple. The image is clear. The Templo Mayor is the architectural image of the mytho-historical account of the events at Coatepec or Serpent Mountain. Just as Huitzilopochtli triumphed at the top of the mountain, while his sister was dismembered and fell to pieces below, so Huitzilopochtli's temple and icon sat triumphantly at the top of Templo Mayor with the carving of the dismembered goddess layed out horizontally far below, the recipient of falling bodies. This drama of sacrificial dismemberment in the song is solidified in the up and down symmetry of the architecture. A number of scholars have begun to interpret the gender significances in this symmetry and myth.

We learn from the combination of violent stones and pictorial and written sources how this mythic structure i.e. the Templo Mayor contributed to the sanctification and enlargement of human sacrifices. As the Aztec Empire expanded, the priest kings felt forced to use incremental human sacrifice as a policy of conquest and persuasion.

---

[13]See Henry B. Nicholson's detailed interpretation of the Coyolxauhqui stone in "The New Tenochtitlan Templo Mayor Coyolxauhqui-Chantico Monument" in press, in Festschrift honoring Professor Gerdt Kutscher, Ibero-Amerikanisches Institut, Berlin, Germany.

They drew their inspiration in part from the myth of Huitzilopochtli's birth and the dramatic stone of Coyolxauhqui that came to serve as the altar for bodies to land on and perhaps be skinned on at the stairways base.

## Part 3
## What is the meaning of Aztec sacrificial exchanges with the gods? "...and flayed the skin off the faces... and kept those for festivals when they celebrated..."

> "Among the most surprising discoveries at the excavations at the Templo Mayor of the Mexica were the rich offerings found there. From the very beginning of our work, we were aware of the importance of these offerings. Because of this, we formulated a specific technique that included extreme care in the process of exploration. This technique allowed us to record clearly the location and internal association of each object and to document the relationship between a group of offerings in regard to a number of other questions...no specific (native) document was written describing how the objects were deposited, what ritual accompanied them, and when they were placed there. The ancient priests had been careful not to transmit information about something that was of greatest importance to them because this was not just any building but their principal temple, the heart and center of their universe...These gifts were the means of communication between humans and the gods, a message expressed in the placement of every object." Eduardo Matos Moctezuma in preface to Leonardo Lopez Lujan's *The Offerings of the Great Temple of Tenochtitlan,* p. xxi-xxii

The third passage I am selecting from Diaz del Castillo's eyewitness account refers to the Aztec rite of Tlacaxipeualiztli, or the Feast of the Flaying of Men which was carried out each year during the second month of the solar calendar. This passage presents one of the most difficult Aztec images to understand—the image of brutal human sacrifice and the skinning of victims. But the passage hints at more i.e. the wearing of skins by Aztec priests, the use of these second skins in rituals and finally cannibalism. In fact, we have detailed information about this ritual in the written record, especially in the second book of Bernardino de Sahagun's *Florentine Codex.* Using that account alone and without much need of archaeology we can gain insight into the paraphernalia, choreography, and purpose of ritual skinning. These purposes included the acquisition of charismatic objects filled with divine fire, (as in the divine song of Huitzilopochtli taking the "emblems" of his sibling and wearing them) the renewal of corn and the preparation for war.[14] It also appears that the rite of heart sacrifice, skinning and "drunken orgies" refers to the sacred offerings and exchanges with particular Aztec Gods. One important element *not* mentioned in the Spaniards report is that these skins were deposited in boxes kept in the floor of the temple as part of a regular schedule of buried offerings to the gods who resided within the body of the temple. Impressed with this combination of sacrifice, skinning and depositing these powerful skins in the temple's floor, we turn to both the ethnohistorical interpretation and the archaeological extension of the meaning of these "ofrendas" or gifts.

In what follows I will a) briefly describe the rite of flaying and offering and b) move to the archaeological record to show how the material context of the 118 "ofrendas" found *in the floors of the* Templo Mayor enlarge our understanding of "gift-exchange" among the Aztecs in ways the written record simply cannot. Helpful in this evolution in our knowledge of the meaning of offerings are two notions central to Aztec ritual the notion of the *teotl ixiptla,* the living god image and the notion of the *altepetl,* the mountain of water still influential among native communities in Mexico today.

*The Flaying of Men and Offerings*

In the month of Tlacaxipeualiztli, (the Flaying of Men) the people celebrated a festival in honor of Xipe Totec. One of the central acts was the sacrificing and flaying of captive warriors who were led through an elaborate series of rituals in the calpullis and main ceremonial center of Tenochtitlan. Prior to the actual sacrifice and flaying, the warriors were transformed into teotl ixiptlas or living images of gods. In one account, a captive was bathed, purified and dressed as the teotl ixiptla, the living image of the god Xipe Totec 40 days before the feast day and displayed in public in each of the city's barrios. The captive warriors were taken to Xipe Totec's temple and "put...to the test" when yopi tortillas, representing their hearts were torn from them. Then they were adorned as sacrificial victims, displayed four times before the people, accompanied by their captors who were also ritually adorned to designate their honor. At the height of this festival, the victims were given new names and the names of gods, forced to dance with their captors and eventually sacrificed either at the top of Xipe's temple or on the gladiatorial stone with "the entire city" present. Their heart's were "torn from them", their blood poured into "the eagle vessel". The slain captive was now called eagle man and his body was rolled "breaking to

---

[14]See my chapter "Give Me Some Skin: The Charisma of the Aztec Warrior" in *City of Sacrifice: The Aztec Empire and the Role of Violence in Civilization* (Boston: Beacon Press, 1999).

pieces, they came head over heels...they reached the terrace at the base of the pyramid." Their bodies were dismembered and divided up so that parts could be ceremonially eaten. Before being dismembered the sacrificed captives were flayed and their skins worn by individuals who moved through the neighborhoods of the city and fought intense mock battles in the streets or collected gifts from the homes of citizens.

At first glance, this short description indicates the central role that the transformation of the human body played in the ritual theatre of Aztec religion. A more sustained view shows the importance of social and symbolic movements and the redistribution of the charisma of the warrior throughout the ceremonial landscape of Aztec Mexico. This feast of the flaying of men transforms the city into the perfect battlefield where "no one fears to die in war".

Among the many fascinating details of this rite, impressively recounted in written sources is the notion of the teotl ixiptla that is central to understanding what is so significant about the archaeological discoveries of what was buried in the floors at the Templo Mayor. Alfredo Lopez Austin describes the meaning of the god-images this way. The deity impersonators were

> teteo *imixiptlahuan*...men possessed by the gods, who, as such, died in a rite of renewal. The idea of a calendric cycle, of a periodic returning, in which the power of a god was born, grew decreased and concluded made it necessary in a rite linking the time of man to mythical time that a god would die so his force might be reborn with new power. It was not men who died, but gods-gods within a corporeal covering that made possible their ritual death on earth. If the gods did not die, their force would diminish in a progressively aging process. Men destined for sacrifice were temporarily converted into receptacles of divine fire, they were treated as gods, and they were made to live as the deity lived in legend. Their existence in their role of the ixiptlatin, or 'images', could last from a few days up to four years."

As suggested in both the Diaz del Castillo's account and the myth of Huitzilopochtli's birth, the "collection" of this divine fire in the material forms of bodies, skins, hearts, emblems was a crucial part of the rebirth of the "force" of a god and for the Aztecs. In the written record we often see how this collection takes place in rites of heart sacrifice that always involved offerings/gifts to the gods. What the archaeology of the Templo Mayor has added to this view of "sacred collecting" and offerings is that the practice was, in part, anchored and monumentalized in the floors of the Great Temple in ways largely unnoticed in the written accounts. It is not that skins or "hearts" survived the hundreds of years since the conquest, but what has survived has been an astonishing diversity of ritual offerings to gods, offerings that represented the "hearts" and divine fire of the people and their gods.

### *Great Temple as Receptacle of Divine Fire*

As the excavation of the Great Temple proceeded, archeologists were surprised, as Matos Moctezuma notes above, by the number, symmetry, symbolism of the over 118 offering caches buried in the floors. We know from a series of colonial documents that the Spaniards became aware of precious objects buried in the Aztec temple floors. Andres de Tapia reported that Cortes actually dug into the floors and walls of the Great Temple and found a "deposit of blood, seeds, and an earthenware water jar. They opened it and extracted gold jewel and there was some gold in a tomb at the top of the tower." (Tapia 1963:70) This brief reference, skipping over the other objects usually find in these kinds of deposits is typical of others including Diaz del Castillo's account of the superimposition of a church built in honor of Saint James on top of the temple in Tlatelolco. He notes "when the foundations were laid bare, in order to make them more solid, they found much gold, silver, jade, pearls, irregular seed pears and other precious stones."[15] At different times during the colonial period, both Spaniards and Indians pillaged offerings and pre-Hispanic burials at various sites. Regardless of this awareness or even 20th century excavations at various temple complexes in Mesoamerica, no one imagined the numbers, symmetry, symbolism and diversity of offering caches found at the Templo Mayor. I cannot go into a detailed description of what the 20 years of excavation has uncovered but the work of Proyecto Templo Mayor uncovered the following patterns.

The 118 offerings of symbolic tribute have been uncovered at strategic points around the base of the pyramid at every stage of its construction. The offerings were buried, for the most part at axial points i.e. in line with the centers of stairways, or at the points joining different temple sections and at the corners. These offerings contain seashells, finely carved masks, statues of deities, sacrificed humans and animals, knives and jewelry. The numbers and diversities of ritual objects given to the gods of the Great Temple are stunning. Consider the contents and provenience of just one of the offerings, Chamber 2 located at the base of the stairway in front of Tlaloc's shrine, in which a large number of finely carved masks were mixed with images of the gods, Tlaloc, Xiuhtecuhtli (Fire God) and Chalchiuhtlicue (Goddess of Precious Stones), a sacrificed puma and other greenstone images in one burial. The three layers of offerings contained *among other items*: 3,997 conch shells; 2,178

---

[15]See the excellent study of all aspects of the offerings in Leonardo Lopez Lujan's *The Offerings of the Templo Mayor of Tenochtitlan,* (Niwot, University Press of Colorado, 1994) For a summary of the ethnohistorical record, see pp. 5-9.

greenstone beads; 87 sculptures and 56 masks from the Mezcala region; and a puma's skeleton covering the eastern side of the deposit.

Like the centzon huitznahua of Huitzilopochtli's divine song and the Spaniards who came from afar, many of the most valued objects accumulated at the Templo Mayor were from distant places. Over eighty per cent of these objects are from distant and frontier provinces under Aztec domination including a large percentage from the peripheries of the Aztec world, the oceans. Their presence in the heart of the city displays the attempts to integrate valued and symbolic objects from the periphery of the Aztec cosmos into the foundation of the central shrine as a means of sanctifying the conquests and the expansion of Aztec sacred social order. For instance a number of offerings contain huge and small shells, usually oriented towards the south, which were brought from the distant seacoasts. They represent the powers of fertility associated with the great bodies of water. These powers are also represented in the crocodiles and swordfish buried at the temple.

The work of Leonardo Lopez Lujan speaks directly to the task of this conference i.e. understanding how material contexts shape, not only our information about religion but also the way we ask and explore questions of interpretation and meaning-in this case the meaning of accumulating sacred fire in the form of ritual offerings to gods. Lopez Lujan argues that the ritual specialists at the Great Temple were concerned with the "management of inner space" of the caches. The objects in the offering caches were never placed in a random order. "It seemed evident to us that the patterned distribution of the gifts followed a code of expression that could be deciphered by examining the contexts. For this reason I tried to explain the relationship between the unearthed material and ritual behavior."[16] It appears that this management of the inner space of these accumulated "gifts" was guided by a symbolic language that was developed to establish effective communication with the living and dying gods, vital forces and sacred entities that dwelled within the great shrine.[17] Whether as skins worn in public and deposited in boxes at the foot of the Great Temple or the amazing diversity of

---

[16]Leonardo Lopez Lujan, *The Offerings of the Templo Mayor of Tenochtitlan,* p xxiv.

[17]Ibid., Lopez Lujan believes there is a language to these offerings. "The information...shows that archaeological contexts have a great similarity to ritual syntax and to verbal language. If this is correct, we will find two kinds of archaeological syntax: an "internal" one, corresponding to the distribution of objects within a container or receptacle, and an "external" one, related to the arrangement of the offerings with respect to architectural structures. In this sense, we could speak of a 'language' of the offerings that resembles the basic principles o writing—a langue not only expressed in signs and symbols, but also with grammatical (or contextual rules." p. 144.

accumulated objects buried in the floors of the shrine, the Mexicas were apparently focusing their most precious gifts into the interior space of their axis mundi.

*Ethnography of the* ***Altepetl***

This combination of lofty pyramid, mythic steps and skins, masks, ashes, stones, pumas and crocodiles offered as gifts in the inner space of the Great Temple point to the most important example of the imagination of matter of all-the Mesoamerican notion of the altepetl. As Diaz del Castillo's description of that human sacrifice showed, the Mexicas were thoroughly galvanized toward the prestige and power of their temple. They were sacrificing enemy warriors at their sacred hill in order to not only destroy them but to gain sacred power from Huitzilopochtli.

But we should not be seduced into thinking that archaeology and its emergent questions tell all there is to know or where to look. In fact, a recent interpretive work based in part on contemporary ethnography responds effectively to the questions of "why so much emphasis on the *interior* of the shrine?" and "why so many ritual offerings?" Alfredo Lopez Austin has written a book seeking to understand two conflicting Mesoamerican notions of paradise entitled *Tamoanchan/Tlalocan: Places of Mist.* After studying for several decades the ancient concepts of the Nahuas concerning "aquatic processes of the cosmos" including the creation of corn, (and working at the Templo Mayor during the 20 years of excavation) Lopez Austin decided to utilize 20th century ethnographies to enhance his evolving model of paradise. The continuities were dazzling and he discovered a symbolic complex that links pre-Hispanic, colonial and contemporary native views to the Templo Mayor. The basic notion is called the "altepetl" and consists of the following. The control over the growth and reproduction of humans, plants, animals and wealth belongs in the hands of the gods who dwell in a great hill. The gods live in this altepetl, this mountain of water and guard the "hearts" "seeds" or the "shadows of seeds" which are the invisible life forces of animals, humans, minerals, currents of water, and all plants and insects. It is known that these "hearts" come from and return to the hill's interior depending on ritual exchanges, i.e. offerings and petitions made by humans on one side and on the other side of the exchange the collection and release of the "hearts" by ancestors and gods residing in caves inside the hill. The paradigmatic altepetl is located in the east quadrant of the cosmos where the creator gods and the extraordinary humans (hombre-dioses) who share the essence of these gods reside. All other hills designated as altepetls by diverse communities, as well as sacred centers for pilgrimages and great temples are considered replications of this great hill. It is the role of priests and warriors to keep the living images that contain the "hearts", "seeds" and "shadows of seeds" within the temples. In other words, the temples are sacred granaries, houses for the economy of the gods.

Humans, in order to participate in the cycles of rebirth must make offerings to the sacred hill in many forms including offerings of objects that are symbolic seeds such as human hearts, heads, skins obtained in sacrifices.

> "Human beings, like all beings in the world, have a 'heart'...which comes, like all other 'hearts' from the great storehouse of wealth. It comes from the great mythical storehouse, spends some time on earth, returns to the storage area, and waits for the moment of another birth...Like the spirit of maize...A recycling return to the storehouse is required not only for the 'hearts of maize or of humans. The 'hearts' of all the different beings have to comply with the cycle."

As a sign of how this notion permeated Mesoamerican life, the altepetl or mountain of water also referred to "the people", "the government", "the city", and "the community". The capital city of Tenochtitlan was the Huey Altepetl, or Great Mountain of Water. This term appears abundantly in all elements of the written ensemble.

I leave it to the reader and the next generation of interpreters to relate the altepetl as "unearthed" in 20th century ethnography back to the three questions of loftiness, the gendered steps and the buried caches at the Great Temple.

## Final Cut

I have tried to both summarize some useful responses to the questions I raised at the beginning of this paper and suggest new responses as a way of moving onto different questions and interpretations suggested by archaeology. I believe we can claim that archaeology with its attention to the "foundations" has been crucial in finding out some "patterns in those actions as a way of inferring the shared understandings which sustained them" (Clendinnen). Now, when we turn back to both Diaz del Castillo's stereotyped account and the teocuicatl's version, enlivened by Proyecto Templo Mayor, we see the action differently. The Spaniard saw the humiliation of fellow soldiers at the summit of the Great Temple just before their brutal murders. And most interpretations of the royal myth are satisfied with the dismemberment of Coyolxauhqui and that cosmogonic sacrifice. But given the sheer number of objects, rebuildings and victims we encounter during our journey through these different accounts, and especially in the archaeology we are forced to pay attention to the entire myth/song.

The text moves on beyond Huitzilopochtli's attack on his sister to emphasize the sacrifice of *all the others.* "He pursued them, he chased them, all around the mountain…four times…with nothing could they defend themselves…Huitzilopochtli chased them, he drove them away, he humbled them, he destroyed them, he annihilated them…he stripped off their gear…he introduced them into his destiny, he made them his own insignia." The myth is not about a single sacrifice of divine siblings but about the increment of sacrifice where a warrior god killed an abundance of other warrior gods who had traveled from afar and attacked the temple and goddess at the altepetl, the sacred mountain. Huitzilopochtli took their hearts and insignias and wore them himself, reinvigorated just after his birth. The Aztecs we learn from historical sources successfully integrated many city-states into their empire and sent thousands of enemy warriors and women rolling down those stairs to land on Coyolxauhqui's stone. However, some communities were alienated into the direction of other kingdoms and the capacity for rebellion increased. Nowhere was this pattern of social fission clearer than in the alliance building process that Cortes' directed as he traveled through the outskirts of the empire and met both vicious resistance and widespread support from communities both loyal and disloyal to Moctezuma's capital. All the more reason then for the desperate Aztecs to sacrifice those Spanish warriors at the Templo Mayor during their "rebellion" against the capital. In the eyes of the eagle and jaguar knights the Spaniards were the threatening personification of the four hundred children who had come out of the darkness, marching from the periphery of the cosmos to destroy the deity, the city, the temple, the altepetl.

# 13

## Anglican Church-Building and the Problem of Textual Interpretation

Peter W. Williams
*Miami University*

Interpreting the meaning of modern religious buildings in more than a one-dimensional manner is a task that has only recently been undertaken by scholars of religion. Until a few years ago, virtually the entirety of such literature was that generated by architectural historians, who were preoccupied with the development of stylistic features and only incidentally, if at all, concerned with the other levels of meaning that lay implicit in houses of worship. The transmission and evolution of the elements of architectural style as revealed, for example, in the metamorphoses of the New England Congregationalist meetinghouse from the early colonial era into the nineteenth century is certainly an interesting task, and one that has been done very capably by a variety of scholars. However, stopping with the architectural elements themselves is to truncate a fascinating story just as it is beginning. Style itself, for example, can be read in the narrow sense of its particular physical elements, such as porticos, columns, and pediments or, more broadly, in its meaning as a system of conspicuous display of fashion that indicates to what degree the displayer is au courant with the latest and most prestigious modes of material consumption and expression. This leads us into issues of social class as well as the dispersion of style from imperial core to colonial periphery. To say only this much is to give some sense of the dimensions of the questions of interpretation of the artifacts of the built environment.

However, the scholar of religion can add considerably more to the interpretive exchange. At the most obvious level, religious buildings have to be looked upon as places designed for a particular activity, namely, the rituals of worship, which are designed by religious communities as a central means of communication with the divine. The design of a church or other religious building, especially its interior, is thus laid out with an eye for the accommodation of a particular set of practices, which may involve the reading aloud of scripture, the procession of appropriately garbed celebrants, and/or the performance of sacramental rituals intended to purify from sin, to mark the transition from one phase of life to another, and the like. These considerations may affect the overall shape of a building; square, circular, rectangular, or cruciform; as well as the provision of seating, aisles, balconies, niches, and various forms of liturgical furniture. They may also dictate certain modes of decoration, such as sculpture and stained glass windows, or, whether by neglect or direct prohibition, their exclusion. To what degree such buildings might themselves be regarded as in some sense as *sacred spaces;* as intrinsically set apart and distinguished from ordinary secular or profane space; is another distinctively religious issue raised in such analyses.

The Church of England brought into being through the political needs and ambitions of Henry VIII was completely indifferent in its early decades to such considerations which the Protestant Reformers on the Continent had debated with varying results. (Luther was the most conservative, the Anabaptists the most radical.). Worship continued exactly as it had in the medieval centuries until Henry's demise, at which time his Archbishop of Canterbury, Thomas Cranmer, began to devise a new vernacular liturgy which in its succeeding avatars began to introduce a new and much more explicitly Protestant understanding of ritual worship into the public domain. After Cranmer's execution during the reign of the Catholic Mary Tudor and the emergence of a Puritan party within the Church of England under Mary's half-sister Elizabeth I, a whole panoply of issues of belief and worship came into open debate within the Church of England which were not settled definitively until the overthrow and restoration of the Stuart monarchs had been accomplished in the middle of the seventeenth century." During the whole period from Henry's break with the Pope to the accession of Charles II in 1660, little church building took place; most of the controversy was over what was to be done with the churches that had been around since medieval times. It was only after the Restoration of the Stuarts that a wholesale new program of church design and building began to take place in England and, with it, the development of a new paradigm of housing for public worship.

Prior to the campaign of church building that ensued from the Great Fire of London of 1666, two major paradigms had been at war in England, as well as in parts of the Continent, for the nature of houses of worship. One was that which had developed during the Middle Ages when the hegemony of the Catholic Church, based in Rome, had gone effectively unchallenged for centuries. Two of the major principles at work in the design of the vast physical plant which had spread during these centuries throughout Britain as well as most of the rest of western and central Europe were those of *sacramentalism* and *hierarchy.* As Erwin Panofsky demonstrated in his classic study, *Gothic Architecture and Scholasticism,* the medieval cathedral especially (as well as individual churches to a lesser degree), were virtual *summas* in the scholastic sense of the term; that is, summaries, in pictorial form, of the history of the Christian church, including in their sculptural schemes, as well as their painting and stained glass, epitomes of the Old and New Testaments, the history of the Christian church, and the inhabitants of the celestial realm. The entire building thus served the function both of instruction and mediation. The often illiterate worshiper could learn the teachings of the Christian faith through observation of the lessons and knowledge contained within the building's fabric. In addition, he or she would participate in the sacramental rituals which the church had been designed to house and to facilitate.

The principle of hierarchy was also demonstrated in the design of churches and cathedrals, the basic shape of which had been derived from the Roman *basilica,* a building form originally designed for secular administrative purposes within the context of the old Roman Empire and built on a scale to inspire awe for the law which was there dispensed. The basilica, which was after Constantine's revolution transmuted first into the Romanesque and then into the Gothic style of church design, was rectangular in form, and placed the seat of power at the far end of the building from the entry through which ordinary folk would gain access. In its ecclesiastical guise, a stylized arrangement of spaces emerged which became long normative. Entry was through the short west end, and was mediated through a *narthex,* or vestibule, which provided a transition between the profane external world and the sacred realm of worship. Immediately inside was the *nave,* where worshipers sat or stood during the service. Beyond this, and again demarcated by such devices as steps, rails, or screens, was the *choir,* where monks or boys chanted parts of the service (in monastic and cathedral churches), and then, ultimately, the *sanctuary* (from Latin *sanctus,* holy), in which only the clergy and their assistants were permitted and in which the sacramental mystery of transubstantiation was performed.

The outbreak of the Protestant Reformation early in the sixteenth century brought within some of its wings ; notably, the Reformed tradition that arose from the work of Zwingli, Calvin, and others in Switzerland; a profound challenge to the notion that humanly created space could be endowed with sacral or sacramental qualities, as had been the presumption during the Middle Ages and which continued on in the Roman Catholic and Eastern Orthodox traditions. The Reformed tradition manifested itself in Britain in the form of Puritanism, a movement for thoroughgoing reform of belief, worship, and conduct. The Puritan movement began to coalesce during the reign of Elizabeth and found brief public triumph during the Interregnum between the first and second Stuart ascendencies from 1647 to 1660 under the direction of first Oliver Cromwell and, briefly, his son Richard. The Puritan attitude towards sacred space was enunciated clearly in the Westminster Confession of 1646, the twenty-first chapter of which stated that "[n]either prayer nor any part of religious worship is now under the gospel, either tied unto or made more acceptable by any place in which it is performed, or towards which it is directed." For the most part, however, English Puritans expressed their sentiments not in words but by deeds, such as the rampant iconoclasm demonstrated in Cromwell's campaign to obliterate as much statuary, stained glass, and other manifestations of pictorial religious expression which his party considered idolatrous in its ostensible aim of attempting to capture the sacred in material form. Even during this brief period of Reformed ascendancy, however, little of a positive nature took place in terms of a public building program, other than the erection of a few private chapels for Puritan squires.[1] The development of a distinctive positive form for Reformed worship did begin to emerge during the same century in the New World, however, a story to which we shall return in due course.

The struggle between Puritan "Roundhead" and Royalist "Cavalier" during the seventeenth century was, as all struggles are, about power, but in this case a power couched extensively in religious terms. Although Henry VIII's break with Rome was clearly an assertion of monarchical over papal power, the implications for religious authority in this struggle were thin. Whether in Anglican or Roman guise, the physical structure of church and cathedral and the liturgies performed therein were expressions of the power of an almighty God who employed the hierarchical agencies of both church and state to achieve his purposes, that is, obedience to his will and law. These latter were not only revealed directly in Scripture but unfolded gradually over the centuries through the interpretations of the institutional church. The introduction of the Reformed faith into Britain in the form of Puritanism had brought with it a profound challenge to such authority in its exaltation of Scripture as the unique and unalterable source of divine will and law. Scripture thus became the model for both civil and ecclesiastical government and, since

[1]"Nonconformist chapel," in Jane Turner, *Encyclopedia of Art.*

it nowhere mentioned bishop, the latter functionaries were banished from any role in church governance. No compromise between the two paradigms seemed possible to the contestants in the struggles of Stuart times.

After the restoration of the monarchy in 1660, however, a disaster of natural rather than human origins provided the setting for the emergence of such a third paradigm. The great fire of London of 1666 had destroyed or badly damaged eighty-seven of the urban churches which had proliferated during medieval times.[2] Sir Christopher Wren was commissioned to rebuild London's "churchscape," and those that remain of the fifty-one which he designed together constitute a remarkable architectural legacy in their elegant adaptation of classical principles to the often cramped and irregular sites which were the legacy of medieval planning (or the lack thereof.) We also have documentary evidence that Wren was designing not just with aesthetic but with theological and liturgical principles in mind. In or around 1711 he wrote the following summary of these principles:

> ...in our reformed Religion, it should seem vain to make a Parish church larger, than that all who are present can both hear and see. The Romanists, indeed, may build larger Churches, it is enough if they hear the murmur of the Mass, and see the elevation of the Host, but ours are to be fitted for Auditories. I can hardly think it practicable to make a single room so capacious, with Pews and Galleries, as to hold over 2000 Persons, and to hear all the Service, and both to hear distinctly, and see the Preacher.[3]

Wren was clearly working within the Reformed tradition of emphasis on the preached Word as the primary means of contact between the divine and the human, as reflected in the centrally-located massive pulpits and the absence of altars that characterized the earlier building or, more usually, remodeling projects undertaken by Calvin, Zwingli, and the Huguenot and Puritan successors. However, some new elements were present here. Wren's churches, which established the prototype not only for Gibbs and Hawksmoor, his English successors, but also for Anglican and other churches in the North American colonies, were clearly products of the Enlightenment as well as the Reformation. Their neo-classical features and their clear glass windows betokened a new emphasis both on elegance and on clarity. They were also distinctly Anglican churches. As James Fenton points out in a recent essay review on works about Wren and other architects of his time, Wren and his contemporaries and successors looked not to the very earliest Christian

---

[2]Whinney, 45; Fenton, 27.
[3]Whinney, 48.

era for their models, when worship was out of prudence and necessity conducted largely in private homes or literally underground in catacombs. This was the period which commended itself most to more radical Protestants, such as the Puritans, who were forced in many cases to emulate their forebears in retreating into private homes or even barns to evade the watchful eye of the Establishment. Rather, they took as their models the post-Constantinian churches which were built on Roman prototypes (e.g., the basilica) after the Emperor Constantine had made Christianity not only legal but, indeed, the preferred religion of the late Empire. As Fenton comments, "What we see...is an attempt to stop primitive Christianity, as an ideal, getting out of hand, and undermining the prestige and position of the Established [i.e. Anglican] Church.[4]

The transit of English church-building fashions and principles led during the colonial period to some interesting variations of the established themes. The oldest surviving English church in the colonies is Old Saint Luke's in Isle of Wight County, near Smithfield, Virginia. Although local tradition has always favored a date of 1632, based on an inscription found on a beam, scholars today believe that 1685 is more probable. (Many church tour guides, in Virginia and elsewhere, frequently emphasize features that are reputedly the oldest, largest, and/or most expensive of their kind, even if the evidence is scanty or doubtful.) The name here is also misleading, since it dates to the nineteenth rather than the seventeenth century. (Most colonial Virginia churches have names such as "Hickory Neck" or "Merchant's Hope," derived from their locality or, as in the later case, an unknown source, possibly a corruption. The "high church," or more Catholic, practice of bestowing saints names on buildings is either a medieval carry-over or the result of nineteenth century movements which we shall discuss shortly.)[5] Old Saint Luke's is particularly interesting because it demonstrates a transition between one style and another in a colonial context. Essentially a Gothic country parish church with buttresses, pointed-arch lancet windows, and a screen separating the sanctuary from the nave, it also has some of the geometrical motifs of the new neo-classical style popularized by Wren and others.

The leading interpretation of Old St. Luke's and the other thirty-six surviving colonial Anglican churches in Virginia; the most powerful and populous of the southern colonies, in which Anglicanism and slave-holding were both legally established; is provided by architectural historian Dell Upton is his 1986 study, *Beliefs and Holy Places.* Upton offers some interesting observations in his introduction as to the

---

[4]Fenton, 26.
[5]Upton, vii.

principles which guided him in this study, which prior to his work had been primarily the province of antiquarians concerned with uncontextualized detail. For example, he states that

> I will argue that while pious impulses and a desire for religious edification moved many Virginians to attend church, these are not sufficient to explain churchgoing in the colony, for the churches were inseparable from the secular life of the parish community. Holy things *and* profane, fused in an eloquent manner, animated the Church and gathered the parishioners, in a process in which the church building and its contents were catalysts. The construction and use of the church were symbolic acts. To build a church was to build the world; not a model of the world or an image of it. The church was one way for eighteenth-century Virginians to explore and ultimately to describe their environment. It provided a meaningful context within with to comprehend and digest change.[6]

Upton is thus concerned not simply with tracing the transit of stylistic components and fashions, although these architectural materials are among the sources which he does utilize, along with documentary evidence from parish records. He has an anthropologist's interest in evoking a whole system of culture from the various pieces of evidence at his disposal. He continues in his introduction:

> When I examine a church, I cannot believe that the parts of it that are common, that are Virginian, are merely lapses in the builders' attempt to reproduce European forms. They are as noteworthy as that which is English and fashionable I assume that the users' alterations to the church are as significant as the builders' intentions. The Anglican church is not just Wren and the Renaissance, it is The Builder's Dictionary, and the Reformation, and the gentry, and slave and indentured labor, and the taxation system. It is the vestries, and the builders, and the parishioners, and Virginia and England.[7]

These colonial Anglican churches, though differing in detail, do have a number of significant commonalities and, as Upton suggests, can be read in a variety of intersecting and overlapping contexts. First, they are, of course, Anglican churches, though reflective of the "low church" or Protestant understanding of the tradition that was prevalent in the colonies during this period. They are primarily houses of worship in what had by now coalesced as a distinctive Anglican tradition, employing the *Book of Common Prayer* together with Scripture as the primary texts to be read aloud in prescribed fashion to the assembled worshipers. To this end, each was equipped with four "liturgical stations" for the performance of Anglican worship rituals. These

[6]*Ibid.*, xxi.
[7]*Ibid.*, xxii.

included a reading desk, from which the Bible was read; a pulpit, from which the same Scripture was expounded; a communion *table* (in preference to the term *altar,* which was too Roman Catholic in its connotations); and a font for baptism. In the now-established Wren tradition, these churches lacked for the most part any extensive ornament other than brickwork, and were devoid of the pictorial or material representations of Jesus and the saints characteristic of Catholic worship. Similarly, the windows were furnished with clear rather than stained glass. The interior plans were generally square or rectangular, without a distinct area for the altar-table as would be found in medieval (or later Anglo-Catholic) churches in which the sanctity of the altar was to be visually and spatially emphasized. Finally, their size was highly conducive to the auditory function; the hearing of the proclaimed and preached word; which Wren had delineated.

As Upton suggests, it is difficult to infer a rich devotional life on the part of the parishioners from the extent evidence. What are much more obvious are the social and political meanings which the material evidence supports. A particularly dramatic example is Bruton Parish Church is colonial Williamsburg, the third such structure to stand on the site. Bruton is located on the main axis of the now-restored colonial capital, the Duke of Gloucester Street, between the College of William and Mary's so-called "Wren building" at one end and the House of Burgesses at the other. (The Governor's mansion is nearby but off-axis.) These are the four largest buildings of a very small town, and clearly are intended, from both scale and siting, as instrumentalities of the state. Within the church, the Governor's Pew, with a splendid embroidered chair and canopy, indicates that the individual occupying it is a man of distinctive power, even compared with the holders of the more favorably sited, and therefore more prestigious, box pews nearby. All churches were required by law to exhibit on their walls the Decalogue (Ten Commandments, or divine law) and the King's Arms, which were conspicuous symbols of royal authority. Clearly, these churches were not simply houses for liturgical functioning, but also instruments of royal power and control.

Royal power, however, was not the only kind of force and influence which these churches proclaimed. Virginia society was dominated by the planter class, an elite of gentlemen who owned the plantations and the slaves whereby the tobacco that was the lifeblood of the economy was produced. This gentry also controlled the churches and their clergy, since the closest bishop resided in London and the clergy were thus dependent on the genteel vestrymen for their livelihoods. The interior layouts of the churches reflected the status differentials in the society at large, since the most prominent of the box pews were reserved for the most wealthy and influential. Individual churches, such as Christ Church in Lancaster county, were sometimes the preserves of particular families, in this case that of Robert "King" Carter, whose pew stood diagonally opposite the pulpit and who lies buried just outside the church. (The pews of many members of his family are in the chancel itself).[8] Upton goes on to argue that the root metaphor for the Virginia parish church was in fact the house; the house, more particularly, of the gentleman, from which hospitality could be dispensed both to peers and to the lesser orders.

A similar pattern of Anglican church building took place in New England during the colonial period, although characterized by some interesting twists and turns from that in Virginia. The original European settlers of this set of colonies were Anglicans in name only. With the exception of the "Pilgrims" who settled the Plymouth colony with the advent of the *Mayflower* in 1620, the larger company of Puritan settlers, beginning with John Winthrop and his followers aboard the *Arbella* in 1630, maintained what was in practice a convenient fiction that they had never technically separated from the Church of England, but were only withdrawing from it geographically in order to initiate a root-and-branch reformation of that institution which would have been politically impossible had they remained in England. Although never formally repudiating the Established Church, these Calvinist dissenters came to American shores with the intent of creating, quite literally from the ground up, a set of social, political and, preeminently, religious institutions based on what they saw as the practices of the Hebrew monarchy in the case of the civil realm and the most "primitive" Christians in the case of the religious.

The unique architectural creation of the seventeenth century settlements in New England was a new kind of place worship, the *meetinghouse.* Where their counterparts in England and Scotland had generally been reduced to adapting secular structures or extant Anglican churches for this purpose, the New Englanders, who had colonized a region where no permanent habitations of any kind already existed, were free to innovate, following earlier Calvinist theology and, most likely, secular architectural precedent, perhaps in the form of medieval English guildhalls.[9] The one surviving seventeenth-century exemplar of this genre is the Old Ship Meetinghouse in Hingham, Massachusetts, built in 1681 and today, in somewhat more ornate external form, housing a congregation of liberal Unitarian-Universalists who can trace their institutional, though not their theological, ancestry directly to the time of

[8]Upton, 179-80 and *passim.*
[9]See Donnelly, *passim.*

founding. Externally, Old Ship resembles not a church but rather a substantial house, with the primary entrance on one of the longer sides. This was one of a number of architectural moves which, though we have no documentary evidence to this end, seems clearly intended to differentiate from the traditional "churchly" pattern of horizontal (basilican) from with entry on the short, west end. (Altars traditionally were oriented; faced east—through an association of Jesus with the rising sun.) Upon entering, one is confronted with an elevated, centered, and sizeable pulpit; the communion table was simply a hinged board which could be extended for the monthly celebration of that ritual. Pews were of the box variety; as in colonial Anglican churches, those nearest the pulpit were the most prestigious, and reserved for the wealthiest and most influential families in the community. Ornament, other than perhaps in later versions some elegant wood-carving, was absent, following in the iconoclastic or aniconic traditions of Geneva. One should also note the place of preeminence accorded clergy in this society; although they could not hold civic office, their prestige, as exemplified in the massive meetinghouse pulpits, indicated the influence in a coordinate church and state.

The metamorphoses of the meetinghouse that occurred during the eighteenth century in New England raise some interesting questions of interpretation. Following the Glorious Revolution in England in 1688-89, in which the restored Stuart monarchy in the person of James II was again and definitively deposed, the English government began to take a far more active interest in the affairs of New England than had been possible during the earlier period of civil war and interregnum. The result was the installation of a royal governor in Boston and, with him, a material Anglican presence in the form of King's Chapel (established 1686) and Christ (Old North) Church (1723) of Paul Revere fame ("one if by land, two if by sea...). The latter structure, which still serves an Episcopal parish as well as a steady constituency of tourists, in many ways resembles its Virginia contemporaries, although its soaring steeple and spire are more directly reminiscent of their more elaborate prototypes designed by Christopher Wren in the mother country.[10]

The erection of such Anglican structures in the North American colonies seems logical enough, and reinforces the notion that religion and its building can be an integral part of the imperialist enterprise.[11] It

[10]St. Andrew's-by-the-Wardrobe is the probable model. See Southworth, 50.
[11]See Gowans for an interesting account of how this pattern extends from England through New England and ultimately, during the nineteenth century, into Hawaii in the form of the neo-classical Congregational churches erected by missionaries there.

is also a good example of how the "high style" of architectural design had now penetrated the colonies, where the cost of such buildings was affordable and the style appreciated and sought after as a badge of good taste and modishness. What is more problematic, however, is why the course of Puritan/Congregationalist architecture than developed immediately afterwards and continued for over a century should have taken the direction that it did.[12] In 1729, Congregationalists in what is now the heart of downtown Boston erected the second incarnation of their Old South Meeting House on the site of what had once been Governor John Winthrop's garden.[13] At first glance, this structure, which later housed several of the public assemblies leading up to the Revolution and which is now maintained as a museum on the "Freedom Trail," appears to be a "knockoff" of Old North in its overall configuration and, especially, its Wren-style tower, steeple and spire. Closer inspection, however, reveals that the main entrance is not on the short side under through the tower, as one might expect, but rather around the corner on one of the long sides. Upon entering here, is in Old Ship, one is faced directly by a dominant pulpit, with other internal arrangements reflecting a slightly more ornate version of their humble seventeenth-century predecessors. The entire course of meetinghouse building until well into the nineteenth century throughout New England and its territorial extensions, such as Connecticut's post-Revolutionary beachhead in the "firelands" of northeastern Ohio, is characterized by similar and progressively more elaborate construction in the Wren-Gibbs tradition.[14] Written documents are silent as to the motivation for this shift, which has sometimes been written off as "steeple envy" or a desire by an increasingly wealthy and worldly Puritan community for the status which such modish building represented. It also seems to correlate with a decline in strict Calvinism and the breaking up of New England Congregationalism into a variety of theologically contending fashions,

---

[12]In the New England context, "Puritan"—originally a derogatory nickname applied to the Calvinist faction within the Church of England—and "Congregationalist," denoting a form of time of American independence, the latter had largely displaced the former, since the close relationship between church and state that had characterized the colonial establishment had largely vanished.

[13]Southworth, 16.

[14]Wren's neo-classicism was enhanced a generation or so later in the work of Sir James Gibbs, whose trademark was a massive columned portico. St. Martin-in-the-Fields in London (1722-26) remains his masterwork. This style is frequently referred to as "Wren-Gibbs" or "Wren Baroque." By the late eighteenth century it had metamorphosed into the "Adam style" in Britain and the "Federal style" in the United States.

including the liberal proto-Unitarianism that by the time of Independence had become dominant in the Boston area.

The progress of Anglicanism in what became in the late eighteenth century the United States of America was interrupted by two major developments. The Revolutionary War was opposed by many Church of England clergy resident in the colonies, a considerable number of whom fled to Canada or back to England. The terms of the new Constitution as well as the religious demography of the new nation also rendered continuing establishment (governmental recognition and support) status impossible, and a Protestant Episcopal Church, organized in 1784, took its place among the array of denominations that constituted the religious makeup of the United States. The net result was a period of several decades of regrouping, until the new means of governance were fully in place and the suspicions of disloyalty that had arisen during the war had been dissipated.

When new Episcopal churches began to be built throughout the new nation, some, such as Boston's Cathedral Church of St. Paul (1820) followed the popular Greek revival style that was by this time becoming a virtually official national style, embodied in everything from governmental buildings to private homes to Jewish synagogues.[15] More representative of what was to come, however, was Trinity Church (1813-14) on the town green in New Haven, Connecticut, which still stands next to two different Congregational churches in the Wren-Gibbs tradition, an odd redundancy dating from the splits induced by the Great Awakening revivals of the 1740s. Trinity, the interior of which now bears little resemblance to the original, was among the first manifestations of the Gothic revival in the United States, and its exotic appearance inspired considerable comment among a citizenry accustomed to the more austere beauties of classicism in its various modes. Although the Gothic would never become as wildly popular as the Greek revival as a general building style, it would soon not only dominate the design of Episcopal churches for the next century but would also have a profound influence on the religious buildings of other traditions, ranging from Baptist to Jewish.

The reasons for the popularity of the Gothic mode during the nineteenth century can be dealt with at a variety of levels. Its origins lay in the appeal of "Gothick" to a small number of enthusiasts for the exotic in eighteenth century England such as Horace Walpole, which led to architectural creations that were more fanciful than serious or accurate. By the early nineteenth century, however, an interest in things medieval in general and Gothic in particular began to deepen, as that period of

[15]Southworth, 11-12.

cultural and social development was seen to offer an instructive counter-paradigm to the runaway industrial and urban development that overtook first England and then the United States. (Alice Chandler and Jackson Lears provide instructive accounts in their works cited here of the diffusion and development of these ideas in Britain and America respectively.) Suffice it to say here that the term "organic" had a particular resonance. The Middle Ages were construed by many as having possessed a social structure in which the different classes were bound to one another by a firm sense of mutual obligation, as opposed to the radical individualism and self-seeking which characterized the reign of laissez-faire capitalism. Similarly, the Gothic style was interpreted in the context of nineteenth-century Romanticism as having derived its essential features from the imitation of natural forms and, in the articulation of its structural elements, to exhibit an organic unity absent in the more mechanical shapes of classicism.

A more immediate source for the appeal of Gothic to both British and North American builders of Anglican churches beginning in the mid-nineteenth century can be easily discerned and documented in the writings of the Cambridge Camden Society, also known as the "Ecclesiologists," which arose in the 1830s. This group was a contemporary counterpart of the better-known Oxford Movement, or Tractarians, who argued for an interpretation of the Church of England's identity that more closely corresponded with catholic rather than Protestant tradition, stressing sacramentalism and the apostolic succession of bishops. Their counterparts at Cambridge shared many of these concerns, but emphasized especially the importance of the physical setting for worship, which they believed had been neglected during the period of neoclassical dominance. Rather, they stressed the normative character of English Gothic parish churches of the fifteenth century, a time when the entirety of the church converged in a seamless, organic web of Christian sacramental symbolism.[16] They particularly stressed the necessity of structurally differentiating the *chancel;* the part of the church which housed the sanctuary and, if present, the choir; from the nave, in which the congregation was seated, thus emphasizing the enhanced sacrality of the former part.

These Ecclesiologists published widely both their rather dogmatic views as well as plans for new churches based on an archaeological study of specific English parish churches which they believed to illustrate particularly well their principles. Their work was furthered in North America by the New York Ecclesiological Society of 1848, which was particularly influential in the mid-Atlantic states. An early example

---

[16]Addleshaw and Etchells, 204 ff. See also Stanton and White.

of its impact can be found in St. James the Less in what is now Philadelphia, built in 1846-48 by a local businessman and modeled on a specific church in Cambridgeshire. The cause was taken up and spread much more broadly by an English immigrant Anglican architect, Richard Upjohn, whose first major achievement was Trinity Church at Broadway and Wall Street in Manhattan (1846). Although fiscal constraints at times prevented Upjohn from achieving as pure a rendition of medieval style as the Ecclesiological ideologues would have preferred, he nevertheless more than any single person was responsible for the proliferation in this country of a Gothic that was reasonably faithful to the structural principles as well as the decorative features of medieval architecture. In addition to the more monumental sort of church rendered in stone that New York's Trinity represented, Upjohn also invented a new style; "Carpenter Gothic"; in which board-and-batten construction (vertically placed boards of alternating width) was utilized to achieve a Gothic-inspired look in more easily affordable wood. Upjohn himself designed many such individual churches and provided generic plans for others; many more in the idiom, designed by local builders, spread across the nation and the entire denominational spectrum like mushrooms during the ensuing middle decades of the nineteenth century. Although such a style could indeed represent the "true principles" of the Cambridge Movement, as many examples in Wisconsin in particular illustrate, in most cases "Carpenter Gothic" was simply a pleasing, rustic-looking design that could be accommodated to virtually any liturgical purpose.[17]

In both England and America, the Gothic progressed in a variety of directions as an increasingly normative style for a communion that was by no means internally homogeneous. Within both the Church of England and its earliest independent offspring, the (Protestant) Episcopal Church in the United States, three distinct factions emerged by the Victorian era which had very different notions of what an Anglican church was about. The original division, already present in earlier centuries but involved with a somewhat different set of issues, was between the "high church" and "low church" factions, which advocated respectively an interpretation of Anglicanism aligned with Roman Catholic and Reformed Protestant emphases. (The above-mentioned Oxford Movement was exemplary of the former in its concerns with sacramental worship and the "high" character of the episcopate; "low churchmen," or Evangelicals, emphasized a more traditionally Protestant

---

[17]Wisconsin and adjacent parts of the upper Midwest are sometimes jocularly known as the "Biretta Belt" of American Episcopalianism, a reference to the penchant among High Church (Anglo-Catholic) Episcopalians for such elements of Roman Catholic clerical garb as the *biretta* (kind of hat).

concern with Scripture and preaching as the locus of religious authority.) Later in the century, a "broad church" movement, influenced by the emergent Protestant liberalism of the day, began to develop which sought to embrace all factions within Anglicanism, reach out to other (mainly Protestant) churches, and involve the church in social causes. Each of these factions employed the Gothic, but with different rationales.

Although the more Protestant of Anglicans had some reason to be suspicious of Gothic, a rationale was provided for its acceptance through the writings of the English art critic John Ruskin, whose ideas were enormously influential on both sides of the Atlantic. In such works as *The Stones of Venice* and *The Seven Lamps of Architecture,* Ruskin presented Gothic as a supremely moral sort of architecture, in which the primary Christian virtues were manifested through beautiful design and honest craftsmanship. Such ideas helped persuade Ohio's low church Episcopal bishop, Charles Pettit McIlvaine, to commission a chapel for Kenyon College—the Church of the Holy Spirit (1868-71); in a Gothic mode which bore none of the sacramental symbolism that Ecclesiological principles had called for. (McIlvaine had refused to consecrate a church which featured an altar rather than a communion table.)[18] Phillips Brooks, later bishop of Massachusetts and closely identified with many of the emphases of the emergent broad church movement, differed from McIlvaine in his repudiation of the latter's extreme low church views, but shared his Protestant distrust of Roman Catholicism. Thus, while rector of Boston's Trinity Church, Brooks instructed the designated architect of that congregation's splendid new home in Copley Square to utilize the Romanesque rather than the Gothic style since the former was closer (at least chronologically) to "primitive" Christianity. H.H. Richardson, who was then beginning a career as one of the most influential architects in America's history, utilized French and Spanish prototypes to produce a masterpiece that emphasized the preaching function for which Brooks was famous. Trinity, however, was by no means a "plain style" meetinghouse that the Puritans would have recognized as one of their own. Rather, it incorporated the work of the finest designers of the time; stained glass artists, muralists, wood and metal craftsmen; to produce a virtual museum of contemporary religious art which had now lost the suspicion; as the Gothic architectural style still did for Brooks; of "Romanism."

At the other end of the Anglican spectrum, what had been called the high church party had now metamorphosed in both Britain and the United States into "Anglo-Catholicism," which added a highly elaborate ritualism to the earlier tenets of the Oxford Movement. In England,

[18]Butler, 113-14.

architects such as William Butterfield went beyond the strict archeological principles of early Ecclesiologist teaching to create an even more elaborate and richly textured Gothicism than the Middle Ages had known.[19] In the United states, these same tendencies, which incorporated Ruskin's admiration for Venetian as well as English Gothic, manifested themselves in, for example, Boston's Church of the Advent (1875-88) on Beacon Hill. Among its early parishioners was Isabella Stewart Gardner, whose Italianate house remains today as the shelter for her collection of one of the nation's earliest and finest collections of European art.

Closely associated with the Advent parish was Ralph Adams Cram, a convert to Anglo-Catholicism whose work, beginning with All Saints Ashmont church (1892-94) in Boston's Dorchester neighborhood, carried the Gothic to a new level of craftsmanship and breadth of appeal. Although Cram preferred to lend his talents to the Anglican cause, he also designed numerous and frequently monumental churches for other communions, including the Polish Catholics of St. Florian's parish in Hamtramck (Detroit), Michigan, and Fourth Presbyterian on Chicago's Michigan Avenue. His churches were not only fine pieces of architectural design but also incorporated the work of allied liturgical craftsmen in glass, metal, and wood. Cram's architecture not only reflected his theological and liturgical convictions but also were intended to promote a social and cultural vision; expressed in his many articles, addresses, and books such as *The Gothic Quest* of 1907; in which he idealized medieval life at the expense of virtually everything which had ensued. Although he has in recent years been interpreted as both an irrelevant reactionary and a closet homosexual, his appeal was clearly broad in his own day, and many who commissioned his architecture; such as then Princeton University president Woodrow Wilson; presumably agreed with very little of his philosophy.[20]

The proliferation of urban church and cathedral building invites analysis at a variety of levels, and is the subject of my own on-going research.[21] One context is the sudden fashionableness of all things English; including Anglicanism—during this period as part of the quest of a newly rich haute bourgeoisie for cultural respectability. Another is the enthusiasm for the arts which the availability of disposable wealth on the one hand and the new respectability of art for Americans legitimized

---

[19]Young, 23; Smart, *passim*.

[20]Lears and Shand-Tucci, respectively. Wilson, ironically, lies buried in Washington's National Cathedral—another monument of Gothic revival architecture—even though he was a Presbyterian.

[21]See Williams 1999 for a provisional report and relevant bibliography for this paragraph.

by Ruskin and, in this country, James Jackson Jarves and Charles Eliot Norton, made possible. This latter drive resulted in the founding of great cultural institutions and the metamorphosis of many churches into art galleries themselves. (Boston's Trinity is a good early example; it directly faces the monumental Boston Public Library.) The theme of public culture as a vehicle for social control of the immigrant masses by the new urban elite is paralleled in a new competition with Roman Catholics, whose great Saint Patrick's Cathedral on Manhattan's Fifth Avenue may have prompted the building of the Episcopalian counterpart, Cram's St. John the Divine, in retaliation. Furthermore, whatever the rationale for these churches offered by Cram, many were interpreted by their commissioners as means of social display, control, or outreach in the context of the current economic system rather than as the vanguard of a medieval revival.

The Depression and World War II brought the Gothic phase of church building to a halt; when prosperity and peace had returned, Modernism; exemplified in the United States by Frank Lloyd Wright; had displaced revivalism in architectural fashion, and the surplus wealth and abundant craftsmanship of earlier years had dried up. With the widespread adoption of liturgical reforms focused in the Roman Catholic Church, especially at Vatican II, Anglican architecture in the United States became considerably less distinctive, especially as diminishing membership reduced the demand for new construction; instead, preservation, such as the "battle of St. Bart's" in Manhattan, has often been more significant.[22] Similarly in Britain, the even more dramatic attenuation of church-going during the twentieth century has resulted in little new recent construction, other than selective post-war restoration such as that of Coventry Cathedral and several of Wren's City churches.

## Possible Student Projects

This brief and selective survey of the development of Anglican architecture in the United States and Britain; which could easily be extended to include Canada and other parts of the former Empire in which Anglicanism is still represented; has hopefully given a sense of the multiplicity of elements that help to shape the course of religious architecture. Using this as a model and the author's *Houses of God* as a guide to interpreting and finding further resources about American religious buildings of many traditions, the student may want to identify a particular religious building for extensive analysis. Virtually any building will do, but the richness of the analysis will be enhanced by the

[22]St. Bartholomew's is the richly-decorated creation of Cram's partner, Bertram Grosvenor Goodhue. See Brolin for details.

availability of written and, especially in the case of newer buildings, oral sources. In addition to published or unpublished histories and archival materials, students may wish to interview clergy, parishioners and, if available, architects to find out how each interprets the structure to which they all have some claim. To this information can be added various lines of interpretation: architectural style; liturgical use; economic resources; social status and ethnic identity; regional and denominational traditions. The meaning that emerges may not be simple, but consist of overlapping or even contradictory layers and components.

## Bibliography: Works Cited and Suggestions for Further Reading

Addleshaw, G.W.O., and Frederick Etchells, *The Architectural Setting of Anglican Worship* (London: Faber and Faber, 1948/56).

Brolin, Brent C., *The Battle of St. Bart's* (New York: William Morrow, 1988).

Butler, Diana Hochstedt, *Standing Against the Whirlwind: Evangelical Episcopalians in Nineteenth-Century America* (New York and Oxford: Oxford University Press, 1995).

Chandler, Alice, *A Dream of Order: The Medieval Ideal in Nineteenth-Century English Literature* (Lincoln: University of Nebraska Press, 1970).

Davies, Horton, *Worship and Theology in England* (5 vols.; Princeton, N.J.: Princeton University Press,1965-70).

Donnelly, Marian Card, *The New England Meeting Houses of the Seventeenth Century* (Middletown, Conn.: Wesleyan University Press, 1963).

Du Prey, Pierre de la Ruffiniere, *Hawksmoor's London Churches* (Chicago: University of Chicago Press, 2000 ).

Fenton, James, "The Master Builders," *New York Review of Books* 47, 15 (10/5/00), 22+.

Gowans, Alan, et al., *Fruitful Fields: American Missionary Churches in Hawaii* (Honolulu(?): Department of Land and Natural Resources, 1993).

Holmes, David L., *A Brief History of the Episcopal Church* (Valley Forge, Pa.: Trinity Press International, 1993).

Jeffrey, Paul, *The City Churches of Sir Christopher Wren* (London and Rio Grande, Ohio: The Hambledon Press, 1996.)

Lears, Jackson, *No Place of Grace: Antimodernism and the Transformation of American Culture* 1880-1920 (New York: Pantheon, 1981).

Muccigrosso, Robert, *American Gothic: The Mind and Art of Ralph Adams Cram* (Washington, D.C.: University Press of America, 1980).

Norton, Bettina A., *Trinity Church* (Wardens and Vestry: Boston, 1978).

Pierson, William H., *American Buildings and Their Architects: The Colonial and Neoclassical Styles* (Garden City, N.Y.: Doubleday, 1970).

——— *American Buildings and Their Architects: Technology and the Picturesque, the Corporate and the Early Gothic Styles* (Garden City, N.Y.: Doubleday, 1978).

Shand-Tucci, Douglass, *Boston Bohemia 1881-1900: Volume I of Ralph Adams Cram: Life and Architecture* (Amherst: University of Massachusetts Press, 1995).

Smart, C.M., *Muscular Churches: Ecclesiastical Architecture of the High Victorian Period* (Fayetteville and London: University of Arkansas Press, 1989).

Southworth, Susan and Michael, *A.I.A. Guide to Boston* (Chester, Conn: Globe Pequot Press, 1987).

Stanton, Phoebe M., *The Gothic Revival and American Church Architecture* (Baltimore: Johns Hopkins Press, 1968).

Tucci, Douglass Shand, *Built in Boston* (Boston: New York Graphic Society, 1978).

Turner, Harold W., *From Temple to Meeting House* (The Hague, Paris, New York: Mouton, 1979).

Turner, Jane, ed., *The [Grove] Dictionary of Art*, on-line edition.

Upton, Dell, *Holy Things and Profane: Anglican Parish Churches in Colonial Virginia* (Cambridge, Mass., and London: MIT Press, 1986).

Whinney, Margaret, *Christopher Wren* (New York and Washington: Praeger, 1971.)

White, James E., *The Cambridge Movement: Protestant Worship and Church Architecture* (New York: Oxford University Press, 1964.)

——— *Protestant Worship and Church Architecture: Theological and Historical Considerations* (New York: Oxford University Press, 1964).

Williams, Peter W. *Houses of God: Region, Religion and Architecture in the United States* (Urbana and Chicago: University of Illinois Press, 1997). The American buildings and the movements they illustrate discussed in this text are all dealt with here, together with a more extensive bibliography and contextual treatment of their times and places.

——— "The Iconography of the American City: A Gothic Tale of Modern Times," *Church History* 68, 2 (6/99), 373-397.

Young, Elizabeth and Wayland, *London's Churches* (Topsfield, Mass.: Salem House, 1986).

# The Social Meanings of Church Buildings: A Response to Peter W. Williams

Danny L. Jorgensen, Ph.D.
*University of the South Florida*

My remarks are directed to a critical appreciation for what we learn, especially about religion, from Peter Williams' discussion of Anglican churches.[1] It admittedly took me more than a few careful readings of his essay as well as hours of analytic reflection to compose a response to this query. Some part of this difficulty is that Professor Williams interweaves a variety of considerations involving multiple layers of complexity. Some of the predominate concerns include: changes in and the spread of church architectural styles in Europe and America; certain historical aspects of European Christianity, the Protestant Reformation, and American Protestantism; other social features of religion; and the design or form of churches particularly in relationship to religious activities and certain social structures. Yet, he never tells us precisely or explicitly what scholarly problem or question he is addressing, exactly how these matters might be resolved methodologically, or why these concerns are significant for the scholarly study of religion.

What I glean from Professor Williams' introductory comments is that he hopes to enhance our interpretative understanding of the meaning of religious buildings and, specifically, Anglican churches. Achieving this objective presumably involves a new and different theoretical and methodological approach. Until recently, he maintains, the interpretation

[1]Peter W. Williams, "Anglican Church-Buildings and the Problem of Textual Interpretation," Chapter x in this volume.

of religious structures has been dominated by architectural historians. He finds their concerns to be "one-dimensional" due to a preoccupation with the stylistic features of buildings (p. 1). Clearly, however, this is not because he thinks that matters of style are unimportant. Indeed, a considerable portion of the subsequent interpretation is concerned with changing architectural styles and their dispersion from one context to another.

Professor Williams argues instead that there are additional levels of meaning "implicit in houses of worship" (p. 1). Accordingly, church buildings—presumably as a meaningful form of human expression—tell us something about social stratification (class) as well as the social dispersion of style. But, Professor Williams argues that we can do even more than this. That is, by examining the design or form of a building, we can learn something about it's function (or how it was used by people). Furthermore, he notes, we should consider how sacred spaces differ from secular or profane ones. It is this last issue—of the interface between material and nonmaterial culture—that I find to be the more fascinating and salient.

The first extended analysis Williams provides begins with a review of Erwin Panofsky's work on the medieval cathedral.[2] It is interesting, although not surprising in light of the nonmaterial culture of Roman Catholicism, that these buildings pictorially summarized the Church's teachings and thereby served the purposes of instruction and mediation. It also is significant that the design of the cathedral functioned to promote and reinforce the religious principle of sacramentalism as well as hierarchical religious and social structural ideals and conditions. Here again, of course, any other finding would be surprising given what we known about the nonmaterial culture of medieval Roman Catholic Europe. This provides the context for Williams to notice how certain fundamental ideological oppositions between Catholicism and Protestantism were reflected in corresponding architectural differences, especially the design of places of worship in England. Even so, he appears to be more interesting in tracing out the spread of Protestant style churches from England to colonial North American, than with a sharp comparative analysis of the interaction between the nonmaterial and material culture, religious and secular.

Williams' second, even more extensive, interpretation focuses on how the structure of colonial North American society, combining the sacred and secular, is manifest in church buildings. Borrowing heavily from Dell Upton, he observes that Anglican churches in Virginia

[2]Edwin Panofsky, *Gothic Architecture and Scholasticism* (New York: Meridian Books, 1957).

symbolically represented the fusion of the sacred and secular as well as reflected the political and social structure of the community.[3] These Anglican churches, for instance, were modeled after the gentleman's house, sustained a connection to royal power and control, and reflected other social structural features, such as social stratification. Unfortunately, Williams does not systematically pursue this fruitful line of analysis further or apply it comparatively when shifting attention to churches in New England.

Professor Williams's discussion consequently confirms that material culture provides a wealth of valuable information about the meanings of human existence. For religions that construct buildings, these artifacts provide key information about religious ideologies, activities, associations and communities, as well as other aspects of the nonmaterial culture and society. Yet, he also touches on many other highly relevant theoretical and methodological issues that are left merely implicit or simply not pursued by this discussion.

I am not a historian and it therefore is difficult for me to judge whether or not the contention that this academic field only recently has begun to investigate sociocultural aspects of religion and society, other than style, when thinking about material culture is justified. For many social scientists and other scholars of religion, however, this is not a recent concern. Most all of the classical social theorists—such as Karl Marx, Max Weber, and Emile Durkheim—focused on the symbolic construction of meaning, including those involving nonmaterial culture to some extent, and they also accorded religion with monumental priority. Contemporary scholars—like Peter L. Berger, Mary Douglas, and Clifford Geertz, among many others—have advanced these classical sociological statements especially as they pertain to religion.[4] Material culture in relationship to social meaning, and especially religion, also is a fundamental concern of anthropology (and archeology, about which I know almost nothing).[5]

---

[3]Dell Upton, *Holy Things and Profane: Anglican Parish Churches in Colonial Virginia* (Cambridge, Mass.: MIT Press).

[4]Peter L. Berger, *The Sacred Canopy: Elements of a Sociological Theory of Religion* (New York: Doubleday, 1967); Mary Douglas, *Natural Symbols: Explorations in Cosmology* (New York: Pantheon Books, 1970); Clifford Geertz, *The Interpretation of Cultures: Selected Essays* (New York: Basic Books, 1973).

[5]See, for instance, Ian Hodder, *Symbols in Action: Ethnoarchaeological Studies of Material Culture* (New York: Cambridge University Press); Ian Hodder (ed.), *The Meaning of Things: Material Culture and Symbolic Expression* (Boston: Unwin Hyman, 1989); Stephen H. Riggins (ed.), *The Socialness of Things: Essays on the Socio-semiotics of Objects* (New York: Mouton de Gruyter, 1994); and Margaret J. M. Ezell and Katherine O'Brien O'Keeffe (eds.), *Cultural Artifacts and the*

Material objects, not unlike texts or other features of nonmaterial culture, do not speak for themselves. They require a perspective or theory where by some factual state of affairs is recognized interpretatively and then, hopefully, arranged into larger meaningful patterns and, ultimately, generalizations about these regularities. Material culture, specifically, presents special interpretative problems.

Ideational aspects of a culture, such as religious texts or activities, inherently are comprehensible at the most basic, native level through the medium of the language that contains their symbolic meanings. Physical artifacts may acquire a certain symbolic meaning, in and of themselves, but they usually are dependent more or less on the language, ideas, and activities of the nonmaterial culture. A knife is a knife—rather than say a letter opener, a pointer, or some naturally formed object with no particular meaning—because of how this object is typed and typified symbolically. A knife or pointer, furthermore, becomes a sacred rather than a secular object when some religious meaning is attached to it.

Decoding the meaning of some artifact therefore always depends on the interconnection between the nonmaterial (the meanings attributed to things) and the material culture (the objects or things). This sometimes is difficult. Is the object a knife, for instance, or a pointer? Is it a sacred object? Or, under what circumstances does it become a sacred object? Most all of Professor Williams' interpretations of Anglican churches presuppose that we already know the social and historical context (the nonmaterial culture) relevant to Anglican churches. These interpretations move from the nonmaterial culture to the meaning of material culture. The meaning of the material culture, in turn, is verified by what we know about the nonmaterial culture.

There is nothing wrong, methodologically, with this interpretative strategy. It, however, is only implicit in Williams' analysis and it therefore is employed in a rather ad hoc fashion. Ad hoc methodologies raise the possibility of misunderstandings, even tautologies, and they do not prepare us to deal with unanticipated results. What happens, for instance, when our knowledge of the nonmaterial culture leads to one set of expectations but the material culture presents something contrary. This precisely is the problem discussed by Jacob Neusner's essay on Jewish texts and the lived religion as it is evidenced in the material culture of the synagogue.[6] These methodological problems are compounded, perhaps obviously, when we do not know much about the

---

*Production of Meaning: The page, the Image, and the Body* (Ann Arbor, Michigan: University of Michigan Press, 1994).

[6]Jacob Neusner, "The Synagogue in Law: What the Texts Lead Us to Expect to Find," Chapter x in this volume.

ideational culture upon which the meaning of an object depends. This, I assume, most commonly is the case faced by some anthropology and most of archeology.

All of this is to say that it would be very useful to have explicit theoretical perspectives and methodologies for dealing with the nonmaterial-material culture dialectic. These matters, however, necessarily will have to wait for future reflection and discussion.

# Studies in Judaism

IN PRINT

Jacob Neusner
*The Emergence of Judaism:*
*Jewish Religion in Response to the*
*Critical Issues of the First Six Centuries*

Jacob Neusner
*The Unity of Rabbinic Discourse:*
*Volume One*
*Aggadah in the Halakhah*

Jacob Neusner
*The Unity of Rabbinic Discourse:*
*Volume Two*
*Halakhah in the Aggadah*

Jacob Neusner
*The Unity of Rabbinic Discourse:*
*Volume Three*
*Halakhah and Aggadah in Concert*

Jacob Neusner
*Dual Discourse, Single Judaism:*
*The Category-Formations of the Halakhah*
*and of the Aggadah Defined, Compared, and Contrasted*

Jacob Neusner
*The Halakhah and the Aggadah:*
*Theological Perspectives*

Jacob Neusner
*The Hermeneutics of the Rabbinic Category-Formations:*
*An Introduction*

TITLES IN THE SERIES, Continued

Jacob Neusner
*The Aggadic Role in Halakhic Discourse:*
*Volume One*
*An Initial Probe: Three Tractates*
*Moed Qatan, Nazir, and Horayot*
*The Mishnah and the Tosefta: The Division of Purities*
*The Mishnah, the Tosefta, and the Yerushalmi:*
*The Division of Agriculture*

Jacob Neusner
*The Aggadic Role in Halakhic Discourse:*
*Volume Two*
*The Mishnah-Tosefta-Bavli to the Division of Holy Things*
*The Mishnah-Tosefta-Yerushalmi-Bavli to Tractate Niddah*

Jacob Neusner
*The Aggadic Role in Halakhic Discourse:*
*Volume Three*
*An Initial Probe: Three Tractates*
*The Mishnah-Tosefta-Yerushalmi-Bavli to the*
*Division of Damages and to Tractate Niddah*
*Sifra and the Two Sifrés*

Jacob Neusner
*A Theological Commentary to the Midrash:*
*Volume I*
*Pesiqta deRab Kahana*

Jacob Neusner
*A Theological Commentary to the Midrash:*
*Volume II*
*Genesis Rabbah*

Jacob Neusner
*A Theological Commentary to the Midrash:*
*Volume III*
*Song of Songs Rabbah*

TITLES IN THE SERIES, Continued

Jacob Neusner
*A Theological Commentary to the Midrash:*
*Volume IV*
*Leviticus Rabbah*

Jacob Neusner
*A Theological Commentary to the Midrash:*
*Volume V*
*Lamentations Rabbah*

Jacob Neusner
*A Theological Commentary to the Midrash:*
*Volume VI*
*Esther Rabbah I and Ruth Rabbah*

Jacob Neusner
*A Theological Commentary to the Midrash:*
*Volume VII*
*Sifra*

Jacob Neusner
*A Theological Commentary to the Midrash:*
*Volume VIII*
*Sifré to Numbers*

Jacob Neusner
*A Theological Commentary to the Midrash:*
*Volume IX*
*Sifré to Deuteronomy*